Hannes Råstam was an investigative reporter for SVT (Swedish Television). He won a number of awards for his work, including the Guldspaden (the Golden Spade), the Stora Journalistpriset (the Great Journalism Award), the Prix Italia, the Golden Nymph and FIPA d'Or. After a battle with cancer, Råstam passed away while finishing this, his first book.

THOMAS QUICK

THE MAKING OF A SERIAL KILLER

HANNES RÅSTAM

TRANSLATED BY HENNING KOCH
Foreword by Elizabeth Day

CANONGATE
Edinburgh · London

P … Ltd,

3

The moral right of the author and translator have been asserted

Published by agreement with the Salomonsson Agency

Originally published in 2012 in Swedish as *Fallet Thomas Quick* by Ordfront

Extract from *Doctor Glas* by Hjalmar Soderberg. Published by Harvill Press. Reprinted by permission of The Random House Group Ltd.

British Library Cataloguing-in-Publication Data
A catalogue record for this book is available on request from the British Library

ISBN 978 1 78211 070 5

Editors: Leyla Belle Drake and Mattias Göransson
Fact checkers: Jenny Küttim and Thomas Olsson

Typeset in Adobe Garamond by Palimpsest Book Production Ltd, Falkirk, Stirlingshire

Printed and bound in Great Britain by CPI Group (UK) Ltd, Croydon, CR0 4YY

To my children

CONTENTS

PART II

PART III

FOREWORD BY ELIZABETH DAY

Many of you will find it hard to believe the story you are about to read.

I first came across the extraordinary tale of Thomas Quick, the serial killer who never was, when I read a brief news article in August 2012 about a book that had just been published in Sweden. The book, which went on to be a bestseller, was written by investigative journalist Hannes Råstam and exposed one of the country's biggest miscarriages of justice in recent times. It told the story of how a patient incarcerated in a psychiatric hospital had confessed to more than thirty murders he never committed.

The man was called Thomas Quick. He was once believed to be Sweden's most notorious serial killer. Throughout the 1990s, his bespectacled face stared out from front pages and television screens. The newspapers even gave him his own nickname – 'The Cannibal'.

On the strength of his confessions, Quick was convicted of eight murders. But when Råstam started investigating the case in 2008, he discovered that there was not a shred of technical evidence that existed to back up the confessions. There were no DNA traces, no murder weapons and no eyewitnesses – nothing apart from Quick's first-hand accounts, many of which were riddled with inaccuracies and had been given when he was under the influence of narcotic-strength drugs.

The book you now hold in your hands is testament to Råstam's bloody-minded genius, to the fact that he asked questions and kept asking them, even when it became clear that the Quick scandal reached the highest echelons of Swedish society and even when there were plenty of people who wanted him to stop, who dismissed Råstam's painstaking research as wild theorising and who didn't want to admit that something, somewhere had gone so terribly wrong.

Because to admit that Råstam was right was to admit that an innocent man had been wrongfully incarcerated for years. It was to admit that there were murderers at loose who had never been brought to justice for their crimes. That the police, the lawyers and the therapists were all responsible for astonishing lapses of judgement, and an ensuing travesty of justice. And it was to admit that what happened in Sweden could conceivably happen again elsewhere, with equally devastating results.

Perhaps the most extraordinary part of this story is that Råstam was right.

When I read that small news item back in August 2012, it struck me that if I had been watching the tale of Thomas Quick unfold in an episode of a Scandinavian television drama, I would have felt the plot was too far-fetched. But there it was in black and white: this actually happened. I was intrigued. A cursory Internet search showed that Quick, now living under his birth name of Sture Bergwall, was still incarcerated in Säter – the same psychiatric hospital where he had made his 'confessions'. He had been acquitted of five of the murders and was awaiting the outcome of two further retrials. I travelled to Sweden to meet him and wrote a piece about the case for the *Observer*.

I was aware, throughout my trip, that the feature I was writing would not have been possible without the sheer dedication of Hannes Råstam. He was a brilliant investigative journalist. In Sweden, where he started out as a professional bass player before making a career change and becoming a documentary researcher in his late thirties, Råstam had won a clutch of prestigious awards. He was renowned for his fearlessness in tackling big subjects – from exposing police cover-ups to tracking down sex-traffickers – and for his relentless pursuit of the truth.

At journalism school, his teachers said that if they sent a group of students to cover a car accident, everyone else would have returned to their desks and written the article while Hannes would still be at the scene, examining a wheel nut. The lawyer Thomas Olsson, who worked with Råstam on many of his stories and who now represents Sture Bergwall, says this attention to the tiniest element of an investigation was typical. 'Hannes was devoted to what he believed was the journalistic mission, and, as a consequence of that, extremely careful with the details,' Olsson says. 'Every statement or detail was turned around several times and had to be confirmed before publishing. I once told him that if the court was as careful about the evidence as he was, there would be no risk whatsoever that anybody would ever be wrongfully convicted of a crime.'

He respected the facts. And it was this that led Råstam to the Thomas Quick case. There had long been controversy over the convictions in Sweden but no one had ever been able to nail down exactly why.

Råstam was the first journalist to gain Bergwall's trust. He had a rare capacity to listen and to keep an open mind, and the two men became friends. 'Hannes was a very intense person with an ability to really listen to other people and also to share,' said Bergwall when I met him. 'It was the first time that I remember thinking, *Something's going to happen*. I felt *Yes! Something's going to change*, and I was ready to come clean . . . It was so liberating to finally tell the truth.'

In order to establish Bergwall's innocence, Råstam spent years ploughing through thousands of documents, re-interviewing key players and putting together a complex timeline of events on the Quick case. His friend and journalistic colleague, Mattias Göransson, recalled that it took nine seconds for Råstam's laptop to calculate the size of his Quick archive. By the end of his investigations, the folder contained 12.5 gigabytes of data and 5,218 documents. To have been able to shape all of that into this coherent and gripping narrative is, in itself, an incredible feat.

Some of what you will read in this book will be discomfiting. A few of the psychiatric transcripts, for instance, are deeply unsettling and border on the bizarre. But this is the language that was used; this is how confused and desperate the whole process had become.

When you read further, you begin to wonder why the close-knit group of people around Quick seemed so eager to believe what he was telling them, and so unwilling to voice dissent from the prevailing view. Råstam would no doubt say it was because they wanted to believe their charge was guilty – the more entwined they became in the case, the more their professional reputations were at stake. In stark contrast, Råstam refused to believe anything until it was shown, beyond doubt, to be the truth. He would keep digging until he got there.

Jenny Küttim, Råstam's researcher on the Quick case, says that all his work displayed 'an obsessiveness towards journalistic truth'. 'He taught me to read all the pages and the footnotes and to read the articles referred to in the footnotes,' she explains. 'He taught me to speak to the people responsible and always keep an open mind – never stop collecting facts. He always questioned the context, the conclusions and people's agendas. That was his strength.'

I wish I had met Hannes Råstam. I wish he could be writing this foreword instead of me. But in April 2011 he was diagnosed with cancer of the liver and pancreas. He was in the middle of writing this book when it happened. For a while, no one wanted to believe the worst. He kept working, with the help of his literary agent, Leyla Belle Drake and Mattias Göransson, who would often sit by his bedside while he dictated key passages. In January 2012, the day after he completed the manuscript, Råstam died.

'The most vivid memory I have is the last time we saw each other,' recalls Thomas Olsson. 'It was early summer and I had gone down to his summer house outside Gothenburg to discuss the manuscript. He had cooked some food and we sat in the sunlight in his garden, drank a beer and discussed the Quick case. After a pause, I asked him how he felt over the uncertain outcome of the treatment of the cancer. He answered, "You know, Thomas, I have lived a good and interesting life. I want to live, but I am not afraid to die . . . and I want to finish the book." In that moment I understood that he knew he was going to die and that he would do so happy with all the things life had given him.

'I think it shows that he was not only a devoted journalist, he was also a person who loved life. Only if you love life is it possible to die happy over the things you had, instead of being furious over the things you will miss.'

His death at the age of fifty-six is not a just ending to Råstam's life story. But he would be the first to say that justice can often be elusive. It's asking the questions that counts.

Elizabeth Day
London, April 2013

'We want to be loved; failing that, admired; failing that, feared; failing that, hated and despised. At all costs we want to stir up some sort of feeling in others. Our soul abhors a vacuum. At all costs it longs for contact.'

From *Doktor Glas* by Hjalmar Söderberg

PART I

'Once you know the terrible truth of what Thomas Quick did to his victims – and once you have heard his deep, bestial roar – only one question remains: Is he really human?'

Pelle Tagesson, Crime Correspondent, *Expressen*, 2 November 1994

SÄTER HOSPITAL, MONDAY, 2 JUNE 2008

THE SERIAL KILLER, sadist and cannibal Sture Bergwall had not been receiving visitors for the past seven years. I was filled with nervous anticipation as I was let into the main guarded entrance at the regional forensic psychiatric clinic in Säter.

'Hannes Råstam, Swedish Television. I'm here to see Sture Bergwall . . .'

I dropped my press pass into the little stainless-steel drawer under the bulletproof glass between me and the guard. He confirmed that my visit had been logged and approved.

'Go through the security gate. Don't touch the door!'

I obeyed the scratchy voice from the speaker, passed through an automatic door, then a couple of metal detectors and finally through one more automatic door into a waiting room where a care assistant rummaged through my shoulder bag.

I followed my guide's firm steps through an inexplicable system of corridors, stairs and elevators. Her heels tapped against the concrete floors; then silence, the rattling of keys at every new steel barrier, the bleep of electronic locks and slamming of armoured doors.

Thomas Quick had confessed to more than thirty murders. Six unanimous courts had found him guilty of the murders of eight people. After the last verdict in 2001 he withdrew, announced a 'time out', reassumed his old name – Sture Bergwall – and went quiet. In the seven years that followed, a heated debate about whether Quick was a serial killer or a pathological liar had bubbled up at regular intervals. The protagonist's own thoughts on the matter were unknown to all. Now I was meeting him, face to face.

The care assistant led me into a large, deserted ward with plastic floors so polished that they shone. She took me to a small visiting room.

'He's on his way,' she said.

I felt unexpectedly uneasy.

'Will you wait outside the room during my visit?'

'This ward is closed, there are no staff here,' she answered curtly, then as if she had read my mind she fished out a little device. 'Would you like an attack alarm?'

I looked at her and the little black device.

Sture Bergwall had been detained here since 1991. He was considered so dangerous that he was only allowed to leave the grounds every six weeks for a drive, on the condition that he was accompanied by six warders. *A case of letting the madman see the horizon to keep him from getting even madder*, I thought.

Now I had a few seconds to determine whether the situation called for an attack alarm. I couldn't quite bring myself to reply.

'There's also a panic button next door,' said the care assistant.

I almost had a sense that she was teasing me. She knew just as well as I did that none of Quick's victims would have been saved by a panic button next door.

My train of thought was cut short by the appearance of Sture Bergwall in the doorway, all six foot two of him, flanked by two care assistants. He was wearing a faded sweatshirt that had once been purple, worn-out jeans and sandals. With a nervous smile he offered me his hand, leaning forward slightly as if not to force me to come too close to him.

I looked at the hand that, according to its owner, had slain at least thirty people.

His handshake was damp.

The care assistants had gone.

I was alone with the cannibal.

THE SÄTER MAN

THE UNSETTLING NEWS was delivered via the media. As usual.

The reporter from *Expressen* was in a hurry and got straight to the point: 'There's a bloke down in Falun who's confessed to the murder of your son, Johan. Do you have any comment on that?'

Anna-Clara Asplund was standing in the hall – still wearing her coat, with the front door keys in her hand – at the end of her day's work. She had heard the telephone ringing as she was unlocking the door.

'I'm in a bit of a hurry,' the journalist explained. 'I'm having a hernia operation tomorrow and I have to hand in the article.'

Anna-Clara didn't understand what he was talking about. But she did have a clear sense that the old wound would once again be torn open. From this day on, Monday, 8 March 1993, she would be forced back into the nightmare.

A forty-two-year-old patient at Säter's forensic psychiatric clinic had confessed to the murder of her son, the journalist told her. 'I murdered Johan,' the man had claimed. Anna-Clara wondered why the police had informed *Expressen* before contacting her.

Anna-Clara and Björn Asplund descended into hell on 7 November 1980. 'A completely normal day', as people like to say. It's always a normal day when it happens. Anna-Clara made breakfast for her eleven-year-old, Johan, before saying goodbye and rushing off to work. Her son left home at about eight o'clock. He only had a

300-metre walk to school, but Johan never got there. Since that day he had been missing without trace.

On the very first day the police deployed huge resources – helicopter surveillance, thermal cameras and search parties – without finding any sign of the boy.

Johan's case became one of the great mysteries in Swedish criminal history. The parents took part in endless interviews, documentaries and debates. Again and again they described what it was like to lose their only child, not knowing what had happened to him and having no grave to visit. But to no avail.

Anna-Clara and Björn Asplund had separated when Johan was three years old, but they had a good relationship and supported each other on their long hard road after Johan's disappearance, helping each other through the hopeless encounters with journalists and the legal establishment.

From the beginning they were both convinced that Johan had been abducted by the man Anna-Clara used to live with. Unrequited love and uncontrollable jealousy were said to be the motives. He had gone off the rails.

The ex-partner said he had been at home on that fateful morning, sleeping in till nine. But eyewitnesses had seen him leaving the house at a quarter past seven. Others had seen his car outside the Asplunds' house at about eight. His friends and colleagues reported his strange behaviour after Johan's disappearance. Even his best friend went to the police and told them he was convinced that Anna-Clara's ex-boyfriend had snatched Johan.

In the presence of two witnesses, Björn Asplund said to him, 'You're nothing but a murderer. You have murdered my son and you will not get away with this. To everyone I meet from now on I will say it was you who murdered Johan.'

That the accused man did not protest, or even try to sue Björn Asplund for slander, was seen by the parents as yet another indication of his guilt. There were circumstantial evidence, witnesses and a motive, but no definite proof.

Four years after Johan's disappearance, the Asplunds hired a barrister, Pelle Svensson, to bring a private civil case against Anna-Clara's ex-partner, an unusual move that also carried with it considerable financial risk if the case was dismissed.

After a sensational trial, the district court found that the accused had indeed abducted Johan. He was sentenced to two years in prison. It was a unique case and a great victory for Anna-Clara and Björn Asplund.

However, their success in the district court was overturned after the defence turned to the court of appeal, which ordered the release of the ex-partner one year later. The Asplunds were instructed to pay their opponent's legal expenses of 600,000 Swedish crowns, a fee the government later dropped for reasons of 'clemency'.

Since then, seven years had passed without any sign of Johan. No one was looking for his murderer any more.

But now Anna-Clara stood immobile in the hall with the telephone receiver in one hand and her front door keys in the other. She tried to grasp what the reporter was saying, that the investigation into her son's murder had been reopened and that a psychiatric patient had confessed to the crime. So no, she could not think of any suitable comment for the newspaper.

Anna-Clara Asplund contacted the police in Sundsvall, who confirmed what the reporter had told her. The following day she learned from *Expressen* that the psychiatric patient was claiming to have strangled Johan and buried the body.

The reporter had also managed to get hold of Björn Asplund, who took a fairly sceptical view of this new information. He still believed that Johan had been murdered by the man they had taken action against in the district court. But he was keeping an open mind on the matter.

'If it's shown that a totally different person has taken Johan's life I'll just have to swallow my pride,' he told *Expressen*. 'The most important thing is that we know the truth.'

Expressen continued following the case and a few days later Anna-Clara Asplund was able to read more details of the confession made by the Säter patient.

'I picked up Johan outside the school and lured him into my car,' the Säter Man – as he was known in the press from that day on – said to *Expressen* on 15 March. 'I drove to a wooded area where I sexually assaulted the boy. I never meant to kill Johan. But I panicked and strangled him. Then I buried the body so no one would find it.'

The forty-two-year-old was clearly a very sick person. As far back as 1969 he had committed sexual assaults against young boys. His most recent crime had been in 1990, when he and a younger accomplice had been arrested for a bank robbery in Grycksbo outside Falun and confined to Säter Hospital. It was here, during a therapy session, that he had confessed to Johan's murder. According to *Expressen* he had said, 'I can't live with this any more. I want to start clearing things up; I want atonement and forgiveness so I can move on.'

You can't live with it any more? Anna-Clara thought, and put away the newspaper.

The public prosecutor, Christer van der Kwast, was an energetic man of about fifty with very short dark hair and a neat beard. He was renowned for his ability to present his views in a forceful tone and with such conviction that they were accepted as given, by both subordinates and journalists. All in all, he was a man who exuded self-confidence and seemed to relish taking command of his troops, plotting the course by which the whole army should march.

Van der Kwast called a press conference at the end of May. In front of a crowd of expectant journalists, the prosecutor announced that the Säter Man had identified various places where he had hidden the body parts of Johan Asplund. Police technicians were currently searching for his hands in a location outside Falun. Other parts of the dismembered body had allegedly been hidden in the Sundsvall area, but despite careful searching with a cadaver dog, so far nothing had been found.

'The fact that we have not found anything doesn't necessarily mean there's nothing there,' the prosecutor commented.

No other evidence had been found to connect the suspect to Johan Asplund's disappearance and van der Kwast was forced to concede that there was little basis on which to call a trial. Yet suspicions remained, he pointed out, because although there was insufficient evidence in this case, the Säter patient was still tied to an entirely different murder.

Van der Kwast told the press that in 1964 the man in question had murdered a boy of his own age in Växjö: fourteen-year-old Thomas Blomgren.

'The details provided by the Säter patient in his account are so comprehensive and well supported by the investigation that under normal circumstances I would not have hesitated to bring charges against the man,' said van der Kwast.

His argument was doubly hypothetical, partly because the statute of limitation for the murder – which at that time was twenty-five years – had expired and partly because the Säter Man had been only fourteen years old at the time of the murder and therefore too young to be tried in a criminal court. Nonetheless, the murder of Thomas Blomgren became highly significant in the continuing investigation: that the Säter Man had murdered at the age of fourteen was undoubtedly compromising.

However, Christer van der Kwast did not reveal how the Säter Man was connected to the murder of Thomas Blomgren, and as there couldn't be a prosecution in the case, the investigation was never made public. Nevertheless, the Säter Man's lawyer, Gunnar Lundgren, fully agreed with the prosecutor's views and asserted that his client's statement was credible.

Increasingly unpleasant details were emerging in the media coverage of the Säter Man's background and character. He had committed an 'attempted sex murder' of a nine-year-old boy at Falu Hospital, according to Gubb Jan Stigson in the *Dala-Demokraten*: 'When the nine-year-old screamed the man tried to strangle him. The forty-three-year-old himself describes how he tightened his grip on the boy's throat until blood spurted from his mouth.'

According to *Dala-Demokraten*, the doctors had been warning since 1970 that the Säter Man was a likely child killer, and the newspaper cited a forensic psychiatrist's statement confirming that he suffered from 'a constitutionally formulated, high-grade sexual perversion of the type known as *paedophilia cum sadismus*'. He was not only a threat but also, under certain circumstances, extremely dangerous to the safety, well-being and lives of others.

On 12 November 1993 Gubb Jan Stigson revealed that the police investigation regarding the Säter Man had been widened to include five murders. In addition to Johan Asplund in 1980 and Thomas Blomgren in 1964 he was under suspicion for the murders of fifteen-year-old Alvar Larsson from Sirkön, who disappeared in 1967, forty-eight-year-old Ingemar Nylund, who was murdered in Uppsala in 1977, and eighteen-year-old Olle Högbom, who disappeared without trace in Sundsvall in 1983.

According to Stigson, the Säter Man had confessed to all five murders. Increasing numbers of journalists were claiming that Quick was Sweden's first real serial killer.

'He is telling the truth about the boy murders', *Expressen*'s full-page article announced on 17 June 1994. The Säter Man had confessed to yet another murder and this time the investigators had finally had a breakthrough. It concerned fifteen-year-old Charles Zelmanovits, who had disappeared after a school disco in Piteå in 1976.

The Säter Man had confessed that he and an older friend had driven from Falun to Piteå in search of a young boy to assault. They came across Charles and lured him into the car. In a nearby wooded area the Säter Man had strangled the boy and cut up the body, taking some of the body parts with him.

According to the investigators, Quick had not only provided the sort of information that had enabled them to find the various body parts, but also specified which body parts he had taken home with him.

For the first time, van der Kwast had the sort of evidence the police hadn't managed to obtain in their other investigations: a confession involving actual body parts and a statement demonstrating that the Säter Man had information that could only possibly be known by the perpetrator.

'The 43 year-old is a sex killer', *Expressen* declared in an article on 17 June.

'We know he is telling the truth about two of the murders,' van der Kwast confirmed.

IN THE HEADLINES

WHEN THE SÄTER Man's therapist, Birgitta Ståhle, went on holiday in July 1994 there was widespread concern about how he would manage without the constant therapeutic support that had become increasingly important to him. On Monday, 4 July his team of carers had planned a lunch at the golf club restaurant in Säter. The Säter Man was accompanied on the outing by a young psychiatry student who was standing in for Ståhle.

She and her patient left Ward 36 at a quarter to twelve and strolled in the direction of the golf course, when he suddenly told her that he urgently needed to relieve himself. He went behind a derelict building that had once served as Säter's security ward. As soon as he was out of sight, he ran along a path through the woods to a road known as Smedjebacksvägen, where, according to plan, an old Volvo 745 was waiting with its motor running. In the driver's seat sat a young woman and, beside her, a man of about twenty who was on trial release from Säter Hospital. The Säter Man jumped into the back seat and the driver pulled off with a wheel-spin.

The car's occupants laughed excitedly: the escape had gone according to plan. The man in the front seat handed over a little plastic bag, which the Säter Man opened and expertly, with a moist fingertip, emptied of every last grain of the white powder inside. He put his finger in his mouth and, using his tongue, fixed the bitter load to the top of his palate, then leaned back and closed his eyes.

'Damn, that's good,' he mumbled as he worked the amphetamine paste in his mouth. Amphetamine was his favourite drug and, unusually, he actually liked the taste.

His young friend in the front seat passed a razor, some shaving foam, a blue baseball cap and a T-shirt to the escapee in the back, then gave him a shove.

'Come on, we don't have time to mess around.'

As the Volvo swung onto the S-70 trunk road towards Hedemora, the assisting psychiatrist was standing by the club house wondering if she should be worried. She called out but there was no answer, and before long she realised that he was neither behind the wall nor anywhere else. It was inconceivable that her sincere and amiable patient should let her down in this way, but after a few moments of fruitless searching, she had to go back to Ward 36 to report that the patient had absconded.

By this time the fugitive was clean-shaven and wearing his disguise. He relished the freedom and the amphetamine rush while their aimless journey continued northwards on Highway 270.

By the time the police in Borlänge put out a call for the Säter Man, forty-two minutes had elapsed and no one had any idea that he was approaching Ockelbo in an old Volvo.

The evening newspapers picked up on the story straight away and immediately extended their print runs. *Expressen*'s headline went in as hard as it could:

POLICE HUNTING
the escaped
SÄTER MAN TONIGHT
'He is highly dangerous'

Up until this point the newspapers had protected the identity of the Säter Man for ethical reasons, but when the most dangerous man in Sweden goes on the run, public interest demands a name, photograph and biographical information:

> The 44-year-old 'Säter Man' is now known as Thomas Quick, after changing his name. He has confessed to the murders of five boys, and the police and public prosecutor believe he can be tied

> to two of these. The man has told *Expressen* that he would prefer just to live in the woods with his dogs – last night the police conducted a search for him in the forests around Ockelbo.

Once the woman driver realised the nature of the crimes for which Thomas Quick was under investigation, she had second thoughts and pulled over by an abandoned farmhouse to drop off the men. The companions found two unlocked bicycles there and, after getting them into some sort of working order, set off for the nearest town. Cycling along, they saw several police cars and were overtaken by just as many, while police helicopters circled overhead. No one seemed at all suspicious of the odd couple on the rusty bicycles.

A large force of police officers equipped with automatic weapons, bulletproof vests and dog patrols searched for them until midnight without picking up their trail.

After spending the night in a tent, the fugitives parted company in the morning. The amphetamine was finished, they were tired and it was no longer fun to be on the run.

While the police were searching the forest, a man in a baseball cap walked into a Statoil petrol station in the small town of Alfta.

'Do you have a payphone I can use?' he asked.

The proprietor did not recognise the man whose image was on the cover of both evening newspapers. Calmly he showed him the telephone. The customer made a brief call to Bollnäs police.

'I'm handing myself in,' he said.

'And who might you be, then?' asked the duty constable.

'Quick,' replied Thomas Quick.

The escape triggered a heated debate about lax security in the country's psychiatric institutions. Most indignant of all was National Police Commissioner Björn Eriksson.

'It's so tiresome that these things happen,' said Eriksson. 'There are so few really dangerous people around; it really ought to be possible to guard them. In the police force, we prioritise the safety of the public over rehabilitation.'

The barb of the criticism was directed at Säter Hospital, but on 10 July 1994 an article strongly defending the institution was published in the debate section of *Dagens Nyheter*. It had been written by Thomas Quick himself, who paid effusive tribute to the staff and quality of the care at Säter, while at the same time putting the boot into the press corps:

> My name is Thomas Quick. After my escape last Monday (4/7) and the massive uproar that followed in the media, neither my name nor my face are unfamiliar.
>
> I neither want to, nor would I even be able to defend my escape from Säter Hospital, but I feel it is absolutely necessary to highlight some of the good work that has been done and continues to be done at this clinic; this is utterly lost in the general screeching of the journalists in their hunt for sensational stories, and it even overwhelms the good intellectual forces attempting to be heard in this domineering choir of voices.

Many were surprised by his words, which indicated that Quick was an articulate, intelligent person. For the first time, the public gained an insight into the mind of a serial killer. They also learned about the process that had played itself out in all of Thomas Quick's murder confessions.

'When I came to the regional psychiatric unit in Säter I had no memory of the first twelve years of my life. Just as effectively repressed were the murders which I have now confessed to and which are being investigated by the police in Sundsvall.'

Thomas Quick heaped praise on the staff who had helped him to recover his repressed memories of the murders, and he described how the therapists had supported him in this painful process: 'My anxiety, guilt and sorrow over what I have done are so boundless, so heavy, that in real terms they cannot be borne. I am responsible for what I have done and also for what I do henceforth. The misdeeds I am guilty of cannot be remedied in any sense, but today I can at least say what they are. I am prepared to do so in my own time.'

Quick explained that he had not escaped in order to commit new crimes, but rather to kill himself: 'After I had parted from my companion, I sat for thirteen hours with a sawn-off shotgun pointing at my forehead. But I couldn't do it. Today I can take responsibility for yesterday, and I think it was this sense of responsibility that stopped me ending my life and made me telephone the police to ask to be arrested. That is what I want to believe.'

CHARLES ZELMANOVITS

ON 18 OCTOBER 1994 Piteå District Court received an application for a summons from the prosecutor Christer van der Kwast with the following brief description of the offence: 'On the night of 13 November 1976 in a wooded area outside Piteå, Quick took the life of Charles Zelmanovits, born 1961, by strangulation.'

The trial in Piteå was set to begin on 1 November and, in the face of the impending legal inquiry into Quick's confessions, the media released more and more details on the background of the alleged serial killer. While previously it had mainly been the tabloids that took an interest in Quick's bizarre stories, now the broadsheets threw themselves into the ring. On 1 November *Svenska Dagbladet* published an article with descriptions of Thomas Quick that from this point were taken as hard facts. The journalist Janne Mattsson wrote:

> Thomas Quick was the fifth of seven siblings. His father was a nursing assistant in a home for alcoholics and his mother a caretaker and cleaner at a school that has since closed. Both parents are deceased. [. . .] What lay hidden behind the outer façade remained a well-kept family secret. From the age of four, Thomas Quick claims to have been a victim of his father's constant sexual predations and was forced to have oral and anal sex with him.
>
> During one of these assaults, something took place that was to shape Quick's life and morbid sexuality – his mother suddenly appeared and saw what was happening. She was so

> shocked that she miscarried. Screaming at four-year-old Thomas, she accused him of having murdered his little brother.
>
> The father echoed these accusations and implied that the boy had seduced him. The mother's relations with her son were henceforth marked by hatred, after the loss of her unborn child. She put all the blame on her son's shoulders, and this is a burden which he is incapable of carrying.
>
> On at least one occasion she tried to kill him, Quick alleges.
>
> He also alleges that his mother began sexually assaulting him alongside his father.

Janne Mattsson further stated that Quick had already committed two murders while still a teenager:

> By the time he was thirteen, Quick had had enough of his father's abuse and he fought off one of his attempted rapes. On this occasion Quick reports that he wanted to kill his father, but he didn't dare.
>
> Instead he took on his father's perverted urges, but with even greater morbid and sadistic aspects. Six months later, at the age of fourteen, he murdered a boy of his own age in Växjö. [. . .] Three years later, on 16 April 1967, a thirteen-year-old boy fell prey to Thomas Quick's hand.

Although Quick was not yet officially linked to the murders and had not been successfully prosecuted for or convicted of any of them, the media assumed that he was guilty. The same was true of the accusations against the parents, who had allegedly subjected their son to systematic rape, assault and murder attempts.

The stance of the media during this period can be explained by three factors. First, there were Thomas Quick's confessions. Second, the public prosecutor, Christer van der Kwast, had made categorical statements that there was other evidence connecting Quick to several of the crimes. Third, these statements were mixed with information about sexual transgressions demonstrably committed by Thomas Quick against young boys in 1969, as well as extracts from statements made by forensic psychiatrists on the danger he posed to the public.

In this way, a complete, apparently logical life story was created for the monstrous killer who would now be prosecuted for the first in a series of murders.

Once again, the article in *Svenska Dagbladet* cited the forensic psychiatrist who had examined Quick in 1970, claiming that Quick was suffering from 'a constitutionally formulated, high-grade sexual perversion of the type known as *paedophilia cum sadismus*'.

Falu District Court had convicted Quick of the assaults on the boys and he was committed to protective psychiatric care. Four years later, at the age of twenty-three, Quick was judged healthy enough to be released.

'With hindsight, it was obviously a mistake to release him,' the article summed up, before closing with the anticipation of a guilty verdict in the approaching trial for the murder of Charles Zelmanovits: 'They released a live-wired bomb packed with repressed angst. It was this angst that would eventually bring Quick and a homosexual acquaintance to Piteå in order to desecrate, kill and cut up a fifteen-year-old boy.'

Although a great many shocking details had already been published in the newspaper, the actual encounter with Thomas Quick in Piteå District Court was a disturbing experience for those present. The journalists competed in their declarations of disgust and loathing for the monster on the stand.

'Is a Human Being Capable of Such Cruelty?' was the headline run by *Expressen* at the end of the opening day in court. The newspaper's very own 'Quick expert', Pelle Tagesson, went on:

> Once you know the terrible truth of what Thomas Quick did to his victims – and once you have heard his deep, bestial roar – only one question remains:
>
> Is he really human?
>
> The scenes that played out yesterday in Piteå District Court must have been the worst ever to take place in a Swedish court of law.

The Säter Man, Thomas Quick, was facing charges for the murder of Charles Zelmanovits.

He wept – but no one felt sorry for him.

In *Aftonbladet*, Kerstin Weigl wrote that Thomas Quick was 'beyond all understanding'. Fortunately the memory expert Sven Åke Christianson was there to explain what normal people couldn't understand. 'I don't think a normal person could ever process what he has done. It's inconceivable, that's why we push it away,' he said, adding that there was a sort of 'logic' underlying Quick's actions. 'Quick was raped by his father from the age of four. His childhood was stolen from him. He cannot endure his fear, so he attempts to transfer this fear to someone else who can take it on. He has an illusion that he can destroy someone else's life and thereby re-create his own. But the effects are short-lived. He has to kill again.'

By the end of the first day's proceedings, any doubt concerning Thomas Quick's guilt seemed to have vanished: 'The man is a serial killer, paedophile, necrophile, cannibal and sadist. He is a very, very sick man,' declared *Aftonbladet*.

A video from the forest in Piteå showed Quick explaining, in tears and with heart-rending moans, how he had murdered and cut up Charles Zelmanovits. No one in the courtroom was left unmoved.

Kerstin Weigl continued:

> For my own part, after hearing those sounds, I cannot have the slightest doubt. The words came in bursts, with deep convulsions as if he was vomiting. Yes – this must be a true account.
>
> Seventeen years after the murder, Quick was able to point out the place where the boy's body parts were found. He sat on the stone where he had desecrated and cut up the body. He explained exactly where he had hidden what.

The trial in Piteå District Court in November 1994 was a walkover for prosecutor Christer van der Kwast. The members of the District Court unanimously found Thomas Quick guilty of the murder of Charles Zelmanovits.

Their confidence massively boosted, the investigators continued to unravel the case. Up until then they had been focusing on Quick's whereabouts at the times of unsolved murders of young boys, or whenever boys had gone missing under mysterious circumstances. Less than a week after the verdict in Piteå, the entire investigation was thrown on its head when Thomas Quick telephoned the home of senior officer Seppo Penttinen at Sundsvall police to say, 'It would probably be a good thing if I was confronted with information about the double murder in Norrbotten about ten years ago. I know I was up there at some point . . .'

APPOJAURE

MARINUS AND JANNY Stegehuis from the Netherlands were a childless couple aged thirty-four and thirty-nine respectively. For three years they had been saving up for their dream holiday in the Nordic Alps and in the summer of 1984 it was finally going to happen.

On 28 June they left their home in the town of Almelo at dawn and drove without stopping to Ödeshög in Östergötland, where some relatives of Marinus lived. They were on a tight budget and couldn't afford overnight stays in hotels. After spending three days in Ödeshög, they continued their journey to Finland, where they had friends whom they knew from a church choir.

When Janny and Marinus left Mustasaari in Österbotten they pointed their Toyota Corolla north, towards the real adventure. They went across Nordkalotten via North Cape and then down through the Swedish Alps, where they planned to live in the wilderness and take each day as it came. They looked forward to fishing, experiencing the wildlife and photographing nature.

The journey was harder than they had anticipated due to a great deal of rain, wind and temperatures close to freezing. They were plagued by mosquitoes. But things were to get even worse. An engine problem outside Vittangi resulted in two tows, a night in a hotel and expensive repairs in a garage.

With empty pockets they left Kiruna and headed south. On the evening of 12 July they put up their tent on the tip of a spit at the northern end of Lake Appojaure. Janny wrote in her diary:

> Drove to Sjöfallets National Park. Beautiful surroundings. Took some photos. Filmed reindeer and saw a stoat at the roadside. Put up the tent at 16.30 on some wooded land. The mosquitoes continue to torment us. From Kiruna went 150 km in drizzling rain. Then it cleared up. Now it's raining.

They rigged up their gas stove outside the tent flap so they had some shelter from the rain while preparing a simple meal of sausages and green beans.

Just before midnight on Friday, 13 July, the police in Gällivare received a call from Matti Järvinen, a resident of Gothenburg holidaying in the Swedish mountains, who reported that he had chanced upon a dead person in a tent at a picnic spot next to Lake Appojaure. Detective Inspector Harry Brännström and senior officer Enar Jakobsson set off at once and after driving eighty kilometres through the rain in the bright northern summer night they reached the place the tourist had described. Before long they found a collapsed two-man tent. Carefully they raised the poles at the short end and unzipped the flap. The scene that met their eyes was described in the police report:

> By the long wall on the west side lies the corpse of a man. He is estimated to be between 30 and 40 years old. The body is on its back. [. . .] The heaviest bloodstains are on the face and around the neck and on the right shoulder. A dense area of absorbed blood is on the right side of the jumper by the sleeve seam at nipple level. Other visible parts of the jumper are bloodstained. The dead man has stab wounds or slashes to his right upper arm, to the left side of his throat as well as to the right of his breast beside the nipple. There is what looks like a contusion across his mouth. [. . .]
>
> To the right of the man, as viewed from the tent flap, lies the dead body of a woman. Her head, the right cheek resting against the floor of the tent, lies alongside the man's hip. The body is lying on its right side and is bent to an angle of almost 90 degrees. The left arm is extended and rests at an angle of about

> 45 degrees from the upper body. The upper parts of the body are wrapped in a patterned duvet cover of the same kind as the one the man lies in. The duvet cover is very heavily bloodstained.

Outside the tent the police found what might have been the murder weapon – a thin-bladed fillet knife made by Falcon, a Swedish manufacturer. The blade had snapped off and was later found between the woman's arm and body. It had broken when the knife struck bone with great force.

Between the tent's opening and the lake a grey-green Toyota Corolla with Dutch number plates was parked. The car was locked, the interior was in good order and there was no sign of unlawful entry.

The police were quickly able to identify the victims. The crime scene gave a strong indication that this had been the work of a lunatic, pure and simple.

The following day the bodies were transported to Umeå, where the medical examiner Anders Eriksson made a thorough forensic examination. In two autopsy reports he describes a very large number of stab and slash wounds.

The investigators concluded that the murderer had stabbed the sleeping couple in a frenzied fashion through the fabric of the tent. Both the woman and the man had woken during the attack – they had defensive wounds on their arms – but neither of them had even been able to get out of their sleeping bags. The incident itself must have happened very quickly.

The news of the murder shook the whole country. Perhaps the worst part of it was the cowardice of whoever had sneaked up on an unknown, wholly defenceless couple in their sleep; or perhaps it was the anonymous, faceless nature of the attack, with the knife stabbing through the thin canvas of the tent, making it impossible for the victims to understand what was happening or see who was attacking them; or was it the frenzy revealed by the large number of wounds? All the evidence at the scene pointed to a perpetrator without any kind of motive. The double murder of the Stegehuises was so strange and twisted in every respect, the only explanation was that it must have been committed by someone unfathomably sick.

The brutal crime in the Swedish wilderness also attracted a good deal of attention outside the country. In the police investigation that followed, more than a thousand people were questioned without any progress being made.

When lengthy murder inquiries are solved it is usually found that the perpetrator has made an appearance somewhere in the investigation documents, but in this case there was no trace of the man who confessed to the crime ten years later. Another fact puzzling the investigators was that Thomas Quick – who up until that point had been known as a murderer only of boys – was confessing to the brutal knife killing of a couple in their thirties.

In the first police interview, held on 23 November 1994, Quick described taking a train from Falun to Jokkmokk, a place he was familiar with from his time as a student at the High School in the academic year 1971–2. He stole a bicycle from outside the Sami Museum and rode off without any particular destination in mind. By coincidence he ended up on the road known as Vägen Västerut, which runs from Porjus towards Stora Sjöfallet.

At the picnic spot by Appojaure he caught sight of the Stegehuises, then later that night he attacked them with a hunting knife he had brought with him.

Quick's account was vague. He even explicitly stated that he wasn't absolutely certain that he had had anything to do with the murder. What made him doubt it, he said, was the nature of the violence, and also because one of the victims was a woman.

In his second interview Quick changed his story, bringing in a second man whom he had arranged to meet in Jokkmokk. This accomplice was a well-known hardened criminal named Johnny Farebrink, whose name, unlike Quick's, had already cropped up in the investigation.

Thomas Quick claimed that they had driven in Farebrink's Volkswagen pickup to Appojaure, where together they stabbed the Stegehuises to death. More interviews followed and Quick's story grew more detailed. Quick told the police that he had met with a school friend from his old high school and that he and Johnny had visited another person in his home in Porjus.

The news that Thomas Quick had an accomplice in the murder

of the Stegehuises was picked up by the newspapers. At the time, Johnny Farebrink was serving a ten-year sentence for another murder, and when *Expressen* asked him to comment on Quick's accusation, he responded, 'This is bloody rubbish! I don't know this guy. I've never met him.'

However, four months into the investigation, prosecutor van der Kwast was convinced. 'Thomas Quick's confession corresponds with the facts established by the murder investigation,' he said in an interview with *Expressen* on 23 April 1995. 'I can only say that the deeper we dig into this story, the more certain we are that Thomas Quick is not lying or fantasising. Thomas Quick was in the vicinity of Appojaure when the murders took place and he had local knowledge from his time as a student at the folk high school in Jokkmokk.'

Thomas Quick had now confessed to seven murders, which – if he was telling the truth – would make him Sweden's worst serial killer. Two highly experienced police officers from the Palme Unit, which was investigating the murder of the late prime minister, were transferred to the Quick case, including the chief officer, Hans Ölvebro. The inquiry was now of the very highest priority.

On 9 July a specially chartered private jet took off from Arlanda bound for Gällivare. In luxurious armchairs sat Thomas Quick, his therapist Birgitta Ståhle, the public prosecutor Christer van der Kwast, the memory expert Sven Åke Christianson, and a number of other officers and care assistants. The purpose of the trip was to carry out a reconstruction of the murder of the Stegehuises.

Also on the plane was Gunnar Lundgren, Quick's lawyer. Considering the fact that this was now a high-profile and important criminal investigation, a county barrister like Lundgren no longer seemed appropriate. After conferring with Seppo Penttinen and Christianson, the decision had been made that Quick should switch to Claes Borgström, the celebrity lawyer. Borgström accepted the brief, but he was at the very beginning of a five-week holiday. For this reason Gunnar Lundgren had been reluctantly invited to take his place in one of the plane's leather seats.

The following day Thomas Quick guided the investigators towards Porjus and Vägen Västerut, eventually turning off the forest path to the picnic spot by Appojaure. Here, police technicians had set up the crime scene to look exactly as it did on the night of 13 July 1984. Hans Ölvebro and Detective Inspector Anna Wikström took part in preparing the scene. The gas stove, sleeping bags and other props were arranged just as they had been found after the murders. A specially ordered tent from the Netherlands, exactly like the one in which the Stegehuises had slept on the night of the murders, had been erected at the edge of the forest. Inside, Ölvebro lay in Marinus Stegehuis's place on the left and Wikström in Janny Stegehuis's place on the right.

Armed with a stick as a knife, Thomas Quick sneaked up to the tent. He threw himself at it and stabbed in a frenzied manner at the canvas, before making his way inside through the opening. He grunted and roared while Anna Wikström, genuinely terrified, called for help. Quick was overpowered and the reconstruction was brought to a halt.

His actions did not in any way correspond with the known facts of the sequence of events.

After a break, the reconstruction recommenced and now Thomas Quick performed with great concentration and in accordance with the known facts. He calmly described to Penttinen every lunge he made with the knife, while also outlining his collaboration with his accomplice, Johnny Farebrink. He demonstrated how the long tear had been made in the short end of the tent, through which he had made his way inside.

Seven hours later, when the reconstruction was over, both the investigators and the prosecutor expressed their satisfaction with the outcome. Van der Kwast was quoted in *Expressen* on 12 July saying, 'It's gone very, very well.' He now held the view that Thomas Quick had convincingly shown in the reconstruction that he really had murdered the Dutch couple: 'He was both willing and able to show in great detail how the murders happened.'

An increasing number of real and self-proclaimed experts set out to explain the experiences and circumstances that had turned the boy, Sture Bergwall, into the sadistic serial killer known as Thomas

Quick. Kerstin Vinterhed, a highly respected journalist who wrote for *Dagens Nyheter*, described his childhood home as a place 'entirely silent and cut off from the outside world. It was a home where no one visited, where no children were ever seen playing nearby.'

Again, Quick's childhood was covered – including his father's rapes, his mother's cruelty and the two murder attempts against him. His transformation into a murderer was thought to have happened after his father's last assault, which took place in the forest when Thomas Quick was thirteen. Thomas wanted to kill his father, but changed his mind when he saw how pathetic he looked with his trousers around his ankles.

'And then I ran away. And it's like a single, giant step from that moment to the murder I committed in Växjö six months later when I was fourteen,' Quick explained.

'So it was as if you were killing yourself, was it?' Kerstin Vinterhed wondered.

'Yes, I was killing myself,' Quick confirmed.

There was a belief that during this murder, just as with all the others, Thomas Quick was both the assailant and the victim. The murders were in actual fact a sort of re-enactment of the assaults to which he had been subjected in his childhood. This was the theoretical model used in the psychotherapeutic treatment of Quick and was also a method approved by the investigators.

Thomas Quick's siblings, nephews and nieces responded with powerless shame to the horrifying accounts in the media of the parents' dreadful cruelty. The Bergwall family no longer talked about Sture. If necessary, he was referred to as 'TQ'. Sture Bergwall did not exist.

They maintained their silence for a long time. But in 1995 the oldest son, Sten-Ove Bergwall, stepped forward as the family's spokesman. In the book *Min bror Thomas Quick* ('My Brother, Thomas Quick') he gave his version of what it was like to grow up in their family home. He spoke for the whole family when he called into question his brother's traumatic childhood memories.

'I don't doubt that it seems true to him. It's a known tendency for people to be encouraged to produce false memories in therapy,' he said to *Expressen*, with firm assurances that his parents could not have been guilty of what Thomas Quick was alleging.

Sten-Ove explained that his purpose in writing the book was not to make money, but rather to reclaim the childhood that Thomas Quick had taken from him by the statements he had made. He also wanted to clear the names of his late parents, as they weren't able to defend themselves against Quick's accusations.

'I'm not suggesting that we grew up in a perfect family, but none of us siblings have memories that back up his story. We were not a bunch of people living in isolation, we were not rejected and mysterious. We socialised with people, we travelled a lot and visited relatives at weekends, at Christmas and on birthdays.'

However, when it came to the murders that Thomas Quick had confessed to, Sten-Ove had no doubts: 'When I heard that a man had confessed to the murder of Johan Asplund, I knew instinctively that it was my brother. And I was sure that more things would come to light.'

The trial for the Appojaure murders began in January 1996 at Gällivare District Court. At the trial in Piteå, Thomas Quick had insisted on closed doors while he was being cross-examined, but in Gällivare he conducted himself with great confidence in the courtroom. In front of an audience he accounted for the murder of the Dutch couple in a convincing manner. He described how he had taken a train to Jokkmokk, wanting to find a teenage boy, and there he met a group of German youths and selected one of the boys as his victim.

On a stolen women's bicycle he had cycled to Domus supermarket, where he met Johnny Farebrink, a 'gruesome and deeply depressed knife-lunatic'. After a drinking session they had gone together to Appojaure, where the Stegehuises were camping. According to Quick, their reason for going was that Johnny Farebrink had 'aversions' to the Dutch couple, while Quick was keen to target the German boy he had met in Jokkmokk, and got the impression that the boy was the Dutch couple's son.

'When I asked her directly, the woman denied her own son. I was furious,' Quick told the court.

The murder of the couple, which had earlier seemed inexplicable, was now revealing a certain underlying logic, though a crazily contorted one.

'I tried to lift her up so her face was right in front of mine. I wanted to see her fear before she died,' Quick went on. 'But I didn't really have the strength, so I just stabbed and stabbed.'

Counsel Claes Borgström asked Quick what had turned him against the woman.

'Because of her denial, I identified her with *M*, and there was also a physical resemblance,' answered Quick.

M was Quick's name for his mother. The murder was thus a murder of his own mother.

A relative of the Stegehuises, with whom the couple stayed in the first few days of their holiday, had come to Gällivare in order to try and understand why Janny and Marinus had been killed. After listening to Quick's account of the double murder, the relative made a statement to *Expressen*: 'Quick is a pig, he doesn't deserve to live.'

The outcome of the trial for the murders in Appojaure was hardly a foregone conclusion. There were questions about a number of aspects of Thomas Quick's story, especially concerning the information about an accomplice. The investigators had not found anything or anyone to back up Quick's information about Johnny Farebrink: no one had seen them together and the drinking session they allegedly indulged in was denied by everyone who was present. For these reasons he was not a co-defendant in the case.

A local artist who had been a student at the same high school as Quick in the 1970s did testify that she was almost sure she had seen him at the train station in Gällivare at the time of the murders in Appojaure.

The district court also believed that Quick's presence in Jokkmokk on the day before the murder was confirmed by the testimony of the owner of a stolen bicycle. She said that the bicycle's gears were broken in precisely the way that Quick had described.

Seppo Penttinen, who had conducted all the interviews with

Quick, testified in court as to the reasons why Quick had constantly changed his story over the course of the investigation. It was because Quick 'had to protect his inner self by inventing something that verged on the truth'. Yet the central aspects of Quick's memories were clear and distinct, according to Penttinen.

Sven Åke Christianson explained Quick's difficulties in remembering his murders and described two contradictory mechanisms in the function of human memory. Remembering what harms us is, on the one hand, an important survival mechanism. On the other hand, we cannot constantly 'go round remembering all the misery we've been through'. It is important to be able to forget, Christianson asserted.

Thomas Quick's memory function had been examined by Christianson, who concluded that it was absolutely normal. He claimed that there wasn't anything to suggest that this might be a case of a false confession.

A medical examiner and forensic technician gave convincing testimony that Quick had described all the most serious injuries sustained by the Stegehuises during questioning, and that his story had been confirmed by forensic evidence found at the scene.

The district court was also impressed by Seppo Penttinen's account of how Quick had been able to describe the murder scene in the very first interviews, and stated in its summing-up: 'On the basis of what we have seen, the district court finds beyond any reasonable doubt that Quick is guilty of these crimes. The circumstances of the crimes are such that it must be considered as murder.'

Thomas Quick had now been found guilty of three murders. But the investigation was still in its very infancy.

YENON LEVI

The accepted definition of a serial killer is taken from the FBI and stipulates that he or she must have committed three or more murders on separate occasions. By contrast, multiple murders that lack a 'cooling-off period' in between are categorised as 'spree murders'.

So far, Thomas Quick had 'only' been convicted of three murders on two separate occasions and thus he didn't meet the formal criteria to be classed as a serial killer. However, during the investigation into the murders in Appojaure the list of confessions to other murders had grown considerably, and Quick was very definitely a serial killer *in waiting*.

These confessions were not always initially made to the police. Pelle Tagesson of *Expressen* was able to reveal in August 1995 that Thomas Quick had confessed during an interview with him to having 'murdered in Skåne' and, by inference, was accepting responsibility for the sadistic sex murder of nine-year-old Helén Nilsson of Hörby in 1989. In the same interview, Quick also confessed to the killing of two boys in Norway and two males from 'central Sweden'.

Christer van der Kwast was clearly put out by Quick's bypassing both therapists and investigators to make his confessions directly to the media. 'I can only hope that he also confesses to me,' he commented.

By leaving clues and making suggestive allusions about murders, sometimes to the police and sometimes to therapists or journalists, Quick was playing a game of cat and mouse that irritated more people than just van der Kwast.

Journalists and the media were assuming an important but unclear role in the investigation. Quick was free to meet any reporters he liked and he always read what had been written about him. Van der Kwast could do little but accept that he had to learn from *Expressen* that Quick had committed one of his 'new' murders in the region of Dalarna, which immediately led the investigation to the notorious murder of the Israeli citizen Yenon Levi on the edge of the village of Rörshyttan on 11 June 1988.

Yenon Levi was a twenty-four-year-old tourist who was found dead beside a forest track in Dalarna. An extensive police investigation had led to a suspect, but the evidence was not sufficiently conclusive to go to trial.

The murder in Rörshyttan had been bubbling under the surface of the Quick investigation for quite some time. About a month after the reconstruction in Appojaure, Thomas Quick called the chief interrogator, Seppo Penttinen, at home. Penttinen drafted a memo of the conversation:

> On Wednesday, 19 August at 19.45 the signatory below was telephoned by Quick. Quick said that he was feeling very bad psychologically and that he wished to talk about certain events he was feeling anxious about. With regard to the case of the Israeli man in Dalarna, Quick says that he was helped by another person to carry out the murder.

Quick stated that they had met Yenon Levi on a side street in Uppsala. His accomplice had spoken English to Levi, who then accompanied them in Quick's car to Dalarna, where the two men murdered the Israeli.

> Quick held him while the other punched him and struck him with 'a heavy object from the boot of the car'. The body was left at the scene where the man was attacked, and it was not arranged in any particular way. The body ended up more on its back than on its side and definitely not on its stomach.
>
> Quick mentioned that he has kept up with what has been

written in the press about the case, but he has avoided looking at the photos and he hasn't read everything written about it.

Quick's confession to the murder of Yenon Levi was not greeted with enthusiasm by the investigators. Seppo Penttinen told Quick that so much had been written regarding this murder in the newspapers that it would be difficult to say anything about it that wasn't already generally known.

Once the preliminary investigation into Appojaure had been completed, further interrogation concerning the Yenon Levi murder was nonetheless carried out. Quick was now suggesting that he had been alone when he caught sight of Levi in Uppsala and convinced the man to accompany him to Falun. Close to Sala they stopped by a holiday cottage, where Quick killed Levi with two blows with a stone to the head. Afterwards, the body was dragged onto the back seat and the journey continued to Rörshyttan, where Quick turned off onto a forest track and dumped it in the woods.

The investigation into the murder of Yenon Levi was long-drawn-out and difficult for everyone involved. Quick's account of the murder was constantly changing. Sometimes he claimed there was an accomplice involved, sometimes not. The actual place where the murder took place varied, as did the information about where he had first met Levi. Quick was even more confused about the murder weapon he had used.

In the early stages of the preliminary investigation, Thomas Quick had claimed that the murder weapon was a stone, which was incorrect. During further questioning, at various times he suggested that the murder weapon was a car jack, a rim wrench, a short-handled camping axe, an iron bar lever, a piece of firewood or a kick or two. All of these proposals were also incorrect.

Over the course of almost a year, Seppo Penttinen held fourteen interviews with Quick and carried out one reconnaissance of the crime scene and two reconstructions. During the second reconstruction, Quick referred to the murder weapon as 'a sort of wooden texture'.

'Do you see anything here that corresponds to the length of it?' asked Penttinen, while at the same time indicating a measure of about a metre between his hands. Quick immediately went and picked up a wooden stick of more or less that length, which conveniently enough was lying nearby.

Christer van der Kwast did not subscribe to the view that Quick's constantly changing story was damaging his credibility. 'The difficulty has been that the memories of the murders have been fragmented and unstructured and that sometimes it has taken a very long time before he can piece together the various fragments into a cohesive whole,' he explained, sounding very much like Quick's therapists at Säter Hospital.

After one and a half years of therapy, police questioning and repeated reconstructions, Thomas Quick had managed to structure his fragmented memories into a more or less cohesive story: Quick and his accomplice had initially forcibly removed Yenon Levi from a train platform at Uppsala station to a car park, where he was bundled into the car. Thereafter the accomplice had kept Levi in check by holding a knife to his throat, while Quick drove them to the murder scene.

On 10 April 1997 Christer van der Kwast handed in a court application to Hedemora District Court. The crime description was short:

> Thomas Quick took Yenon Levi's life by blunt violence against Levi's head and upper body between 5–11 June 1988 in Rörshyttan, in the municipality of Hedemora.

This was the third murder trial in which Thomas Quick was alleging that he had killed with the help of an accomplice. Also for the third consecutive time, the accomplice had not been called to appear at court. His full name was given in the verdict and his participation in the murder of Yenon Levi described in detail, but as he had denied the charge and there was no evidence against him, no further action could be taken against him. 'Questioning NN with regard to this case would not be productive for us,' Christer van der Kwast concluded.

Hedemora District Court was forced to acknowledge that during the trial 'no evidence had been presented that directly connected

Thomas Quick to the crime'. However, the court believed that Quick's account of the murder had been coherent and free of serious inconsistencies. He had provided a great deal of accurate information about the murder scene, the victim's clothes and wounds – details that, according to the court, corresponded very well with facts established by the autopsy and the forensic examination of the scene.

Quick had also referred to other specific details which seemed to suggest that he really had murdered Yenon Levi: for instance, he described finding a carved wooden knife in his backpack which the victim had mentioned in a postcard to his mother.

Seppo Penttinen explained to the court that Quick's discrepancies weren't particularly remarkable. The convoluted process of arriving at the correct murder weapon, for example, had always seemed reasonable to Penttinen because he 'had had the impression that Thomas Quick knew all along that it was a club-like piece of wood, but for reasons of personal distress he had not been able to say so'. Penttinen also gave testimony on the emergence of Quick's story in questioning and the manner in which the interviews were conducted, which was considered highly important in the sentencing. There was a view that Quick had provided detailed information which only the murderer could possibly have known.

On 28 May 1997 Thomas Quick was found guilty and convicted of the murder of Yenon Levi:

> In conclusion, the court finds that Thomas Quick's account has high evidential value. By his confession and the investigation as a whole it is placed beyond all reasonable doubt that Thomas Quick has committed the act for which prosecution has been brought. Thomas Quick shall therefore be held responsible for wilfully taking Yenon Levi's life.

Thomas Quick was handed back into continued psychiatric care.

He had now been found guilty of four murders on three different occasions and could therefore, even by the FBI's strict definition, call himself a serial killer.

THERESE JOHANNESEN

During the investigation into the murder of Yenon Levi, Thomas Quick continued remembering that he had also killed an assortment of other people. One of many new confessions concerned the murder of nine-year-old Therese Johannesen, who on 3 July 1988 disappeared without trace from her home in a residential area known as Fjell, outside Drammen in Norway.

Therese Johannesen's disappearance was Norway's most notorious criminal case to date and led to the biggest police operation in its history. At its peak, some 100 police officers were working on the case. In the first years they questioned 1,721 people. In total, 4,645 tip-offs and leads were passed on to the police, who logged 13,685 observations and movements of cars in the area. But without any success.

In the spring of 1996, Swedish and Norwegian police established close working relations to look in more detail at the murders of Therese Johannesen and two African asylum seekers who had disappeared from a refugee centre in Oslo in March 1989. Quick had confessed to murdering all three of them.

Experience suggests that serial killers usually have a certain modus operandi. Some seek their victims within a particular geographical area; others have a particular type of victim, such as young boys, prostitutes, couples making love and so on. Some murder their victims in a particular way. Ted Bundy, for instance, lured his victims – always white, middle-class women – into his car, where they were killed by a blow to the head with a crowbar.

In light of this, there was scepticism in some quarters when Quick departed from his own stated preferences and practices and confessed to the murder of a girl who had lived in Norway. Even his previous lawyer, Gunnar Lundgren, who up until that point had never expressed the slightest reservation, was dubious about this new confession. 'It's so off-key, so completely different from his usual behaviour,' he said.

While admitting that the murder did certainly diverge from established patterns, Christer van der Kwast, who was in charge of the investigation, believed that 'the investigators must therefore broaden their perspectives' and understand that killing for its own sake can give the serial killer sexual satisfaction.

On 26 April 1996 Quick left Säter accompanied by a group that consisted of police officers, care assistants from Säter Hospital, memory expert Sven Åke Christianson, psychotherapist Birgitta Ståhle and prosecutor Christer van der Kwast.

Quick was taken on a tour of Fjell. He described to the police where he had first chanced upon Therese, where he rendered her unconscious by dashing her against a stone, and how he carried her into his car and took her away from the scene. He also described how in 1988 there had been a bank in the street and wooden planks on the ground, adding that the balconies had since been repainted in a new colour. This information was found to be correct and Quick was notified that he was under suspicion for the murder of Therese.

The following day, Thomas Quick found himself at the head of a long convoy of cars travelling along Highway E18 towards Sweden. Close to the settlement of Ørje, the convoy swung onto a forest road, where Quick had promised to lead the police to a sandpit where he had hidden Therese's body. As he walked them round the area, Quick described how he had cut up the body into small parts, which he lowered into the middle of a small lake known as Ringen. After considerable discussion, the investigators decided to drain the lake in order to find Therese's body parts. The most expensive crime scene investigation in Nordic history took place over the next seven weeks. The lake was drained and all the sediment at the bottom was pumped up until the investigators had reached levels dating back

10,000 years. Water and mud from the bottom were filtered and searched twice without so much as a splinter of bone being found.

'Thomas Quick has either lied or mistaken the location. We have reason to doubt his credibility,' said Drammen's chief of police Tore Johnsen when the last pumps at Lake Ringen were turned off on 17 July.

When the Norwegians reassessed the enormous amount of Therese-related material that had been amassed, they did not find a single sighting, of either people or cars, that could be connected to Thomas Quick.

Many were convinced that this would be the end of the investigation into Quick's involvement in the murder of Therese, and possibly even the end of the whole Quick inquiry. Yet one year later Thomas Quick was back in Ørje Forest with his entourage of investigators and care assistants.

'He performed stupendously. This extended reconnaissance was enormously straining for him,' said the lawyer Claes Borgström afterwards.

'Now I'm convinced that it was Quick who murdered Therese,' said Inge-Lise Øverby at the Prosecution Authority in Drammen. 'We have established that Thomas Quick really was here in the forest. We have very strong circumstantial evidence that he was also in Drammen at the time of Therese's disappearance.'

The police had found a tree marked with a symbol that Quick claimed he had carved; a saw-blade that Quick said he had left on the scene had also been recovered and a blanket that allegedly belonged to Quick.

But the police's most important find was a charred spot where Quick said that he had burned Therese's body parts. At one of these aforementioned places the cadaver dog Zampo picked up the scent of human remains. Among the ashes, forensic technicians had found some scorched pieces that, according to experts, were fragments of a child's bones.

'Quick's Victim Found', *Dala-Demokraten* announced across its entire front page on 14 November 1997.

Triumphantly, Christer van der Kwast declared that for the first time they had been able to follow Quick's confession all the way to the discovery of a murder victim. He described Therese's bone fragment as a breakthrough for the entire investigation.

'The remains of a person of Therese Johannesen's age have been found in a place near Örje, where Thomas Quick says that he hid the body parts of the nine-year-old girl in 1988,' Gubb Jan Stigson summarised in *Dala-Demokraten*.

The find in Ørje Forest meant that the Quick investigators now identified new priorities and focused all their energy on the investigation into Therese's murder. The prosecutor charged Quick with the murder of Therese Johannesen at Hedemora District Court, announcing with great confidence on 13 March 1998: 'In this case we have a strong concentration on technical evidence.' Oddly enough, the trial for a murder committed in Norway was entrusted to Hedemora District Court, although the proceedings were held in the high-security courtroom of Stockholm District Court. This, apparently, was for reasons of 'personal safety'.

Christer van der Kwast emphasised that Quick had given them thirty unique details connecting him to the crime. 'Quick has provided exclusive information of a scope and direction that connect him to the relevant places and to the girl,' he maintained in his summing-up.

Counsel Claes Borgström had no reservations about the evidence against his client: 'There is no conclusion to be drawn other than that he committed the act for which prosecution has been brought.'

When Quick gave his own summing-up in the district court, he tried to provide a psychological explanation for his murder of Therese. 'My guilt is fixed and heavy and a suffering to me, but I want you to understand that I have re-enacted my own experiences from my damaged childhood,' he said.

As expected, Hedemora District Court reached the verdict that Thomas Quick had beyond all reasonable doubt murdered Therese Johannesen, sentencing him to continued psychiatric care. Quick had been found guilty of his fifth murder.

THE DOUBTERS

The critics who had questioned Quick's guilt in the early stages, during the trial for the double murder in Appojaure, hadn't had very much exposure and were soon forgotten. But in the spring of 1998, while the Therese Johannesen case was under way, a heated Quick debate flared up which would this time become entrenched and give rise to an embittered, apparently endless exchange of hostile fire.

The debate began with an article in *DN Debatt* written by the journalist Dan Larsson, a former miner from Malmberget who had taken up a new job as the crime correspondent for *Norrländska Socialdemokraten*. Having followed Quick's trials for the murders of Charles Zelmanovits and the Stegehuis couple, he was absolutely convinced that Quick was innocent. In his article, Larsson pointed to a number of dubious issues, including the fact that all the investigations had been led by the same small, cohesive band of individuals. He also alluded to the way that Quick, in every successful prosecution against him, had mentioned an accomplice whose participation had to be strongly called into question.

Four days later, *DN Debatt* published an article written by Nils Wiklund, a university lecturer of forensic psychiatry, who wrote:

> The Thomas Quick murder trials are unique in a number of ways. Western judicial procedure is based on an adversarial confrontation, where the court of law seeks to arrive at the truth by evaluating the prosecutor's argument as well as that of the defence, which seeks to present things in a different way.

During the Quick trials, Wiklund went on, the adversarial principle had been abandoned because the prosecution and defence adopted the same position. His observation was certainly true of the ongoing trial, in which Claes Borgström not only clearly accepted his client's guilt but also turned to the journalists, psychologists and lawyers taking part in the case and urged them to 'be responsible'.

'The repeated attempts of the defence lawyer to silence public debate is both upsetting and irresponsible. He should have tried to achieve an impartial examination within the framework of the court's examination,' Wiklund went on.

The heat of the debate was further fuelled when Johan Asplund's father, Björn, called for Christer van der Kwast to be put on trial. He alleged that van der Kwast's failure to prosecute Quick's accomplice in the Therese Johannesen trial amounted to gross professional misconduct. Quick had identified an accomplice and had stated that this person had helped to abduct the girl as well as raping her in a car park. Björn Asplund wrote:

> If the Assistant Chief Prosecutor Christer van der Kwast believes that Quick is credible, how can it be that this named person who is known to the police (also to Kwast) is not brought in by the court for questioning?

Acting as an accessory to murder and gross sexual assaults on children are crimes that fall under general prosecution. Asplund therefore believed that van der Kwast had failed to fulfil his duty to prosecute and as a consequence should be tried for misconduct.

Anna-Clara and Björn Asplund had followed the trials closely from the very beginning and they were both convinced that Quick's confessions were false. They fought hard to 'separate Quick from Johan'.

Other media channels threw themselves into the debate and more critics signed up, including the barrister Kerstin Koorti. In SVT's (Swedish Television) news programme *Aktuellt*, she declared that she didn't believe Thomas Quick was guilty of a single murder. She described the Quick trials as 'one of the greatest miscarriages of justice of the twentieth century'.

Criticism of an even more serious nature was published in the debate section of *Svenska Dagbladet* on 12 June 1998. Under the headline 'The Quick Case – a Defeat for our System of Justice', the witness psychologist Astrid Holgersson criticised the team of prosecutor, police and psychiatrist who had 'single-mindedly focused on looking for anything that implicated Quick in the murders'.

Astrid Holgersson had reviewed interrogation reports from several of the murder investigations and she gave tangible examples of how Christer van der Kwast had prompted Quick to come up with 'the right answers' during questioning. It was generally known that Quick, in the early stages of the investigations, had made a number of incorrect statements. However, no systematic analysis of his witness testimony had ever been made, Holgersson said. Instead, the courts had been persuaded to accept unscientific psychological explanations for Quick's errors. She gave an example from the verdict for the murder of Yenon Levi:

> The court noted that 'the final version has emerged after a number of interviews' but did not attempt any critical analysis of how it emerged. There was acceptance of psychological speculation on the reasons for this, namely that 'Quick had problems in confronting some of the details'.

Sven Åke Christianson was in the direct line of fire of Astrid Holgersson's criticisms. His contribution to the investigation was described as unethical and unscientific. 'With suggestion and manipulative methods', he had tried to help Quick to cobble together an account that didn't contradict the facts of the crime. Holgersson also pointed out that Christianson was performing a secondary professional role on the side of the prosecution while at the same time serving the district courts 'as an expert capable of assessing the value of his own findings in the investigation'. Accepting both of these roles, according to Holgersson, was plainly 'unethical'.

Astrid Holgersson further maintained that Christianson had 'impacted on public opinion in a biased fashion – in direct conflict with the role of professional psychiatrists at court hearings – by spreading his subjective views on the question of guilt in various lectures that he gave on the "serial killer" Quick'.

In the anthology *Recovered Memories and False Memories* (Oxford University Press, 1997), Christianson had published an article in which he stated that Quick was a serial killer, which presumably should have been the very issue for the courts to determine. Holgersson quoted from Christianson's article about Quick's repressed memories which were recovered in therapy:

> The memories of the murders caused overwhelming anxiety as these were re-creations of the sexual and sadistic assaults to which the serial killer had himself been subjected as a child.

Astrid Holgersson commented:

> As mentioned before, there is no actual evidence for the supposition that Quick is a serial killer, that he was subjected to sexual abuse as a child or that this should be considered a distinguishing feature of serial killers.

The members of what Holgersson denoted 'Team Quick' – prosecutor Christer van der Kwast, chief interrogator Seppo Penttinen, therapist Birgitta Ståhle and memory expert Sven Åke Christianson – kept their heads down and remained silent throughout the exchange. The one person who did come forward as a defender of the investigation was Claes Borgström. He had already taken a few hard knocks, as a number of critics had remarked on his passivity during the investigation and trial.

Borgström's response to Holgersson's critique in *Svenska Dagbladet* under the headline 'An Unusually Nasty Conspiracy Theory' was laced with sarcasm and irony:

> One must really thank Astrid Holgersson for her scientifically well-founded judgements on these horrific crimes that won't leave those affected by them any peace for the rest of their lives. All she has to do is go through a few papers and have a look

at a few video clips. She will find the truth lying there, ready and waiting.

The Quick feud reached its peak in August 1998 with the publication of Dan Larsson's book *Mytomanen Thomas Quick* ('Thomas Quick, the Mythomaniac'), which was primarily concerned with the double murder in Appojaure. Larsson believed that those murders were the work of a local bodybuilder who was abusing amphetamines, alcohol and anabolic steroids. Gubb Jan Stigson reviewed the book in the news section in *Dala-Demokraten* under the headline 'New Book on Quick an Embarrassing Bungled Job'. Even though the newspaper had set aside a full page for the review, Stigson concluded by stating: 'The failings in Larsson's background material are so numerous that there simply isn't enough space for them all here. This examination will therefore continue in tomorrow's edition of *DD*.'

And sure enough, the 'review' did continue the following day. By this stage, the Quick feud had forced all the participants into diametrically opposed positions and had become an irreconcilable battle of personal prestige in which it was no longer possible for any of the parties to retreat a single inch from their stated positions.

TRINE JENSEN AND GRY STORVIK

THOMAS QUICK CONTINUED making new confessions of murders. By the summer of 1999 he had reached twenty-five, of which he had been convicted of five. The growing pile of unexamined crimes to which he was confessing made *Dagens Nyheter* rank him as 'one of the worst serial killers in the world'.

But something had changed since the Quick feud. Had it sown the seeds of doubt that were now taking root among crime reporters? Or were they and the general public simply growing tired of Thomas Quick?

At any rate, the press archives speak their own clear language: Thomas Quick no longer generated big headlines. Nor was anyone surprised when 'the boy killer' Quick, in the spring of 2000, was prosecuted for two typical heterosexual murders of young women in Norway: seventeen-year-old Trine Jensen, found raped and murdered in August 1981, and twenty-three-year-old Gry Storvik, murdered in June 1985. Both women were natives of Oslo and their bodies were found just outside the city.

Police technicians had found traces of sperm inside Gry Storvik. Thomas Quick admitted that he had had sexual intercourse with her prior to the murder, despite his clear-cut homosexual disposition since the age of about thirteen. These two new murders meant that Quick had made the full journey from a boy killer to an omnivorous serial killer without any preferences, patterns of behaviour or geographical limitations.

DNA analysis revealed that the sperm did not belong to Thomas

Quick, but even this didn't give rise to any noticeable consternation. The guilty charge against Quick for murders six and seven was only briefly alluded to in *Expressen*. Falu District Court made a statement to the effect that there was a lack of technical evidence connecting Thomas Quick to the crimes. Despite this, the court reached the same verdict as in the other cases:

> On a balanced judgement of what has been shown, the district court finds that Thomas Quick's confessions are supported by the investigation to such a degree that it must be considered beyond all reasonable doubt that he has committed the acts as stated by the prosecutor.

'There's no need to speculate about whether he is lying. He has qualified knowledge of the murder', was Sven Åke Christianson's comment on the verdict.

'Yesterday, Thomas Quick was convicted without technical evidence for the murders of Trine Jensen and Gry Storvik', Norway's *Aftenposten* pointedly concluded.

And that was all.

JOHAN ASPLUND

THE STORY OF Thomas Quick begins and ends with Johan Asplund.

When, during therapy in 1992, Quick started remembering the murder of Johan, he was very unsure whether he had had anything to do with it. It is unlikely that he would have suspected at this point that he would eventually remember committing another thirty murders.

If Thomas Quick had begun by confessing to the murder of Yenon Levi, the matter would have ended up in the Avesta police district rather than with the Sundsvall police. But the murder of Johan came first and the Quick file therefore landed on the desk of prosecutor Christer van der Kwast and the Sundsvall police, where senior officer and narcotics investigator Seppo Penttinen was charged with heading the investigation.

It would be understandable if Seppo Penttinen had harboured a dream of being the one to solve the murder of Johan Asplund, Sundsvall's greatest crime mystery. Over the years, the police had invested enormous amounts of manpower and resources with a view to producing some sort of technical evidence as the Quick case progressed.

After the verdicts for the murders of Gry Storvik and Trine Jensen, the investigation took a firm new grasp on Johan's murder inquiry, as it had done so many times before.

'We're getting very close now with Johan Asplund,' said van der Kwast.

'Again!' commented Björn Asplund acidly. 'There's bound to be another murder in Norway he'd rather talk about . . .'

But this time the investigators were determined to bring Johan's case to court and reach a verdict. On Valentine's Day 2001 van der Kwast called Björn Asplund to let him know there was now enough evidence to instigate proceedings against Thomas Quick for the murder of Johan.

Both Björn and Anna-Clara Asplund welcomed the decision and approved the prosecution. 'We just want an end to this after twenty years,' they said. 'But we'll question every detail during the trial.'

'The details provided by Quick show that he has been in physical contact with Johan,' van der Kwast assured everyone at the press conference after the announcement of the trial. 'Even his descriptions of things in Bosvedjan indicate that he was actually there on that morning.'

But Johan's parents were dismissive of the prosecutor's line of reasoning.

'He did not murder my son,' said Björn Asplund with absolute confidence, pointing to the fact that there was no technical evidence at all. 'I don't believe he is guilty of a single murder.'

The most significant failing in the Quick story, Asplund argued, was that none of Quick's murder convictions had been tested in a higher court. But that would change now.

'If against all probability he is found guilty, we'll take it to the court of appeal. And then the bubble around Thomas Quick will hopefully burst.'

During the trial, the district court believed that Quick had given details about the residential area of Bosvedjan which proved that he had been there on the morning of Johan's disappearance. He was able to describe a boy who lived in the same house as Johan. The fact that Quick could make a drawing of the boy's jumper was viewed by the court as significant. He had also given precise information about distinguishing marks on Johan's body.

Sundsvall District Court reached a unanimous verdict on Quick having committed the offence beyond all reasonable doubt. On 21 June 2001 Quick was convicted of his eighth murder.

Only then were Johan's parents informed that because they had supported the prosecution they were not entitled to appeal against the verdict.

And with this the murder of Johan Asplund had come to a close.

TIME OUT

THREE SIGNIFICANT EVENTS took place in November 2001.

On 10 November an article was published in *Dagens Nyheter*, written by the historian Lennart Lundmark. It was entitled 'Circus Quick, A Travesty of Justice':

> The guilty verdicts against Thomas Quick are an all-time low not only for the Swedish judicial system but also for Swedish crime reporting. There is no doubt that the entire story will be refuted.

A few days later, on 14 November, Leif G.W. Persson, the criminologist and professor of police studies, mocked the entire Quick investigation during the Legal Fair at the Stockholm Exhibition Centre. Levelling his comments at the impaired judgement of the investigators, Persson expressed his doubt that Quick had committed a single one of the murders for which he had been convicted.

The following day, Thomas Quick published his third article in *DN Debatt*, 'Thomas Quick in the Wake of Accusations of Mythomania: I Will Not Take Part in Further Police Investigations', in which he stated:

> From now on I will take some time out, maybe for the rest of my life, from police investigations into confessions I have made for a number of murders.

Thomas Quick fiercely attacked Leif G.W. Persson, Kerstin Koorti and all the others who had called his confessions into doubt and were now making it impossible for him to continue cooperating with the police investigation.

> To be met year after year by entirely unfounded statements from a troika of false prophets claiming that I am a mythomaniac, and to see this little group so uncritically treated by the mass media, is, and will continue to be, far too much of a strain. I resign from any further cooperation with police investigations, also for the sake of the victims' loved ones who have accepted the evidence just as the courts have done. I do not want them to have to feel unsure about what has happened.

Three months later Thomas Quick took back his original name, Sture Bergwall. The man who had been created less than ten years earlier no longer existed.

The Thomas Quick era was over.

The judicial case of Thomas Quick, on the other hand, lived on in the culture pages of the newspapers, where the investigation and the verdicts were challenged by more and more people. Even some of the police detectives involved in the investigations came forward to express their doubts.

But Sture Bergwall remained at Säter Hospital, in silence, year after year.

When I visited him on 2 June 2008 his time out had lasted for almost seven years.

Why had Quick gone silent? Was it really because his credibility had been questioned by Leif G.W. Persson and other sceptics? Or were there other, hidden reasons?

WHY DID THEY CONFESS?

I BECAME A journalist rather late in life – when I was thirty-seven years old – but I immediately managed to sell a number of stories to Swedish Television's (SVT) investigative journalism programme *Striptease*. I enjoyed the work, I had unlimited energy and I felt everything was going astonishingly well. Before I knew it I was a permanent employee.

My interest from the very beginning was focused on crime and justice reporting, and within a couple of years, working with the reporter Janne Josefsson, we chanced upon a scoop that I was certain I would never be able to trump. It concerned the drug addict Osmo Vallo, whose time of death happened to coincide with a hundred-kilo police constable stamping on his back while he lay on the ground with his hands cuffed. There was no connection between his death and the police's treatment of him, according to the medical examiners.

Our examination of the case forced two new autopsies of Osmo Vallo's body, resulting in the conclusion that the cause of death was precisely the effect of the policeman stamping on Vallo's back.

We were awarded the Swedish Great Journalism Award for our reporting on Osmo Vallo. In my first years as a journalist I received a number of other national and international prizes and honours.

These successes gave me a great deal of freedom at SVT, where my superiors saw in me a trusty provider of broadcast-quality reportage. After ten years as a researcher, working with the reporters Johan Brånstad and Janne Josefsson, I became a reporter in my own right in 2003. I began with the most politically incorrect and taboo-laden subject one could imagine: 'The Case of Ulf'. This concerned a man sentenced to eight years in prison, though he denied all charges, for sexually abusing his daughter. Following my report on *Uppdrag granskning* (Investigation Assignment) the accused appealed and, after three years in prison, was able to leave the court a free man.

Most likely it was this case that led to my home telephone ringing one September evening in 2007. I heard an elderly man's voice asking me if I was the one who had made television documentaries on old legal cases. I couldn't deny that I was. He told me about a large number of deliberately started fires, 'more than fifty', in and around the town of Falun between 1975 and 1976.

I thought this was beginning to sound like yet another of those extraordinarily deterring tip-offs I received more or less by the minute.

'A group of youths and children got blamed for it,' he said. 'I haven't thought about it very much over the years, but now as I'm growing older it's started eating away at me . . . I'm calling so you can help put things in order.'

'OK?' I said, puzzled.

'You see, the one who started those fires . . . was me.'

The hairs on my arms stood up. I realised I'd never be able to stop myself trying to find out if what he was saying was true.

'OK,' I said. 'I'm willing to dig out the verdicts and other material on the fires to check what you've told me. How do I contact you?'

'You don't,' said the anonymous voice. 'I have children, I live in an area far from Falun and I'm not prepared to reveal my identity.'

'Are you serious? I'm supposed to put in weeks of full-time work "to put things in order" for you, without even knowing who you are?'

'I'll call you in two weeks. If you do a bit of background research about the fires, you can test my knowledge with a few questions. I promise you'll be convinced I really am the "Falun Arsonist".'

Things worked out exactly as my informer said they would. He called back two weeks later, by which time I had read some of the verdicts and newspaper articles on the case. I asked him several questions about the fires, which he was able to answer convincingly.

There was only one problem. Of the ten suspects questioned by the police, nine had admitted their guilt. Surely the case was cut and dried? But the anonymous caller stood his ground: these young people were innocent.

So I tracked them all down and got the same story from each of them – they had had nothing to do with the fires; the arson story had ruined their lives. They had been arrested and subjected to tough police questioning. Their interrogators had denied them both legal representation and the possibility of calling their parents. But if they made full confessions they would be released and could go home. And so they confessed.

They did it to get out of an unbearable situation. But their confessions were used by the social services to have them put into institutional care and they ended up in children's homes. As adults, many of them had tried to keep this aspect of their past secret, even to their children and spouses. They were in despair that I had shown up to rake over the ashes. Participating in an investigative programme was out of the question for most of them.

Gubb Jan Stigson had covered the hunt for the Falun Arsonist in 1975–6 and had written countless articles on the fires. When I stepped into his office at *Dala-Demokraten* on a bright winter's day in January 2008, I wasn't thinking about Thomas Quick at all.

Stigson sat behind his crowded desk, with his feet on the table – he was wearing clogs – and his hands behind his neck. He didn't rise to greet me, merely nodded nonchalantly at the visitor's chair on the other side of the desk. Some of the faded piles of paper looked as if they had been there for years.

I spotted an unframed and yellowing diploma curling up around a lone drawing pin above Stigson's black tufts of hair. It read: 'The 1995 Grand Prize of the Publicists' Club to Gubb Jan Stigson. For his passionate and patient work as a crime reporter for more than 20 years.'

Once we had got my main errand, relating to the Falun Arsonist, out of the way he fixed his peppercorn eyes on me.

'We should help each other expose the liars spreading false information about Thomas Quick,' he suggested in the melodious dialect of Dalarna. 'People who say Quick is innocent don't know what they are talking about!'

I wasn't surprised. Stigson was the most dedicated fact-grubber when it came to Thomas Quick, and he was still pushing his line of argument in the Quick feud, ten years after it first broke out.

Nor was it the first time I had listened to Stigson's arguments; he had been trying to convince me for years to take a long, hard look at the case of Thomas Quick, who, he was convinced, was guilty of all eight murders as charged. I had replied that it would not be much of a journalistic feat to reveal that past court judgments had been correct. A handful of critics maintaining Quick's innocence didn't change this fact.

By coincidence, I had discussed the matter only a week earlier with Stigson's chief enemy, Leif G.W. Persson.

'Thomas Quick is just a pathetic paedophile,' Persson had told me. 'By managing to get the bastard convicted, the police, prosecutors and therapists have only helped protect the real murderers. It's a sad story. I'd even call it the greatest miscarriage of justice we've ever seen in this country. Remember, there is not a shred of evidence against Thomas Quick except his confessions.'

'But surely you can't deny that Quick said quite a lot about the murder victims, the crime scenes and the victims' injuries?' I objected. 'How did he manage that?'

Persson scratched his beard and muttered in his inimitable way, 'That's pure nonsense, criminological tittle-tattle spread by Quick's coterie of reporters, investigators and the prosecutor. Quick doesn't actually know very much when he's first up for questioning.'

'Quick's coterie of reporters' was Persson's reference to Gubb Jan Stigson – the other members of the 'media coterie' had stopped writing about Quick years ago. Nothing provoked Stigson more than when the Professor of Police Studies made light of Thomas Quick's earlier criminal record.

Take, for instance, the following lines from one of Persson's columns:

> Thomas Quick was known to the police long before he became a serial killer. Over the years he has been brought to book for various rather pathetic petty crimes that reeked of stupidity.

Stigson had carefully memorised every such example. Persson was like a red rag waved before the man from Dalarna.

'Leif G.W. Persson describes repeated sexual assaults against children and attempted murder as "pathetic petty crimes".'

The subject made Stigson's voice more strained than usual, rising to falsetto as he launched into his rant, repeating facts he knew inside and out: 'Thomas Quick was diagnosed early on as a sadistic paedophile – *paedophilia cum sadismus* – and was judged to be "not only a threat but also, under certain circumstances, extremely dangerous to the safety, well-being and lives of others". This was written in 1970! And in 1974 in Uppsala he stabbed a man with a knife so badly that he only survived by a miracle. These are the actions that G.W. calls "pathetic petty crimes"! Do you understand how dishonest these people are?'

Gubb Jan Stigson often quotes forensic psychiatric statements or court verdicts. With his detailed grasp, he can attack his opponents by pointing out factual errors in their comments and articles.

Besides Leif G.W. Persson, the person Stigson most detested was the writer and journalist Jan Guillou. Demonstratively he waved a couple of A4 sheets in the air: rejected articles on the subject which he had sent to national newspapers.

'In Jan Guillou's book *Häxornas försvarare* [The Witches' Attorney] I've counted forty-three factual errors in the chapter on Thomas Quick! For years I've been trying to challenge him to a public debate. But he doesn't have the courage! And the national newspapers won't take my articles,' he said.

It was with a certain relief that I said farewell to Stigson and walked out into an unwelcoming, bitterly cold Falun day to knuckle down to my investigative report on the Falun Arsonist, which was increasingly proving to be about the phenomenon of false confessions.

Why will certain people, under police questioning, confess to serious crimes even if they are absolutely innocent? It seems almost inconceivable. Most people would never think they could do something so idiotic. And yet, in Falun, nine young people had confessed to starting a large number of fires. Later they claimed they had had nothing to do with it. In the early stages I found it very difficult to believe them.

Once I started looking into the research on false confessions I realised just how common they are. Nor could they be described as a recent occurrence. When the baby son of the celebrity Charles Lindbergh, the first man to fly solo across the Atlantic, was kidnapped in 1932, over two hundred people came forward to make confessions. Almost as many have confessed over the years to the murder of the Swedish Prime Minister Olof Palme.

Since its establishment in 1992 the American organisation Innocence Project had managed, by use of DNA technology, to help release 282 people innocent of the crimes for which they had been convicted. The organisation confirmed that about 25 per cent of these had confessed their guilt entirely, or to some degree, during police investigations. That they later retracted their confessions did not help them in their court cases.

Children, young people, people with mental illnesses or impairments and drug users are by far the largest group. When subsequently asked why they confessed, the most common answer given is, 'I just wanted to go home.'

My research into the phenomenon revealed that some of the most significant legal scandals have come about because of false confessions. In Britain, for instance, there were the draconian sentences handed out to the Birmingham Six and the Guildford Four. Sweden seemed to be one of the few judicial states in which the problem of false confessions was more or less unknown.

I went to New York, where I interviewed Professor Saul Kassin, one of the world's foremost experts on the subject.

Saul Kassin wasn't surprised for a second to hear of the young people in Falun who had confessed to the crimes. The most surprising part of the story, in his opinion, was that a thirteen-year-old girl, who had been kept under arrest in isolation while subjected to tough questioning, continued to deny any involvement for three days.

'It's very unusual for a thirteen-year-old to hold out for three days!' he told me. 'Most will confess in a few hours or a day.'

Professor Kassin was able to back up his views with a series of astonishing cases in which teenagers had confessed to extremely serious crimes even though they demonstrably had nothing to do with them.

When I met the 'youths' who had confessed to arson, they were in their fifties. Finally, eight of them agreed to participate in my documentary. It was enormously liberating for them to tell their stories. The police who had conducted the investigation agreed that it had not been done properly and that they hadn't managed to uncover the truth about the arson case.

The programme was aired on SVT's *Dokument inifrån* ('Inside Document') on 30 March 2008, and by way of a conclusion I said, 'I can't quite stop myself from asking – how many others are there who have confessed to crimes they never committed?'

THE LETTER TO STURE BERGWALL

I HAD NO idea whose version of events was correct, Gubb Jan Stigson's or Leif G.W. Persson's. The entire Quick debate seemed quite absurd to me. Six district courts had unanimously found Thomas Quick guilty of eight murders. In other words, they had taken the view that he was guilty beyond any reasonable doubt. Yet a number of perfectly rational people were claiming that he was innocent of *all* these murders.

Surely it couldn't be possible? Logic would seem to suggest that if there was enough evidence to convict Quick for eight murders, it must also be a relatively easy matter to show that Persson, Guillou and the other doubters were mistaken.

On the other hand, if Quick really was innocent, then what Leif G.W. Persson had said would be true: this would be the most significant Swedish miscarriage of justice of all time.

For my own part I had no particular opinion on Quick, nor did I have any ambition to reveal the truth of his guilt, or not, as the case may be. Rather, my idea was to make a documentary about the feud and its colourful principal characters.

At the same time there was probably a subconscious connection between my recent knowledge of false confessions and my keenness to get started on Thomas Quick, who for more than ten years had been referred to as the country's worst 'serial confessor' of crimes he had not committed.

After my documentary on the Falun Arsonist had aired on television, I read a number of the books that had been published on Thomas Quick and, on 22 April, I wrote my first tentative letter to him.

> Sture Bergwall,
>
> By coincidence I found your book *Kvarblivelse* [What Remains] in a second-hand bookshop and I am reading it now with great interest, if also with a certain unease.
>
> [. . .]
>
> I am aware that you turned your back on journalists a number of years ago, which I can appreciate as a perfectly reasonable decision, but nevertheless I want to ask if it would be possible to meet you. I want to emphasise that this should *not* be viewed as a request for an interview! Nothing that we discuss in any meeting will be published, I am only asking for an unprejudiced meeting. I am convinced that such a meeting would be productive, not only for me but also for you.

The reply came just a few days later. I was welcome at Säter Hospital.

MY CONVERSATIONS WITH JAN OLSSON

TO PREPARE MYSELF I read the court's verdict and various articles on the subject. The volume of material was overwhelming.

On 29 May 2008 – three days before my first meeting with Sture Bergwall – I phoned Jan Olsson.

Now retired from his position as a detective chief inspector, Jan Olsson had more than thirty years' experience as a murder investigator and forensic technician. He had been the assistant head of the forensic division in Stockholm and the head of the National Police Board's profiling group. What interested me most about him was that he had been in charge of the forensic investigations into the murders of the Dutch married couple at Appojaure and Yenon Levi at Rörshyttan.

He had made no secret of his belief that Thomas Quick was wrongly convicted, and he had written articles on the subject. The fact that he was a policeman set him apart in the diverse crowd protesting Quick's innocence.

I wanted to hear, in his own words, precisely what had convinced him that Quick was wrongly convicted. Olsson was a pleasant man who took his time, carefully outlining about ten different aspects that had given rise to his misgivings. His arguments centred on the two murder cases he had worked on. From what I understood, Olsson's criticisms were of three failings that might be categorised as systemic faults:

1. From an early stage, the investigators had searched for whatever backed up Quick's story. Information that seemed to exonerate him was not considered or further examined.

2. The same prosecutor had been in charge of the investigations into all the cases, and only one interrogator was allowed to question Quick. After the first conviction it became almost impossible for the investigators to challenge Quick, and with each new conviction it became even more difficult. In a sense, according to Olsson, the investigators had become 'the prisoners of the prisoner'.

3. The adversarial relationship in the legal process means that a trial should be a contest between the prosecutor and the defence lawyer. Because the defence led by Claes Borgström did not question the evidence against Quick, the system had collapsed.

After two long and interesting conversations with Jan Olsson, that evening I read the articles he had written over the years. One of the articles published in *DN Debatt* on 3 October 2002 concludes as follows:

> Thomas Quick himself says that he has murdered all these people. All I have to say to him is: Make those of us who doubt you and spread this doubt into the world shut our mouths. Make me stand here, humiliated at having been so wrong to suspect you. You only need to show a single piece of tangible evidence to make it so. One of the body parts you claim to have kept, an object you have stolen from one of your victims. Until this happens I urge the Prosecutor-General to re-examine this case.

I had myself been considering whether I might offer to be an aide to Sture Bergwall, to help him put a stop to the braying of Jan Olsson, Jan Guillou, Leif G.W. Persson, Nils Wiklund and all the others who said that he was just making it up. If Quick really had 'treasure troves' of body parts, he could safely reveal these to me without having to 'give them up', which, it had been alleged, was the main psychological block to revealing the locations of the bodies. I imagined I might be able to bring some item from a hiding place, have it analysed and then the whole thing would be over.

Caught up in these naive ruminations, I was woken by the phone ringing. From the display I could see it was time for a third conversation with Olsson.

'Yeah . . . hello . . . It's Janne. Jan Olsson. I just wanted to mention something that occurred to me. A little piece of advice for you.'

'Please, go ahead,' I said.

'You're reading all the interrogations with Quick. Think about one thing: has he ever given a single piece of information that the police didn't already know? I'd say that's what you ought to be thinking about.'

I thanked him for the advice and promised to stick to it faithfully. It was probably very good advice.

But for the rest of the evening I thought about all the information Thomas Quick had provided during questioning which was supposedly unknown to the police: Therese Johannesen's eczema scars in the crooks of her arms, the pinpointing of the spot where burnt remains of a child were found, the location of the stab wounds in Appojaure, his shepherding of the police to the place where Gry Storvik was found murdered, all the details about the murder of Thomas Blomgren in 1964. And so on . . .

If the 'doubters' knew how Quick could be in possession of all these details, they certainly hadn't managed to explain it to me yet.

THE HERMIT

AFTER THE CARE assistants had left us alone in the visiting room, Sture Bergwall got out some coffee cups and a Thermos. I produced a few tired-looking cheap pastries from Willy's in Säter. For a while we indulged in small talk about my drive from Gothenburg, how spring was on its way and other trivialities.

We spoke about how he had been inside these walls since Ingvar Carlsson had become prime minister and Mikhail Gorbachov had been at the helm of the Soviet Union! Sture had arrived at Säter before the first web page on the Internet had been created.

'I've never had a conversation on a mobile phone,' said Sture, who had understood from watching television that nowadays everyone walked around with a telephone pressed to their ear.

'How do you survive such a long period of isolation?' I asked. 'What do you do with all this time?'

His answer flowed like water, as if he had been waiting a long time to give it.

'My day starts at exactly 05.29. Usually I just wake up, or else there's the alarm clock. Then I listen to *Ekot* [News] on the radio and get up at 05.33. After the morning procedures I walk to the canteen at 05.54 to get coffee and buttermilk. I'm so punctual that the assistants say they can set their watches by me!'

He took a bite of his pastry and washed it down with a mouthful of coffee.

'At exactly 06.05 I ring the bell to be let outside. On the dot!

That's the only way to survive in here,' he explained. 'I have to be incredibly routine-ey. Incredibly routine-ey!'

I nodded, understanding very well what he meant.

'Today is the two thousand, three hundred and sixty-seventh day in a row that I've taken a walk round the exercise yard. I do it every day.'

Sture looked at me as if expecting a reaction.

'Two thousand, three hundred and sixty-seven days,' I repeated, impressed.

'My walk in the exercise yard is for exactly one hour and twenty minutes, in the pattern of a figure of eight. At 07.25 I take a shower and then I have a coffee and read the newspapers. Then I start my work of solving crossword puzzles. I subscribe to a number of difficult crossword magazines. I've never left a crossword unsolved. Sometimes it can take days to solve the last few clues, but I always solve them. Often I send them in – I use the name of someone who works here so I don't attract any attention – and I've won small prizes quite a few times, a lottery ticket or something. It's like a job. The crosswords keep me busy from eight thirty to four in the afternoon. In the daytime I always keep the radio on. Always P1! The programmes I like are *Tendens* ['Tendency'], *Släktband* ['Family Ties'], *Lunchekot* ['Midday News'], *Vetandets värld* ['The World of Knowledge'] and *Språket* ['Our Language']. At six in the evening I retire to my room and after that I don't want to be disturbed by anyone. Then the evening routines begin, and they are mainly about watching television. I go to bed at nine thirty. At ten o'clock I turn out the lights and go to sleep.'

It was exactly as I had suspected. Sture Bergwall had no contact with anyone outside the hospital. No one at all. Hardly even with his fellow patients.

'Sture, you've confessed to a large number of murders. And you've been convicted for eight of them. Do you still stand by your confessions?'

Sture looked at me in silence, before answering.

'The confessions stand firm. They do . . .'

There was a lull in the conversation while we let this decisive prerequisite for our meeting sink in. I looked at the mysterious man sitting before me.

Either he was the worst serial killer in northern Europe, or he was a mythomaniac who had duped the entire Swedish judicial system.

Nothing about the man gave me the slightest clue as to which alternative seemed most likely.

'You're living under rigorous security conditions,' I said, trying to move things along. Sture listened attentively. 'The clinic seems more or less escape-proof: steel doors, reinforced glass, alarms.'

He mumbled his agreement.

'I'm wondering . . . What would happen if you were allowed to rejoin society?'

Now Sture was looking at me with incomprehension.

'Would you fall back into criminality, start murdering and cutting up children again?'

His heavy gaze grew even sadder.

'No, no, no!'

Slowly he shook his head, then stopped and sat there with his eyes looking down at his lap.

'No, I wouldn't.'

I didn't give up.

'So what would happen if you were allowed to live in society under supervision?'

'The doctors believe that I need to be kept in psychiatric care—'

'I know that,' I interrupted. 'I've read what they have to say about it. But now I'm asking *you*. You strike me as fairly normal. Reasonable.'

'Yes?' his voice rose in that characteristic way of his. He smiled and looked as if I had said something absurd. 'Wasn't I supposed to be?' he added rhetorically.

'No you weren't! You're regarded as Sweden's most dangerous and craziest basket case. Haven't you understood that?'

Sture didn't seem to have taken offence, but the question remained unanswered: what would happen if Sture Bergwall were released?

The question was justified.

The man in front of me appeared to be sensitive and kind. It was difficult to merge one's impression of him with that of the cruel, sadistic serial killer.

And what conclusions might I infer from that?

None at all, I thought.

The silence was broken by the care assistants from Ward 36 coming to take the serial killer back to his cell.

We said our farewells without agreeing to meet again.

UNCLE STURE

I SPENT THAT summer reading pre-trial investigation material and contacting a number of police who had worked on the Quick inquiries, Sture Bergwall's family and friends, the families of the victims and the accomplices he had pointed out. The list was apparently endless. Many of them were welcoming and generous. For obvious reasons it proved difficult to establish a line of communication with the people responsible for the care of Thomas Quick at Säter Hospital. My expectations were close to zero when I telephoned Säter's retired chief physician at home.

Göran Källberg was not enthused when he heard about my plans to make a documentary about Thomas Quick. I said that I didn't want to discuss the question of guilt, but rather how the investigation and psychiatric care had been managed. As soon as he heard this, his tone softened considerably.

It was obvious that the Quick case was troubling Göran Källberg, but for reasons that were unclear. He was critical of prosecutor van der Kwast's handling of the relationship with Säter Hospital. He was also self-critical with regard to certain elements in the psychiatric care.

'In any case, patient confidentiality makes it impossible for me to discuss an individual patient,' he explained.

I asked what his position would be if Sture Bergwall gave him authority to speak freely. He didn't want to answer this, but he was prepared to think about it.

His ambivalence was obvious. Something was bothering him,

something he very much wanted to talk about. But he struggled with it. I understood that this conversation had placed Göran Källberg in a dilemma of sorts.

'I feel a great deal of loyalty to Säter psychiatric clinic and the people who work there,' he said. 'On the other hand, I don't want to participate in the cover-up of a miscarriage of justice.'

What was he saying? A miscarriage of justice? I did my best to hide my excitement. So this was how the ex-chief physician of Säter Hospital regarded the case of Thomas Quick – as a miscarriage of justice.

Göran Källberg indicated that his concerns centred on the events around the time of Quick's withdrawal, his 'time out'. He told me that on his own initiative he had asked a couple of different judges about the possibilities of overturning the verdicts and demanding restitution for Quick. The answer he received was that in principle it would be impossible. He had no choice but to leave it there.

However much I thought about it I couldn't imagine what it was that Källberg considered to be a possible reason for the conviction to be overturned.

One thing I have learned in my years as an investigative journalist is the importance of chronology: to clearly define the order in which things occurred, so that one can rule out incongruities – meaning certain things that couldn't possibly have happened at the same time – and separate cause and effect.

By meticulously arranging the eyewitness accounts of the death of Osmo Vallo on a timeline, I was able to show that the police's version of events was not credible. In the same way, accusations against the man convicted of incest in 'The Case of Ulf' were disproved by the simple fact that he was elsewhere at the time when he was supposedly assaulting his daughter. After the Gothenburg riots, by breaking things down into units of time – in this case, using the large volume of video footage taken at the time of shots being fired on Vasaplatsen – Janne Josefsson and I were able to show what had actually happened.

Now my attention was focused on the investigation into the

murder of Yenon Levi in 1988. The murder took place in Avesta police district, where the police inspectors Lennart Jarlheim and Willy Hammar had done an impressive job of mapping out Thomas Quick's life chronologically, from the cradle to Säter Hospital.

By way of a summary they had established in 1956, the Bergwall family had moved to a flat at 4 Bruksgatan in Korsnäs outside Falun. The father, Ove, passed away in 1977 and, after his death, Sture took care of the household and his sick mother, Thyra, up until her death in 1983.

During these years Sture had been declared medically unfit for work because of his psychological problems, and he was claiming disability benefits. Helped along by his mother's pension, they managed to pay their way. He spent a lot of time with his siblings and their families and had particularly strong ties to his nieces and nephews. At home he kept himself busy with rug-weaving, household chores and by spending time with his mother and her friends.

Sture Bergwall's life seemed to be improving when, in August 1982, he opened a tobacco shop with his older brother, Sten-Ove. One year later their mother died, and he was now living by himself in the parental home.

A number of youths would hang out at the kiosk in the evenings; one in particular, an eleven-year-old referred to as Patrik Olofsson, started helping out with minor chores and also enjoyed taking care of Peja, Sture's Scottish deerhound. Sture was soon on friendly terms with the Olofsson family.

In 1986 the Bergwall brothers wound down their entrepreneurial project and Sture became unemployed. He opened a new kiosk on Drottningplan in the town of Grycksbo with a new business partner – this time Patrik's mother, Margit Olofsson.

The new kiosk quickly became a hang-out for teenage boys in the area, who increasingly also visited Sture at home. Sture had started taking driving lessons and on 27 March 1987, after many attempts, he passed his driving test. His first car was a 1965 red Volvo PV. Sture's popularity among the boys was at its peak when he began to organise 'heavy metal' trips to Stockholm in his twenty-two-year-old car. They went to concerts by Kiss, Iron Maiden and WASP.

Having previously survived on disability benefits, Sture Bergwall had now become a shopkeeper. During the Grycksbo years he worked as a bingo caller and newspaper delivery man too, and he was demonstrably popular with customers, colleagues and employers.

Patrik Olofsson spent more and more time with Sture and even lived with him during certain periods, with his parents' approval. The relationship between Sture and the Olofsson family was now so tight that it seemed perfectly natural for Sture to celebrate Christmas with them.

But the story ended in catastrophe for the Olofssons. The husband and wife separated, a deep disagreement arose between Sture and Mrs Olofsson, the kiosk went out of business and Patrik turned his back on his family. Sture's time in Grycksbo came to an end when his and Patrik's financial and social predicament drove them to rob the town's branch of Gotabanken.

The foolishness of the robbery was almost mystifying: Sture was a customer of the bank, which was next door to his previous kiosk. On the morning of 14 December 1990 the robbers forced their way into the home of the bank manager and took the family hostage. They had disguised themselves with Santa Claus masks and balaclavas. As an extra precaution Sture spoke with a Finnish accent, but after a while he forgot about this and went back to his usual way of speaking. Both of them were recognised without much difficulty and they were arrested by police immediately after the robbery.

Patrik was eighteen years old. He received a prison sentence of three and a half years. Sture was clinically assessed and committed to psychiatric care at the Säter clinic, where he had more or less stayed ever since, apart from the few occasions when he had been granted leave to travel to Stockholm, Hedemora and other towns in the regions of Dalarna and Norrland.

It was the time before the robbery that particularly interested me.

During extensive questioning, the teenage boys had described how Sture had made ice hockey goals for them, organised treasure trails and made popcorn. For a while, Sture had rented a holiday cottage where a number of the boys would occasionally have sleepovers. On no occasion had he tried to molest any of them and none of the boys had even suspected that he was homosexual. One evening a few of the boys had gone to Sture's home to watch a horror film. When things got particularly scary, Sture had held one of the boys' hands. On the way home, the boys had talked about it. They thought it was weird that a grown man would want to hold a thirteen-year-old's hand.

This long-standing innocent relationship with the boys of Grycksbo did not chime with the image of the serial killer who switched personality and compulsively raped, desecrated, murdered and cut up boys.

I contacted a few of the Grycksbo boys and met with one of them. None of them could quite reconcile the image of Thomas Quick with the Sture they felt they had known so well.

Preoccupied with these thoughts, I travelled to Dalarna at the end of August for a second meeting with Sture.

On the way to Säter I stopped at Falu District Court to look through the investigation material on the murder of Gry Storvik. I turned a page and it was like being punched in the gut when I saw the forensic technician's first photo of the body. The murderer had carelessly flung her out into a litter-strewn car park. A naked woman's body, still girlish, lay face down on the asphalt. Not satisfied with killing Gry, the murderer had also apparently intentionally and aggressively placed her in an exposed position for public display.

The effect of the photograph was unexpected. I felt upset, confused and embarrassed by the picture in front of me.

Whether he was guilty or not, this was a snapshot of the incomprehensible series of tragedies implied by Quick's confessions. After all, if Quick really was innocent of these crimes, the convictions were in effect an amnesty for the real murderers who had done this to Gry Storvik and the other victims.

This was precisely what Leif G.W. Persson had said, but it was only now that I properly understood. Again I looked at the photograph of Gry in the investigation file. It had been taken on 25 June 1985. It was now 28 August 2008 and the murder would become statute-barred in one year and ten months.

In 660 days the murderer – if he were someone other than Thomas Quick – would walk free for ever.

SÄTER HOSPITAL, THURSDAY, 28 AUGUST 2008

AS SOON AS Sture and I had made ourselves comfortable, I was keen to hear his feelings about his time in Grycksbo.

'When I read the interviews with the boys in Grycksbo and all the other people who knew you back then, I got the impression that this was a very happy period in your life.'

'Yes, that was a very good period,' Sture confirmed. 'Actually the best time of my life.'

Sture talked about various events, happy memories, his and Patrik's dogs and Christmas celebrations with the Olofsson family.

'But it all ended up as a complete disaster,' I reminded him.

'Yeah, in the end it went terribly bad, the whole thing!' said Sture, wringing his hands.

'And the effects on Patrik's family,' I continued. 'You worked your way in and then you hurt them terribly. Didn't you?'

Sture nodded. Silent. I could see his mind working. Then he hid his face in his hands and was rocked by deep sobs.

'Sorry, it's just so terrible thinking about it,' he managed to tell me through his convulsions.

I don't think I have ever seen a grown man cry with such abandon. Like a child. It was touching and frightening at the same time.

I was concerned that I had ruined everything I had started to build up, but Sture soon pulled himself together, wiped his tears and went to the locked door.

'Wait here! I'll be back in a minute,' he said, pressing the button.

Before long a care assistant was there to let him out. A few moments later he came back with a big tin box containing hundreds of photographs from his childhood, adolescence and adult years. We sat there for a long time, looking through the photographs. Many were of Sture posing or indulging in horseplay for the camera.

The television producer in me only had one thought: *How can I persuade Sture to lend me this box?*

One of the photos was of a woman in her mid-thirties. She was sitting in a kitchen, smiling at the camera. Sture held the photo under my nose.

'This is a bit odd. This is the only woman I ever had sex with,' he said.

I sensed a certain pride in him.

'The only one?' I asked, dumbfounded. 'Ever?'

'Yeah. Just with her. There are some special reasons for it,' he explained cryptically.

Long after, I learned that these 'special reasons' were that at a certain time in his life he dreamed of having children. Maybe he could manage to live with a woman despite his sexual orientation? The attempt was unsuccessful.

For my own part, that photograph and what Sture had just told me had another significance. *Gry Storvik*, I thought to myself. The woman working as a prostitute in Norway, who had been murdered and dumped in a car park with a man's sperm inside her body. *That woman in the photo is not Gry Storvik! With whom you claimed you had intercourse.*

So why had Sture told me this intimate detail? Had he given himself away? Or was he consciously leading me down this train of thought? No, we had never spoken of either Gry Storvik or any other murder, so why would he think I knew about his claim to have had sexual intercourse with Gry? My thoughts swung back and forth along these lines as we continued looking through the photographs.

As my visit started drawing to a close I asked, in a slightly absent-minded way, 'Do you think you could lend me a few of your photos?'

'Of course,' he said. 'I'd be happy to.'

I made do with five photographs: Sture in the kiosk; Sture and the guys on a hard rock outing; Sture looking with mock alarm into his empty wallet; Sture at the kitchen table; Sture posing outside the Olofssons' holiday cottage, where allegedly Yenon Levi was murdered.

That Sture let me take the five photographs was a clear indication of trust. As we parted, I knew that Sture would participate in my documentary. One way or another.

A DISCOVERY

BY THE END of the summer of 2008, both Gubb Jan Stigson and Leif G.W. Persson were becoming irritated with me.

'If you still haven't twigged what this is about you must be bloody stupid!' said Persson petulantly.

Stigson thought my mental faculties were just as impaired, since I hadn't understood that Quick really was the serial killer he had been convicted as.

'Take the murder of Therese Johannesen, for example. Therese was nine years old when she disappeared from a residential neighbourhood known as Fjell in Norway on 3 July in 1988. Seven years later Thomas Quick confesses to the murder. He's in Säter Hospital by then, he's capable of describing Fjell; he's shown the police to the spot, he's told them there was a bank there in 1988, he knew that the balconies had been repainted – all completely correct! He's said there was a children's playground being built and there were wooden planks scattered about on the ground. How could Quick know all that?' he asked rhetorically.

'If what you're saying is right, then I suppose at least he must have been there,' I admitted.

'Oh yes, of course,' said Stigson. 'And then he showed the police a wooded area where he murdered her and hid the body. That's where they found pieces of bone that proved to be from a human aged eight to fifteen. In one of the fragments there was a groove from a saw blade! Thomas Quick was able to show where he had hidden a hacksaw blade which fitted into the groove in the bone.'

Stigson shook his head.

'And then they say there's no evidence! I mean, the evidence is absolutely overwhelming, which is exactly what the Chancellor of Justice, Göran Lambertz, wrote after he'd reviewed all of Quick's verdicts.'

'Sure, it sounds convincing,' I said.

Gubb Jan Stigson had such a rabid, unshakeable and one-eyed view of Thomas Quick that I was reluctant to argue with him. Even so, I was grateful to him. He was a well-informed and invaluable person to talk to, who had also generously supplied me with material from the extensive investigations.

On one occasion he photocopied all three hundred articles he had written on the subject.

But his most important contribution was probably that he put in a good word for me with his allies – Seppo Penttinen, Christer van der Kwast and Claes Borgström. I don't know exactly who he spoke to, but I do know that he opened many doors for me.

Penttinen wasn't dismissive when I phoned him, despite his great suspicion of journalists who wanted to talk about Thomas Quick. He made it quite clear to me that he would never agree to be interviewed – he never agreed to interviews on principle – but he sent material that he felt I ought to read, including his own article 'The Chief Interrogator's View of the Mystery of Thomas Quick', published in 2004 in the *Nordisk kriminalkrönika* ('Nordic Crime Chronicle'), where, among other things, he wrote, 'To demonstrate what sort of evidence underpinned the successful convictions, the investigation into the murder of Therese Johannesen in Drammen might serve as a typical example.'

Even van der Kwast had emphasised the Therese investigation as the one where there had been the strongest proof against Quick. If Stigson, Penttinen and van der Kwast were agreed on this, there was no longer any doubt about which case I would try to get to the bottom of, to examine whether there was any basis for the murmurings about a judicial scandal.

Thomas Quick revealed things about his victims that only the perpetrator and the police could have known. Sometimes he even said things that the police were unaware of. This was clearly stated in the sentencing documents.

In several instances it was also difficult to see how he could have been aware of some of the murders at all. This was not least true of the Norwegian murders, which had hardly been covered in the Swedish media. How could Quick, locked up at Säter Hospital, even have had the knowledge to talk about the murders of Gry Storvik and Trine Jensen? Or show the way to the remote places where their bodies had been found?

I felt that many of those who had doubted Thomas Quick's testimonies had dismissed the question of the information he had provided too lightly. Some of Quick's so-called unique information could be explained, yet some of it seemed mysterious even after careful scrutiny of the investigation documents.

Quick had given descriptions of the victims' injuries, details of the crime scenes and information about the victims' clothes and belongings that had apparently not been mentioned in the media.

How did Quick know that a nine-year-old girl named Therese had gone missing from Fjell in July 1988? Hedemora District Court had recognised the significance of this in its summary of the evidence.

In its verdict for the Therese case, the district court writes: 'Information about this event available to Quick in the media – in so far as it has been shown – would have been limited.' And Quick had also given testimony on the subject: 'He has no memory of having read anything about these events before his confession', the sentencing document states.

The collected investigation material into the case of Thomas Quick amounts to more than 50,000 pages. I decided to organise the sections pertaining to Therese Johannesen along a timeline, and sat down to read all the interviews and documents from when Quick first started talking about her disappearance. How did he and the investigation get embroiled with Norwegian crimes in the first place?

I found a report in the police investigation stating that Quick had had contact with the Norwegian journalist Svein Arne Haavik.

Thomas Quick hadn't initially attracted any attention at all in Norway, but in July 1995 Haavik wrote him a letter in which he explained that he was working for Norway's biggest newspaper, *Verdens Gang*, which had recently published a series of lengthy articles on Thomas Quick. Haavik requested an interview with the serial killer.

The police report gives the following information:

> Shortly after, Haavik was telephoned by Thomas Quick, who asked Haavik to send all the newspaper articles about him and his murders in Norway.
>
> Haavik therefore sent Thomas Quick the newspapers from the 6, 7 and 8 July 1995.

The series of articles began on 6 July 1995 with a three-page opener. The front page was filled with a brooding photograph of Thomas Quick looking into the camera.

'Swedish mass murderer admits: I MURDERED A BOY IN NORWAY.'

Thomas Quick poses across an entire spread, wearing a T-shirt, jeans, Birkenstock sandals and white socks. The reporter describes his 'murders of bestial cruelty' and also reveals a snippet of new information: 'Under a cloak of secrecy, Norwegian and Swedish police have for several months been investigating at least one murder of a young boy in Norway.'

'I can confirm that a part of our investigation concerns a Norwegian boy whom Quick has told us he killed. The problem has been that we have yet to identify him, but we have some ideas about who the boy might be', *Verdens Gang* quoted from a statement by prosecutor Christer van der Kwast.

The following day the next article continued with Thomas Quick's description of the boy he had killed in Norway as '12–13 years old and cycling'.

The concluding article, on 8 July, was a long piece with the headline: 'Where Quick's Possible Victims Went Missing'. A half-page photograph shows a refugee centre in Oslo and there is also a smaller image of two African boys.

> The boy who went missing disappeared from this refugee centre in Skullerudsbakken in Oslo, which has since closed down, and was most likely the same boy that Thomas Quick (45) has admitted that he killed.
>
> In March 1989, two boys of about 16 and 17 went missing on separate occasions from the Red Cross reception for lone minors.

In other words, when Quick first mentioned Norway it was in reference to the murder of a boy – not a girl. But where did this information come from?

I dug my way back through the investigation material and found that Quick had told Seppo Penttinen in November 1994 about a dark-haired boy of about twelve of 'Slavic appearance' whom he called 'Dusjunka'. He associated the boy with the town of Lindesberg and a Norwegian place which he referred to as 'Mysen'.

Penttinen wrote to the police in Norway to ask whether they had a case with a boy of such a description who had gone missing. They did not, but his Norwegian colleagues sent information about two asylum-seeking boys of about sixteen or seventeen who had disappeared in Oslo.

Once the article appeared in *Verdens Gang*, the information became a self-fulfilling prophecy.

After a long period of making suggestive comments, Thomas Quick confessed to Penttinen in February 1996 that he had murdered two African boys in Oslo in March 1989. Penttinen immediately started preparing a trip to Norway.

In the interrogations that followed, I was able to read how Thomas Quick denied having read anything about any Norwegian murders in the newspapers, despite the fact that he asked for the serialised articles from *Verdens Gang*. He gave assurances that he had not seen any photographs of the missing asylum-seeking boys.

I could therefore confirm the following with absolute certainty: Quick had actively sought out information about feasible murders in Norway, he made use of this information during questioning, then lied about not having seen any information about the murders.

The series of articles which Thomas Quick received from Norway also offered another snippet of information. Next to the main article was a smaller item where *Verdens Gang* speculated on whether Thomas Quick might have been involved in Norway's most notorious unsolved crime.

> Therese Johannesen (9) went missing from the neighbourhood of Fjell in Drammen on 3 July 1988. Her disappearance triggered the most extensive manhunt in Norwegian history.
>
> During this period of time Quick has said that he committed murders in Norway.

Admittedly, the article doesn't provide any further details on either Therese or Fjell, but it does contain a number of critical pieces of information: the name of the girl and the place and date of her disappearance.

It is proven that Thomas Quick had access to these facts by the end of July 1995, and it is therefore hardly surprising that in the very first interview he was able to say that Therese was nine years old and went missing from Fjell in the summer of 1988.

But with questions that were not answered in the article in *Verdens Gang* he had less success.

As in most of the murder investigations, Quick's confession to the murder of Therese Johannesen had started during therapy. 'Events had floated up' and Birgitta Ståhle felt bound to report them, she said. Quick had been incoherent and 'Ståhle described the circumstances as *twisted*', Penttinen noted.

The idea was to get the whole story out on Wednesday, 20 March 1996. Birgitta Ståhle and Thomas Quick walked into the music room at Säter Hospital, where Seppo Penttinen and Detective Inspector Anna Wikström were already sitting waiting in the red and black armchairs.

Penttinen asked Quick to describe the residential area of Fjell.

'I can see properties,' said Quick. 'Not apartment blocks. Family houses.'

The place name Fjell (Mountain) may have given Quick the wrong associations, because he described the place as a bucolic idyll with scattered family homes here and there – possibly the Norwegian word for a city neighbourhood, *bydel* (a part of a village in Swedish), may have caused him some confusion, too. He claimed to have travelled there via an unpaved road.

'It's very small,' Quick clarified in the interview.

In actual fact Fjell is a typical 1970s concrete suburb with high-rise blocks, viaducts, shopping centres and 5,000 inhabitants in a fairly concentrated area.

Quick's voice grew increasingly quiet and finally he whispered, 'This is going to be bloody difficult!'

If at the time of questioning Penttinen was aware of how badly Quick's description corresponded to reality, he hid it well. He kept plying him with new questions:

> PENTTINEN: Do you know what time of day this is, more or less?
>
> TQ: Should be more or less lunchtime.
>
> PENTTINEN: What does lunchtime mean for you?
>
> TQ: The middle of the day.
>
> PENTTINEN: Do you remember what the weather was like?
>
> TQ: The weather was quite good, high clouds. Summer . . .

Therese disappeared at twenty past eight in the evening. Quick's remark on the decent summer weather did not ring particularly true, as at the time of Therese's disappearance Fjell was experiencing some of the worst torrential rainfall in ten years.

After the interview, Seppo Penttinen summarised Quick's descriptions of Therese's appearance and clothes:

> He stated that she had fair, shoulder-length hair, her hair bounced when she ran. She was wearing trousers and possibly a jacket. Later in the interview he said there was something pink, and he has a memory of it being a T-shirt with buttons. Her panties were patterned. She was wearing a wristwatch. Quick made an association of the strap being thin with a simple buckle and he had a colour impression of the watch as light green or pink.

Improbably enough, all these descriptions were wrong, and one would be quite justified in describing the account as a 'total miss', as certain critics of the Quick case have pointed out.

In the original police investigation after Therese's disappearance, a great deal of care was given to the girl's description, including every possible detail, with her clothes carefully specified. The most recent photograph was also there.

The girl in the colour photograph is standing in front of a brick wall, looking candidly into the camera. Her hair is black, her skin a golden brown, her eyes dark brown. A happy smile reveals a gap of two missing front teeth, pulling the corners of her eyes into a squint.

Quick spoke about Therese's big front teeth. Maybe they had grown since the photograph was taken?

When I called Inger-Lise Johannesen, Therese's mother, she told me they hadn't even started coming through.

Thomas Quick's blonde version of Therese is quite simply a stereotype of a Norwegian girl, a guess with reasonably good odds, statistically speaking, of being correct. In the end, everything was wrong except the information Thomas Quick had read in the little side article in *Verdens Gang*.

THE DEAD END

ONE LATE AFTERNOON on 23 April 1996 the police's little convoy of vehicles drove via Örebro and Lindesberg on Highway E18 into a little settlement known as Ørje on Svenskvejen ('the Swedish road') towards Oslo. Thomas Quick sat in the middle seat of a white minibus next to Inspector Seppo Penttinen.

The aim of the trip was for Quick to show where and how he had murdered two asylum-seeking African boys and nine-year-old Therese Johannesen in Norway.

The details Quick had given corresponded exactly with the case of two boys who had gone missing from the Red Cross asylum-seekers' centre on the outskirts of Oslo.

During the trip to Norway he outlined the route for how to get there. Before the trip he had made a drawing of the building, which was a fairly unusual old wooden house with a number of unique details. When they arrived, they found that the house looked exactly as in the drawing.

Quick showed them the way to a place known as Mysen, where apparently one of the boys had been killed. The boys' bodies had then been moved by Quick to Sweden, where he had cannibalised his victims before burying them in Lindesberg.

Detective Inspector Ture Nässén told me how Thomas Quick and the investigators drove to the football pitch in Lindesberg. There, the forensic technicians dug up a large area that Quick had pointed out. The cadaver dog Zampo reacted to the presence of human remains. When no body parts were found, Quick said that he had made a mistake; they should be searching the football pitch in Guldsmedshyttan instead. Despite determined digging and further sniffing by the cadaver dog, nothing was found there either.

While the excavations were in full swing in Guldsmedshyttan, something quite remarkable happened. Ture Nässén received confirmation that the two murder victims the police were looking for were in fact alive. Both had made their way to Sweden, where one of them had settled. The other was living in Canada.

And so two of Thomas Quick's Norwegian murders no longer existed. Undeterred, their investigations into the third murder continued with renewed energy. After an inquiry lasting some two years, and twenty-one interviews about Therese Johannesen, in which Quick changed his story countless times, his insights into the murder were deemed to be of such accuracy that Hedemora District Court found him guilty.

With my newly acquired insights into witness psychology, and having recently learned of Svein Arne Haavik's efforts as an informer, I realised that Quick's testimony wasn't worth a great deal. Nonetheless, there were the remaining bits of evidence: the pin-pointing of the crime scene in Ørje Forest, the fragments of bone . . .

I needed to go to Drammen, so I called Inspector Håkon Grøttland and invited myself.

'You're welcome,' he agreed.

RECONNAISSANCE IN ØRJE FOREST

IN SEPTEMBER 2008, the photographer Lars Granstrand and I crossed the border at the same place as the Quick investigators during their journey to Norway twelve years earlier.

At Drammen police station we met with Håkon Grøttland, who had participated in all of Quick's trips to Norway.

'He's not like us – he's not rational or logical,' said Grøttland.

He explained the specific difficulties investigators had faced in their dealings with Thomas Quick.

'Quick says "yes" and shakes his head at the same time! And he says "left" when he means right. There are simpler things in God's world than trying to figure out Thomas Quick.'

Personally, he hadn't been able to understand him, Grøttland explained. But Seppo Penttinen and Birgitta Ståhle knew what Quick meant.

Håkon Grøttland had worked on the Therese Johannesen investigation when she disappeared in July 1988. After that, he was part of a Norwegian police unit investigating Thomas Quick and he was still convinced that Quick had murdered Therese Johannesen.

'What is it that really convinces you?' I wondered.

'Just imagine Quick sitting there in a psychiatric clinic in Sweden, having all this detailed knowledge about Therese and Fjell and Ørje Forest. So we go out and check what he has said, and we find that it's actually true.'

I agreed it was difficult to find any other plausible explanation than the fact that Quick was guilty.

Grøttland gave us a lift to Fjell, where Therese had lived with her mother. We drove past the Fjell Centre and the video rental store where Therese had gone to buy sweets with the sixteen crowns and fifty öre she had in her pocket. Grøttland parked the car and showed us a wide-open area of grass, with a high-rise apartment block towering against the sky – Lauritz Hervigsvei 74. Grøttland pointed to the row of windows on the fifth floor.

'That's where she lived. And Quick stood here when Therese came walking from over there,' said Grøttland, pointing at a slope leading down to the road we had just driven along. 'It was here he took her.'

I counted the eight floors of the block, thirty-five large windows on each floor.

So Thomas Quick had supposedly abducted Therese in front of 280 large windows, right under the eyes of her mother, who had described how she stood on the balcony keeping an eye out for her the whole time.

'Christ, it's like abducting a child right in front of the main stand at Råsunda Stadium,' the photographer whispered into my ear.

Thomas Quick was never seen by anyone in connection with any of the thirty murders to which he had confessed and had never left any signs of his presence. That was why I had assumed he must always have exercised extreme caution.

During the investigation into Therese's murder, as we know, some 1,721 people were questioned by the police, but none of them had seen anything that could be related in any way to Thomas Quick. Nor did any of the 4,645 tip-offs that came in have any connection with Thomas Quick. I looked up at Therese's balcony and confirmed to myself that everything must have happened in full and public view.

'Then he smashed her head against a boulder on that slope, went and got his car and put her inside,' Grøttland explained.

'Seems incredibly risky,' I said.

'Yes, obviously,' answered the inspector.

*

The following day I met Grøttland's colleague, Ole Thomas Bjerknes, who had also worked on the Quick investigation. He showed me Hærland Church, where supposedly Quick had killed Therese. Then we went to Ørje Forest and drove several kilometres down bumpy forest tracks before reaching the area where Quick had disposed of Therese's body.

Bjerknes was teaching at the Norwegian police high school. That same day he had given a lecture about the Quick investigation, and he happened to have brought along three video tapes of raw footage from the Norwegian reconnaissance trips with Quick. I tried not to sound too keen when I asked if there was any chance of being able to have a look at the tapes. To my surprise, he readily handed them over. I took the coveted tapes, promising to return them to him before leaving Norway.

The same evening I sought out a television production company in Drammen and managed to hire the equipment needed to copy the tapes. I started at eight o'clock in the evening, in my hotel room. There were about ten hours of reconnaissance on the three tapes. The tapes to which I was transferring the material had to be changed every hour.

The most interesting footage was of Thomas Quick sitting in the car, while another camera filmed out of the windscreen. The camera pointed at Quick – from time to time also taking in Seppo Penttinen on his right-hand side – but the road was shown in a little superimposed box on the top left of the screen.

Quick's eyes rolled about. Sometimes they seemed to drop or stare with a crazed expression. It was extremely perplexing and unpleasant. The Thomas Quick of these recordings was an altogether different person from the one I had met at Säter Hospital about a week before. I wondered what could have triggered this personality transformation. Even his way of talking was different.

To keep myself awake through the night I forced myself to watch all three video tapes as I was copying. Often it was uneventful and excruciatingly dull, moving along without a word being uttered for half an hour, or with long sequences in which the cameraman had put down the camera and it had continued filming the car seat. Because I was copying I couldn't fast-forward; I had to suffer every minute of it.

It was already past midnight as I slotted in a new tape. We were now with a hand-held camera in the car behind Thomas Quick's van. Quick had requested that the car should stop but the camera kept rolling. In the recording, you can hear a care assistant coming into Quick's car and offering him medicine.

> CARE ASSISTANT: Are you taking your Xanax?
> TQ: Mm.
> CARE ASSISTANT: Can you get it down without water?
> TQ: I have . . . Coca-Cola . . .

On the tape, Thomas Quick speaks with a sluggish voice as if he is finding it difficult to formulate words at all.

> CARE ASSISTANT: Put it in your mouth . . . Is one enough? . . . Shouldn't you have another one right away?
> TQ: Yes, maybe . . .

Thomas Quick's answer is something between crying and talking, a sound made by a person going through terrible suffering.

I hear Quick taking another pill and after that the journey can go on.

The clinical drug Xanax is a tranquilliser classed as a narcotic, of a type known as a benzodiazepine, notorious for being extremely addictive and with a number of serious side effects.

What I had just seen convinced me that Thomas Quick was as high on drugs as he looked. I also recalled Göran Källberg's insinuations. Could this be what he had been alluding to, namely that Quick had been medicated with such strong drugs that his confessions must be viewed as unreliable? I watched the material with renewed interest. My tiredness had been swept away.

*

Again I changed the tape. Now Thomas Quick is in the first car in a convoy of four or five, heading towards Ørje Forest. He is leading a procession that includes a chief prosecutor, a police interrogator, a lawyer, a psychotherapist, a memory expert, several drivers and nurses, as well as a large number of Swedish and Norwegian police officers. Quick has announced that he will show them the way to a gravel pit where Therese Johannesen's body has been buried. The gravel pit is in Ørje Forest – he knows the way.

The convoy moves east along Highway E18 towards Sweden, and Quick complains about all the houses. He says that this also disturbed him after murdering Therese. Finally the situation becomes critical. The road signs indicate that the Swedish border is getting very close, and Quick has been quite clear about Therese's body being buried in Norway.

> TQ: . . . we're approaching the border and I have to find a road before . . .
>
> PENTTINEN: Before we get to the border?
>
> TQ: Yes.
>
> PENTTINEN: Yes, that's how you described it earlier.
>
> TQ: Yes.
>
> PENTTINEN: Do you recognise that, Thomas?
>
> TQ: Yes.

What Quick claims to recognise is Klund Church. After a good deal of conferring they decide to turn off onto a forest track on the right.

There is a road barrier and Quick says it was also there the last time round, but 'then there was no problem getting past it'.

Seppo Penttinen nonetheless has his doubts and he asks if there is really such a place as the one Quick has described down this road.

> TQ: It should be a sort of levelled area, of that characteristic, and then there should be . . . as if at some point it has been a kind of, of . . . I've had trouble describing it during questioning as well . . . like a gravel pit or soil pit or . . .

PENTTINEN: You mean like someone's been removing some kind of gravel?

TQ: Yes.

The convoy heads down the forest track, which proves very long. They shake and rattle, kilometre after kilometre. It already seems quite inconceivable that this track made for forestry vehicles should lead to a gravel pit.

Quick had said earlier that the church could be used as a marker to gauge how far down the road they should drive, but the steeple has long since disappeared from view.

TQ: Mm. I'm feeling that we have gone very far in relation to my memory of the distance I went.

PENTTINEN: Yes. Have we gone too far?

TQ: I don't know.

Quick says that he's had certain 'points of recognition' along the road, so they continue. I note that Quick is now noticeably slurring his words. He says that it is difficult for him to go down this road. After a while he starts flapping his arms.

PENTTINEN: You're waving your hand. What are you trying to say?

TQ: I don't know.

PENTTINEN: Should we carry on?

TQ: Yes, let's carry on. The fox must be red.

PENTTINEN: I can't hear what you're saying.

TQ: The fox must be dead.

PENTTINEN: The fox?

TQ: The Jewish boy.

PENTTINEN: The Jewish boy must be dead?

Thomas Quick seems to be lost in the mists, and Penttinen is concerned.

PENTTINEN: Are you with us, Thomas?

TQ: Mm.

But Thomas is not with them. Mentally he is in an entirely different place.

PENTTINEN: (*repeats*) Are you with us, Thomas?

Quick again hums an answer.

PENTTINEN: We're coming up to a crossing here. Now you have to decide the way, Thomas. Should we go to the right? You're nodding to the right.

The car turns right.

PENTTINEN: Here there's a turn to the left.
TQ: Keep going straight.
PENTTINEN: Shall we carry on?
TQ: Mm.
PENTTINEN: Straight on.
TQ: We can go where you find . . . so we can . . .
PENTTINEN: Turn round?
TQ: Mm.

Thomas Quick's droning voice now only hums his answers and soon he closes his eyes.

PENTTINEN: Now you're closing your eyes. How are you?
TQ: Stop a while. Over there.

The convoy stops. Quick sits in silence with his eyes closed. The terrain where the car has stopped does not correspond in any way to the description given earlier by Quick. There is no levelled piece of land here and certainly no gravel pit. The van has stopped on a long slope in a rolling Norwegian forest.

Quick sees a hill. He decides to walk to the top and is accompanied by Seppo Penttinen, Birgitta Ståhle, Claes Borgström and Detective Inspector Anna Wikström.

PENTTINEN: Are we within walking distance now of the place where Therese is?

TQ: Yes.

Quick is so unsteady on his legs now that Ståhle and Penttinen have to keep him on his feet by taking an arm each. You can see that they've done this before. They make their way up to the top of the hill, where the whole group stands in silence. Finally Penttinen speaks up.

PENTTINEN: You're looking down at the road, by that curve down there. And now you nod. Is there something special about that place? Try to describe it.

TQ: (*in a monotone, almost whispering*) The curve leads . . . up steps.

PENTTINEN: What did you say? The curve what?

TQ: Leads steps up.

It is difficult to make much sense of Quick, who seems completely drugged.

PENTTINEN: Can you see the place from here?

Quick is immobile. He closes his eyes.

PENTTINEN: You're nodding and closing your eyes at the same time.

Quick has opened his eyes and sees something at the bottom of the slope. They agree it's a shoulder of rock.

'Shall we try to get down to that spruce tree?' Quick suggests at long last.

They walk towards a little spruce tree and, when they get there, stand in silence once again. Quick whispers something inaudible. He's helped to light a cigarette.

'Is the curve in that direction?' he wonders, pointing with his arm.

'It is,' Birgitta Ståhle confirms.

'I want to have a look at it,' says Quick, and starts moving in the direction he has just been indicating.

The ground is covered in old branches and it is difficult to make much progress. Quick starts stamping on the branches. Penttinen grabs him.

Quick has a total freak-out and starts shouting, 'You bastard! Bloody bastard swine! You bloody bastard swine! Bloody bastard swine!'

Quick stamps and thrashes with his arms but is quickly overpowered. He ends up at the bottom of a heap of police and care assistants. Seppo Penttinen turns to the camera, as if to make sure that this is being properly documented. There is something triumphant about Penttinen's expression when he looks into the camera, filming this dramatic moment.

Someone has indicated to Christer van der Kwast that dramatic things are unfolding in the Norwegian undergrowth. He comes running into shot, wearing a shiny black suit. Quick is lying down, growling intently, a low, rhythmical sound.

Everyone in the company knows that Quick has undergone a transformation; he has assumed one of the multiple personalities he harbours within. This is a figure referred to by him and his therapist as Ellington – the evil figure of the father, the murderer – who has taken over Quick's psyche and body.

'Thomas,' says Penttinen in a pleading tone, while Quick continues making his noises.

Birgitta Ståhle tries to connect with her patient. 'Sture! Sture! Sture! Sture! Sture!' she says.

But Quick carries on being Ellington, and he growls back. 'Gone for ever,' he says in a thick, dark voice. 'Gone for ever!'

He growls again. 'And people will step on your slut snout,' he roars.

Ståhle makes another attempt to gain access to her patient, who is now calming down.

Quick is helped onto his feet and the whole group moves silently towards a height, where Quick sits down with his back to the camera. Penttinen, Ståhle and Anna Wikström are holding him. They remain sitting in silence for a long time.

'Tell us now,' Penttinen asks.

'Wait a moment,' says Quick, irritated. 'I have to . . .'

'What are you going to tell us?' Birgitta wonders.

'No, no! Don't disturb me!'

Quick isn't ready to start talking yet. No one has asked him what happened to that gravel pit he promised them. Or what he meant when he said that Therese would be found in an area of 'levelled ground'.

Quick starts whispering and, in a scarcely audible voice, speaks of how Therese 'was gone for ever when I left her'. The boys were still here but she was gone for ever. Therese's body is within an area between the spruce tree and the hilltop, he says.

'It's not enough, Thomas,' says Penttinen. 'It's too big.'

They reach a stalemate. Quick has not been able to deliver a body, nor a gravel pit and not even a levelled area of ground. And Penttinen is not accepting a vague suggestion that Therese is somewhere in the forest. He is demanding more than that.

Quick asks to speak privately with Claes Borgström. They step aside and the camera is turned off.

When recording is resumed fifteen minutes later, Quick disjointedly slurs something about 'a boy is mutilated by a car on packed earth'. He says that he has just been up on a hill and seen a boggy pond 'with certain stones'. This is the spot where 'the broken girl has been hidden', he says.

Quick wants to mark out a triangle in the forest where Therese's body may be found. Together they establish the outline of this triangle, the base of which is formed by a line from a spruce tree to 'almost down to the pond'. From this baseline, the tip of the triangle reaches 'two-thirds of the way up to the top of the hill'.

When the group has completed this time-consuming exercise, they start walking in the direction of the pond. Penttinen explains how he has to hold on to Quick, 'in view of what happened earlier'.

Quick growls by way of an answer.

'Are you having difficulties looking at the pond, Thomas?' asks Penttinen.

Quick growls.

'Talk so we can understand,' says Penttinen.

By now, they have reached the pond.

'When you walk by this pond, you start reacting to something,' says Penttinen. 'Do you recognise it in some way? Yes, you're nodding. What does that mean?'

'I want us to go a little further,' says Quick. 'I might need a bit of support.'

Quick is now so heavily drugged that he is walking with great difficulty. He has clearly been given more tranquillisers.

'I can't carry you, you have to understand that,' says Penttinen.

However, Quick doesn't seem to be understanding very much at all at this point. What he says is almost impossible to make out, and although he's being propped up he is struggling to make forward progress.

'We're waiting, Thomas, there's no hurry. We'll keep going for as long as you can stay on your feet.'

'Can I have a look at the pond?' asks Quick.

'But you have your eyes closed, Thomas!' says Penttinen. 'Try to open them. We're right here.'

Quick asks if Gun is there. Gun is Sture's twin sister, whom he has not seen for a number of years.

Anna Wikström explains that she is not Gun.

'It's Anna standing here,' she says.

Quick keeps his eyes shut.

'I'm going to look at the pond,' he says.

'We're here,' says Penttinen.

'Try to look,' Wikström urges.

'I'm looking,' says Quick.

'Why do you react like that?' Penttinen wonders.

'Because those boulders there . . .'

Again Quick runs out of words. A moment later he asks to speak to Birgitta Ståhle without the camera and microphone. By the time the video camera is turned back on after a twenty-minute interval, Quick has made a new statement. Claes Borgström has to explain what he has said. Quick will not answer any further questions.

Penttinen seems overwhelmed by the gravity of the moment, if also slightly concerned that Quick, in the last hour, has given several different versions of what happened to Therese. He knows that it is Quick's normal pattern of behaviour to make 'conscious deviations' from things that are difficult, in a psychological sense, to approach. Now he wants to assure himself that this emerging version is the truth.

'Before Claes explains I want some clarification,' says Penttinen.

He leans towards Quick and talks to him intimately.

'These two places we've filmed here which you've distinctly pointed out, are they 100 per cent certain for you? Without any variations, in the sense of deviations?'

Quick, speaking with difficulty, assures him that this time he is telling the truth: 'The deviations have partly been about this story about gravel . . .'

He sounds as if his batteries have run out mid-sentence.

'The gravel pit?' Penttinen fills in.

'Yes, that's right,' says Quick.

As soon as Quick has stepped aside it is time for Claes Borgström to give a little presentation to camera, with the boggy pond in the background.

'So what's happened here is that at point one, this crotch-like formation, he massacred Therese's body. In other words there are no whole body parts left. No larger pieces of bone. Then he's taken the body parts, after massacring the body, into this depression here. Then finally he's swum out into the middle of the pond and let go of them, then gone back and fetched more. Some of them have sunk to the bottom and others have floated off in various directions. So there's a point three in his story and it's the pond.'

That was all Claes Borgström had to say on behalf of his client. The reconnaissance in Ørje Forest was over and the last video tape had come to an end.

Noise and static started on the TV and I felt almost as divorced from reality as Thomas Quick when I looked around my room, brightening now in the light of early morning, at the First Hotel Ambassadeur in

Drammen. The copying had taken almost twelve hours and it was eight in the morning. I was bewitched by what I had seen in the films: a sizeable delegation of Swedish civil servants allowing themselves to be led about by a drugged psychiatric patient who clearly had no idea where he was. Could they really not have understood? *No*, I thought. *It wasn't possible*. Could they really have believed he knew where Therese was? Even though he first spoke of a gravel pit; then, finding there was no gravel pit, a spruce tree; then within a certain triangle in the forest. Finally, she was 'massacred' and submerged in a pond.

It was difficult to accept that these highly educated representatives of a range of academic disciplines had not seen through the performance. With assumed or actual naivety they all took Quick's information seriously, and it was determined that the pond would be drained.

A very large number of police constables from several of Norway's districts took part in this work for seven weeks, with additional support from home guard personnel and external experts. First, the top layers of soil in the areas pointed out by Quick were peeled back and all the material manually sieved and examined by cadaver dogs and forensic archaeologists. After this unproductive Sisyphean task had been concluded, the even more laborious job of draining the small boggy pond commenced. Thirty-five million litres of water were pumped out and filtered; the bottom sediments were vacuumed until layers that were estimated to be 10,000 years old were reached. When nothing at all was found, everything was filtered a second time, but still not even the tiniest fragment of Therese was found.

Once again, the extremely costly investigation led to the inevitable conclusion that what Quick had said was untrue.

The fact that nothing was found after the pond had been drained called for an explanation from Quick. At this point he changed his mind and said that he had hidden Therese's body in a gravel pit.

While the Norwegians continued scouring the forest and surrounding terrain, Quick was repeatedly questioned by Seppo Penttinen. And so the investigation continued to focus on Ørje Forest until the technicians – finally! – found the remains of a few fires, in which there were burnt pieces of bone.

One of those who examined the finds in Ørje Forest was the

Norwegian professor Per Holck, who soon reached the decision that some of the bone fragments were human in origin and came from a person aged between five and fifteen.

How could you challenge a professor at the anatomical department of Oslo University, who had confirmed that these were indeed the body parts of a child, found precisely where Quick claimed to have disposed of a nine-year-old girl's body by cremation? And still . . .

The story was *too* odd for me to be able to believe it.

I had set myself the task of scrutinising the prosecutor's strongest case, Therese Johannesen, and afterwards I tried to summarise my position. What I had seen had pretty well convinced me that Quick did not murder Therese. It was worrying but also exceptionally impractical. It was becoming increasingly difficult to talk to the protagonists on the opposing sides of the Quick feud.

I had also discovered another thing, which no one else seemed to be aware of: Sture Bergwall, the person I had met at Säter, had nothing at all in common with the drugged mental patient who, under the name of Thomas Quick, had stumbled about in various forests, muttering incoherently about how he had murdered, chopped up, desecrated and eaten his victims. I had also hit upon the only reasonable explanation, namely that Quick had been encouraged to take large amounts of narcotic-strength medications.

I realised I had to control myself. So far, insights and information were still little more than hypotheses. Many questions remained to be answered. Above all I was thinking about that burnt piece of child's bone, found in Ørje Forest, exactly where Quick had said that he burned Therese's remains.

I went back to Sweden filled with a great sense of doubt, well aware that I had now joined the side of the sceptics.

After my return I phoned Sture Bergwall, who was very curious about how my work was going. I told him about my trip to Fjell and Ørje Forest and about my meetings with Norwegian police officers.

'Oh, you're really putting a lot of work into this! So you've been in Norway and Ørje Forest?'

Sture was deeply impressed by my endeavours, but more than anything he seemed interested in the conclusions I had reached.

'So what do you think about it?' he wondered.

'To be honest I have to say that this whole trip to Norway and what I saw there have made me rather hesitant.'

'In that case I'd like you to tell me what's on your mind next time you come up here,' said Sture.

I cursed my own loose tongue, which would most likely mean that my next meeting with Sture would also be the last. We decided that I would come to Säter one week later, on 17 September 2008.

I was going to be honest. If he chose to throw me out, so be it.

SÄTER HOSPITAL, WEDNESDAY, 17 SEPTEMBER 2008

WHEN WE MET for the third time in the visiting room at Säter Hospital, Sture Bergwall said, 'Now I want to hear what you really think about it all.'

It was an unpleasant request.

After all, Quick had said that he took time out because of people disbelieving his confessions. What would happen if I also questioned them?

I tried to temper the bitter pill with a generous measure of humility.

'I wasn't there when the murders were committed. I wasn't at the court hearings. I can't say what's true. All I can do is work with hypotheses.'

I could see that Sture was following my line of reasoning and that he accepted my description of the premises.

'When I was in Norway I had the opportunity to carefully study the video recordings from your reconnaissance of the crime scene in Norway. I'll tell you what I saw: you were given an addictive narcotic, a very strong drug, Xanax, in large doses. While you were being taken round you seemed very much under the influence of it. And when you got to Ørje and you were supposed to show them the place where Therese was buried you didn't seem to have a clue what to do next.'

Sture was listening now, very attentively. His face had a concentrated expression but he did not reveal how he felt about what I was saying.

'You were unable to show the police to the gravel pit, as you'd promised,' I carried on. 'You couldn't show them the way to Therese's body. You behaved as if you'd never been in that place before.'

I looked at Sture, my shoulders hoisted up tentatively.

'I don't know what the truth is. But as I said when I called you, I began to feel very hesitant.'

Sture looked straight ahead with an empty stare. We sat there for a long while, neither of us saying anything. Again, I was the one to break the silence.

'Sture, can you *understand* that this is what I'm seeing in those films?'

Sture was still silent, but he hummed and nodded. *At least he doesn't seem angry*, I thought. I had said what I had to say. I could not take it back and I had nothing to add.

'But . . .' said Sture and then went silent again.

He spoke slowly and with emotion: '. . . if it is true that I haven't committed any of these murders . . .'

Again he sat in silence, staring down at the floor. Then he leaned towards me, threw out his hands and whispered, '. . . if it is true – then what can I do?'

I met Sture's despairing gaze. He looked utterly devastated.

Again and again I tried to say something, but I was so overwhelmed that I couldn't make a sound. Finally I heard myself say, 'If it's true that you haven't committed *any* of these murders, you have the chance of a lifetime now.'

By now, the atmosphere in the little visiting room was so tense that it was physically tangible. We both knew what was about to happen. Sture was very close to telling me that he had lied during all those years when he was Thomas Quick. In principle he had already admitted it.

'The chance of a lifetime,' I repeated.

'I live in a ward where everyone is convinced that I'm guilty,' said Sture quietly.

I nodded.

'My lawyer is convinced that I'm guilty,' he continued.

'I know,' I said.

'Six courts have convicted me of eight murders.'

'I know. But if you're innocent and prepared to tell the truth, none of that matters.'

'I think we should leave it there,' said Sture. 'This is a bit too much for me to swallow in one go.'

'Can I come back?'

'You're welcome back,' he said. 'Any time.'

I have no memory of leaving the hospital, only that a few moments later I was standing in the car park, talking to my producer Johan Brånstad at SVT. Most likely I was incoherently telling him about my overwhelming meeting and its ramifications.

Rather than going back to Gothenburg, as planned, I went directly to Säter Stadshotell and booked a room for the night. Restlessly I paced back and forth inside, trying to concentrate on my work.

I had been given strict orders never to call Sture after six o'clock in the evening. It was two minutes to six. I called the patient line at Ward 36. Someone went to fetch Sture.

'I just wanted to know how you're feeling after our meeting,' I said.

'Oh, thanks,' he answered. 'It actually feels good. I'm feeling it's good, what's happening now.'

Sture sounded happy, and this emboldened me to ask the question.

'I'm still in Säter,' I admitted. 'Can I come and see you tomorrow?'

His reply was immediate, without the slightest pause for reflection: 'You're welcome!'

THE TURNING

'I HAVEN'T COMMITTED any of the murders I've been convicted of and none of the murders I've confessed to either. That's the way it is.'

Sture had tears in his eyes and his voice no longer carried. He looked at me, as if trying to work out whether or not I believed him.

All I knew was that he had lied. But was he lying to me now? Or when he confessed? Or on both occasions? I couldn't be certain, but the prospects of finding out had just dramatically improved.

I asked Sture to try and explain right from the beginning, so I could understand better.

'When I came to Säter in 1991 I had certain hopes that my time here would move things along for me, I'd gain insights into myself and learn to understand myself better,' he began hesitantly.

His life was ruined and his self-esteem about as low as it could get. He was looking for a reason to exist, he wanted to be someone, and to belong.

'I'd been passionate about psychotherapy for a while, especially psychoanalysis, and so I was hoping to improve my understanding of myself in that way,' he explained.

A doctor on the ward named Kjell Persson, who was not a psychotherapist, had taken pity on him, but Sture soon realised that he wasn't a very interesting patient. When Kjell Persson asked him to talk about his childhood he answered that he didn't have any particular memories, he did not feel that anything was worth talking about.

'I realised soon enough that the important thing was to start making up some memories from childhood, traumatic memories about dramatic events. And what a response I got as soon as I started talking about things like that. An incredible response!

'More and more it was about sexual molestation and abuse and how I myself became an abuser. The story was built up in therapy and the things I said about it were helped along by benzo.'

Sture was already addicted to benzodiazepines when he got to Säter in April 1991 and gradually the range of drugs on offer and their dosages increased – mainly, he claimed, because of developments in the therapy room.

'The more I told them, the more benzo I got. In the end I practically had free access to medicines, to narcotics.'

Sture maintained that in all the years of the murder investigations he was constantly drugged with benzodiazepines.

'I wasn't straight for a moment. Not one moment!'

Benzodiazepines are highly addictive and soon Sture could not live without the medicines. He 'reactivated repressed memories' in therapy, confessed to murder after murder and participated in a string of police investigations. In return he gained the attention of therapists, doctors, journalists, police and prosecutors. And he had unlimited access to narcotics.

I thought about all the people around Quick in the years of the police investigations – lawyers, prosecutors and police. Had they been aware that he was drugged? I asked.

'They must have been! They knew I was taking my Xanax, and you could see by my behaviour that I was drugged. How could anyone not see that? It would have been impossible!'

The truth of this last comment was something I had been able to confirm for myself from the video footage taken in Norway. There was no mistaking that he was so heavily drugged at times that he was unable to walk or talk. And the medication was administered quite openly.

'Was your use of medications ever discussed between you and your lawyer?'

'No! Never.'

'No one questioned your intake of medication?'

'At no time! I never heard that question being asked.'

According to Sture, the doctors, therapists and carers had ensured that he had a constant and unlimited supply of narcotic medications.

'Today it would be unthinkable, but at the time I was happy the question wasn't brought up. It meant I could keep using those drugs.'

Sture claimed that he had been constantly drugged for almost ten years. It was during those years that he cooperated with the prosecutions, leading to his convictions for eight murders which he had not committed.

Then everything came to an abrupt end.

'One day, it must have been towards the middle of 2001, there was a decision taken by the new chief physician at Säter, Göran Källberg. All the medications would be dispensed with. No more benzo. I was just terrified of having side effects from the withdrawal.'

I thought about what the retired chief physician Göran Källberg had said a few months earlier, about not wanting to be a part of a 'cover-up of a miscarriage of justice'. I was starting to understand the general thrust of Källberg's thoughts about Quick, the murders and his use of medications.

Sture had felt that there was a sort of silent agreement between him and Säter Hospital, a connection between his confessions for murder and the unlimited supply of medication. Now the terms of the agreement had been cancelled from one day to the next. His reaction was one of anger, bitterness and fear.

'How was I going to live without medicine? What would it mean physically?' Sture's use of benzodiazepines had reached such high levels that it had to be reduced by gradual increments over an eight-month period.

'They were difficult months. I just stayed in my room. The only thing I could do was listen to the radio, P1.'

Sture crossed his arms, clutching at each shoulder.

'I lay like this on the bed,' he said, shivering violently.

'And then suddenly you were clean and felt healthier. But then in practice you were sentenced to life for eight murders?'

'Yes.'

'And you'd contributed to this yourself!'

'Yeah. And I couldn't find a way out. I haven't had a single person to turn to for support.'

'Why not?'

He became silent, then he looked at me with a kind of astonishment, before laughing and saying, 'Where was I going to turn? I could hardly speak to my lawyers, who were also a part of this whole thing that led to my convictions. I've been very alone in this . . .'

'Not a single person to talk to?'

'No, I never found anyone. But maybe there were people . . .'

'The people around you now, in the clinic, do you know what position they take on your guilt?'

'In general I think they think I'm guilty as charged. Maybe there could be the odd exception among the staff. But it's not discussed.'

All police questioning ceased after the article in *Dagens Nyheter* in November 2001 in which Quick announced that he was withdrawing and taking time out. Shortly after, Christer van der Kwast shelved all pre-trial investigations in progress. Quick stopped receiving journalists and entered into his seven-year period of silence.

What is less well known is that Sture also stopped having therapy. Without the medication he had nothing to talk about. He didn't want to carry on talking about the sexual abuse in his childhood and the murders he committed as an adult – nor was he *capable* of talking about these things without the benzodiazepine. It was the medication that had made him so glib that he could take the initiative in his therapy sessions and during police questioning.

'For a few years I didn't see Birgitta Ståhle at all. Then we started meeting once a month for a "social chat". Then as you'd bloody expect she slipped it into a conversation: "For the sake of the loved ones you have to carry on talking." So it's been like a nightmare scenario!'

Another nightmare has been that Sture has almost no clear memories at all about what happened during his years as Thomas Quick. It's generally known that high doses of benzodiazepines knock out the cognitive faculties – learning processes simply don't work.

Initially I suspected that Sture was faking his memory loss, but soon I realised that he really didn't have a clue about significant events – even when speaking of them would have been in his own best interest. It struck me that this was a situation that had made it almost impossible for him to retract his confessions.

'I really hope that the medications have been properly recorded in the patient file,' he said. 'I don't know if they have.'

What Sture had told me meant that the case of Thomas Quick was not only a giant miscarriage of justice but also a healthcare scandal of huge proportions – a prisoner in psychiatric care who had been given inappropriate therapy and insane levels of medication. The convictions for eight murders were a direct consequence of this malpractice. That is, if Sture was telling the truth. And how could I ever check the level of accuracy in his statements?

'It would be useful for me to be able to read your file,' I said.

Sture looked very uncomfortable.

'I don't know if I want that,' he said.

'Why?'

He lingered over his answer.

'I would find it so dreadfully embarrassing to let another person read everything I said and did in those years.'

'Christ! People have read how you assaulted children, murdered them, chopped them up and ate their bodies! What could there possibly be left for you to be embarrassed about? Everything's about as embarrassing as it can get!'

'I don't know,' Sture repeated. 'But I'll think about it.'

His answer made me suspicious. Was Sture denying me his files because they revealed another story?

'You think about it,' I said. 'But if you want the truth to come out, it's conditional on you being absolutely candid. Truth and nothing but the truth . . .'

'Yes, I suppose you're right,' said Sture. 'I'm just so dreadfully ashamed . . .'

We said goodbye after a long and exhausting conversation. As I was preparing to leave and Sture was just about to ring the bell for the care assistant, I suddenly remembered something important.

'Sture, I just want to ask you one last question that I've been obsessing about for six months.'

'What's that?'

'What did you do in Stockholm when you were on leave?'

He smiled broadly and answered without a moment's hesitation. His answer also made me smile.

PART II

'If you're saying that the police, along with a psychologist, have rigged Swedish court cases to put an innocent person behind bars, I will answer that this has never happened in the history of our legal system. If someone could prove that, it would be the biggest scoop in the world!'

Claes Borgström, Thomas Quick's defence lawyer 1995–2000, in an interview with the author on 14 November 2008

LIVING A LIE

I WAS STANDING by the door to the visiting room, waiting for the guard to let me out. But first Sture had to answer my question.

Thomas Quick's trips to Stockholm when he was on leave were noted in the police investigation material. On his return from one of these trips, it was as if he had made 'a hypnotic journey in a time machine' and now had amazing recall of every detail of his murder of Thomas Blomgren in Växjö. At least this was how his therapist interpreted the sudden return of his memory.

'Oh, I can tell you that all right,' said Sture triumphantly. 'I sat in a library in Stockholm reading newspaper articles about Thomas Blomgren. Yeah, I sat there scanning through microfilm. I noted down important facts and made a drawing of the outhouse. I smuggled these into Säter and mugged up on them before I got rid of them.'

Although I had suspected this was exactly what had taken place, it was almost unsettling to learn how infernally crafty he had been. Why on earth had he put so much effort into duping the police?

According to Sture, his goal had not been to trick the police. It had all been about achieving credibility with his therapist and trying to be an interesting patient.

'I was forced to the library by Kjell Persson,' Sture explained. 'You have to understand the enormous pressure I was under in my therapy. We sat there three times a week, a couple of hours every time. And I talked and talked without being able to come up with any real facts. It was also about Kjell Persson and [chief physician] Göran

Fransson wanting to pass on something substantial to Seppo and Kwast. Talking about Thomas Blomgren seemed harmless. It was a statute-barred crime and there was no risk I'd be prosecuted for it.'

I heard what Sture was saying, but however hard I tried to understand, it was all too crazy for me.

'And anyway,' Sture continued with a pointed glance, 'I have an alibi for the murder of Thomas Blomgren! A very strong alibi!'

I still hadn't quite got over what he'd said about the library.

'Me and my twin sister were confirmed on that Whitsun weekend in 1964,' Sture told me eagerly. 'The confirmation stretched over two days! It was at home, in Falun! We were in folk costume! We were part of a folk-dancing group and we were all confirmed together.'

'Are you really sure about this? You're sure you have the right date and the right year?'

'Quite sure,' he said emphatically. 'I was worried all along that they'd find out about the confirmation. My siblings knew about it! And the others who were being confirmed. It wouldn't have been so difficult to find out about it!'

Finally the guard came to let me out. We had to say a quick goodbye.

My head was spinning as I walked out into the autumn air and went to my car. There was a great deal to process here; I remained deep in thought all the way back to Gothenburg.

Sture Bergwall's retraction of his confessions to all the murders had a fundamental impact on the work with my planned television documentary.

He soon got over his initial resistance to letting me have his files and before long I had access to material far beyond anything I could ever have dreamed of. The material primarily consisted of patient notes, records of medications and so on, but Sture had also kept masses of correspondence, diaries, private notes and old investigation documents.

Sture provided me with everything I wanted and didn't even bother reading through what he was passing to me.

'That's my big security, I *know* there's nothing in this material that will contradict me. For the first time I have nothing to hide. Nothing!'

'The truth will set us free,' I answered in a slightly jaunty tone, but at the same time there was a deep underlying seriousness.

If Sture's new version of events was indeed the truth, I knew that the mere fact of telling it would be a great relief to him.

In the time after Sture's turnaround we often spoke about the devastating consequences of any attempt on his part to lie to me. Even the most inconsequential lie would send us both into limbo. In my heart I knew he was telling me the truth. I knew it. But for reasons of plain self-preservation I was determined to question everything he said.

As far as the outside world was concerned he was the foremost lunatic in the whole country, a person entirely devoid of credibility. The fact that he now claimed it was all made up wouldn't necessarily change that perception.

Yet the convictions imposed on Thomas Quick were also based on additional evidence, and I knew that I would have to scrutinise – and rule out – every single piece. If even one item could not be explained in any other way than by Sture's guilt, his entire story would collapse like a house of cards.

With the researcher Jenny Küttim, I was producing a documentary in two parts, scheduled for broadcast on 14 and 21 December 2008. We had exactly three months to complete our task.

We had questions for Sture on a daily basis and relying on the patient telephone in his ward was no longer an option. We got him a simple mobile phone which we posted to him in Säter, so that we could talk as often as we liked.

Sture Bergwall had no money to pay for the legal advice he needed now, but the lawyer Thomas Olsson, with whom I became acquainted during 'The Case of Ulf', accepted the commission on a *pro bono* basis, at no cost to the client.

Jenny Küttim and I devoted ourselves wholeheartedly to checking

Sture's statements and working our way through the colossal amounts of documentation to which we now had access. Sture's patient files stretched from 1970 to the present. They confirmed Sture's own account of a senseless over-medication.

The material makes for remarkable reading. What we were seeing was no less than an inconceivable healthcare scandal.

THE ARRIVAL OF THE SERIAL KILLER

AFTER THE BOTCHED bank robbery in Grycksbo in 1990, Sture Bergwall was initially given a psychiatric evaluation at the state clinic for forensic psychiatry in Huddinge. In her eleven-page social investigation, the counsellor Anita Stersky summarised her patient's life thus far: sexual assaults on young boys at the end of the 1960s, the consequent sentence of psychiatric care, a spell at Sidsjön Hospital in Sundsvall, then the release on trial and subsequent studies at the folk high school in Jokkmokk. 'After this period, things took a turn for the worse,' wrote Stersky. 'SB got involved with homosexuals abusing narcotics and alcohol. Despite this, he had a certain feeling of belonging with the group, which gave him a negative identity but an identity nonetheless.'

Sture was confined to Säter Hospital for the first time in January 1973, then conditionally released to pursue his studies at Uppsala University. Everything seemed to be going well until March 1974, when he attacked a homosexual man, whom he came very close to stabbing to death. The social report listed further periods of confinement, more conditional releases, Bergwall's 'death wish' and suicide attempts; then, in 1977, a definite release from Säter. Of Sture Bergwall's attraction to young boys, Anita Stersky concluded: 'He has learned that he is not allowed to live out his desires.' She added: 'One of the most important factors in SB being able to control these desires was that he completely stopped using narcotics and alcohol.'

There followed a description of the years in Grycksbo: the kiosk venture, life with Patrik, the cancellation of disability payments, bankruptcy, financial problems, his time as a bingo caller and finally the failed robbery of Gotabanken.

In her closing statement as counsellor, Stersky wrote:

> In our conversations, SB has usually been extremely anxious and nervous, and occasionally bursts into crying fits. When we speak of particularly emotional subjects, SB has a tendency to become hysterical. He chews, scratches or pulls at his beard, closes his eyes and shakes in an almost convulsive manner, or he sits stiffly and keeps his eyes closed for several minutes and at such times is not receptive to any attempts to communicate with him. [. . .] In my opinion SB suffers from a significant psychiatric disturbance and needs to kept in confined psychiatric care. This should be arranged for him at a hospital equipped to deal with high-maintenance patients, because of the level of danger he presents.

Sture told me about the almost bottomless despair he felt at this time: 'I had a good life in Grycksbo. Many friends and a job as a bingo caller in Falun. The old ladies liked me; many of them picked the days when I was working to come in. I was the caller, I sold the chips, took care of the old girls, fetched coffee, joked with them. I made them enjoy themselves. It was a nice job and it suited me really well. By getting caught for the bank robbery I burned all my bridges. Relatives, friends, my work, I lost everything.

'I had done bad things before. But that was a long time ago, when I was a young man in the 1960s and 1970s. After the robbery I couldn't even imagine looking into my siblings' eyes again. I was utterly alone and had nothing to go back to. Nothing.'

His time in Huddinge gave him two things, he explained to me.

'At the psychiatric clinic in Huddinge I learned that even a horrifying mass murderer like Juha Valjakkala could awaken feelings of admiration among some of the staff. He'd been kept in a special isolation ward under constant surveillance. There was this terrible fascination for Juha and his crimes.'

With his Finnish girlfriend Marita, Juha Valjakkala had murdered an entire family in Åmsele, in the region of Västerbotten, in 1988. After their arrest in Denmark, Juha was put through an extensive psychiatric assessment at the clinic of forensic psychiatry in Huddinge. Although some time had passed since Valjakkala left the clinic, his shadow still hung heavily over the ward.

'Some of the staff were talking to me about Juha all the time. I was like a vent for their need to talk about Juha and the murders,' said Sture. 'I realised that even a loathsome criminal could be admired and loved.'

That was one thing. The other thing that came up, Sture explained to me, was that Anita Stersky told him about a 'fantastic form of psycho-dynamic therapy' that had been developed at Säter Hospital. He looked forward to that.

The dark blue Volvo passed Säter golf club, slowly turned onto the road known as Jonshyttevägen, or Jon's Cabin Way, and glided along the leafy shore of Lake Ljustern. The passenger in the back seat had no idea that he was destined for international fame and, in terms of the number of murders he had committed, would overtake giants like Jack the Ripper, Ted Bundy and John Wayne Gacy.

But it was early spring in 1991, the piles of sticks and branches built up for Walpurgis Night had not yet been lit and Thomas Quick was still known as Sture Bergwall. He did not know that his life story would occupy psychologists, doctors, researchers, journalists and a large part of the Swedish legal establishment for decades to come. He had no idea that internationally distinguished academics, believing that his case was unprecedented, would follow his remarkable fate with great interest.

When Sture Bergwall arrived at Säter Hospital on 29 April 1991, the concept of the serial killer was relatively new to the average Swede. A number of cases in the USA had caused the FBI to coin the term and develop new methods – in particular so-called profiling techniques – in an attempt to track down the elusive perpetrators. The phenomenon had been the subject of extensive research among American criminologists and behavioural experts in the latter part of the 1980s. A few years later it began to be exploited by writers and film-makers in popular culture.

In the spring of 1991, the new anti-hero of popular culture was taking possession of the stage in grand style, represented by Hannibal 'The Cannibal' Lecter in the screen dramatisation of Thomas Harris's novel *The Silence of the Lambs*. In the film, the brilliant serial killer helps the investigators – with a series of infernally cryptic clues – identify the serial killer 'Buffalo Bill', who catches and kills women with the express intention of sewing himself a suit made from their skins. Dr Lecter offers sharp-witted and psychologically insightful leads in the form of anagrams and personal questions directed at FBI agent Clarice Starling, often with learned references and quotations from Marcus Aurelius, the Roman emperor. But the razor-sharp cannibal's clues are so sophisticated and cryptic that they can only be deciphered with enormous difficulty.

Sture wasn't able to go to the cinema, but he rented the film on video and, like everyone else in Sweden, began to learn how serial killers operated and how they could be hunted down.

At the same time the successful novel *American Psycho* was published, in which the ice-cold sadist, millionaire and serial killer Patrick Bateman looked for amusement and a cure for his overriding boredom by assaulting his victims, with perfectly judged indifference, using electric drills and staple guns. The library at Säter Hospital acquired the book, which Sture Bergwall immediately borrowed and read.

'The main character of the novel, Patrick Bateman, is incredibly intelligent, which I think was important to me. I saw that one could be intelligent and a serial killer at the same time. *The Silence of the Lambs* and *American Psycho* also got a certain status because they were reviewed in *Dagens Nyheter* and *Expressen*'s culture pages. Because of that, serial killers also became interesting to me,' Sture recalled.

For Sture Bergwall, having an identity as an intellectual person was important, and he noted that his doctors and psychologists were interested in the new phenomenon. And with an almost uncanny sense of timing, the successful stories in popular culture were soon finding their equivalent in real life.

One warm evening at the end of July 1991, two police officers were cruising through a district of Milwaukee in Wisconsin known for its prevalence of heavy crime, when a young black man came running up to them with a handcuff dangling from one of his wrists.

The man's name was Tracy Edwards and he told them about a 'strange guy' who had put the handcuffs on him before he managed to escape from the apartment.

The door to apartment 213 was opened at once by the tenant, Jeffrey Dahmer, a handsome, presentable thirty-one-year-old man with blond hair who showed no signs of nerves. He readily offered to go and get the keys to his boyfriend's handcuffs from the bedroom. The policemen gleaned that Dahmer looked to be a decent person living in an apartment which was unusually neat and well furnished for the area. Despite this, something made one of the policemen insist on taking a look at the bedroom where the key was kept.

In the bedroom the policeman discovered a large vat containing 300 litres of acid, in which three human bodies were dissolving. His colleague opened the refrigerator to find four human heads lined up on the glass shelves. No food was kept in the fridge, only human body parts. Another seven craniums were stored in the wardrobe, and Dahmer had baited a lobster trap with the penis of one of his victims.

The well-mannered, attractive young man had drugged his victims, drilled holes in their skulls and poured various chemical substances directly into their brains. Once this was over, he had raped them, cut them into pieces and then eaten choice parts of their bodies.

How does one explain such behaviour? And what does one call a person who has committed such deeds? The newspapers did their best to find suitable labels. 'Satan', 'The Cannibal from Milwaukee' and 'A Living Monster' were some of the names given to Jeffrey Dahmer, but words never seemed to be enough.

However repellent the details revealed about Jeffrey Dahmer were, the media was soon reporting on an even worse serial killer, 'The Russian Devil' – guilty of at least fifty-two murders.

Once again it was an apparently harmless, friendly soul who was uncovered as the personification of evil. Fifty-five-year-old Andrei Chikatilo, described as a 'mild-mannered language teacher', lived a peaceful life with his wife and children in the south Russian town of Novocherkassk. In their twenty-seven-year marriage, his wife had never suspected her husband of hiding any dark secrets.

The serial killer could be anyone. You, me, the neighbour or your spouse.

During their twelve-year hunt for the Russian serial killer, the police had arrested several others. One of these suspects was made to confess and, even worse, was eventually executed for murders that were later connected to Chikatilo.

Another suspect managed to kill himself before the trial.

During Sture Bergwall's first autumn at Säter, an unknown perpetrator started shooting at immigrants in the Stockholm area. Before the shots were fired a small red spot had been observed on the victims, which gave the evening press the idea of calling the perpetrator the 'Laser Man'.

On 8 November the Laser Man shot his fifth victim – the only one who actually died. National police were under pressure, knowing that the Laser Man would carry on shooting immigrants until he was arrested. This was particularly troubling, as the police had no idea where or in what circles such a criminal should be sought.

The modus operandi of the Laser Man was in many ways consistent with the clichés of serial killers. He chose victims that were non-Caucasian; he worked in a defined geographical area; he had no relationship to the ten victims; he was disciplined and hardly left any traces. On the other hand, the Laser Man had usually failed to kill; of his ten victims, only the fifth died of his injuries, which must be put down to luck, as he hadn't fitted the weapon's silencer correctly.

Frustrated at the survival of the first four victims, the Laser Man departed from his earlier methods and sneaked up on his fifth from behind, put the barrel to the back of the thirty-four-year-old man's head and pulled the trigger. Not even the incorrectly fitted silencer could have saved him.

*

At Säter, Sture Bergwall was placed in psychiatric care alongside heavily criminalised, violent men. The status of the patients was largely determined by how interesting their life stories were, and their crimes. In this context, Sture was rather out of his depth.

A SPECIAL PATIENT

KJELL PERSSON AND Göran Fransson were the chief physicians in charge of Säter Hospital in the early 1990s and have stuck together ever since.

During the assessment period, before Sture Bergwall was placed in psychiatric care, Göran Fransson had collected 650 kronor (about £50) for offering his psychiatric opinion on the failed bank robber. This opinion – known as a P7 – is sought in order to determine whether a person arraigned for trial should be given a more extensive psychiatric evaluation.

It does not fall within the brief of a P7 to make judgements on the level of danger a person presents, even less to speculate on the likelihood of the person having committed as yet undiscovered crimes. Yet this was exactly what Fransson felt he was especially suited to do:

> The crime for which he has been convicted shows signs of serious sexual perversions where the risk of repeat offences is high, and in view of this it seems surprising that he has not been prosecuted on other occasions for such crimes.

Göran Fransson's assumption that Sture Bergwall had committed serious crimes which had not yet been discovered would soon prove to be almost prophetic. That the opinion was inappropriate has even been retrospectively conceded by Fransson himself. 'I regret writing that. It shouldn't have been there, in a P7. But I was proved right in the end,' he said in an interview with *Dala-Demokraten* in June 1996.

The belief that Sture had committed other undiscovered crimes in the past was soon well established among those in charge of Sture Bergwall's care. And obviously, whoever seeks shall find.

Sture's patient notes, medication logs and other documents gave me a detailed insight into his day-to-day life at Säter from the very start. Sture participated apathetically in the routine examinations when he was being admitted: he undressed on command and allowed a medical assistant to shine a torch into his eyes, test his reflexes with a rubber mallet to his knees and inspect his skin for signs of puncture marks or anything out of the ordinary that should be taken into account. On the following day he met with a doctor who was destined to make a number of interventions in Quick's life that would prove to have a profound impact. Chief physician Göran Källberg had an introductory conversation with Sture and made the following notes in his patient file:

> He was calm and collected and entirely at ease with the implications of psychiatric care. He has extensive familiarity with closed psychiatric care. We spoke in general about his situation and his difficulties. [. . .] At times he is overwhelmed by powerful anxiety attacks and even during our conversation he became extremely tense, tearful and also irregular in his breathing. Eventually he calmed down. Apart from this, he maintained a good level of formal communication in the conversation.

When Göran Källberg questioned the existing prescription of medications he was surprised by Sture's vociferous protest. He allowed the medication to stay as it was for the time being, but noted in his patient file that Sture was 'clearly addicted to the little dose of Oxazepam which he has been taking for a number of years'.

Sture's day-to-day life at Säter Hospital soon fell into sedate normality. Judging by the file, he kept a low profile and settled in without any problems at all.

But the files also repeatedly mention Sture contacting members of staff to report that he was feeling unwell and having suicidal thoughts. On 17 May 1991 Kjell Persson wrote:

> Sture Bergwall came today and wanted to speak with a doctor. Mentions that he broods a lot at night, feels anxious, breaks into sweats and wants to cry. 'I have to talk and get it off my chest.'

Even though Persson was not a psychotherapist he took pity on Sture and let him come to see him from time to time, precisely to 'get things off his chest'. These informal conversations gradually took the form of counselling sessions. One of Sture's recurring themes was that he had no justification for his existence, that he should kill himself. He bore a burden of deep sorrow for having lost his former best friend, Patrik, who was twenty-two years his junior. As the elder of the two, he felt guilty that Patrik had been imprisoned. Persson made a note in the file on 24 June 1991:

> When one touches upon these and similar matters the patient displays a wealth of tics, convulsive breathing and strange grunting sounds. During rounds today it was reported that there has been less and less of this on the ward. There have not been any other problems.

It seems that Sture Bergwall had a burning desire to be allowed to start psychotherapy; however, it was proving far harder than he had thought. Regardless of whether his panic attacks, tics and grunts were theatrical or the real thing, the doctors remained quite cool in their response. Put simply, they did not view Sture as an interesting patient. On 2 July Kjell Persson wrote in the file:

> The patient has been increasingly plagued by anxiety these last few days, is having problems sleeping at night and broods a great

> deal. He has suicidal thoughts, but says that in actual fact he would not dare hurt himself. This is something he has been experiencing for years, with varying levels of intensity, but he claims that he really did intend to kill himself the evening before the robbery. He claims that he had chosen a place where he would drive his car off the road, when he noticed his dog on the back seat. He said he would like some sort of confirmation that he is so bad that he should really commit suicide.

The file clarified that Göran Fransson had withdrawn the highly addictive medication Somadril ('it drones so nicely in the brain') and the doctors tried one substitute after another. Sture claimed that all the other medications made him even more depressed. Finally, after the Somadril was administered again, a sense of calm was temporarily restored. Göran Källberg noted on 10 July:

> The overall judgement on the risk of suicide does not in my view merit any special security measures. Just for the patient to be able to talk about it and open up seems to provide relief. It should also be noted that the suicidal thoughts are mostly based on a sort of existential problem, in that he sits there looking back at his life and how difficult it has been and how he feels like a failure. There is nothing depressive, melancholic or psychotic about his thinking and argumentation. In other respects it should be noted that the patient has adapted well on the ward. He has a sincere wish to get himself into a better state, but he feels he cannot manage it by his own efforts alone. The patient is very intellectual in his arguments and likes to use theoretical terminology. At the same time he is aware that this is a way for him to distance himself.

During the summer months, as a mark of trust, Sture was allowed outings of a few hours' length in the company of members of the nursing staff. These took place without any hitches. The conversations with Kjell Persson continued, but the doctors were unsure whether there would be any meaningful results from psychotherapeutic treatment. Persson noted in Sture's file on 9 September:

> Ever since being moved to Ward 31, i.e. shortly after his arrival at the clinic, the patient has been pleading for psychotherapy. It is not wholly clear whether he would be a suitable candidate for this, and one must take into account our limited psychotherapeutic resources. As a temporary solution I have therefore set up my communication with the patient under a heading of supportive conversation. It has been found that the patient uses the time sincerely, to reflect on himself, his actions and his situation.
>
> The conversations seem to generate a lot of anxiety and muscular spasms and the patient also pleads for more time, as he apparently feels that this process is helping him organise his thoughts.

Sture was ambivalent during the conversations. On the one hand he begged for communication, on the other hand he was closed. 'He is fond of expressing himself in abstract terms rather than speaking of tangible events in his life,' wrote Persson, then went on:

> What seems central to him at the moment is that he has no justification for his life at all. He behaves impeccably on the ward, but we have not felt he can be trusted with leave, so far we judge him to be too closed and inaccessible, difficult to gain an overall perspective on.

Sture had gone through psychotherapy before. Back then he was also asked to talk about his childhood. At the time he had answered that he had no direct memories, by which he meant that his growing up as one of a large number of siblings in a fairly poor family did not offer any particularly interesting experiences.

Sture noticed that Kjell Persson was fishing for traumatic events in his childhood. His feeling of being an uninteresting patient solidified his sense of failure. It seemed that he was incapable even of being a successful lunatic.

Sture explained it to me: 'I had intellectual interests but lacked an education and had an inferiority complex towards my brothers and sisters. They studied at university and got academic jobs, but I failed and was terribly alone. I had a passion for psychoanalysis and was utterly focused on starting a process of deep therapy. But not really because I wanted to clear up strange thoughts or ideas within myself. It was more the social interaction I was longing for. To be an intellectual, to be able to make associations freely, to sit down and talk with an equal, these things appealed to me. To a large extent it was also about having some confirmation of being an intellectual person.'

The therapy at Säter was based on so-called object relations theory. This offshoot of psychoanalysis first emerged in the 1930s and attaches great importance to the first years of the child's life. In short, among other things the treatment makes the assumption that a number of personality disruptions can be traced back to sexual abuse by parents. Because people do not generally have memories from a very early age, one of the important roles of the therapist is to 'reawaken' such memories or interpret vague intimations so that they become understandable and fit into the therapeutic pattern. A central aspect of the theory is that painful memories can be repressed or even 'dissociated', meaning that they end up scrambled in some way. The therapist must therefore look for the real events underlying metaphysical and often symbolic narratives, memories and dreams.

Sweden's foremost proponent of object relations theory was the psychiatrist Margit Norell, who had broken away from the Association of Psychoanalysts in the 1960s to create her own association for 'holistic' psychoanalysis, before also breaking away from this. At the time of Sture Bergwall's committal to Säter Hospital the seventy-eight-year-old veteran of object relations theory was working as a supervisor for the clinic's psychologists and therapists. According to Sture, she was treated with extreme reverence by the staff, and in his own notes he occasionally referred to her as 'the Great One'.

In Säter's library he immersed himself in the theories underlying the hospital's therapeutic treatment methods, he told me: 'I hadn't been at Säter for very long when I started reading Alice Miller, who wrote about the child and the parents. Her point was that because the child is so dependent on the parents, it can't bear the memory of the parents' sexual abuse. When memories are as difficult as that they're repressed instead and become inaccessible. I soon realised that Alice Miller's theories fitted very well with the clinic's outlook. You had to look to your childhood for explanations as to the way you ended up as an adult. And difficult memories were repressed. When I started my conversations with Kjell Persson I was well aware of what was on his mind, and I was able to express myself so that I got a positive response. I made this adjustment to get what I wanted, which was human interaction.'

Sture used his counselling to discuss all manner of things, including the contents of Bret Easton Ellis's controversial bestseller: 'For me it became important to discuss the book with Kjell, to compare Patrick Bateman's fantasies with my own. The book *American Psycho*, Alice Miller's theories on repressed memories from childhood, the ideas in circulation at the clinic – all these things created a very special and fertile ground for the serial killing. One has to bear in mind that the people committed to the clinic were violent. I was in this environment, I socialised with these people, I became a part of all this. And in the end I wanted to be a part of that world, because I had nothing else.'

DRUG ABUSE AND THERAPY

WITH KJELL PERSSON'S help Sture began to 'reawaken' traumatic memories from his childhood so painful to him that they had been 'fragmented' and hidden away. Successively, fragments of memories were assembled into events, which created an overall impression of a terrible childhood filled with violence, sexual abuse and death.

The effort Sture put into his therapy was viewed very positively and he was now treated with a level of appreciation that he hadn't previously encountered in his life.

One of the consequences of Sture opening up were 'rewards' in the form of leave, which was gradually increased. Persson's notes, in this case from 2 October, were increasingly upbeat in their tone:

> Continued conversation with the patient once a week. He fluctuates between more openness and more introspection. When he is closed to communication he tends to wear a jovial mask, and it is evident that at such times he grows more weary with himself.

By the autumn, Sture had been given three hours of 'leave' per day and, judging by staff notes in the file, was managing this perk without any problem at all. Persson wrote that the patient's care does not 'give cause for even the slightest concern'. He was 'always very polite and accommodating'. In accordance with Sture's wishes, the counselling was increased to two weekly sessions, Persson noted on 4 November, and 'at the very heart of the conversation is his sense of alienation. He does not dare show who he is and he feels very little justification for his life.'

Sture's patient files and earlier court verdicts pointed to a life in which an extensive abuse of alcohol, drugs and prescription medicines had caused him serious problems. This issue was never touched upon in the file notes.

Sture's consumption of legally prescribed narcotics was escalating, yet his well-documented long-term substance abuse never seems to have been meaningfully addressed in the counselling. For later readers of these files, this is a bit of a mystery, as is the fact that Sture preferred to speak of himself as a sex criminal, serial killer and cannibal rather than an ingrained alcoholic and drug addict.

In his first months at Säter, Sture established that while there were individuals that he liked among both the staff and the other inmates, there were also some that he had difficulties putting up with. In both camps there were people he could make use of. One of the people that Sture liked and found useful was twenty-two-year-old Jimmie Fagerstig, an intelligent repeat offender with a violent criminal background whose entire body was covered in tattoos.

'I remember when Sture came to the regional clinic. I thought he shouldn't be there at all. A smart person with a lot of ideas. But he had his anxiety and one hell of a death wish. He asked me to beat him to death with a bit of furniture. He lay down on the floor and said, "Just bloody kill me, Jimmie!"'

Eventually Sture rose in Jimmie's esteem, not because he was the ward champion at Scrabble but because he told him he was serving a sentence for aggravated robbery. Sture was someone on Jimmie's own level, but older and more experienced.

'Yeah, I thought it was pretty cool dressing up as Father Christmas and robbing a bank! So he got some brownie points for a while,' said Jimmie when I met with him.

Their bond was cemented more than anything by their common interest in drugs, and Jimmie was impressed by Sture's amazing ability to get himself extra doses of medicine.

'He'd throw himself on the floor and start screaming. When that happened they didn't come with the dispenser, they just brought the whole jar. "Sture, how many do you want?" He was smart! He put on his panic attacks and got as many Halcions and Xanax as he liked.'

The doctors soon realised that Sture wasn't satisfied with the drugs available in the clinic and was topping himself up from illegal sources. Sture's most important supplier was Jimmie Fagerstig.

'We had so many damned drugs that sometimes they'd call in from outside,' said Fagerstig. 'If there wasn't any junk in Hedemora they called me. "Yeah sure, come at nine", I used to tell them.'

'Fishing with a jar' meant that the inmates lowered a jar of drugs on a string from a ventilation window. When the jar came up again, there was money inside.

During the autumn and winter of 1991, Sture was viewed as sufficiently reliable and stable to be allowed to attend the service at Säter Church unaccompanied, and to go jogging on his own around Lake Ljustern.

But on 18 December he gave his care assistant a shock by absconding with another patient. From the file:

> We waited until 18.00 when the leave expired. He did not come back to the ward. A fax was sent at 18.19 to notify the police in Falun.

When Sture's room was searched, a number of suicide notes to doctors and nurses were found, in which Sture announced that he had decided to kill himself.

> A patient and a fellow patient have thus absconded and the patient has left a pile of suicide notes behind, mostly dated September and October this year, with one addition written on the day of leaving. Among other things the patient apologises for his behaviour. He gives fairly extensive instructions on how to proceed after his death, and he further writes that his body will be found within a close radius of the hospital grounds.

> However, it later emerges that the patient has been down to the hospital cashier's office several times in the morning before absconding to ask for his pension payment, which at that time had still not come in. Staff have searched the hospital grounds without finding anyone. Today, the police have passed us the information that the patient and fellow patient have most likely hired a car in Sala.

On the following day Sture and the other patient returned to Säter in a rented Volvo. Sture admitted that he took amphetamines at the time of the escape, and that among other places they had been in Åre. He said that the purpose of the escape had been to commit suicide by driving the car head-on into a rock wall, but because the other patient was in the car, he was unable to put his plan into action. Sture said to his doctor, Kjell Persson, that the reason for his escape was his bad conscience about buying amphetamines in the Säter Hospital grounds.

File notes after the escape suggest that staff on the ward had begun to suspect that Sture was self-medicating and that he had suppliers other than Säter's own doctors. The personnel were authorised to search Sture after leave outings and he was caught a number of times trying to smuggle banned substances or pharmaceutical drugs into the ward.

In his therapy, Sture had begun to talk more and more about harrowing experiences in his childhood. He told Kjell Persson that he had not previously had any recall of them, but now one nightmarish event after another was surfacing. It began with the suggestion that his parents had been emotionally cold and indifferent to his needs. Then came images of being sexually assaulted at the age of three by his father.

Sture's mother, Thyra Bergwall, was well known in Korsnäs as a warm, considerate woman who kept the family together and pretty much single-handedly brought in the income needed to look after her seven children. In his conversations with Kjell Persson, Sture found memories were resurfacing of his mother's dual nature. He described how she tried to drown him in a hole in an ice-covered lake when he was four years old. Sture lost consciousness but was saved by his father at the very last moment. On another occasion his mother tried to kill him by pushing him into the path of an approaching tram. Somehow he also managed to survive this attempted murder.

Sture's memories of parental abuse grew increasingly torrid. In the end he described the entire family as being involved in the outrages, both as victims and perpetrators. The more extreme the memories recovered by Sture in therapy, the more positive the response of Persson to his patient.

> Over time he has become more and more open in his communication, he has found the courage to scrutinise himself and his sexual perversion in a way that has clearly led to new insights for the patient, including how 'sick' his actions have been, which was something he was earlier repressing and unable to integrate. There is a marked dual nature in the patient, whereby he displays both a timid and an accommodating nature on the ward, yet behind this mask some very stormy emotions lie hidden which he dares not show or speak of.

Kjell Persson's note on 9 April mentions Sture's timid, accomodating nature in his day-to-day life in the ward. However, during their therapeutic conversations he realised that this behaviour was little more than a mask, behind which Sture's 'dual nature' lay hidden. The therapy began to close in on this perceived dual nature, in order to uncover what lay hidden there.

In the same entry, Persson goes on:

> The patient has gone into his childhood experiences, which previously seemed fairly well established, but now a number of fresh memories have come to the fore. He has also been interpreting dreams. In short, one could say that there seems to have been an extremely tense situation in the family, where there was hardly any space for the patient's own needs during his childhood.

In his file notes, Kjell Persson is rather evasive about what he has discovered, as he wants to try and preserve his secret for as long as he can. His own conviction is that, through therapeutic support, he has managed to help Sture regain control of old, repressed memories about the horrifying assaults to which he was subjected as a child. According to the dogma holding sway at Säter, Persson had managed this feat as a consequence of his professional skills as a therapist.

In the spring of 1992, Sture was placed in a high-security ward known as Ward 36. At the same time he was also given more recreational opportunities. Some rather sparse notes record that Sture took walks, jogged round Lake Ljustern and travelled to Avesta while on leave. From time to time he suffered from anxiety, and whenever this happened he was given Diazepam and other narcotic-strength medications, in particular benzodiazepines.

As summer drew near, his doctors felt Sture was now so stable that, from 6 June 1992, he was given full clearance – that is, he had the freedom to move about in the community during the daytime as he pleased.

Yet the brief and harmonious file notes hide the great drama that was unfolding three times a week, with stormy emotions and tales of sexual abuse and violence. Kjell Persson knew that the truth about Sture would not trickle out slowly, rather it would drop like a bomb. And on that day, the patient and his therapist would end up on the front pages of the country's newspapers. But not yet. The therapy had to carry on for a little longer.

THE BATHING TRIP

THURSDAY, 25 JUNE 1992 was a balmy, sunny day, perfect for a bathing trip to Lake Ljustern with Therese, one of Sture's favourite nurses, who was easy to talk to and also seemed comfortable in his company.

They lay on the beach, basking in the sun while distractedly speaking of Sture's life and the crimes he had committed.

'I wonder what you'd think of me if you found out that I'd done something really serious.'

Therese gave Sture a searching look.

'What do you mean, "serious"?'

'Well, something really, really serious. You understand. How would that change the way you saw me?'

'I don't get what you're saying at all! Really, really serious! Why don't you just say what you mean.'

'I'll give you a clue.'

'OK.'

Sture thought about it in silence for a few moments, before spelling out, 'M-U.'

'M-U?'

Therese gave him a troubled smile.

'Sture, I'm not getting any of this.'

She felt that the entire gist of the conversation was odd, maybe also a touch unpleasant, although she kept this to herself. It was hardly difficult imagining what 'something really serious' could mean for a patient who had been sectioned at a secure psychiatric clinic and who had already committed aggravated robbery, sexual assaults on children and grievous bodily harm. She managed to steer him off the subject, but once she got back to the ward she reported what Sture had said.

Göran Fransson and Kjell Persson were jointly responsible for Sture Bergwall: Persson was in charge of the therapy, while Fransson was responsible for his overall care. When Fransson walked into the ward the following day he was given a report on what had been said on the beach. He immediately requested that Sture should come and see him in the music room. As soon as Sture came in, Fransson closed the door behind them.

'Sture, I am very, very concerned about what I was told in the ward this morning. What you asked Therese on the beach yesterday,' he clarified. 'M-U . . .'

Sture lowered his eyes.

'We offered you full clearance because we thought you were stable. We thought we knew where we stood with each other. Do you remember we spoke about this during rounds yesterday?'

Sture hummed his agreement but had nothing else to add.

'Surely you understand you've got us worried! Something *really serious*? What does that mean? And the clue, those letters M-U?'

Sture looked at the floor.

'Do you even know what those letters M-U stand for?'

'Yes, I do. Of course . . . But I can't explain it. Not now.'

'But why did you say this? There must be some reason for it?'

Sture hummed, while Fransson held his tongue.

'All this,' Sture explained with some hesitation. 'It's just my usual way of pushing away people who appreciate me.'

'You weren't pushing anyone away! Therese reported what you said just as she had to do. You have to understand that this poses a problem for all of us. Your leave today . . . Do you see how unsettling that is for us?'

'I could just not go out. I could,' whispered Sture by way of an answer.

'I'm cancelling your full clearance from here on. No free movement until we understand what this means.'

Sture stood silent and immobile with his head down.

'We get very wary when you start saying mysterious things like that, Sture.'

What Sture had been alluding to on the beach outing – that he had done 'something really serious' – played right into the suspicions Fransson had first brought up when he made his short psychiatric assessment and speculated about Sture having very likely committed more violent crimes between the assaults on the boys and the bank robbery in 1990.

'That means I daren't express my feelings any more,' said Sture in a muted voice. 'I can't tell the staff what I am feeling.'

Fransson skewered him with his eyes.

'I promise you, Sture. There's no problem at all about that as long as you don't speak in riddles. Now we have to think about what's happened. And then we'll talk about it later. OK?'

And with this, Göran Fransson walked out of the music room.

Ten days later Sture had once again regained his right to full clearance. The anxieties of the bathing trip seemed to have been forgotten. The hospital authorities were in the midst of discharging him from psychiatric care. Sture Bergwall made an application to the National Registrar's Office to change his name to Thomas Quick, which was approved. He wanted to be free of his past and start a new life with an untarnished name. He had signed a lease on a small flat, a studio room with a kitchen at Nygatan 6B in Hedemora from 15 August, and was 'feeling very well at the moment'. The one cloud on the horizon was where he would get the money to furnish his new home. The only other notes over the summer are about reductions in his intake of medications, running practice and how well he handled his leave to places such as Hedemora, Avesta and Stockholm.

The move into the flat was delayed. In September Sture realised that he wouldn't be able to pay the rent for his flat and he had to give up the lease. He stayed on at Säter and from November he was placed in holding accommodation for patients waiting to be released.

But while the supervisors at the hospital were preparing for Thomas Quick's release, dramatic events were unfolding in secret.

THE GAME TURNS SERIOUS

IN HIS CONTINUED therapy with Kjell Persson, Thomas Quick remembered that he had travelled to Sundsvall, where he had murdered Johan Asplund. As it happened, Johan's disappearance had been one of the most widely publicised criminal cases of the 1980s and Quick wasn't absolutely certain that the memory was authentic. Persson determined that they would go to Sundsvall together on 26 October 1992 to see if his recollections became clearer.

Kjell Persson had checked the address, yet they lost their way on their first attempt. Many years later, Persson testified in the trial for the murder of Johan Asplund, admitting that it was 'possibly on his initiative that they turned off towards the neighbourhood of Bosvedjan'.

In fact it is a good deal more than possible. Both Kjell Persson's own report and the information he gave in the first police interview on the matter indicate that when they came to a junction on the right signposted 'Bosvedjan', Persson suggested that they should turn into it. Quick didn't object, but wasn't able to say whether it was the right way or not.

At one point, Quick had such a severe panic attack that Persson had to interrupt his private reconnaissance. Quick's reaction was interpreted as a sign implicating him in the murder.

After a short visit to Bosvedjan they drove around the environs of Sundsvall aimlessly until they came to an area known as Norra Stadsberget, where Quick was again overwhelmed by intense anxiety.

When it had passed, he suggested that this was where the actual killing had taken place.

After their return to Säter, Persson did not make a note in the file about what had taken place. Their conversations about the murder of Johan continued in secret, three times a week. Neither the police nor the hospital management were informed, despite the fact that Persson was convinced his patient had committed a murder.

If chief physician Kjell Persson hadn't gone on holiday in February 1993 it would likely have taken a good while longer before Quick's accounts of murders became generally known.

But now that he had left the clinic, Quick, who had grown accustomed to his bizarre conversations three times a week, turned to Birgitta Ståhle, a thirty-nine-year-old psychologist and devoted follower of object relations theory.

'Our communication will function as a safety "valve" for Sture, because the therapeutic process he's going through is bringing up so much material for him that he needs fixed points of reference in terms of meeting someone,' Ståhle wrote in the file.

But Birgitta Ståhle did not become the safety 'valve' she had imagined. To use her own metaphor, one might say that the pressure cooker exploded at their first communication. She was so aghast at what Quick told her she immediately contacted Göran Fransson, who was responsible for Quick's care.

'Sture has told me that he's murdered two people, two boys,' Ståhle told him.

Göran Fransson didn't want to admit that his colleague Kjell Persson had been keeping him informed about developments in Quick's psychotherapy. It wouldn't have looked good if he, as the person responsible for Quick's care, was aware of Quick's murder confessions without passing them on.

With Birgitta Ståhle entering into the equation, the bubble of secrecy surrounding Thomas Quick had burst. Göran Fransson ruminated on the matter for eleven days without doing anything. Then on 26 February he sat down to write in Quick's file:

> The patient's therapist is currently on holiday. In the meantime the patient has turned to a few key people on the ward, as well as to the psychologist Birgitta Ståhle, to say that he has committed two murders, one when he was sixteen years old and another about ten years ago. The information relates to two boys, who are thought to have disappeared without their bodies ever being found. I explained to him that this obviously has legal ramifications and he must take this to the police if he is to have any likelihood of reconciling himself with what he has done. He is aware of this but obviously very frightened.

The note gives the impression that Thomas Quick had suddenly confessed to two murders that were previously unknown at Säter. In actual fact he had been talking about one of the murders – Johan Asplund's – since October 1992. His own doctor had made further investigations into the matter. Now that the secret was coming out into the open, Fransson was clearly aware that it might be seen as inappropriate for a psychiatric clinic to start looking into a patient's murder confession without reporting it to the police.

The situation startled Quick. Everything had been exciting, simple and safe while he was talking only to Kjell Persson. He had seen their conversations as a stimulating, intellectual game. Now all of a sudden Göran Fransson was talking about making a police report, bringing a prosecution and going to trial. As a consequence of Sture's glibness with Birgitta Ståhle, Pandora's box had been flung open and his own words were flying round, threatening and frightening, completely out of control. It was impossible to turn the clock back, to reseal the words in the enclosed space of the therapy room.

Back from his holiday, Kjell Persson resumed therapy with Quick and later noted in the file:

> What have further emerged are extreme episodes of terror during the patient's childhood, when he clearly came close to being

> killed by his mother. The most serious of these was an attempted drowning in Lake Runn. The most traumatic events for the patient seem to have taken place when he was 3–5 years old, although the sexual molestation seems to have continued after this period, but it was somewhat less frequent.

What now made Quick the priceless treasure of the clinic was not the sexual assaults in themselves, but rather the connection between these and the violent crimes Sture committed as an adult. According to object relations theory, Sture's violent crimes were re-creations of the assaults to which he had been subjected as a child, or, as Persson put it in the file:

> Alongside the uncovering of these bizarre images from his memory, which from time to time seem crystal clear, his memories of the murder of Johan Asplund have come forth with increasing clarity. Initially his memories of the crime were more like dreamlike fantasies, but gradually during the therapeutic process they turned into increasingly clear, distinct images. While working on these images of the assault and murder of Johan Asplund, they have become interwoven with terrifying images from his childhood, and the crime has appeared as a psychological re-creation of his childhood situation with several angles of possible approach.

One day in February 1993, Göran Fransson knocked on Thomas Quick's door and stepped into his room. He wanted to hear what Quick's position was in relation to his own confessions. Quick told him that his feelings were no longer as clear as they had been earlier. He felt indecisive and unsure of the whole thing.

'I want to give you a chance to go to the police yourself, but if you don't make a report within two weeks I'll have to do it myself,' said Fransson.

Quick understood that the police had to be informed, but he said that he wasn't certain that he had very much he could tell them about the murder of Johan Asplund.

'You have to prepare yourself in writing before being questioned,' said Fransson. 'And obviously we'll ensure that you have hospital staff to accompany you during the interview.'

At Fransson's express request, Quick tried as best he could to talk about the murder of Johan Asplund. He realised that this was not at all the same thing as talking to Kjell in a therapy session. Fransson noted the attempt in the file:

> He describes it more or less as fantasies, which he was unclear whether or not actually happened, but that now, as a consequence of the ongoing therapy, he has confirmed to himself. I confronted him at this point by saying that last week he answered evasively on two occasions to direct questions on the possibility of other crimes. Personally, I find it strange that fifteen years should have passed between these crimes. Then he tells me that he has fantasies or visions of another two, named Peter and Mikael respectively. The order is according to a chronological sequence. However, he is unsure whether or not these have fallen victim to him.

Sture told me how he had agonised during the two-week period Göran Fransson had given him. If he said that he had been lying about the whole thing in therapy he might be able to get out of his precarious situation. But would anyone believe him? What would Kjell Persson say? And Fransson?

He thought about every conceivable retreat, but nothing struck him as realistic. Finally, he contacted Göran Fransson and asked him to call the police. He would let things take their course.

Senior officer Jörgen Persson arrived at Säter Hospital at eleven in the morning on 1 March 1993. Half an hour later, he had rigged up his tape recorder in the small, provisional interrogation room and been introduced to the suspect. Kjell Persson was present as the interview witness. Jörgen Persson checked that the tape recorder was rolling as it should, then sat back in the armchair.

'Well then, Sture, let's start our little chat. I'm from Borlänge police and really I don't know anything much, just that you're here at Säter Hospital and that lately you've started talking about certain things you'd like to tell me about. I don't know anything about old investigations apart from what I've read in the newspaper or whatever, so I'm completely unprepared, so to speak.'

They made sluggish progress during the interview, despite a good deal of pressure from Jörgen Persson. Finally he asked the simple question that set Quick into motion: 'What happened? What do you remember, Sture?'

'I borrowed a car belonging to an acquaintance,' said Quick. 'And made a trip at night and eventually came to Sundsvall. I mean I started when it was dark in Falun and when I got to Sundsvall it was still dark.'

'Yes,' said Officer Persson encouragingly. 'Then what did you do? Where did you head off to?'

'It was a trip without a goal . . . I mean I didn't have a fixed destination. But I came to the outskirts of Sundsvall, anyway.'

'Whose was the car? Who did you borrow it from?'

'I can't remember his first name right now. But his surname. Ljungström, he was called.'

'And how, in what way, did you know Ljungström? Was he a relative? Or an acquaintance?'

'No, he was an acquaintance. We used to meet down by the Lugnet public pool.'

Quick then told Jörgen Persson how he came, in Ljungström's Volvo, to a car park in the residential area of Bosvedjan, north of Sundsvall.

'Can you describe the houses, the colours, what the houses were made of or anything like that?'

'Well, I should let you know that I went there this autumn with the interview witness here, so I could also be remembering that . . . It could be a bit difficult knowing which memory I'm telling you,' explained Quick.

'You've been there to look at the place? So you know what the houses look like, you mean?'

'Yes.'

After hearing this in many ways noteworthy information, the

detective inspector chose not to dig deeper into the matter and instead moved on.

'So what did you do when you were there in the car park?'

'I have to be a bit straight to the point here and use the method that's available to me. I was looking for a boy and I had noticed there was a school nearby. And two boys came walking by, but soon they went separate ways, and I called out once they had separated, so to speak. I don't know if they were together but they came at the same time anyway. The boy who came towards me, so to speak, had an unzipped jacket and I called out to him, asked him for help and told him I'd run over a cat, and he came to the car and I took him into the car and drove away, and went to . . . Stadsberget in Sundsvall and there I killed him. And this boy, in other words, was Johan Asplund.'

Quick went silent.

Officer Persson did not seem to know how to go on from here. He had just heard a full confession to the most infamous murder in Sundsvall in modern times – that of an eleven-year-old who disappeared on 7 November 1980.

'I see,' sighed Jörgen Persson. 'And you've been carrying this inside you for all these years?'

'I've been carrying it for all these years, but not on a conscious level,' Quick answered cryptically.

The questioning continued with a general probing to establish a description of Johan's clothes, but Quick could only remember that he wore a dark blue jacket.

It occurred to Persson then that he was questioning a murder suspect who had no legal representation. It was such a serious issue that he had to deal with it in some way. He said, 'Just so we do things properly here, Sture, I have to tell you that in saying you killed him, you are under suspicion for murder, you do understand that?'

'Of course,' answered Quick.

'And this whole thing about a right to a lawyer, you know about that, you know one has a right to a lawyer in a police investigation?'

Quick said he hadn't thought about it. Officer Persson explained that he had to stick to the rules and inform him of his rights.

'Of course,' said Quick.

'Right,' said Jörgen Persson. 'And how do you see this whole question of legal representation? Can I continue this conversation with you and we'll discuss your legal advice later, or do you want to have a lawyer? At what point do you want a lawyer involved?'

'That's a difficult question,' Quick stated. 'We never thought about that.'

'No,' confirmed Persson, the interview witness. 'I can't answer that.'

'No, we can't,' said Quick.

'And I'm not a lawyer,' said Kjell Persson.

'No,' Quick agreed. 'I think, formally speaking, we should be right and proper in that respect, so maybe he should be here right from the start.'

When he had no backing from either his doctor or the police officer, he continued making his point: 'A lawyer might be good in the sense that he could be the slightly neutral force in all this. I'm thinking that it might be quite good, really.'

But things did not work out this way. Instead, Jörgen Persson turned off the tape recorder and had 'a little discussion about it', as he put it in the report afterwards. When the recording resumed, the interview continued without a lawyer being present.

When, fifteen years later, I read out the interrogation transcript to Sture Bergwall and he heard how, with good reason, he argued that he should have a lawyer present from the very beginning, he said, 'I get so incredibly emotional when I hear how it was done. Upset. And I recognise the situation so well, how much I wanted to please Kjell Persson. If I'd admitted that everything I'd said in therapy was just made up, I'd embarrass Kjell Persson. And I also didn't want to embarrass myself to Kjell.'

For several months, three times a week, he had been talking about the murder with his doctor, who now suddenly figured as the interview witness – with whom Quick, as a psychiatric patient committed into care, was in an extreme position of dependence.

'I mean, it was absolutely impossible for me in that position to say that I had lied my way through hundreds of therapy sessions,' says Sture.

I asked him to explain what he meant when, in the interview in 1993, he said that a lawyer could 'be the slightly neutral force in all this'.

'I meant that a lawyer could be a balancing factor to Kjell Persson and me; that he could ask, "Is this really true, Sture?" And explain that we should take it easy.'

When the interview was resumed, Quick was made to describe in detail how he had tricked Johan into coming closer, how he had pulled him into the car and dashed his head against the dashboard until he passed out.

'Then what happened?' asked Officer Persson.

'We left the area, and I still didn't know, so to speak, where we were going, but in the end we got to Stadsberget in Sundsvall and parked the car there. I brought Johan out of the car with me and we walked a good distance into the woods there. That's where the actual . . . I mean, I strangled him there.'

A little later in the interview, Officer Persson asked what happened to the body.

'It's under a large boulder, under some rocks,' said Quick.

'And at what time did the body end up there?' wondered Jörgen Persson.

'Well, that same morning.'

'Mm,' said Officer Persson. 'Shall we break for lunch, then?'

In the afternoon the interview picked up where it had left off, on Stadsberget, where Quick said that he had strangled Johan and hidden the body.

'So how did you do it, when you strangled him?' asked Officer Persson.

'Using my hands.'

'Had anything in particular happened before you strangled him?'

'No, nothing in particular.'

But when he was asked more questions about his intentions when he lured Johan into the car, Quick recalled that he subjected Johan to a sexual assault before strangling him.

'And then, once he was dead, what did you do? I'm thinking, you said he ended up under some rocks, that's what I'm thinking about.'

At this point the story took a new and unexpected turn.

'I took off his shoes and leg coverings or whatever the hell I should call them. And I'm sort of a bit unclear here. I think, but I don't know for sure, that I hid his clothes in, somewhere where we are, I mean. I rolled up the clothes and put them under some stones or whatever they were. And then I went to fetch a blanket from the car and I put him in that. And so in fact I don't think I hid his body on Stadsberget but I think I drove off with him. And I went by pretty much the same route as when we came and then headed north, so I mean we drove out of Sundsvall again, headed north a distance towards Härnösand. And I mean I think, after that road, I found a smaller road which I turned into and found a place to hide him.'

Quick described a place with 'a dip in the landscape' where he found a few boulders he could remove. Once he had done so, he put the body there and then rolled the boulders back. Jörgen Persson listened patiently to all of Quick's versions of what happened, or may have happened, but he got stuck on details in the account.

'Let's put it like this, Sture: you said "I think" when you were talking about the body. Are you sure you loaded the body into the car again and drove off, or are you not quite sure?'

'I'm not quite sure.'

'So the body could still be there on Stadsberget somewhere, is that correct?'

'Yes,' said Quick.

By now, Officer Persson had fixed on another detail that was coming up in the interview and he found curious.

'How did you know you were going to Stadsberget? You knew the actual name of the area, I'm thinking about that.'

Quick turned to Kjell Persson and answered while facing him.

'I know that from our trip, that it's called Stadsberget, so to speak. I didn't know that before, I don't think.'

'I suppose you have to say what happened,' said Kjell Persson.

But Jörgen Persson didn't let Quick talk about the trip. Instead he turned to the interview witness.

'So you've been up there, have you, to Sundsvall?'

'We've been there, yes. That's right.'

The questioning did not provide any answers as to what the therapist and Quick were doing on Stadsberget and why they went there.

However, one aspect of the story of great interest from a police perspective was that Quick described how the car had been bloodied inside. He explained in painstaking detail how he had stopped at a petrol station on the way home to clean the car and wash away the traces of blood. At the same time, he took the opportunity to telephone his mother, with whom he was living, to tell her not to worry.

Quick turned to his therapist and said, 'I know I'm being difficult, Kjell, but can you check if they've put on coffee?'

When Kjell Persson left the room to fetch coffee, Officer Persson took the chance to ask Quick what happened when he went to Sundsvall with his therapist. To make the officer aware of the purpose of the trip, Quick had to explain the function of the memory when dealing with traumatic experiences.

'This event had been completely hidden to me. There were pieces of it in my conscious memory. Then, my therapist and I worked on it for a long time and very intensively. We have been meeting three times a week and slowly the blockages have worked themselves free. I was about 80 per cent sure that I had killed Johan, but I kept the trapdoor open – I mean, as if this weird thing just couldn't be true. So what did we do? We went to Sundsvall and I didn't know where we were going and all that. The therapist drove the car and I sat next to him and we arrived in Sundsvall and I didn't know where we were going.'

'That sounds about right,' Kjell Persson interjected. He had just come back into the interview room with the coffee.

'But eventually I recognised the place,' said Quick.

'I should add that I knew where we were going,' Kjell Persson pointed out.

'Yes, that's right,' said Quick.

'But I didn't want to. I wanted you to show me the way, to lead us. I had found out in advance where Johan lived. That was where I wanted you to lead us, and I let you do that to a certain extent, although I had to help you a little bit,' added Kjell Persson.

Quick described how he had recognised an Obs! supermarket and was able to give approximate directions from there, although he hadn't managed to point out the exact junction and Kjell Persson had reminded him.

'Yes, yes,' said Quick.

'I noticed that we'd gone wrong,' said Persson.

Finally they reached Johan's house. Quick was keen to give his impression of the moment.

'Well, that's when I knew I'd had an opening. This unreal stuff couldn't be true. But once we were there, then I saw everything and so I knew that it was true.'

'You had that feeling at this point?'

'Yes, exactly.'

'Are you absolutely sure now that it's true?'

'Yes. After the trip. That was the trip that closed, closed . . .'

Officer Persson had been listening to Quick's interpretations and trying to understand his metaphors about open trapdoors and how apparently the trip to Sundsvall had closed everything. At the same time he seemed aware of the lack of tangible evidence to show that Quick was in Sundsvall and had in fact murdered Johan. He found it odd that the confession should come at this point, twelve and a half years after the crime.

'Sture, did you ever do anything, try and tell anyone around you that you did this?' he asked.

'I never knew it was me,' answered Quick.

'You never knew?'

'That's the difficult bit.'

Quick went on to explain how he, like everyone else, had read in the newspapers about Johan's murder and at the time had felt he *might have* been the one who did it. But these feelings were pushed away. He described the long process in therapy, when images from the murder slowly started resurfacing.

'More like fantasies to begin with,' Kjell Persson clarified.

'Yes, precisely,' Quick agreed.

'As I've understood it, that is apparently how you have experienced things,' Kjell Persson filled in.

'Yes, exactly,' Quick agreed.

'Hm,' said Officer Persson. 'So you haven't been back there since to change anything, look for clothes, move the body?'

'No,' Quick quickly affirmed.

'You're quite sure of that? Or is there a possibility that you might have been there?'

'No, I don't think there's any such possibility.'

'And when we went there, it's fair to say we stopped when we discovered that Stadsberget was where it happened, and then we left it at that. Then we went home,' explained Kjell Persson.

'Precisely,' Quick confirmed.

'You couldn't handle any more than that,' the chief physician went on.

'I see,' said Officer Persson. 'So at no point did you go into the woods and traipse about in there?'

'We only went in a very short distance,' answered Persson.

'A very short distance, definitely,' confirmed Quick.

'You recognised the place and then we went back,' said Kjell Persson.

In this first police interview Thomas Quick confessed to another murder of a boy which had apparently taken place before 1967, somewhere in the region of Småland, possibly in the town of Alvesta. Quick described how he had been driving around with a man ten years older than himself – we'll refer to him here as Sixten Eliasson. Sixten was homosexual, but as a member of the Salvation Army he had to hide his sexual orientation behind a matrimonial façade.

'He had a black . . . what are those cars called?' Quick pondered.

'Studebaker,' prompted Kjell Persson.

'Yeah, that's right,' said Quick.

'Quite an unusual car,' the chief physician pointed out.

'Yes,' said Quick, then remembered what sort of car Sixten actually had. It was an Isabella.

'A Borgward Isabella,' Kjell Persson corrected.

'Exactly,' said Quick.

'What happened to that boy, then?'

'Him? He was hidden. I hid him.'

'Do you know where you hid him?'

Quick turned to his therapist.

'I told you about that one, didn't I? That half-rotted ladder I lifted up and there was a space underneath?'

'A ladder, you're saying?' Officer Persson tried to clarify.

'A big ladder, I mean, sort of partly overgrown with vegetation and soil, and I mean it was fairly rotten. But when I lifted it up the ground came away underneath.'

'Yes, yes, something that was not in use but . . .'

'Exactly, it had been lying there for years.'

Officer Persson asked if Quick knew anything else about the boy. What was his name? Where did he come from? How old was he?

'Well, he was my own age or a couple of years younger. And his name was probably Thomas.'

'Has the boy's body been found since the murder?'

Quick didn't remember if he had spoken about this in therapy, and he turned to Kjell Persson, who had no recollection of Quick ever having mentioned it. Quick said that he didn't believe the body was found for many years.

Even though Quick had confessed so readily to the murders of Johan in Sundsvall and Thomas in Småland, Officer Persson was not satisfied.

'I'm thinking along the lines of if there's anyone else you've . . . killed in a similar way to these others you've told me about?'

'No,' said Quick. 'But when you think about how hidden these events have been, I obviously can't give you a categorical no. What I can say is "no, I don't think so". I suppose that's how I can answer a question like that.'

'But is there something in your thoughts that maybe makes you think there could be something more? Is there some image, something you remember inside that makes you . . .'

'No, no memory,' Quick answered patiently, but Jörgen Persson would not let it go.

'There's nothing in your thoughts that makes you think there could be any more?'

'No, nothing apart from this. Like I just said, this has been so well hidden that I can't totally rule out that something else has happened.'

'Do you have any more faint images, memories of anything?'

'No,' Quick answered.

Perhaps the chief physician Göran Fransson had described Quick's 'fantasies or visions on the subject of . . . Peter and Mikael'. In any case, Officer Persson wasn't about to let the matter drop. He insisted on trying to make Quick confess to more murders.

'I was thinking there might be something sort of tucked away,' he tried, 'which you have some vague sense of or a few thoughts about.'

But his efforts were fruitless. Quick refused to go along with the idea that he had committed any other murders. Finally, Jörgen Persson suggested that they should leave it there.

The interview had lasted three hours and Quick was formally notified that he was now suspected of murder.

At Borlänge police station, Chief Prosecutor Lars Ekdahl was given a verbal report on the questioning. It was destined to be the last contact the Borlänge police ever had with Thomas Quick.

AIMLESS WANDERING AND DIVERSIONS

AS THE MURDER of Johan Asplund had been committed in the county of Västernorrland, the case ended up on the desk of Christer van der Kwast at the regional Prosecution Authority in Härnösand.

Christer van der Kwast was forty-eight years old, born and raised in Stockholm. After completing his legal studies he worked as the chief clerk at Södertörn District Court in the late 1960s, then as a trainee prosecutor in Umeå and Östersund.

After finishing a strategically useful course in corporate finance, he was taken on in 1986 as the regional prosecutor in Härnösand, with his principal focus on financial crime. In 1990, the Social Democrats announced that financial crime would be a priority area in the legal system. That same year van der Kwast was made a chief prosecutor. Perhaps his foremost achievement in those years as regional prosecutor was the so-called Leasing Consult case, with a total of twenty individuals prosecuted and a number of trials throughout the 1980s – but many of the cases ended up in the appeals court, with reduced sentences and acquittals. White-collar crime in Västernorrland was not a particularly common problem, and for this reason he had to devote much of his time to other crimes. The only murder investigation he had previously been involved with was that of Eva Söderström, who was stabbed to death. The investigation ran into the sand. He spent most of 1992 on speeding offences.

The conversation with the chamber of prosecutions in Borlänge on 1 March 1993 must have been a welcome change. Admittedly at least ten other nutters had already confessed to the murder of Johan Asplund. Now a patient from Säter would also be joining their number.

Yet the confession had to be checked, and this meant that Christer van der Kwast needed an investigator. He chose Seppo Penttinen, a Sundsvall policeman specialising in narcotics surveillance who, after twenty-three years in his job, still had the title of Senior Police Officer. Very much like van der Kwast, his experience was focused on a different type of criminality. And up until that point he had operated in almost complete anonymity.

That would soon be a thing of the past.

The new investigators had hardly had time to finish their initial questioning at Säter before Anna-Clara Asplund took the telephone call from *Expressen* and was informed that 'a bloke down in Falun' had confessed to the murder of her son, Johan.

It didn't take long before the crime reporter Gubb Jan Stigson had a secret source – 'one of the investigators', according to his article – for the most important story of his career. His first article on Thomas Quick was published in *Dala-Demokraten* on 10 March 1993 under the headline 'Falun Resident Confesses to Murder of Missing Boy'.

'If the confession is true it means that one of Sweden's most notorious criminal cases has been solved,' wrote Stigson. 'One of the investigators' had told him that final proof had not yet been found; Johan's body was still missing.

Although the story was relatively shaky, and 'people with insight into the case had expressed their doubts about the man's story', Stigson couldn't quite help himself from revealing the suspect's identity. He wrote that the man who had confessed to the murder of Johan was a '42-year-old Falun resident, well known as the kidnapper of a bank manager in Grycksbo'. The question of the identity of the 'Falun resident' who had murdered Johan was thereby answered for all who had ever known of Sture Bergwall.

The following day, Gubb Jan Stigson continued his reporting and was able to divulge that 'the Falun resident had pointed out where Johan is buried'.

'He has provided workable information on the body,' the head of the preliminary investigation, Christer van der Kwast, commented to *Dala-Demokraten*. 'This is obviously very interesting to us. The case had earlier been held up by the absence of a body.'

The article was illustrated by a large full-body photograph of Sture Bergwall and his dog Upfold, a Scottish deerhound – most likely the only dog of this breed to be found in Falun. For 'ethical reasons', Sture's face had been blurred out. A few days later, Stigson got hold of another photograph of Sture, sitting on his racing bicycle. Once again, the newspaper had 'preserved his anonymity' by blurring his face.

When the leaks from the investigation started running dry, Stigson called in the bank robber Lars-Inge Svartenbrandt, who had previously been locked up in Säter Hospital with Quick.

'He's probably telling the truth,' said 'Svarten' (Blackie) in *Dala-Demokraten*.

On Saturday, 13 March Kjell Persson drove Thomas Quick to Sundsvall for the second time. Other passengers in the car included Göran Fransson and a psychiatric nurse from Säter Hospital. When they reached the town of Myre in Njurunda they met with Christer van der Kwast, the lawyer Gunnar Lundgren, police inspector C.G. Carlsson and senior officer Seppo Penttinen.

Penttinen took the wheel of the Volvo in which Quick was travelling and they headed directly for Norra Stadsberget in Sundsvall. The trip went smoothly apart from Quick suffering a few anxiety attacks concerning what lay ahead. Once they got there, Quick was led onto the path where he had previously walked with Kjell Persson.

This time, the walk gave rise to enormous anxiety in Quick, who had to be supported under the arms by Fransson and Persson. Quick signalled that he wanted to turn right, only to be overwhelmed by such heavy anxiety that he 'leaned back into the arms of the accompanying doctors'.

Finally they reached the spot where Quick claimed he had killed Johan. He sat down on a boulder, held his arms out at an angle of forty-five degrees and announced that within this area he had hidden Johan's clothes and 'footwear'. When Quick had to specify the exact position he grew vague and could neither say how far into the terrain the police should search nor describe the general appearance of the hiding place. Suffering intense anxiety, he then went on to describe how he had carried Johan back to the car.

In his report, Göran Fransson wrote:

> The patient has now been questioned by police after confessing to the long-unsolved murder of the boy Johan Asplund in Sundsvall. A reconnaissance of the area had been set up for next week, but in view of the leaks within the police and the great press interest, we will make the reconnaissance today under conditions of absolute secrecy. [. . .] During the inspection [of the woods by Norra Stadsberget] the patient suffered from increasingly high anxiety and constantly lost his grip on reality, upon which he asked us to bring him back, which we did with concrete calls emphasising time and place. The last short distance he was more or less carried by the arms by me and Kjell. By then, he was overwhelmed by strong anxiety and hyperventilating. He had to breathe into a plastic bag.

'After a moment of rest and a toilet visit, as well as consumption of coffee and sandwiches, Quick announced that he had enough strength back to resume the inspection,' noted Seppo Penttinen in his police report. The route they took seemed haphazard, with a good deal of uncertainty. Quick said that he 'very likely travelled on smaller roads' towards the Obs! supermarket, which in practice proved impossible; he 'seemed to recall' he went this way, and he 'experienced' that he probably went that way.

The police were forced to make certain 'route adjustments'. Quick was clearly unsure during the inspection and 'tried to work out how, in a logical sense, he would have chosen the route'. Göran Fransson explained in the file how the search took place:

> The patient sort of feels and is helped by Kjell [Persson] to interpret those feelings. When he had a sense that he recognised a particular stretch of terrain he had a very severe panic attack with intense chest pains. He also had a severe headache. He hyperventilated and had to breathe into a plastic bag again. He got another 5 mg Diazepam and 2 Citodon for the headache.

After a two-hour diversion based on Quick's directions, the file makes it clear that a collective decision had been made not to listen to him:

> The police suggested another route than the one he has reacted to, and after driving along this road for about ten minutes we reached an area he had earlier described well during police questioning, where once again he grew extremely anxious but was also more collected than he was earlier.

The cars turned into an open area, where they parked. In his memo of the inspection Seppo Penttinen noted:

> At 16.15 Quick stepped out of the car, saying that he recognised the place. He had had severe panic symptoms in the car and had not dared look out to the right where the rocks drop away with a line of visible boulders. He strolled along the right-hand side of the fields, with the intention of trying to point out the place where he had hidden Johan Asplund's body. At that point he was surrounded by his doctors and his psychiatric nurses. It was difficult for him to turn his eyes to the edge of the rocks.

Thomas Quick now revealed that he had cut up Johan Asplund's body. He indicated where he hid the head 'with a fairly high level of probability' and where the police should look for other body parts. After three and a half hours of reconniassance he was utterly exhausted and Christer van der Kwast made the assessment that the suspect had given them all the information he had. The inspection was concluded.

*

In the spring of 1993, with great optimism, dog patrols with cadaver dogs, forensic technicians and other personnel searched the places Quick had pointed out. Readers of *Dala-Demokraten* were able to follow Gubb Jan Stigson's daily bulletins on the search for Johan Asplund's body.

On 19 March the newspaper ran its seventh article on Quick in ten days: 'It came to nothing,' Stigson wrote, with obvious disappointment.

'We have a strange starting point,' explained Christer van der Kwast in the article. 'For once we have a person who's confessed to a serious crime. Now we have to confirm in some way that what he has admitted to is actually true.'

During the questioning taking place alongside the search, Thomas Quick was constantly coming up with new versions of events. On 18 March he said that he cut the body into several parts using a lopping saw. Seppo Penttinen wondered how he had managed to part the head from the body.

'Was it difficult in any way to make a saw run smoothly through the actual tissue?'

'Yes,' admitted Quick. 'It was quite bothersome.'

He said that the head was left on a rocky ridge in Åvike, just outside Sundsvall. Then he drove to another hill, carried Johan's body to the top and threw it into a ravine.

On 21 April Quick offered that he had wrapped Johan's torso in the seat covers of the car. The head was left behind in Åvike, while all the other body parts were placed in a cardboard box marked 'Korsnäs Bread'. He drove towards Härnösand and stopped on the bridge to Sandö, where he dumped the cardboard box and its contents into the Ångerman river. In the end, the questioning had to be stopped on account of Quick's overwhelming panic attacks.

The car used by Sture Bergwall in the murder of Johan had been borrowed from a homosexual acquaintance, he claimed. There was nothing remarkable about that, until the investigators started looking into the matter.

For the owner of the car, referred to here as Tord Ljungström, the telephone call came as a shock. He couldn't understand why a police detective should want to see him. However, he ensured that the interview was held in a neutral, discreet place, in room 408 at the Scandic Hotel in Falun.

'I don't know anyone by the name of Thomas Quick and no Sture Bergwall either,' Ljungström insisted.

Only when Seppo Penttinen described Sture Bergwall's appearance was Ljungström's memory jogged.

'Could this possibly be the Sture who's been committed to Säter Hospital?'

Ljungström conceded that he did remember him. He described how they had been acquainted some ten or twelve years ago.

'We met maybe seven or eight times and had sexual relations,' he admitted. 'We always met at the sports hall in Lugnet, by the public pool. Always on a Tuesday, because Tuesday was my day off. I was working at a grocery at that time.'

The meetings had always taken a certain form, according to Ljungström. He had arrived in his car while Sture cycled from his home in Korsnäs to Lugnet.

Had he possibly owned a light blue Volvo, a model from 1980, wondered the investigator?

Ljungström answered that he had owned many cars, most of them Volvos, but never a light blue one. What about a dark blue one?

The interrogation report gives a consistent impression of Ljungström trying to be cooperative and answer the questions truthfully. But when Officer Carlsson suggested that Ljungström had lent his Volvo to Sture Bergwall, Ljungström became less cooperative.

'That's absolutely incorrect! I'm very particular about my cars and I've never lent my car to anyone. Well, except my wife, of course,' he added.

Tord Ljungström was willing to answer all kinds of personal questions, but he categorically denied ever having lent his car to Sture. The interview finished without the investigators having managed to budge him by a single inch on that point.

The following day, Christer van der Kwast disclosed to journalists that Thomas Quick had pointed out the person who had lent him the car used for the murder. But he seemed to imply that the 'car lender' was a tricky customer who had tried to give them the slip.

'The individual in question initially denied knowing the forty-three-year-old but later admitted that he was familiar with him. Their relationship was of a sort that would do a great deal of damage to the individual in question if his identity were ever to be revealed.'

The day after questioning Tord Ljungström, Seppo Penttinen drove to Säter to interview Quick yet again. Göran Fransson was also present.

'If we could begin by talking a bit about your driving licence and so forth,' began Penttinen. 'When did you take your driving test?'

'In 1987,' answered Quick.

Everyone in the room must have realised that the answer was a strange one.

'In 1987?' asked Penttinen with sincere surprise.

He twisted and turned and repeated the question, but the answer remained unchanged. Sture obtained his driving licence in 1987 and, prior to this, didn't have any significant driving experience.

'The drive to the Sundsvall area, did that not, so to speak, cause you problems in terms of driving the car on your own?' Penttinen wondered.

'No. Oh no! No problems at all,' Quick assured him.

The following day, Penttinen visited Quick's younger sister, Eva.

'Eva, would you say that Sture was capable of comfortably driving a vehicle at the time we are looking at, 1980?'

'I actually never saw Sture drive a car before 1987,' she replied. 'The first time was in 1987, when he got his licence.'

Eva recalled that Sture was such an awful driver that he'd even had problems changing gears after passing his test.

Hurriedly they summoned the car owner, Tord Ljungström, for more questioning that same evening. Despite great pressure applied by the interrogators, he would not budge from his denial.

'Ljungström is not changing his view that he is 100 per cent sure he never lent the car to Sture Bergwall,' noted Penttinen in the interrogation report. The next day, on 18 March, he was back at Säter Hospital to crack the nut of the car. He put out a set of colour charts. Quick picked a colour known as Tintomara 0040-R90B.

'As light as that?' Penttinen burst out. 'That was the colour of the car?'

'Hm.'

'Right. Well, then I have to inform you that we spoke to Ljungström yesterday and we've been able to confirm that he never owned a blue Volvo like this during the relevant period.'

'Hm.'

'What do you have to say to that?'

'What can I say? That must be right, then.'

By referring to the National Road Administration's vehicle registry, Seppo Penttinen was later able to establish that Ljungström had bought a new 1981 model of a Volvo 244 from Falu Motor AB two weeks before the murder. The car was not blue, as Quick had claimed. It was red.

If Quick's story were true it would mean that the shop assistant Tord Ljungström had bought a brand-new Volvo on hire purchase, for the equivalent of a year's salary, only to immediately lend it to an unemployed man, Sture Bergwall, whom he hardly knew. Also a man who couldn't drive and who didn't have a driving licence.

Quick had also described how Johan had bled inside the car and the cut-up body was later transported in the boot inside a cardboard box so soaked in blood that the base fell out. Ljungström's old vehicle was traced and picked up by the police from its current owner. If Quick's story was true and a cut-up corpse had been handled and transported in the car, there would feasibly still be some contamination from the blood. The Swedish National Laboratory of Forensic Science (SKL) examined the car's seats, the carpet in the boot and other exposed surfaces, without finding any trace of blood.

Ljungström maintained until his death that he had never lent his car to Sture. There was no suggestion that he had committed a crime, only that he had lent his car to someone, and it is difficult to see why he would protect a murderer. In the police interviews he had been truthful about his homosexuality and in answering other sensitive questions, whereas Quick was time and time again caught out telling lies and changing his story. Despite this, the investigators chose to believe Quick's version of events, while Tord Ljungström was assumed to be lying.

On 26 April Thomas Quick, Kjell Persson, Seppo Penttinen and Inspector Björn Jonasson travelled to a settlement known as Ryggen about ten kilometres east of Falun to look for one of Johan Asplund's hands.

First, Quick had to get his bearings and walk round the area with Persson. Having wandered around for an hour, they returned to the investigators and announced that they needed more time. One and a half hours later, after a good deal more walking, Quick was overwhelmed by such terrible anxiety that he had to 'rest'. A hospital vehicle was brought forward. After spending some time with his doctors – and possibly taking some medication – Quick announced that he was ready to show them where the hand was hidden.

Yet he didn't manage to find the little creek where he said he had hidden the hand. There was only a small ditch in the area. Quick kept talking incoherently, describing a torch he had brought with him when he hid the hand, mentioning the stones under which he left the hand, recalling a Mora knife that he hid at the same time and a boom that was lowered. But Quick didn't manage to lead the group to any hand.

The forensic technicians arrived shortly afterwards and examined the scene without finding anything of interest. Once again, Quick had promised to pinpoint where he had hidden body parts, in a place where the police later found nothing.

Kjell Persson wrote a disappointed note in the file. Quick's story 'has been judged by police and prosecutors to be of varying credibility, and as a result of nothing being found the level of doubt is obviously growing'.

On 5 May Quick's lawyer wrote a letter to Christer van der Kwast. The letter revealed that Gunnar Lundgren had had extensive 'discussions' with Quick, who still wanted to solve the murder of Johan. The lawyer concluded his letter as follows:

> However, he has now confirmed to me that he cannot offer to supply any further information but he would rather that you make a decision to prosecute on the basis of the existing investigation, or that you abandon the case altogether.

After considering his options for a couple of weeks, van der Kwast called a press conference where he announced that he lacked the grounds for any prosecution of Quick, although the suspicions still remained and the investigation would continue. In reality the investigation went to sleep very soundly that summer.

Having read the report of the preliminary investigation, what actually emerges is that Thomas Quick did not manage to provide one single item of information that indicated he knew anything at all about Johan's disappearance – while a great deal seemed to speak for his having invented the whole thing.

Meanwhile, at Säter Hospital, Thomas Quick's psychotherapy continued and there were no doubts at all about his guilt there.

At the end of May, Kjell Persson wrote that Quick was quite sure about the reality of the murder of Johan and that it was extremely unsatisfactory that no finds had been made at the scene of the crime. He also pointed out that Quick 'had thoughts and fantasies about other murder cases'.

Thomas Quick's files record many difficult panic attacks and suicide attempts during the investigation. When the questioning ceased in the spring and summer his anxiety tailed off, and by July Quick was allowed full clearance in and out of the hospital grounds. On 2 August his Diazepam was withheld and a week later the other benzodiazepines were also removed from Quick's list of medications. As part of this process, Quick was moved to an open ward.

'The level of danger he poses is perceived as having been considerably reduced, and currently he finds himself in an unusually good psychological condition,' wrote Kjell Persson. This harmonious observation was followed by the ominous note that Seppo Penttinen had been in touch that same day to inform them that the criminal investigation would be ongoing as before.

But despite remaining under suspicion for the murder of Johan Asplund, which should mean that arrest was obligatory by the Rules of Court in the Code of Judicial Procedure, Thomas Quick was spared arrest and no restrictions on newspapers, the telephone or receiving visitors were put in place.

During the period that followed, the file deals almost exclusively with the approval of Quick's leave outings to Borlänge, Avesta and Hedemora, as well as several trips to Stockholm. There is no mention in the file of the purpose of these trips.

There is no doubt about the fact that discussions were under way on the sidelines about the direction of the continued investigation. There were certain additional matters to look into on the Johan Asplund case, but not even Kjell Persson believed that Quick had anything further to divulge there. What the doctors and medics were discussing, rather, was a statute-barred crime – the murder of Thomas Blomgren in Växjö in 1964.

A DEEP-SEA DIVE INTO THE PAST

AFTER DISCUSSION BETWEEN Seppo Penttinen and Quick's doctors, a decision was made to hold further police interviews, at which Göran Fransson and Kjell Persson would also be present.

On Wednesday, 22 September 1993 Thomas Quick travelled unsupervised to Stockholm. As usual, Göran Fransson, who authorised the trip, didn't refer to its purpose in the file.

When, during the first police interview about the murder of Johan Asplund, Thomas Quick confessed to a second murder 'before 1967 somewhere in Småland, maybe in Alvesta', he also mentioned his accomplice Sixten and his unusual car, and that the victim's name was probably Thomas. Now, almost seven months later, it was time for Quick to dig up some facts. So he ordered back issues of newspapers from the archives at the National Library.

The murder of Thomas Blomgren was one of the best-documented crimes of the 1960s.

It was twenty to ten on Whitsun Eve in 1964 when Thomas Blomgren opened the front door of the family's house on Riddaregatan in Växjö.

'Don't worry! I'll be home soon,' he called out to his parents.

His tone revealed that he was half joking, but there was also an underlying seriousness to his words. The last time he had been to Folkets Park (the People's Park) his parents had humiliated him by showing up to fetch him. Thomas walked down Dackevägen, passing many other locals from Växjö who were strolling down to the park at a more leisurely pace. Several of them noticed a man standing under some trees on the corner where Dackevägen meets Ulriksbergspromenaden.

In the police interrogation that followed, the witnesses would describe the man as about forty-five years old, approximately five foot nine, well built, with a round face and dark, back-combed hair, a dark suit, white shirt and dark tie. He was not a local, it was generally agreed. A number of people were curious and took an extra careful look at the man, who was standing by himself in an odd place. He was untroubled by the glances, however, and merely stood there in the bushes as if he were looking out for something.

It was a quarter to ten when the man saw a boy coming down Dackevägen. Thomas turned off Dackevägen and went towards the clump of trees, directly towards the spot where the man was standing. It was his usual short cut to the People's Park.

After seeing Ing-Britt's Cocktail Show on stage, Thomas didn't go straight home, as he had promised his parents. Instead he strolled around the park and when he passed the target-shooting stand, the proprietor asked Thomas to go and buy him a hot dog. He was paid with a couple of tokens and later tried his hand at some shooting.

When Thomas finally left the People's Park, he was more than an hour late and he had only a few minutes left to live.

Meanwhile, the car mechanic Olle Blomgren and his wife, Berta, had grown so anxious that they had gone out to look for their son. At half past one Olle called the police, but despite a great deal of effort and search parties the boy was not found.

At half past ten in the morning on Whitsun, a caretaker named Erik Andersson went to pick up a bag of onions from his brother-in-law's tool shed at Dackevägen 21. When he opened the door, which was latched from the outside, he found the body of a dead boy who'd been thrown in head first among the bicycles and tools. His clothes were disordered, his belt was undone, the trouser button torn off and his face smeared with blood.

Thomas Blomgren had clearly been subjected to an extremely violent sexual assault which also caused his death.

*

Kjell Persson wrote in the file that since his patient's trip to Stockholm, Thomas Quick had 'dived deep into the past' and 'all his memories had come back'. Previously, Quick hadn't even been able to name the town where the murder took place. Now he was suddenly able to provide a remarkably detailed description of the 1964 murder in Växjö.

On Monday, 27 September 1993 Penttinen went back to Säter.

'Let's start with the time aspect, can you be precise about when in the 1960s this happened?' Penttinen was heard asking on the interview tape.

'Sixty-four,' Quick answered without hesitation.

'Are you quite clear about that?'

'Yes.'

'In what way are you able to tie down this year?'

Quick answered that he connected the year to a certain event that took place in the spring of 1963.

'Certain lucid moments,' interjected Kjell Persson, who was also present.

'Yes,' said Quick.

'I don't know if you need to go into detail about . . . it has nothing to do with what happened in Småland,' Persson continued. 'It relates to what you were subjected to yourself.'

What Kjell Persson was alluding to was that Quick, in therapy, had described his father's last sexual assault in the woods in 1963. The murder of Thomas Blomgren was a re-enactment of this final paternal assault on Sture, according to the psychiatric principles that held sway at Säter Hospital. From the assault on him in the woods, as Quick was later to explain, it was only 'a single step' to the People's Park in Växjö on Whitsun Eve, 1964.

Quick remembered that the events in question took place in late spring, and he had recollections of 'lilac and bird cherry'.

Seppo Penttinen had also been swotting up on the investigation documents from the Thomas Blomgren murder. Witnesses had seen a boy with a Beatles hairstyle in the People's Park.

'At that time the Beatles look was all the rage, wasn't it?' tried Penttinen. 'Have you ever been a fan of long hair like that?'

No, he hadn't, said Quick.

'Do you know if you have any photographs of yourself from around that time?'

Quick didn't know.

'No confirmation photos or anything like that? I remember we went to see your sister at home and we looked at some photos. I don't remember if they were from this time.'

'No, I can't say either,' said Quick abruptly.

He preferred to talk about the dance pavilion and the lottery booths in the park. Everything was exactly right. But the name of the town was too traumatic to say out loud.

'I can only say it's a town in Småland and it starts with a "V",' he said.

'So there's no doubt about the fact that you mean Växjö in this context?'

Quick nodded.

During questioning on 1 March, Quick had said that the murder took place in Alvesta or Ljungan. Kjell Persson explained to Penttinen that Quick had to give them the wrong name because the name Växjö gave rise to such painful emotions.

'In a sense it's about undoing what's been done,' he clarified.

These were the same psychological mechanisms that made Quick show them the wrong way when they were inspecting crime scenes, Persson continued. It was because Quick did not 'dare speak plainly about what's going on'.

Penttinen interrupted the psychological explanation by asking Quick how he made his way to Växjö when he was only fourteen years old and lived in Korsnäs, outside Falun, 550 kilometres from Växjö.

'I went to Växjö by car,' he replied.

'So with whom, then?' Penttinen wanted to know.

'Rather not say.'

On 1 March, Quick had described how he had travelled with Sixten Eliasson, the Salvation Army soldier, in his Borgward Isabella. But now Quick explained that he didn't want to answer the question of whom he had travelled with, not now and not in the future either. Nor did he want to explain his reasons for this decision.

Instead, Quick said that he came to the People's Park in the evening, where he remembered Thomas standing by a throwing or target-shooting stall.

Kjell Persson was dissatisfied. He told Penttinen how things worked during their therapy sessions. Quick's recall of the images from his memory were such that Persson felt it was as if Quick was reliving everything, with the actual conversations, the feelings and smells.

'Almost like a hypnotic journey in a time machine,' he went on.

Before, there had been a feeling of presence which he did not observe at all in the police interviews with Penttinen. His way of explaining the change was that they didn't rely on questions and answers like Penttinen did.

'I let it all float free,' Persson explained. 'And I listen and follow as we go along. Hopefully in combination with strong emotions, of course.'

'Is it possible to get to that level with four of us sitting round a table?' wondered Penttinen.

'No, it's impossible,' said Quick.

'There's no way,' Kjell confirmed.

'So we'll have to stick to the normal way of talking, then,' Penttinen agreed with some disappointment.

Kjell Persson wasn't quite willing to throw in the towel just yet.

'I think he can give a pretty good account of what came out on that occasion.'

Persson turned to Quick and clarified his remark: 'When you travelled back in time . . .'

Penttinen asked Quick if that was what he was doing.

'That's what we were doing,' Quick confirmed.

And then Quick described Thomas as small and slight, at least a head shorter than himself, ruddy and wearing a nylon jacket. When Thomas was about to go home from the People's Park, Sture asked his anonymous driver to follow them. Once they were a few hundred metres away from the park, the driver caught up with them and took hold of Thomas's hands. He held the boy's arms while Sture gripped him from behind, his right hand across Thomas's nose and mouth.

The boy got a nose bleed and was soon unconscious.

The driver was caught out by the rapid turn of events and ran to pick up the car.

'I picked him up and carried him. I put him in this shed, closed the door. And then the car came and we left the place.'

As they left the scene, the anonymous driver repeated, 'This hasn't happened. This hasn't happened . . .'

What Quick was saying about the twenty-nine-year-old murder had an astonishing level of detail. It chimed so well with known facts that Seppo Penttinen could hardly have had a moment's doubt that Quick's memories were authentic. Quick was also able to draw a surprisingly detailed sketch of the tool shed where he had hidden the body, even though he had only been at the scene for a minute at most and it was pitch dark at the time. It was even more curious when one considered that six months earlier he had described hiding Thomas Blomgren's body under a rotten ladder in the woods. He also claimed that he had strangled the boy – not suffocated him, which was the actual cause of death.

It was as if the strengths of his new testimony erased all of the earlier contradictions.

Even an out-and-out Quick-doubter like Leif G.W. Persson found his convictions wavering when he was later able to listen to Quick's account of the murder of Thomas Blomgren. Quick had spoken of blood from Thomas's nose running across his right hand and said that he felt the boy's chest through his undershirt. The forensic technicians had found a handprint there in blood, as if the murderer had wanted to assure himself that the heart really had stopped beating. Leif G.W. Persson commented on Quick's description of the bloody hand as 'pretty damn toxic'.

Soon after, Göran Fransson gave Thomas Quick permission for another unsupervised outing, and on 19 October Quick went off to Stockholm. The following day he was questioned again about the murder in Växjö and was able to answer all of the questions put to him by his interrogator.

In Sture's file is Kjell Persson's description of the earth-shattering breakthrough in the therapy. On 22 October he wrote:

> These deep-sea dives have absolutely solidified in the sense that all the memories have come back from the actual train of events, integrating the thoughts that the patient had, various sensory impressions including smell, memories of things the patient said and what others said, and so on.

Kjell Persson was convinced that through his psychoanalytical treatment methods, he had managed to recover Sture's repressed memories of the murder of Thomas Blomgren. Not without disappointment, he was also compelled to state that 'we are still waiting for a definitive breakthrough with the material concerning Johan Asplund, many of the details are still too difficult for the patient to be able to deal with as there are strong emotions involved, especially concerning the sense of exposure and aggression associated with the events'.

Thomas Quick's knowledge of the murder of Thomas Blomgren was seen as such a significant breakthrough in the investigation that Christer van der Kwast no longer had the slightest hesitation that Quick had been tied to his first murder. Through this, the prosecutor suggested that suspicions were also sharpened in relation to Johan.

However, there was no talk of the alleged double murderer being kept under lock and key. Despite having been sentenced to closed psychiatric care and then suspected of two murders, the prosecutor and doctors at Säter were in agreement that he should be free to move as he wished in the community and go on unsupervised trips.

STURE'S ALIBI

WHEN JENNY KÜTTIM, my researcher, and I ordered old newspaper articles about Thomas Blomgren, it was clear that they offered all the correct information given by Thomas Quick on the murder. Sture had told me that he particularly remembered an aerial photograph of Växjö, in which the route from the People's Park to the tool shed had been marked out. Thomas Blomgren's home was also marked. We found the photograph in *Aftonbladet* from 19 May 1964, with the headline 'This is the Route of Death'.

The policeman Sven Lindgren from Växjö was eighty-five years old, but his memory was crystal clear when he spoke about the murder of Thomas Blomgren, which had taken place some forty-four years earlier. He had continued working on the case until it was statute-barred in 1989.

'I know that Thomas Quick is innocent of the murder of Thomas Blomgren,' the old policeman told me on the phone.

He spoke with a halting voice and was so hard of hearing that I had to shout out the words one at a time for him to be able to hear my questions.

The reason for Sven Lindgren's confidence on the matter, he told me, was that he knew the identity of the real murderer. Apparently his colleague from that time, Detective Superintendent Ragnvald Blomqvist, could tell me more. Before long I was in my car and on the road to Småland.

Blomqvist received me in a tidy detached 1960s house in Växjö.

He was equally dismissive of the notion of Thomas Quick's involvement in the murder: 'We succeeded in mapping out Thomas Blomgren's night from the moment he walked out of his home to when he left the People's Park. In effect there was an unbroken chain of events and meetings with people in the park. There's just no room for an unknown boy like Thomas Quick in this narrative.'

Perhaps one of the strongest indicators for Quick not having murdered Thomas Blomgren was a 'highly credible key witness' who had been sitting in a car outside the People's Park as it was closing. At half past eleven she had seen Thomas Blomgren leaving the park in the company of a forty-year-old man. They headed off in the direction of the clump of trees where the same man had been observed earlier that evening.

Quick had claimed that he had been with Thomas Blomgren in the People's Park and that they had left together. This just wasn't possible, according to Ragnvald Blomqvist.

Sven Lindgren made much the same statement to journalists when he first heard of Quick's confession, according to *Dala-Demokraten* on 3 November 1993: 'If it had been a boy from outside he would have figured in the investigation. That's why I don't believe this.'

Ragnvald Blomqvist told me that the police eventually managed to identify 'the man in the copse' and that he was detained on 6 January 1971 and later formally arrested as a murder suspect by Växjö District Court. According to the 'key witness', the detained man was the same person who had left the park with Thomas Blomgren. The suspect was kept under arrest for a substantial period of time, but his defence lawyer appealed against the arrest and Göta Appeal Court released the suspect, though by the smallest possible margin – three judges in favour, two opposing. The superintendents in Växjö accepted the decision of the appeal court but were still convinced that the case was 'solved as far as the police was concerned'.

Reading the 1964 press cuttings, it is clear that the police investigation leaked like a sieve from day one. Pretty much every scrap of information the police had on the murder and the boy's injuries immediately ended up in the newspapers. Several articles declared that this was allegedly a case of a 'homosexual murder' without specifying what this assertion was based upon. The police had in fact secured technical evidence that pointed to a murder of this kind, but at least they managed to keep this piece of information under wraps.

I accompanied Ragnvald Blomqvist to the People's Park and he showed me where the various witnesses had been standing and what route Thomas Blomgren had taken when he left the park in the company of the 'man in the copse'. Blomqvist showed me the place where the small copse had once been. Given that the man detained for the murder was now dead, Blomqvist felt he could tell me the only secret the police had managed to keep for all these years.

'We took soil samples from the ground and samples of the vegetation in the copse and submitted them for analysis. Thomas's belt was unbuckled and his trousers unbuttoned. There were bits of vegetation in Thomas's trousers and underpants. Our technical analysis indicated that the plant material, soil and other fragments, definitely came from this copse. In other words the trousers must have been pulled down in the copse where the vegetation was found.'

The information that Thomas Blomgren's trousers and underpants had been pulled down and that the boy lay on the ground in the copse before the murderer had thrown the body into the tool shed had been kept secret until Ragnvald Blomqvist shared it with me. For this reason, Thomas Quick hadn't been able to read about it in the newspapers and he hadn't been able to speak of it either. According to his testimony, they had gone straight to the tool shed.

Several witnesses in the area had heard a scream around the time of Thomas's disappearance. What the police had also not revealed earlier was that a woman had been walking her dog close to the copse. The dog stood barking towards the trees and refused to move. The police were convinced that it was Thomas who had shouted and the murderer was trying to silence him, but because the woman with the dog had been there for so long, the man didn't dare release his grip and Thomas died by suffocation.

The police officers in Växjö have never been able to understand how Christer van der Kwast could link Thomas Quick to the crime. Even more odd was the fact that van der Kwast didn't want any assistance from the officers who knew this case like the back of their hands. Ragnvald Blomqvist and Sven Lindgren were frustrated that they weren't allowed to participate in the questioning of Quick.

'We knew a lot, and things that hadn't been noted down. If we had been allowed to question Quick we could have caught him lying.'

Blomqvist and Lindgren were both quite clear on this point. But Christer van der Kwast was obviously unwilling to give them the chance.

The mystery deepened further when we looked into Sture's statement that the murder took place at a time when he had a watertight alibi. Jenny Küttim had managed to track down most of Sture's fellow confirmation candidates, who confirmed that the information was correct.

I called Sven-Olof, who now lived in Svärdsjö in the region of Dalarna.

'Oh yes,' he said. 'We were confirmed in Kopparbergs Kyrka [Copper Mountain Church] on the Whitsun weekend in 1964. The confirmation ceremonies were held over two days, and the actual confirmation was on the Saturday afternoon. Candidates were asked a lot of questions. The communion itself was at the morning service on the Sunday. I particularly remember that Sture carried the baptismal font.'

The reason for this was that the Bergwall family were members of the evangelical Pentecostal Church and so hadn't been christened within the Swedish Church. Sture and his twin sister, Gun, were therefore being baptised alongside the confirmation ceremonies. Sven-Olof emailed me photographs in which Sture could be seen carrying the baptismal font.

I was stunned. Thomas Quick's alibi had just been verified for the time of perhaps his most important murder. It was through his detailed description of the Thomas Blomgren killing that Quick had laid the foundations of his credibility as a murderer. That he had started murdering as early as the age of fourteen was an excellent basis on which to build the myth of the crazed serial killer Thomas Quick.

'That was also the weekend he said he'd been down to Växjö for a bit of murdering,' said Sven-Olof, with a smile that could almost be heard over the telephone.

'You knew about that?'

'Oh yeah,' he replied in the sing-song dialect of Dalarna. 'Of course you keep an eye on your mates! Oh yeah. So that was one murder he wasn't guilty of, anyway . . . We never believed it, that's for sure.'

In other words, this was something that Sven-Olof and many others in Dalarna had thought about for many years. They just couldn't see that it was true. Also Sture's twin sister, Gun, confirmed it. In addition, she told us that she had been interviewed by the Quick investigators. So they already knew the lie of the land.

Here was another astonishing piece of information. We had ordered all the files of investigation material and interviews from the Quick inquiry, even the so-called 'slush' – unsorted investigation material that didn't need to be recorded but must nonetheless be kept as official documentation.

Nowhere among these tens of thousands of pages was this interview mentioned.

The driver who had allegedly given young Sture a lift to Växjö was another riddle. Why had this Sixten not been questioned? What did he have to say about Quick pointing him out as an accomplice in the murder of a fourteen-year-old boy? The question troubled me so much that I felt I had to contact him at once. I didn't manage to get hold of his telephone number, but I did find an address and I soon sent a bouquet of flowers to Sixten Eliasson in Dalarna. It may seem rash, maybe even unethical, but I organised an Interflora delivery and had my earnest wish delivered to Sixten's door in Dalarna:

Call me!
Hannes
0708-84 XX XX

When my mobile phone rang I apologised for my methods and explained my purpose, feeling quite guilty when I heard how tortured

Sixten sounded to have this subject brought up again, but my curiosity got the better of me.

'I've already told the police everything I have to say.'

'What? Were you questioned during the investigation?'

'Yeah, yeah. Three times!'

'And what did you have to say about Quick's statement that you drove him to Växjö in 1964?'

'I've already said to the police everything I have to say. I'm not in very good health and this has already ruined my life enough.'

'Can't you just say if you drove him there or not?'

I had to accept that Sixten wasn't going to utter a single word about his part in the investigation, but he had already given me a far more important piece of information than I had dared hope for. There were three existing police interviews with Sixten and it should therefore only be a question of time before I got hold of them.

Yet none of these interviews were to be found among the investigation material. We contacted Christer van der Kwast and Seppo Penttinen, but they didn't acknowledge any hidden interview transcripts. We went through all the cuttings and documents again, but to no avail. But as we did, we noticed that there had been others pursuing the same line of enquiry.

On 24 November 1995 *Dala-Demokraten* was beating its biggest drum. A full page was devoted to Gubb Jan Stigson's latest scoop:

DD-REPORTER REVEALS WHO DROVE QUICK TO VÄXJÖ

'I am absolutely sure of the man's identity'

According to Stigson, the man who drove the car 'had protected a murderer for more than thirty-one years'. Stigson had approached the investigators to tell them that he knew the identity of Quick's driver. Inexplicably – as Stigson saw it – Christer van der Kwast wasn't the least bit interested in the information. He simply refused to take Stigson's calls.

'It's incredibly irritating to make repeated urgent calls to van der

Kwast, only to be told that he's not available,' Stigson said to a colleague at the newspaper.

Gubb Jan Stigson reported the chief prosecutor to the Parliamentary Ombudsman for 'absenting himself from an opportunity to receive information of importance to the investigation'.

In a letter to the Parliamentary Ombudsman, Christer van der Kwast replied that the driver's identity was unknown to the investigation.

Gubb Jan Stigson pondered in his own article on what he should do with his sensational information: 'It's an incredibly difficult question. Obviously there's a big risk that he's close to a nervous breakdown. The crucial matter is that the man gives us all the information he can so that as many murders as possible can be solved.'

Sixten Eliasson had provided me with a belated explanation for the whole messy business – on no account did Christer van der Kwast want to reveal to Stigson or anyone else that their man had already been questioned on three occasions, the result of which was that it had been clearly shown that Quick had falsely accused him.

Despite this, van der Kwast kept insisting that Quick was linked to the murder of Blomgren.

THE WAR OF THE MEDICS

AFTER HIS SUCCESS in the Växjö murder case, Thomas Quick admitted that he had also murdered thirteen-year-old Alvar Larsson, who had disappeared in 1967 on the island of Sirkön in Urshult after going out to fetch some firewood. Quick also confessed to murdering eighteen-year-old Olle Högbom, who had disappeared after a school party in Sundsvall on 7 September 1983. Quick was back on heavy medication. The investigators hardly knew what to think of these new stories of murders. 'Is he Sweden's first serial killer?' *Dala-Demokraten* asked on 8 November 1993.

Gubb Jan Stigson wrote that in addition to the previously known murders of Johan Asplund and Thomas Blomgren, investigations were now under way to see whether Quick was guilty of a further three murders: 'If this proves correct, the 43-year-old will go down in Swedish criminal history as its first real serial killer.'

As Sweden's first serial killer was being unveiled at Säter Hospital, a cat-and-mouse game was in play – very much like the one in *The Silence of the Lambs*, though this one wasn't invested with such sophisticated elegance. Thomas Quick wanted to lead the investigation on to the disappearance of Olle Högbom, which had been handled by the police in Sundsvall – Seppo Penttinen's police district. In one round of questioning about Thomas Blomgren, Quick was keen to talk about an important year in his life.

Penttinen made the following note in the report:

> One of the years he mentioned was 1983. He said that was the year when his mother died, and, in the same week another 'dramatic event in several senses' took place. Quick was anxious when he said this and didn't want to say in plain words what he meant by the statement. Instead he asked if he could give a little clue in the form of a line from a well-known children's song. Then he said 'Mors lilla Olle' [Mother's Little Olle].

Seppo Penttinen didn't have too much trouble deciphering the helpful serial killer's little riddle. Olle Högbom's disappearance was, like the case of Johan, the most infamous crime in his police district in modern times, a mystery where the police did not have the slightest trace or sign of a suspect.

The names Alvar and Olle were added to the list of Quick's potential victims.

A few months earlier, Göran Källberg had taken over as the hospital's new chief physician and as such was now ultimately responsible for Thomas Quick's care. Quick's confessions to the murders of Johan Asplund and Thomas Blomgren had attracted a good deal of press attention and no more than four days into his new job, Källberg brought up the issue with Quick's doctor. Källberg explained that he was dubious about allowing the patient full clearance and leave at a time when his involvement in two murders was under investigation. Göran Fransson swore that he and Kjell Persson had it all under control. They also emphasised that the arrangement had been made with the full knowledge of the chief prosecutor and the police.

What Fransson carefully avoided mentioning was that he and Kjell Persson, with a great deal of secrecy, were continuing to run their own parallel criminal investigation. Accompanied by Quick, the two doctors had gone back to Ryggen to look for Johan's hidden hand. In an unguarded moment, Quick wandered off to a 'hide', where he claimed he had found two fingers. When the doctors asked what he had done with them, he said he had eaten them. Afterwards, Persson and Fransson made an agreement with Quick not to mention the incident to the investigators. A few days later they returned again to Ryggen to look for Johan's body, without success. On later occasions they toured various other locations to look for body parts.

Early in 1994, Källberg was informed that during therapy Quick had confessed to yet another murder. From his notes:

> On 14 January I learned from members of our personnel that the patient has now disclosed that it is a case of six murders of boys, and that the memories of these are beginning to come back to him.

Six murders was, apparently, the upper limit of what the chief physician was prepared to tolerate and he brought up his concern with Kjell Persson once again:

> [I] made it clear that I could not support his full clearance and would not give my support either to him or Frasse [Göran Fransson] if something happened. Frasse has, after all, already told me that it would be a catastrophe for him if something happened. Kjell agrees that it would be catastrophic, but he urges me not to interfere.

After this conversation, Kjell Persson went on sick leave and Källberg agonised over how to handle the situation. When he called 'Frasse' to discuss his decision to cancel Quick's full clearance and leave, he was informed that Fransson was now also on sick leave.

Thomas Quick was then living on Ward 37, an open ward that was a 'twin section' of Ward 36, where violent prisoners convicted of serious crimes were kept locked up. The office for both of these wards was located within Ward 36, and this was where Thomas Quick went to have coffee on the morning of 21 January 1994.

After a brief meeting with the staff, Göran Källberg sought out Thomas Quick and informed him of his decision to cancel his full clearance. With this, Quick was locked up in Ward 36 along with the most dangerous criminals.

Kjell Persson, still on sick leave, was extremely unhappy about this, and a week later he contacted Källberg to let him know his disappointment with the decision, which, in his view, might result in the serial killer Thomas Quick committing suicide before he'd had time to confess and face trial for his crimes. Persson described this as 'a national scandal'.

Göran Källberg dismissed this argument as contradictory, but was unsettled enough by the conversation to place an immediate call to Ward 36 to enquire about Quick's state of mind. He made a note during the call, to the effect that the staff had not noticed 'anything out of the ordinary with the patient. As we speak he's sitting with the staff, playing Scrabble'.

The realisation that there was a serial killer at Säter Hospital created tensions not only internally at the clinic but also between the investigators and the carers. Göran Källberg was soon aware of great consternation within the investigation team that Quick had been locked up. On the same day that the regime at the hospital was changed, Christer van der Kwast called Källberg to explain that the cancellation of his full clearance would put the ongoing investigation in jeopardy.

Christer van der Kwast believed that Thomas Quick 'has to get something in return' for his confessions, but he was given short shrift. In fact Källberg was furious that a prosecutor was trying to interfere in the care of one of his patients. Full clearance and leave in exchange for murder confessions? 'I cannot tolerate reasoning of this kind', noted Källberg in the file.

Källberg could live with the conflict with van der Kwast. What was more serious was that increasing numbers of staff at the clinic were turning against him. Thomas Quick being disappointed was perfectly understandable, but the real problem was the reaction of the two doctors, Fransson and Persson.

Kjell Persson was already planning to leave Säter for a new job at St Lars Psychiatric Clinic in Lund and he now put a great deal of effort into trying to bring his patient with him. Quick fuelled the fire by threatening to stop cooperating with the police if he wasn't allowed to continue his therapy with Persson. Källberg viewed the situation as blackmail – pure and simple.

In February 1994, van der Kwast put in another call to Säter's management to offer his views on how Quick's care should be organised and 'once again emphasised the importance of a close level of communication with senior physician Kjell [Persson] for the sake of the ongoing police investigation'.

When Kjell Persson's efforts to bring Quick with him to Lund failed, he managed instead to arrange a place for him at the forensic psychiatric clinic in Växjö. However, the chief physician of the institution, Ole Drottved, declined Persson's offer to continue therapy with Quick. This would have to be handled by the clinic's own staff.

Christer van der Kwast, who believed that the police investigation was absolutely dependent on Kjell Persson's therapy, intervened again in the question of care and called Drottved, who let himself to be persuaded. Persson would be allowed to preside over Quick's therapy.

Again, chief physician Göran Källberg was presented with a *fait accompli* without having been consulted or informed. 'This is because it has been put into effect by non-medical staff who are not in our employ', he commented bitterly in his file – a pointed reference to van der Kwast.

But there were many who wanted to help stir the pot in the period leading up to the move. Göran Fransson, while he was on sick leave, maintained his communication with Thomas Quick via the ward's patient telephone. A psychiatry student who had functioned as Quick's therapist during holiday periods also threw herself into the ring. In a letter to Quick she tried to make him understand Göran Källberg's decision on the lock-down in Ward 36:

> When it is growing more evident that you have committed six murders, when you are in the midst of a difficult process in terms of your memories of this, it seems reasonable that you should be 'held with a slightly firmer hand'. Unfortunately I think there would be an almighty row if the public found out that a serial killer was allowed so much free movement. You know how people are, and the mass media . . .

When Kjell Persson's sick leave was coming to an end, he refused to go back to the clinic unless he could work 25 per cent of his normal working hours and devote himself exclusively to Thomas Quick. He wanted to rid himself of such duties as making ward rounds and dealing with other patients. If he didn't get what he wanted, he would put himself back on full sick leave.

The request was conveyed to Källberg at a meeting on 7 February, after which Persson immersed himself in a telephone consultation with van der Kwast to schedule police questioning in the coming period. Having concluded this, he left the clinic and went home.

In the midst of this messy conflict, the investigation pressed on with further interviews. It can be seen from Göran Källberg's notes that at this time he was beginning to have doubts about the method of the therapy Quick was being put through. Källberg and Kjell Persson happened to meet on a train, and they spoke about how the therapy would be organised if Quick moved to Växjö.

> Kjell also tells me that he is now taking on a great challenge with the therapy. At the same time [I am] slightly dubious about whether this really is therapy. [Kjell] tells me that he mostly sits in silence and the patience starts remembering as soon as Kjell sits down in the room.

On 21 February Göran Fransson, who was still on sick leave, communicated his unwillingness to go back to his job at the clinic, where 'he feels exposed to some sort of plot and that someone wants to do him harm'.

Göran Källberg wrote in his memorandum after the telephone call that he viewed Fransson as 'clearly paranoid'. In short, the atmosphere at the regional clinic in Säter was not at its best.

Kjell Persson never went back to his job at Säter. Instead, he focused all his energy on the transfer of Thomas Quick. For his own part, he was going to be working at St Lars in Lund, commuting twice weekly to Växjö for the therapy sessions with Quick.

Shortly before Quick's departure, Persson was informed of the rules in force at Växjö, including the prohibition of all forms of benzodiazepine. This was an unexpected problem. Would Quick agree to it? And if he did, would he have to be detoxified before he was moved to Växjö?

On 28 February Källberg wrote:

> Have initiated a reduction in the dosage of benzodiazepine for TQ. Unfortunately it has not been clear to me just how much he is taking. He is also motivated to quickly cut his intake.

Sture Bergwall tells me that all this was just a pretence: 'It was a shocking piece of news that they weren't offering benzo at Växjö. At first Kjell said it would sort itself out, he'd talk to chief physician Drottved. When they wouldn't agree to it, Kjell said it would all sort itself out once I got there.'

Thomas Quick suffered withdrawal symptoms during his detoxification which lasted a few weeks, but he was eager to get it over with as quickly as possible. After all, once he was there everything was going to 'sort itself out'.

On 3 March Källberg noted that 'TQ is having withdrawal symptoms but he wants to carry on with the rapid detox'.

Less than two weeks later a removals van took Thomas Quick and his belongings to the regional psychiatric clinic in Växjö, which immediately proved to be an entirely different institution to Säter Hospital. The hope that things would fall into place as far as provision of benzodiazepines was concerned was quickly scuppered. The Växjö clinic emphasised 'security aspects, the establishment of boundaries and assessments of the dangers posed by patients', Quick was told.

The move was also a disappointment for Kjell Persson, who had been looking forward to resuming his successful therapy with Quick. According to Sture, Persson visited him twice for the purpose of the therapy, but on both occasions he came in vain.

'I couldn't speak a single word. I couldn't describe anything without benzo, so we just sat there,' he said, laughing at the memory.

Nor did the infamous patient from Säter live up to the expectations that had grown among the staff at Växjö, who noted in the file:

> The patient has been kept in our admissions ward for the last two weeks. The ward staff perceive him as withdrawn and introspective in any communication.
>
> Via his therapist Kjell [Persson] the patient has communicated that he can't put up with the methods of care practised in our clinic. The therapist Kjell also takes the view that he cannot continue his therapeutic programme under existing routines here.

Thomas Quick would only communicate with staff via Kjell Persson, and the management of the clinic confirmed that it had proved impossible to integrate the two different care regimes of Säter and Växjö, 'which means that we cannot satisfy the patient's views and wishes on full clearance, medications, etc.'.

By the time this note was made, Thomas Quick had already called Ward 36 at Säter Hospital to say that he couldn't stand it any more. He wanted to go back.

'We'll come and pick you up tomorrow', was the immediate decision.

The following day three care assistants went to Växjö to effect the move. Sture enthusiastically told me about the journey back to Säter: 'It was wonderful! As soon as we got into the car they got out a paper bag of Diazepam! Home at last!'

They stopped off in Gränna to eat at a restaurant and bought sweets at Svampen in Örebro. When they came back to Ward 36 all the staff were waiting for Quick with open arms. At the front stood Birgitta Ståhle.

Now things would really get started.

BIRGITTA STÅHLE TAKES OVER

AFTER HIS RETURN to Säter Hospital on 30 March 1994, Thomas Quick moved into his old room and the doctors put him back on a moderate dose of benzodiazepines. A liberating sense of calm descended over the clinic which had for so long been riven by dispute.

For Quick, on the other hand, the loss of his therapist Kjell Persson was difficult to endure. Birgitta Ståhle wrote in the file that Quick, after his stay in Växjö, was extremely impatient to continue his therapy and also very clear about the need to do this within the framework of the clinic at Säter, because he felt so secure and at home in his ward. He asked Ståhle to help him and she agreed.

As the chief physicians Fransson and Persson had left the field, Birgitta Ståhle emerged as the undisputed winner of a bitter contest in which she had not even needed to participate.

At three o'clock in the afternoon on 14 April 1994 the new core of the Quick investigation assembled in the music room of Ward 36. In the four red and black armchairs sat Seppo Penttinen, Thomas Quick, Birgitta Ståhle and the lawyer Gunnar Lundgren. The fifth wheel of the cart was Sven Åke Christianson, a lecturer in psychology from Stockholm University, who was there in his capacity as a memory expert with a particular interest in serial killers.

In advance of the session, Thomas Quick had passed on the message that he had important information about the murder of Johan Asplund. He had consumed large amounts of benzodiazepines over the course of the day. His account grew painfully detailed and fuzzy while Seppo Penttinen listened patiently, asking questions and trying to move the story on.

Towards the end of the long interview things became extremely problematic when Quick, via Ståhle, revealed to the police that the doctors had been conducting their own investigation.

> TQ: I think we made some real finds as well.
>
> PENTTINEN: What was that, then?
>
> TQ: Two . . . Two . . . One of those and one of those . . .
>
> PENTTINEN: Mm. You're looking at two bones of your long finger. Where are they now?
>
> TQ: I have to go outside while Birgitta says where they are.

Thomas Quick left the room and Birgitta Ståhle took over to explain what had emerged in their therapeutic conversations regarding Johan's recovered finger bones.

'This is the difficult part,' she began hesitantly. 'This is what he told me. Now. Er . . . because he told me he found pieces of bone from the hand by the stream and he showed them to Göran and Kjell but then he ate them, so they're no longer available to us.'

Penttinen sat in silence.

That two doctors had been running their own investigation and actively keeping this information from the investigators was probably shocking enough. Even worse was that Quick had allegedly eaten the only technical evidence to have emerged in the entire investigation.

Birgitta Ståhle's short intervention was recorded on tape and would be transcribed and become public on the day the prosecution was announced for the murder of Johan Asplund. Seppo Penttinen had already heard enough.

'I see,' he said tersely. 'We're pausing this interview at 16.06.'

Kjell Persson's successor, Birgitta Ståhle, never involved herself in investigative activities, choosing instead to cooperate fully with the police. She conducted therapy sessions with Thomas Quick at least three times a week and reported anything of police interest to Seppo Penttinen.

The greatest difficulty was that Quick, when he came to Säter Hospital, was unaware of having committed any murders at all. These memories were completely repressed, as were all the sexual assaults to which he had been subjected in his childhood.

Under Ståhle's custodianship Quick managed to go back mentally into his childhood in Falun in the 1950s. In the therapy he seemed to be transformed into the little boy Sture, who, with a child's vocabulary, recounted his experiences in detail while Ståhle continuously made notes and recorded his reactions.

Similar situations had been described by Kjell Persson as 'a hypnotic journey in a time machine'. The psychological term for such time travel is 'regression', which implies that the patient goes back to an earlier stage of development, often for the purpose of reliving and working on traumatic experiences.

Thomas Quick's term for the experience was 'time-fall' and it did in fact seem that in the therapy he was able to go back in time at will, either to his supposedly terrifying childhood or to those occasions when he had committed murders as an adult. According to the theories in practice at Säter Hospital, his violent crimes were 're-enactments' of the traumas of his childhood, so that in effect the violent criminal harboured within himself both the victim and the perpetrator. The connection between the victim and the perpetrator in the same person meant that the reconstituted memory of a sexual assault in the perpetrator's childhood could be used to gain an understanding of how the abuse had been re-created by the adult. Sture Bergwall had re-enacted his parents' sexual assaults by raping and murdering young boys.

Over a period of time, Birgitta Ståhle's therapy with Thomas Quick developed into a garden of repressed memories, several of which were germinated and developed into stories that held up all the way through legal processes to court verdicts for murder.

Nowadays, the reliability of such repressed memories extracted in therapy is viewed with scepticism, not least in legal systems around the world, but in the 1990s these ideas were at the very heart of the treatment of Thomas Quick and other violent prisoners at Säter.

Neither the doctors nor the psychiatrists at Säter ever questioned the fact that Quick had no memories of any of his murders even though he was, apparently, the worst serial killer in Sweden. There was a broad consensus that experiences of this kind were so unendurable that the memories were 'dissociated' and hidden in the far reaches of the brain. Nor did anyone at any stage examine Ståhle's competence at extracting such memories by use of regression techniques.

As the fragmented memories gradually returned, an intellectually stimulating process took over in which the pieces were joined up – 'integrated' – while Birgitta Ståhle and her curious patient watched in terror as the image of the serial killer Thomas Quick materialised before their very eyes.

I knew that Ståhle was having weekly coaching from object relations theory guru Margit Norell for her therapy with Quick, but their reasoning and approach were a well-kept secret. There was no documentation about it apart from Sture Bergwall's meagre and unconfirmed memories.

Birgitta Ståhle had been keeping careful notes on every therapy session, and after Sture retracted all his confessions he demanded to see these notes, which, legally speaking, were a part of his file. Her answer was astonishing: Ståhle maintained that she had destroyed them all.

Sture also told me that Margit Norell and Birgitta Ståhle had written a book about Thomas Quick. The authors had said it would be a groundbreaking work on a par with Sigmund Freud's case study of 'the Wolf Man'. But for unknown reasons the book was never published.

Sture and I realised that we would never have access to the manuscript.

Evidently my only source of information on Birgitta Ståhle's ten-year period of therapy with the serial killer Quick was Sture Bergwall, the person with possibly the least credibility in the whole country.

After Sture Bergwall's retraction of his confessions, the hospital management imposed a variety of reprisals on the troublesome serial killer. Among other things the doctors withdrew his so-called 'fresh air' outings, and it was decided that the blinds that afforded him a measure of privacy and protected him from direct sunlight in his room should be removed. The bookcases with books and CDs that had been in his room for almost two decades were also removed.

When Sture was packing the contents of the last bookcase into a cardboard box, he found an unmarked scuffed folder at the bottom of a pile of old vinyl records. Sture opened the file and read the lines at the top of the first page in amazement:

> INTRODUCTION
> The purpose of this book is to describe a very difficult and unusual therapeutic process which I, in my capacity as supervising therapist, have been monitoring in the years 1991–95 . . .

Sture could hardly believe his eyes: he had found Margit Norell and Birgitta Ståhle's manuscript, which we had all thought was lost. He continued reading:

> Before the therapeutic process began, Sture had no memories at all from before the age of 12. His awareness of the murders he had committed – the first of them at the age of 14 – had initially only come up in the therapeutic process. In no case was he ever the object of suspicion or under investigation for any of these crimes. Whenever a murder and the particular details of it were sufficiently clarified in the therapy, Sture himself asked the police to come and question him and investigate the matter.

A few days later I held the priceless manuscript in my hands, all 404 pages of unedited text, sections of it indigestible in its thorny, psychological jargon – but nonetheless it was the therapists' own account of their process with Thomas Quick.

In my early research on Thomas Quick I had often come across the expression 'the Simon illusion'. I understood this to be a central theme of the therapy but had some difficulty grasping the precise meaning of the illusion. As soon as I got the chance I asked Sture to explain.

'Simon came into the picture in my therapy with Birgitta Ståhle. He was born in connection with a sexual assault on me by both my father and my mother. I can't remember how I described it, but he was killed by dismemberment. I mean the head was cut off. Then the foetus was wrapped in newspaper and put on the back of a bicycle and then me and Dad went and buried it on Främby Point.'

Sture was four years old when he witnessed the murder of his little brother, and an idea took hold of him that he should try to 'mend Simon', and make him whole and alive once again. Somehow this idea transformed into the concept of Sture being able to 'gain life' by killing. In his therapy with Birgitta Ståhle this train of thought became the explanation behind Sture's development into a murderer of boys.

No one had ever heard of Simon before Thomas Quick started talking about him to Birgitta Ståhle, and according to Sture these were pure fantasies that had come up in the therapy room.

I sat with the manuscript in which Ståhle described in her own words how Thomas Quick regressed in the therapy and was transformed into the four-year-old witnessing how his parents murdered and cut up his little brother Simon:

> The face is contorted with the terror of dying, with a gaping mouth. I, Birgitta, can communicate with Sture, which demonstrates that although he is in deep regression he nonetheless still has a connection with the here and now.
>
> The first lunge with the knife stabs into the right-hand side of the torso and is delivered by the mother. Thereafter the father takes the knife. The Sture-shell repeatedly says not the throat, not the throat, then holds up the throat. The knife stabs and cuts up the torso and then the right leg is removed.
>
> M [Mother] takes flesh from Simon and puts it in the Sture-shell's gaping mouth.
>
> The Sture-shell says, 'I'm not hungry.' Sture says that M and F embrace and it gives him an unpleasant feeling. Then he reaches out to take Simon's hand. Realises that it is loose, it is unattached. Says, 'I've broken off my little brother's hand.'

In the therapy, Simon's birth and the parents' killing of him were perceived as truths. Sture's experience of the murder as a child would later be re-enacted in the murders of Johan Asplund, Charles Zelmanovits and the other boys. The memories were repressed but the adult Sture was able to 'recount' his experiences by means of the murders and by desecrating and cutting up the bodies, just as his parents had cut up his little brother.

In the book, Sture's mother is referred to throughout as 'M' or 'Nana', euphemisms for a creature of such evil that her real name would be too frightening to speak out loud. Birgitta Ståhle returns in several passages to the evil mother's heinous deeds:

> Sture starts talking spasmodically. Nana has just pressed her hands round Sture's throat. 'He feels her hands. Now she goes to Simon', where Sture remains behind his closed eyes. She was there, right in front of Simon's undamaged face. The body was broken but Sture can concentrate on the face so he doesn't have to look at the broken body. Sture sees Nana's bloody, clenched hand. He grows silent, then he says, 'Maybe that red stuff is fruit syrup?' . . .

According to Margit Norell, the fact that Thomas Quick believed the blood on his massacred younger brother was fruit syrup could be seen as evidence that he was telling the truth. She wrote in the manuscript:

> So how can we know if what Sture is describing is the truth?
>
> When it comes to the experiences of the child: the childlike language, the typical childish reactions, the manner of the regression, the emotional expressions – and the ever clearer memories.
>
> As for the repressed adult experiences: the reconstructions and their correspondence with police records and, lastly, the connection between the two.

Investigators searched in vain for Simon's buried body on Främby Point. They ordered the mother's medical records from Falu Hospital, and these indicated that Thyra Bergwall had not given birth to a child at this time nor suffered a miscarriage. No one close to the family had noticed any pregnancy and neither had Sture's six siblings. Despite this, no one in the investigating team seems to have had the slightest doubt about the authenticity of Sture's account. Not the police, not the prosecutor, not the courts and not Margit Norell.

> Like all children, Sture has tried to maintain a positive image of his parents. He has done so particularly with his father, who was sometimes capable of showing kind sides – even if rather sentimental in their form. But mostly it was his mother who was frightening to Sture, and one of the forms this took was that he no longer dares remember her face or look at it. When this is no longer possible – in connection with the death and cutting up of the Simon foetus – Sture divides his image of the father into two parts – P and Ellington – where Ellington represents the terrifying, evil part of his father.

During one regression, Thomas Quick talked about a 'time-fall to the level of 1954' – P had left the room after the murder of Simon and soon after came back wearing a clean shirt. *It's a man who's borrowed Daddy's shirt*, thought Sture the child, and named his father's evil incarnation, Ellington. In the therapy Quick often used the euphemisms 'Ellington' and 'P' for his father, but he was able to enunciate the word 'Father' without any particular problems. Using the word 'Mother' when speaking of her was, however, an impossibility.

It's a strange story. But stranger still is the evolution of the Ellington figure.

In the therapy, Ellington changed from having been his father's evil alter ego to a personality that quite often took possession of Thomas Quick's body. Birgitta Ståhle witnessed the transformation many times and recorded one instance of this in the manuscript:

> I can promise you that the transformation I saw was the Devil incarnate in literal form, and Sture's response to this. He bares his throat and after that there is denial in his words, no, this is

not my father, it's a record that's jumped out of him and is saying this.

What the Devil has said to him is – you shall taste death.

Ellington's different roles in Thomas Quick's story is one of many examples of how the figures in Quick's descriptions are constantly changing form; no one personality is fixed and is always symbolising someone else. Ellington is the father figure into whom Quick is transformed when he commits his murders.

During the first period of therapy with Birgitta Ståhle the relevant cases were Alvar Larsson, Johan Asplund, Olle Högbom and a boy who was sometimes called 'Duska' and sometimes entirely different names. The last name added to the existing list from Kjell Persson's time was Charles Zelmanovits, and it was in this case that Ellington made his entrance as a murderer of boys.

Charles was fifteen when he disappeared on the way home from a school disco in Piteå on the night of 13 November 1976. Since Thomas Quick's return from Växjö, the murder of Charles had become the priority case in the therapy sessions and the police investigation.

LEADING QUESTIONS

IN THE SUMMER of 2008, long before the dramatic meeting at Säter where Sture admitted to me that his confessions were all false, I visited Falu District Court to copy their documents on Sture Bergwall's youthful transgressions and the murders of Gry Storvik and Trine Jensen. There, they were not only helpful but also talkative, and a young law clerk told me that a Norwegian production company had also ordered copies of the two investigation reports of Thomas Quick's murders.

'When they got the invoice for 40,000 crowns they refused to pay,' he told me.

I was curious and slightly concerned about the possibility of a competing television production in Norway, but soon learned that it was a series on psychological profiling.

One of the world's leading profilers, former FBI agent Gregg McCrary, had compiled psychological profiles of the individuals who had murdered Therese Johannesen, Trine Jensen and Gry Storvik.

Gregg McCrary had not been given access to the interrogation transcripts or other information about Thomas Quick, only technical forensic reports, interviews with people connected to the victims and similar materials. Of course, he hadn't been told that the same person had been convicted of all three murders.

Quite shamelessly I decided to sponge off my Norwegian colleagues and booked an interview with Gregg McCrary in Virginia, USA.

He received me at the end of September in his grandiose property in a gated community behind walls and manned sentry posts. To McCrary it seemed quite obvious that three different people were responsible for the Norwegian murders for which Thomas Quick had been found guilty. None of his psychological profiles of the criminals bore any kind of resemblance to Thomas Quick, and in two cases he concluded that the guilty person would have needed very good local knowledge, which Quick didn't have.

When I told McCrary about my own investigation, he said, 'The only thing we know for sure is that he's a liar. First he confessed to the crimes, later he changed his mind about it. What matters now is that we decide which of the two versions is the truth. He may have committed a few of the murders, he may be guilty of them all. In regard to the three murders I am familiar with, I'm positive he's innocent. And I am extremely dubious about the others.'

He carried on: 'I've been called in many times to check interviews when there's a suspicion of a false confession. The first thing I usually do is to quickly leaf through the interrogation transcript to see who's doing the talking. The preponderance should always be on the suspect, if it's not there's a big risk that the interrogator is passing information to the suspect.'

Gregg McCrary told me about cases he had worked on himself, where it was found that false confessions had been made, even though the suspects had provided information which only the perpetrator and the police should have been in a position to know.

The interrogators had been absolutely sure that they hadn't revealed any information of such kind, but after carefully scrutinising the transcripts they noticed that this was precisely what had happened. Information can be revealed by tiny insinuations, or just the way a question is phrased.

The interrogator is supposed to ask open-ended questions: 'What happened? Tell me!' If the interrogator asks leading questions answerable with a 'yes' or 'no', the interview is not being handled correctly.

The substance of McCrary's insights was like an echo of what the Quick-critical policeman Jan Olsson had said to me early on: 'Think about one thing: has he ever given a single piece of information that the police didn't already know? I'd say that's what you ought to be thinking about.'

CHARLES ZELMANOVITS'S DISAPPEARANCE

CHARLES ZELMANOVITS LAY on the floor while his younger brother, Frederick, tried to help him squeeze his slim body into the even slimmer Wrangler jeans.

Fred struggled and pulled at the waistband; Charles sucked in his stomach and finally managed to get the brass button through the buttonhole. Stiff and clumsy, he got onto his feet and ran his hand across the denim, which was stuck to his thighs like an eel skin. As the trouser legs reached his feet, they widened to cover them completely.

Frederick Zelmanovits was only twelve years old but he clearly remembered the evening of 12 November 1976, just before the unfathomable happened. I met him in the little restaurant he ran in Piteå and found that Charles's younger brother had aged; his flowing locks had thinned, turned grey and been cut short. He had children and soon he would be turning forty-five.

He spoke of the disappearance of Charles, which had left a permanent feeling of emptiness in his chest: 'It was my best friend who disappeared.'

Charles was the one Frederick always turned to when there were arguments in the family, or whenever he had problems of any kind. That last evening with Charles had been quite normal. Frederick remembers how earlier on he had thrown a dog bowl of water over Charles. Then he had helped him get his jeans on and the dog bowl was forgotten.

Charles and Frederick had mixed their blood, one thumb pressed to another, before they left their childhood home in Spain and moved with their family to Piteå, in the cold and dark of the north. It was their mother, Inga, who had insisted on the move from Fuengirola so the boys could have a better education. Her Spanish husband, Alexander, was a surgeon, but he had taken a position as company doctor for Munksund Sawmills.

Inga Zelmanovits had always spoken Swedish with her sons, so Charles had no problems with the language when he started at Pitholm School – just the odd word came out wrong sometimes. He was accepted by the other pupils and soon became one of the most popular boys in the class, which was possibly helped along by his gleaming ash-blond shoulder-length hair, his almond-shaped brown eyes and a smile that revealed a perfect row of teeth.

But despite all his good points, Charles was still a foreigner and an outsider. That was how it was in Piteå in 1976.

On the evening in question, Charles had been reminded that his position among his circle of friends shouldn't be taken for granted. His classmate Anna had the house to herself over the weekend, so there was a party at her parents' lavish villa. Everyone was coming, but no one had thought to invite Charles.

He gave his jeans a final check, then put on the long leather coat which had been hand-sewn to order in Spain. In his pocket was a secret bottle of Bacardi even his blood-brother didn't know about – but the world has knowledge of it now, thanks to the police's scrupulous mapping-out of his last evening.

Charles drummed up his courage and dialled the number. Anna answered and Charles could hear that the party was already in full swing, even though it was only half past six. Of course he was welcome, she said, no problem.

Before long Charles was ringing the doorbell. The other boys had beer, wine and spirits, which they offered to the girls. Charles pulled out his bottle of Bacardi and sat down on a footstool.

By half past eight most of them were drunk, someone called a taxi and the party came to an abrupt and chaotic end. Charles and a few others who couldn't squeeze into the taxi ended up walking the three kilometres to the school disco at Pitholm School.

As soon as he walked into the school canteen Charles saw Maria.

And she saw him. They danced and kissed a bit before she went outside with him. They brought the rum with them to a hidden spot. It was six degrees outside. They had sexual intercourse but it was over almost before it started. Maria was in a bad mood when they went inside again.

But Charles was soon back outside with all the seventeen- and eighteen-year-olds who hadn't been allowed inside the school disco. His rum was almost finished and Charles was quite drunk. He didn't have a clue where Maria was.

'Charles!'

Leif was calling him. Charles was fond of nineteen-year-old Leif, who was an unusually decent guy and was Maria's friend.

'You want a nip?' asked Charles, holding out the bottle to offer him the last few drops.

Leif shook his head and said, 'Maria told me about it. You've really upset her. And made her angry.'

Charles finished off the last sip without answering. But Leif wouldn't let it go.

'You can't just get your bloody end away and then not give a damn about her for the rest of the night. You have to be with her tonight! Then after that you can do what you want . . .'

Charles couldn't think of anything appropriate to say by way of a response and just stood there with his empty bottle. Leif repeated how much he disliked the way Charles had behaved and then left him by himself in the dark.

The rumour spread like wildfire: 'Charles fucked Maria.'

After all, she was the best-looking girl in the school, even the eighteen-year-olds thought so. Before long the gossip was that 'the Greek' had raped her.

Lars-Ove was eighteen and had stayed sober so that he could be the designated driver that night. When he caught sight of Maria he suggested a drive in his car. They drove into the centre of town, but things didn't work out as Lars-Ove had hoped – Maria was upset and spoke only about Charles.

Charles was still at the disco at Pitholm School. He looked for Maria until he was the last person left and then hurried homewards.

After a few kilometres down the long straight road known as Järnvägsgatan (Railway Road) he caught sight of a large gang of schoolmates. He ran until he caught up with them, but Maria wasn't there.

Charles exchanged only a few words with his friends from the party earlier at the villa before hurrying on. The last his friends saw of him was when he passed under the street light by the T-junction at the end of Järnvägsgatan. No one saw if he took a right or a left turn into Pitholmsgatan.

He never reached home.

When Charles disappeared into the darkness, his younger brother, Frederick, was sleeping, so he was unaware of what had happened until he awoke the next morning.

'There were loads of police outside and soon enough I guess I understood what they were doing there. In the beginning we thought he'd come back, but as time passed it got worse and worse.'

Frederick described Charles's disappearance as a family catastrophe. He tried to put into words the endless torment of uncertainty, how his parents' spirits were broken, telephone calls from someone who said, 'Hi, it's Charles', and then hung up. He described the foolish hope that he would find Charles standing there one day, that he was not dead and everything would be as it had been before.

'Of course you always wanted to think that he was out there somewhere. But time passed. It was quite chaotic.'

Frederick never believed in the suicide theories or that Charles had been unwell or hadn't dared go home. Frederick said it was inconceivable that Charles would have disappeared on purpose.

'Someone did something to him, that's always been my firm belief.'

Sunday, 19 September 1993 was a beautiful morning in Norra Pitholmen. A young hunter had made plans to spend the best part of the day in the forest, on land where his family had hunting rights.

With a firm grip on his shotgun, he hurried to keep up with his dog, which had almost reached the clearing at the top of the slope.

The dog barked to signal wildfowl. The hunter was peering up into the sun when he stumbled over something. The object looked like a large, greyish white mushroom but felt hard as a stone. It was too large to be an animal bone, too round for an animal cranium. With one foot he scraped away the moss, picked it up and found himself standing with a human cranium in his hand.

His discovery was puzzling. A body couldn't have lain here for a long period of time without being found. They often used beaters here for the hunting and he had passed the spot countless times. A few years earlier his father had cut down the forest a stone's throw away. The hunter looked at the cranium one more time before carefully putting it back on the ground, memorising the place and hurrying away after his dog.

Churning thoughts of the skull wouldn't give him any peace and after an hour of unproductive stalking he went back to have another look at the object. He remembered the boy who had gone missing without trace seventeen years before, and it dawned on him that he had to go home and call the police.

The police patrol confirmed the presence of several more bones and decaying garments in the area. They found what looked like the sleeve of a brown leather jacket.

'The person associated with this cranium is currently not known to us,' wrote Detective Inspector Martin Strömbäck in his report, although he didn't have the slightest doubt about the identity of the dead person.

Charles's father was no longer alive, but Frederick and his mother, Inga, were soon notified that Charles had been identified by means of his dental records.

'At least it was something definite . . . A lot of people say it's such a relief when a body is found, but I have a hard time feeling that. What's the meaning of a body? I want to know what happened. For a number of years we were clear about the fact that he no longer existed. When the body was found the uncertainty returned: OK? Why is it lying there? What really happened?'

*

It wasn't until three months later, on Friday, 10 December, that the newspapers reported that Charles Zelmanovits's remains had been found.

The riddle of the missing fifteen-year-old had been partially solved. The Zelmanovits family had received written confirmation that Charles was dead. How he had died or why he had ended up in the forest on Norra Pitholmen were questions that the investigation could not answer. The forensic technicians hadn't found anything to suggest that Charles had been the victim of a crime.

A few days after the publication of the articles on Charles Zelmanovits, Thomas Quick mentioned during a therapy session with Kjell Persson that he had 'come into contact with new material'. He had become aware of some memories of murdering a boy in Piteå in the 1970s.

Kjell Persson replied that he had read an item in the newspaper about that particular case, because the police had found Charles's remains in a forest outside Piteå.

'Oh really,' said Quick, surprised. 'I never saw that.'

It was after eight in the morning on 9 February 1994 when the lawyer Gunnar Lundgren walked out of his magnificent Dalecarlian mansion, got into his Honda and drove just short of fifty kilometres to Säter Hospital.

Lundgren was sixty-one years old and the best-known lawyer in Dalarna, having defended the most notorious criminals in the region, including the bank robber Lars-Inge Svartenbrandt, the mass murderer Mattias Flink and now also Thomas Quick, the alleged serial killer. A confident person, Lundgren didn't hesitate to express controversial opinions in public, as was clear when he explained his views on his assignment to act as Thomas Quick's lawyer: 'Quick has confessed to five murders, but the police are still not entirely convinced that he's telling the truth. I am. It is therefore going to be my assigned task to convince the police that my client has murdered people.'

Barely an hour later, Gunnar Lundgren walked into the music

room of Ward 36 and greeted his client and the chief interrogator Seppo Penttinen before taking a seat in the usual red-and-black-striped armchair opposite Thomas Quick. The last time they sat here they had been talking about the statute-barred murder of Thomas Blomgren.

But he was no longer firing blanks. If there was any substance to Quick's latest confession, he would be charged with the murder of Charles Zelmanovits.

Penttinen switched on the little cassette recorder. He made himself comfortable and turned to Quick, who was trying to concentrate on the task that lay ahead of him.

'Sture, if you could start by explaining what you were doing in the area at the time you made contact with this lad.'

'Well, it was the same thing as the other trips. It was an unpl . . . unplanned, planned, unplanned trip. Er . . .'

Quick told them that he got there in a car.

'In which case it would be interesting if you can tell us what car that was,' said Penttinen.

Sture told me that he remembered the problems he had had with the car he claimed to have borrowed from Ljungström at the time of the murder of Johan Asplund. This time he wanted to avoid similar difficulties at all cost. For this reason he answered curtly that he didn't want to say what car he had been using. Not yet.

Penttinen turned off the tape recorder while Quick conferred with his lawyer. Quick told Lundgren that he knew what car he had been travelling in, but for secret reasons was unable to divulge this information today.

The crime had figured in his therapy for a while, Quick explained, under the designation 'the dark boy'. Then the first name had 'emerged'.

Yet 'the dark boy' is not a particularly apt description. Charles was not dark; his skin tone was fair and his hair ash blond. This was backed up by the police description from 1976, in which Charles's hair was described as 'dark blond'.

Quick also said that Charles didn't have long hair, which was an inaccurate description of his centre-parted shoulder-length hair.

'What about his clothes?' asked Seppo.

'Today I'd like to say that he had one of those denim jackets with a woolly lining.'

At a later stage in the interview Quick tried to hedge his bets by describing the coat as being made of a slippery material and he would guess it was a black down jacket.

At the time of his disappearance, Charles wore a striking, expensive, full-length leather coat. It seems unlikely that it would be confused with a denim jacket with a lining or a black down jacket.

Nor did Quick remember Charles's especially tight jeans, even though he said that he removed his trousers.

'Sort of trousers for special occasions, so to speak. I don't know what you call that material, er . . .'

'You don't mean denim?'

'No.'

'Is it a thinner fabric?'

'And with a clasp here,' said Quick, pointing at his own waistband.

Thomas Quick seemed to be describing a pair of gabardine trousers and he also indicated that Charles was wearing boots, whereas in fact he was wearing brown suede Playboy brand shoes. He also said that he had buried Charles's body, although it was a rather shallow grave.

But on this point the forensic technicians were able to make a categorical statement after examining the scene. 'There is no indication that any of the findings have been buried', was the conclusion given in the report. And Quick's method of killing the boy was so odd that it gave rise to further questioning.

'I used a, one of those little, er . . . er . . . shoe horns made of metal,' Quick told them.

The forensic examination of Charles's remains had not pointed to any signs of Charles being the victim of a crime.

Charles's remains had been scattered over a fairly large area and the technicians stated that the bones had been pulled out of the clothes by wild animals. Some of the largest bones of the body were missing altogether.

Bearing in mind that Quick had previously told them about how he cut up Johan Asplund's body, Seppo Penttinen's next question was entirely logical: 'Was there any kind of cutting up of the body?'

'No, not . . . not that. No severing of any body part in that way,' explained Quick.

Seppo Penttinen came back to the question of whether the body was cut up during questioning on 19 April. The new information Thomas Quick gave on this point became the strongest evidence for his guilt.

Before the interview began, they discussed the question of whether there had been any cutting up of the body and, if so, whether Quick had removed any of the body parts from the scene. This conversation took place, as on so many other similar occasions, without the tape recorder being switched on and without an interview witness or the presence of a lawyer. When the tape recorder was switched on the question was cleared up by means of Penttinen making suggestions that Quick confirmed.

PENTTINEN: You were sort of developing a line of thinking when we had a break before we started this interview that you had taken some limb with you from this place, and then in that conversation you mentioned that something had happened to his legs, and while I'm talking about this now you're nodding in agreement. Do I understand you correctly that you removed a leg?

TQ: Yes.

PENTTINEN: How much . . . What part of the leg? You showed me in that conversation that it was around the knee.

TQ: Yes.

PENTTINEN: Would that be both legs or just the one we're talking about?

TQ: Well, one more than the other.

PENTTINEN: How do I interpret that if you say that it's one more than the other?

TQ: Er . . . I-i-it's both, but yes . . .

PENTTINEN: You took both of the lower legs away with you?

TQ: Yes.
PENTTINEN: You're nodding there as an answer.

This was precisely in line with the police investigation. But some forensic technicians returned to the relevant area a few months later to make a more thorough inspection. On 6–7 June they searched a larger area and in so doing found one of the lower legs that Quick had indicated he'd brought back to Falun with him.

Penttinen was in Piteå when the new bone was found and he wasted no time in scheduling a new round of questioning with Quick on 12 June 1994.

When I read the interview report I was struck by the fact that although Quick had already indicated which limbs he had removed from the scene, Seppo Penttinen pretends that the subject hasn't been mentioned before.

PENTTINEN: Is there some limb you're 100 per cent sure should not be on the scene?
TQ: Yes.
PENTTINEN: Can you say what sort of limb that would be?
TQ: Leg.
PENTTINEN: A leg. Is it the right or the left one, can you confirm that with any degree of confidence?
TQ: Not with any confidence, no.
PENTTINEN: But a leg with a shin bone and a thigh bone?
TQ: Yeah, yeah . . .
PENTTINEN: Which won't be found there?
TQ: No.
PENTTINEN: Is there any uncertainty about that?
TQ: Definitely not the thigh bone.

Order had thankfully been restored, the number of Charles's disappeared and recovered lower legs had gone back to two. But there is cause to reflect on what sort of interrogation methods were being used – when Quick evidently had the opportunity to correct the erroneous information he had given earlier.

Penttinen does not ask if there are any limbs missing. Instead he asks if *some* limb is missing. The answer is given in the question – the right answer being *one* limb.

Quick cautiously answers 'leg' without making it absolutely clear if he is using the singular or plural.

'A leg,' Seppo Penttinen clarifies and asks if this would be the right *or* the left leg. Then he establishes that they are speaking of a bone consisting of a thigh bone and a shin bone.

When they first inspected the scene, forensic technicians confirmed the presence of a number of fox earths south of the spot where the body was found. Most of the bones located after the removal of Charles's remains were within a large fan-shaped area spreading out towards the fox earths to the south. The investigators mentioned a bone from an arm: 'Everything points to an animal having ripped the fabric and bone from the leather sleeve.'

Talking to the forensic technicians, their view, even today, is that there is nothing to indicate anything other than that foxes or other wild animals dispersed the body parts over a wide area, and that some of the bones may have been dragged underground into the fox earths.

Quick claimed that he cut up the body using a saw of the kind used to lop logs for firewood. The medical examiners haven't found any evidence of the sort of damage a saw would give rise to; on the other hand, there are plenty of signs of damage by animals.

Quick claimed that he removed the jeans – which were almost impossible for Charles to put on while he was alive – prior to cutting up the body. Evidently he mistook these tight jeans for a pair of gabardine trousers.

'Which leg taken from there could be described as the whole leg,' Seppo asked. 'Is it the whole left leg?'

'Yes,' answered Quick.

But if Quick did indeed take one of Charles's legs from the scene, it must have been the right leg. According to the medical examiner, the thigh bone found nearby was the left one.

The forensic technicians have marked eighteen locations on a map where bones and parts of clothes were found, after quite clearly being dragged away by wild animals. The bones found at the furthest distance from the original position of the body were the largest bones of the body – that is, the pelvis, a thigh bone and a shin bone.

If we study the interrogation using the methodology of Gregg McCrary, the conclusion we reach is astonishing.

In the part where Quick describes how he has cut up and removed bones, the questions are closed throughout – in other words, the correct answers are contained within the questions. In the two crucial sections of the interview on the body parts, Penttinen accounts for over 90 per cent of what is said (142 words) and Quick for only 10 per cent (15 words). In the second interview, the split is 83 per cent for Penttinen and 17 per cent for Quick.

But the most troubling aspect is the formulation of the questions themselves, the way that Penttinen's questions repeatedly contain the answers he is looking for.

Quick only needs to say 'yes', nod or mumble an answer. And he does exactly that.

Sture is rarely any help in clarifying what actually took place during the investigations. His recall of the reconstructions and questioning is completely wiped clean, he claims, because of being heavily medicated with benzodiazepines.

There is a slight glimmer of hope when I ask him how he first found out that Charles Zelmanovits had disappeared in Piteå in 1976. Sture seems enthusiastic about finally having something tangible to say regarding the investigation.

'I clearly remember sitting in the day room in Ward 36, reading *Dagens Nyheter*. I saw an article on how they had found Charles's remains.'

My first search for 'Charles Zelmanovits' in a database of *Dagens Nyheter* articles is disappointing. The article Sture claims to have read is not there.

Dejected, I call to let him know that there is no such article in existence. Maybe he has made a mistake?

'No, no! I even remember the article was in the column on the far left of the page,' says Sture with absolute conviction.

Jenny Küttim eventually found the article manually in SVT's press archive, published in *Dagens Nyheter* on 11 December 1993, on the left-hand side of the column, exactly as Sture said.

The headline ran: '16 Year-Old Murder Mystery Solved'.

I noticed that the caption writer had mistaken the year. When the article was written, it was not sixteen but actually seventeen years since Charles's disappearance. Interestingly, the year 1976 was not mentioned in the article.

If Thomas Quick had relied on this article alone as the source for his confession he must have tried to calculate in which year he would have murdered Charles. He would have counted back sixteen years and ended up in the autumn/winter of 1977. And that is precisely what he did.

Quick had already been talking to his therapist about the murder of Charles for three months when the first police interview was held. Seppo Penttinen asked whether Quick could remember in which year it took place.

'Ten years after the Alvar event,' said Quick, referring to the murder of Alvar

Larsson on Sirkön in 1967.

'Ten years after,' answered Penttinen. 'In which case it would be 1977.'

'Yes,' said Quick.

Thomas Quick also confirmed the year 1977 by claiming that the murder was committed as a reaction to his father's death in September of that year. These mnemonic constructions increased the credibility of Quick's story, but however well backed up it seemed, Penttinen was well aware that Quick had ended up in the wrong year.

'Is that an absolutely definite thing that it was in 1977? Could there be some sort of variation there?'

'When it happened the Alvar memory popped up. And I remember thinking I was seventeen then and I'm twenty-seven now,' Quick persisted.

The lawyer Gunnar Lundgren intervened and removed them from their predicament by suggesting that they should come back to the date on another occasion.

'It was a bit vague today,' said Lundgren. 'I think you and I can work it out in some way later on.'

In fact they never went back to the question of the date of the murder, nor did they go into why he had suggested that the murder was connected to his father's death and took place exactly ten years after the killing of Alvar.

Seppo Penttinen was obviously aware that Quick's confession was coming close on the tail of the mass media reporting on the discovery of the bones in Piteå and so he asked the obvious question: 'Have you read anything in the newspapers about this?'

'If I have I can't remember. Kjell [Persson] mentioned it when he said his surname, and there'd been an article about it.'

Thomas Quick's knowledge of Charles Zelmanovits no longer seemed so impressive. He had only talked of the murder after *Dagens Nyheter* published an article on the bones that had been found. He had relied on *Dagens Nyheter*'s erroneous information about the year, retrospectively tying this to his father's death and the murder of Alvar Larsson.

These were some of the first instances I came across that even the murders Thomas Quick had been found guilty of were based on false confessions. A thousand and one questions remained to be answered before I was prepared to believe that six courts of law had convicted an innocent psychiatric patient of eight murders he had never committed.

As I carried on reading the interrogation transcripts I was amazed to find that pretty much every statement Thomas Quick made on Charles Zelmanovits was incorrect.

Quick stated that he met Charles south-west of Piteå, whereas we know that Charles disappeared in Munksund, north-east of central Piteå. After their initial meeting, Quick described how he and an accomplice drove through central Piteå on their way to the murder scene. The fact is that Charles disappeared in the vicinity of his home and the place where his remains were found lies some four kilometres away, directly east on Norra Pitholmen.

According to Quick, they had caught sight of Charles late in the afternoon or in the evening. As we know, Charles was with his friends the whole evening, right up to the point where he disappeared after one in the morning.

Quick said that there was snow cover in Piteå, but on 12 November 1976 there was no snow at all, as there had been several days of rain and thaw.

The forensic technicians confirmed that the body had not been buried, as Quick claimed.

Thomas Quick suggested that Charles voluntarily agreed to have sex with him, which seems less than likely given that Charles had just had sex with his school friend Maria a few hours earlier.

How did Seppo Penttinen and Christer van der Kwast respond to these anomalies? Quick had even suggested that he had managed to persuade a married man without a criminal background to drive 1,500 kilometres on winter roads to find a young boy – did they not consider how unlikely this seemed? And why would they drive all the way to Piteå?

What prosecutor Christer van der Kwast thought about all this is not mentioned in the investigation material, although he did approach the psychiatrist Ulf Åsgård for guidance on the psychological issues. Åsgård, who worked for the National Swedish Police Board, declined as he was busy with the Palme Unit. Instead, van der Kwast had to settle for the services of an unknown lecturer and memory expert from Stockholm University who could think of nothing he'd rather do than throw himself into a study of the psyche of a real serial killer.

COGNITIVE INTERVIEW TECHNIQUES

AT THE SAME time as the first police interviews with Thomas Quick were being conducted in March 1993, *DN Debatt* published an article by Sven Åke Christianson, a senior lecturer in psychology, who mercilessly criticised Sweden as 'a third-world country in terms of its commitment to psychological research and the use of psychological knowledge in the judiciary and the police service'.

Christianson's article proposed a number of solutions to the problems facing the Thomas Quick investigation:

> At the moment, psychological research is being conducted into how violent criminals and psychopaths perceive and approach emotional situations. Special studies are also being made of serial killers to try and establish personality types, background factors, the sort of victims they select and how they operate. This type of research should be of extreme relevance to the police, in view of the violent crimes that are so prevalent in our time.

To latter-day readers, the article almost seems like an application to join the Quick investigation. Christianson seductively offered up all manner of questions his expertise might help to answer:

> Psychological awareness of how to relate to psychiatrically disturbed people or people in emotionally charged conditions would be of great help to both interrogators and prosecutors.

Despite the fact that Sweden hadn't previously had a serial killer of this kind, Christianson dwelled on the unusual phenomenon:

> Studies have been made of grossly violent men and serial killers; how they behave, what drives them, how they see their own crimes and what they remember of them. Some are what we term psychopaths, such as the serial killer Jeffrey Dahmer in the USA. He kept pieces from the corpses of fifteen people in his home.
>
> What needs are being satisfied in these psychiatrically disturbed people?

Sven Åke Christianson arrived at Säter Hospital on 14 April 1994 and immediately set about testing Thomas Quick's memory functions.

Sture Bergwall still remembers their first meeting. 'I found it difficult to believe that this slight little man was a psychology lecturer.'

Christianson's enthusiasm at having been offered a job with an investigation that would require all his specialist skills was unmistakable. In addition to memory research he had a burning interest in serious, violent crime and serial killers. Alongside his assignments within the justice system, Christianson spent his spare time at Säter, engaging himself in conversations with Thomas Quick. These conversations sometimes continued for seven or eight hours at a time, and tended to explore all manner of questions on the subject of the serial killer's behaviour. Christianson was the theorist in these conversations, while Quick was the practitioner expected to come up with answers to the academic's deep, probing questions on the bizarre inner life of a serial killer.

'Sven Åke Christianson was a real serial-killer freak who intended to write books on Thomas Quick and other serial killers, books this thick,' Sture told me, holding his arms straight out to indicate their imagined thickness from cover to cover.

'Jeffrey Dahmer was one of his favourites in these conversations, the serial killer who kept chopped-off heads in his flat. I remember when Sven Åke asked me how Jeffrey Dahmer felt as he was cutting up his victims. And he asked me to describe the feeling of eating the victim, *the sensual and erotic feeling of it.* Sven Åke felt that Jeffrey Dahmer *must* have had a sensual feeling. And I was supposed to describe that.'

Sture also told me that Christianson carried out various exercises with him. Prior to his departure for Piteå, where Quick was supposed to show the investigators how he had murdered Charles Zelmanovits, Christianson took him out into the grounds of Säter Hospital.

In a copse behind the hospital museum Quick was told to pretend he was carrying the body of Charles Zelmanovits. He was supposed to make a 'trial walk' with the body from the forest road to its final resting place.

'He asked me to remember my emotional state of mind. I was meant to feel that I was excited and tense, but also that I was weighed down with a great sorrow about the dead body. Also anger, I was supposed to feel that. "Don't forget you're carrying a heavy body," he said.'

Sture remembered that as he trudged up the wooded slope, pretending to be carrying the body and the sorrow, Christianson walked beside him with a watch in his hand, counting his steps out loud.

'When I had walked 300 steps, Sven Åke said, "We're here now!" Then he asked me if I had any new memories about Charles Zelmanovits. "Oh yes, I certainly do," I told him. In that way I affirmed him, as well,' Sture Bergwall recalled.

During the same period Sture also remembers a trip in a car on a forest road to Björnbo, some thirty kilometres from Säter.

'Me and Seppo took the car out, with three care assistants. We were inspecting different kinds of ditches. We sat in the car and kept going until the road came to a dead end.'

Before long they found a ditch that was very wide and apparently very similar to another ditch in Piteå. Sture claims that Penttinen made him aware of what sort of ditch they were after – not in so many words, but with a certain finesse.

'I mean, that's the secret. He said, "Maybe the ditch looked a bit like this?" And then I understood that the ditch did look like that. "Yeah, this is what it looked like," I said.'

Both the re-enactment on the hospital grounds and the investigators' approach of taking Thomas Quick into the forest to look at ditches were practical examples of the new ideas about 'cognitive interview techniques' as proposed by Sven Åke Christianson. By re-creating the same 'inner and outer environment' as at the time of the murder, it would supposedly become easier for Quick to access his memories of the crime. In this context, even leading questions might be justifiable, according to Christianson.

On the specific occasions described by Sture there was such an obvious risk of the investigators providing him with decisive information that I couldn't quite take his words at face value. The whole thing went absolutely against all established investigative methodology. Could this really be true?

While on a personal level I believed what Sture was telling me, it struck me that I had once again run into information so outlandish that unless I could back it up in some way it would be entirely useless to me.

On the afternoon of 20 August 1994 a private chartered plane landed at Piteå Airport. The passengers on board included Thomas Quick, Birgitta Ståhle, Sven Åke Christianson, the investigators and nursing staff from Säter Hospital.

Piteå-Älvdal Hospital had placed a whole ward at the disposal of the Quick investigation team. It wasn't particularly comfortable, but everyone could at least stay in the same place and the safety of both Quick and the general public could be guaranteed.

The following morning, the entire group – now also accompanied by Christer van der Kwast and Anders Eriksson, the medical examiner from Umeå – went to the police station in Piteå, where Commissioner Harry Nyman had prepared a welcoming spread of coffee and pastries.

Shortly after, Thomas Quick was travelling in an unmarked police car with Christianson, Ståhle, Penttinen and a nurse from Säter, who were all waiting tensely for the alleged serial killer to lead them to the place where he had murdered and hidden Charles Zelmanovits.

Various documentary sources from the car journey indicate that Quick didn't have a clue where the car was supposed to be going.

'As I said during questioning, I don't have much of a sense of direction here,' he excused himself.

Because Seppo Penttinen knew the way, they weren't entirely clueless. The car drove out of the town centre along a road known as Timmerleden (the Timber Route) and then continued a few kilometres on the Norra Pitholmsvägen. Before long they were out in the sticks.

Although they were quite close to their destination, Quick still couldn't get his bearings, so Penttinen kept moving in the right direction. When they were only 500 metres away, Quick had to take over and show them the way.

'We're now in the area that's of interest to us,' said Penttinen to Quick.

Along the remaining short stretch of road there was a junction, where Quick had to determine which way they should turn. He chose to go left. The car continued for two kilometres before Penttinen revealed that this was wrong. They turned back and tried the right-hand turning instead.

Soon Quick noticed a number of police officers a short distance into the forest. They drove past. After continuing a few kilometres they reached a settlement and Quick realised they had gone too far. Again they turned back, passed the place where the body had been found and parked by the side of the road. Quick knew that he was very close to the spot. He indicated that he wanted to walk. After fifteen to twenty metres on the forest road he stopped.

'We looked for ditches like this when we did an inspection in Säter,' he said.

There it was – proof that it had happened exactly as Sture described it to me.

A single, stray comment in hours and hours of wandering about in the Piteå forest, absolutely puzzling to all but those who were most closely involved with the case, and for the same reason so very easy to overlook.

When they reached the ditch closest to where the body had been found, Quick noticed that a path had been formed by the police and technicians who had examined the location in the last few weeks.

'Think we have to go in here,' said Quick.

After a few steps he hesitated.

'I can't cope with walking on my own to the place.'

He was ushered into the forest and on the video tape you can hear Quick saying, 'It's supposed to be as far as the trial walk I did with Sven Åke. Three hundred steps . . .'

Once again the cognitive interview techniques were reaping rewards.

Quick was supported and led into the forest by Seppo Penttinen. After they had gone 300 steps the relevant spot was visible. Forensic technicians had dug up the ground in their search for bones removed by foxes and other wild animals, and a large area of the ground had been disturbed.

Penttinen noted in his memo of the reconnaissance that Quick 'is extremely bothered by the ground being disturbed and the moss torn up'.

During earlier questioning Quick had described sitting on a stone or a tree stump. Once he was at the scene he found a large boulder near the place where the remains were found. He tried to show how he had sat there after Charles had been murdered.

Despite the dark November night there had been no problems, said Quick. He had seen both his accomplice and Charles quite clearly. Anyone who has been in a forest at night will immediately realise the problem. In a Norrbotten forest at two in the morning, you would be hard pressed to make out your hand in front of your own face. Quick nonetheless claimed that he had been able to see the ground in front of him and could differentiate between spruce and pine. No one questioned how this could have been possible.

In accordance with Sven Åke Christianson's cognitive interview techniques, the police had brought along a dummy to represent Charles Zelmanovits. Penttinen asked Quick to place the dummy on the ground exactly as he had placed Charles's body.

The dug-up section of ground showed the position of the body but not which way the head was pointing. Quick had a 50 per cent chance of getting it right. The dummy ended up 180 degrees in the wrong direction.

Penttinen asked if the body had really faced in that direction.

'Yes, I'd say so. I'd say so,' said Quick.

At this point, Sven Åke Christianson stepped in, gesturing with his hands to help Quick access his emotional recall.

'Shall we try and put it in that direction as well? So he can get a feeling for that?'

However, Quick refused to move the dummy, so Penttinen had to turn it round himself in accordance with Christianson's suggestion. Finally the dummy ended up in the right position.

'I don't know if the video camera is picking it up, but Thomas is nodding vigorously,' Penttinen clarified into camera.

Anders Eriksson asked a few questions about the cutting up of the body, which Quick had problems answering. He was unsure whether he had lopped off one of the arms. If so, he believed it was left at the scene.

'What about the hands, did something happen to them?' asked Penttinen.

But Quick couldn't bear the exchange any longer.

'I can't take it, can't take it. I can't cope any more.'

Quick was crying uncontrollably, sobbing and shaking.

'Give me another Xanax. I don't give a damn if I overdose . . .'

'Of course.' There was a chorus of voices in the background.

'You haven't had one for quite a while,' said Birgitta Ståhle.

A care assistant from Säter brought the jar of pills and Quick got what he wanted. Twilight was beginning to fall over the forest and Quick began to weep in a monotone that soon turned into a strange sort of guttural braying.

Once Quick's moaning and weeping had calmed down, the large group left the forest feeling absolutely triumphant. With a measure of forethought, Harry Nyman had booked a table at Paltzerian in Öjebyn, north of Piteå – the only restaurant in the world that exclusively served *palt*, a northern speciality made from offal and rye.

Sture remembers the restaurant visit with mixed feelings.

'They were all so happy and pleased! The one who was most

pleased of all was Seppo Penttinen. Many different kinds of *palt* were brought in and we munched them all down with a lot of chatting. As if the murderer was being celebrated after the successful reconnaissance! It was repulsive and macabre . . .'

Christer van der Kwast was delighted. When he got back home he wrote a letter to the police in Piteå:

> I want to pass on my warmest thanks for the excellent assistance provided to us by the police force in Piteå, overseen by Commissioner Harry Nyman on the occasion of the reconnaissance undertaken with Thomas Quick in Piteå on 21 August and for the additional arrangements that were made on the same occasion.

A MACABRE SHOW

IN THE MEDIA reporting on Thomas Quick that summer the image of the archetypal evil serial killer grew increasingly defined

Experts on the topic had popped up everywhere, and now they were making confident statements on how Thomas Quick had definitely murdered the five boys, in accordance with his own confessions. A professor of forensic psychiatry, Lars Lidberg, who had been recruited by prosecutor van der Kwast, single-handedly determined Quick's guilt in so far as the Zelmanovits case went before the court had even passed its own judgment.

'It is my view that Thomas Quick is guilty of the murders of these boys to which he has confessed. There is nothing to suggest that he is fabricating, exaggerating, wants to make himself important or is seeking to impress others by talking about his experiences,' Lidberg told *Expressen* on 3 November 1994.

Obviously a serial killer like Thomas Quick had to be kept under lock and key, but incarceration alone was not enough, Lidberg went on: 'If he won't agree to castration voluntarily, there is the possibility of forcibly injecting him.'

No punishment was severe enough, no security measures too elaborate for the serial killer Thomas Quick.

'People like this only get worse and worse, they can never stop,' van der Kwast explained in *Expressen* on 18 October 1994.

Thomas Quick's file from this period is extremely limited in scope, but it does reveal that his intake of benzodiazepines was steadily increasing and the notes provide several snapshots of a patient sliding out of control:

> *2 May 1994*
> Today Thomas had a severe panic attack in the afternoon, approached the staff and said, 'I'm going mad, help me.' He was given a Xanax pill, and was helped to the music room, where he lay on the floor screaming, held down by staff from time to time. After about 45 minutes it passed.
>
> *6 June 1994*
> Thomas had a severe panic attack as a result of therapy. We held onto him for a moment and he was given a Xanax pill. Once the anxiety passed the conversation continued. Thomas had another attack at about 13.00, when we found him in the therapy room. He had removed his clothes and was extremely anxious. We decided to put him in a straitjacket.

Care assistants have to be called repeatedly to give medication to Quick or to hold onto him so he doesn't harm himself during the therapeutic conversations. These file notes about a patient who requires large amounts of narcotics and has to be put in a straitjacket might be viewed by the modern reader as signs of failure in his psychiatric care. But Quick's reactions to Birgitta Ståhle's treatment were viewed as genuine evidence that the therapy was working. His extreme state of anxiety was seen as a logical consequence of his regression during the therapeutic process. Ståhle wrote in the file:

> The regress [*sic*] means that the patient makes contact with his early traumatic childhood memories, and also how these are retold by the patient in his adult life through the assaults and murders which he has spoken of during the current police investigation.

Before the trial for the murder of Charles Zelmanovits, the lawyer Gunnar Lundgren wrote to the district court to explain the particular psychological and medical factors that applied to his client:

> When he is confronted with and is about to talk of dramatic details and horrors in this current legal process, there is a risk that he will be so severely affected by anxiety that one may be forced into a number of adjournments. Apart from being afflicted by cramps he also has great difficulty speaking. This can, however, pass fairly quickly with a few moments' rest and a few pills.

A great deal hung in the balance in this court case, as an acquittal would most likely have meant the end of any further investigation into Thomas Quick. Many members of the public had turned up to see the beast first-hand and hear about his terrible deeds.

When the public was let into the courtroom on 1 November they were met by a macabre sight that could hardly have disappointed those who wanted a bit of sensationalism. Christer van der Kwast had arranged a table of items that the members of the court, the prosecution team and spectators in the gallery would constantly have before their eyes during the proceedings. On the table lay a lopping saw, the remains of a partially decomposed leather jacket and a Playboy shoe that had seen better days.

Charles Zelmanovits's mother, Inga, and younger brother, Frederick, passed the table with a shudder, turning their eyes away but not before they had recognised Charles's shoe and parts of the jacket that he had worn seventeen years earlier. And the saw . . .

Throughout the main proceedings these items were an eerie and tangible reminder of what this case was about, but they also created a false impression of being some sort of technical evidence.

Admittedly, the saw had been found about a hundred metres from Charles's remains, but the forensic investigation hadn't been able to identify any damage to the bones from a saw. Quick hadn't even said that he had left a saw in the forest. The same applied to the parts of the leather jacket – another troublesome reminder that Thomas Quick, despite all the questioning, had never managed to say exactly what outdoor garments Charles had been wearing. The Playboy shoe on the prosecutor's table was just as puzzling. In interview after interview Quick had maintained that Charles was wearing boots.

Christer van der Kwast's fateful cabinet of curiosities lacked one item that would have constituted strong evidence against Quick, who had said a number of times that Charles had been wearing a robust leather belt with a large metal buckle. Charles's younger brother had been summoned to the court to talk about this belt. The district court wrote in its verdict:

> Frederick Zelmanovits states that he cannot say with absolute confidence whether Charles owned the sort of belt referred to. Though he remembers that he had one such belt himself, at the time of his brother's disappearance.

In its verdict, the district court confirmed that 'the brothers could have shared the belt'.

If Quick was speaking the truth, there ought to have been a leather belt somewhere near Charles's remains. The forensic technicians had carefully searched the forest outside Piteå with metal detectors. The buttons and studs of the decomposed jeans were found, but no belt was ever located.

For this reason the belt was missing on the prosecutor's table. Instead it had been decorated with three other objects.

Of all the things that happened in the district court in Piteå, one in particular made an unforgettable impression: the screening of the video from the reconstruction in the forest.

The Quick reporter from *Expressen*, Pelle Tagesson, still remembers his impression of those days in Piteå: 'I met Quick during the trial and thought he seemed a fairly normal bloke. Then I saw the films of the reconstruction. It was absolutely rattling! I remember feeling uneasy about having shaken his hand.'

Despite the inconsistencies of the case, Pelle Tagesson grew utterly convinced of Quick's guilt when the prosecutor showed the video in which the suspect was making those bestial, guttural sounds. All doubts were swept aside: 'It's impossible to act out what happened in the reconstruction.'

*

Before the trial, Christer van der Kwast had written to the district court suggesting that they would need additional expertise in the field of psychology. He recommended that the members should rely on the services of Sven Åke Christianson.

As Christianson had been working as a part of the investigation on behalf of the prosecutor for a lengthy period of time, it would obviously be inappropriate, almost impossible, for him to accept an assignment from the district court to assess his own findings. This did not prevent him from accepting the offer.

Christianson provided two specialist statements, one of them 'concerning the conditions of Thomas Quick's testimony from a psychological perspective':

> In terms of what the perpetrator is able to remember, I have concentrated on the patterns of behaviour and memories of serial killers as well as the background factors for this type of crime.

This formulation makes it quite clear that his starting position was that Quick was a serial killer. Even before the trial he had publicly pointed him out as both a serial killer and a cannibal.

'It's a primitive way of behaving – his actions are those of the child within himself. And when one eats parts of someone's body it can be an illusion that the victim lives on inside, that the children are still alive inside his body,' Christianson explained in an interview with *Expressen* on the first day of the trial.

Everyone seemed to have forgotten that Thomas Quick hadn't yet been found guilty of a single murder.

In his testimony, Professor Lars Lidberg was crystal clear on the question of guilt and causality for the behaviour of the serial killer.

'The significant thing in Quick's case is that Quick has been subjected to sexual molestation from the father and mother, and that a connection has been made between sexuality and aggression.'

He did not reveal how he was in a position to know that any such violence or sexual assaults from the parents had ever taken place, and simply based his scientific reasoning on the assumption as if it were a fact.

Quick's compulsive and repeated killing accorded very well with how 'Quick hides parts of people he has killed and keeps certain body parts as some form of talisman,' Lidberg went on.

As Quick had already confessed to the murder of Charles Zelmanovits, the trial was ultimately about determining whether or not this could be a false confession.

Sven Åke Christianson, in his testimony, described various types of false confessions and finished with this conclusion: 'These are not relevant to Quick's case.'

When it was time for Quick to testify in court, the defence demanded that it must happen behind closed doors, which the district court granted. Once the public had left the courtroom, Quick assured the court that he had not at any stage read anything about Charles Zelmanovits's disappearance. This was important information. Unfortunately it was also untrue. Not only did Quick confess to the murder after reading about the discovery of Charles's remains in the newspaper – but as he was under no restrictions he was able to carefully monitor any on-going reporting on the matter. In Margit Norell and Birgitta Ståhle's manuscript of their book on Quick, I also found a passage revealing that he eventually managed to acquire an even sharper information source. The authors quoted Quick:

> When I read the investigation reports I saw and I felt Charles's whole life for the first time. He was not just someone I killed; he powerfully turned into the whole person Charles whom I had murdered.

In other words, when Quick was brought to trial in Piteå he had read the entire preliminary investigation report, with technical examinations and many interviews.

These gave Quick an overall picture of 'the whole person Charles'. Also in the patient files I found a note about Thomas Quick 'going through the preliminary investigation of Charles Z during the autumn'.

Therefore it's hardly surprising that Thomas Quick, behind the closed doors of the district court, managed to portray what had happened with sufficient detail.

And yet how could the district court find Quick guilty of murder when almost everything he had said under police questioning was incorrect? Why was the sentence unaffected by Quick's inability to find his own way to where the body had been found?

The simple answer is that the members of the district court were unaware of practically all the aspects of the investigation. They hadn't read any of the interviews with Quick.

Under Swedish rules of procedure there is no obligation for a court to immerse itself in the investigation material; in fact, this is one of the cornerstones of Swedish law, known as the Immediacy Principle of the Code of Judicial Procedure (Chap. 17.2§). According to this basic principle, the members of the court are only permitted to attach significance to what they observe in the main proceedings.

The lawyer Gunnar Lundgren could have – and many would probably say should have – called the interviews with Thomas Quick to the court's attention. He could have read out passages from the reports to show that Quick knew nothing about Charles Zelmanovits or Pitholmen at the beginning of the investigation. He could have informed the court that Quick had provided contradictory accounts and that he had been encouraged by leading questions.

But Lundgren had no such objections. He quite simply took the view that the district court should find Quick guilty of the murder in question; he even expressed this view in the courtroom.

The phenomenon that was later criticised by the forensic psychologist Nils Wiklund and Detective Chief Inspector Jan Olsson – the suspension of the adversarial process – was already taking place in the first Quick trial.

The prosecution for the murder of Charles Zelmanovits was Lundgren's one and only case as Thomas Quick's defence lawyer. Later, in an interview, he gave his opinion of the role of the lawyer in cases where the defence pursues an identical line of argument to the prosecution.

The reporter from *Aftonbladet* asked if Lundgren had helped his client 'get caught for as many crimes as possible'.

Lundgren agreed with this assessment: 'Yes. He wanted to confess to what he had done and so it was my responsibility to help him with that.'

There was a united front in Piteå District Court: prosecutor, investigators, the defence lawyer, the suspect, therapists, doctors, experts and journalists. All seemed to be pulling in the same direction, so how could it have ended in any other way?

In its verdict of 16 November 1994, the district court wrote:

> Quick has admitted to his deed and his confession is backed up by the information he has provided. However, there is no technical evidence to connect Quick to the crime.

The last part was obviously a weakness in the prosecution's case. Nor had any witnesses seen Quick in Piteå at the time of the murder. But these things, according to the district court, were counteracted by other circumstances:

> Quick's statements on the body parts he removed from the scene conform very well with the evidence, in the sense that these body parts are missing from the crime scene. This fact makes a very strong supporting case for the accuracy of Quick's information.

The forensic technicians who examined the scene where the remains were found concluded that there were no signs of a crime having been committed and definitely no signs of the body having been cut into pieces. The investigators had noted that Charles's bones had been dragged in the direction of some fox earths to the south of the remains. The absence of certain bones was therefore not evidence that the body had been cut up.

The views of the forensic technicians were not taken into account. Quite the opposite: the missing leg bones were judged to be 'very strong supporting evidence' for Quick's guilt.

Thomas Quick, who had gone back to Säter after his testimony, received the court verdict delivered by fax to the hospital reception. Eagerly he rifled through the pages until he reached the important part:

> By way of a summarising judgment the district court finds Quick guilty beyond any reasonable doubt of the act for which prosecution has been brought. The circumstances of the crime are such that the crime should be considered as murder.

Because of the lack of technical evidence, the pronouncements of specialists in psychology and psychiatry carried a great deal of weight in the judgment. Professor Lidberg, in an interview in *Aftonbladet* on 15 April 1997, did not hesitate for a moment about his own significance in the outcome of the case.

'Thomas Quick was convicted on my evidence in Piteå. I am wholly convinced that he was guilty of the charges and that was also the view taken by the court.'

Lidberg's conclusion that he had single-handedly determined the outcome of the case is certainly an exaggeration of his own importance, but quite clearly the guilty verdict was a great success both for him and for Christianson.

Christer van der Kwast had been concerned about their difficulties in coming up with a single piece of evidence for any of Quick's confessed murders. He therefore had every reason to be very satisfied.

'With this guilty verdict I have been given a green light so that an investigation can be conducted as we have done here. A confession, reconnaissance of the crime scene and a profile of the perpetrator are enough for a successful prosecution, despite a lack of traditional technical evidence.'

Future events would soon prove that van der Kwast had made an entirely correct assessment. That 'traditional' evidence was no longer required would soon become a matter of concern for many more people, but with the recent verdict in his hands, van der Kwast was full of confidence.

'I am counting on this having a very positive impact on the ongoing investigation,' he said.

NOCTURNAL DOUBTS

'I WONDER WHAT you'd think of me if you found out that I'd done something really serious.'

It was with this comment that it had all begun, during a bathing trip with a young care assistant from Ward 36 in June 1992.

At that time Quick was still called Sture Bergwall and was regarded as so harmless that he was being reintroduced into the community with his own flat in Hedemora.

This cryptic and ominous question had, justifiably so, given rise to concern among the carers at Säter Hospital, and soon Quick had confessed to his first murder and hinted at more.

Confessions by innocent people are not particularly rare – especially among patients in psychiatric clinics – but for a real serial killer who has never been suspected of a single murder to start confessing to a series of murders is, according to researchers, unique. It has never happened before.

Psychological profiling is one of the few tools available for tracking down serial killers. When Quick first started confessing, there was almost no awareness of this technique in the Swedish police force.

But during the hunt for the Laser Man, the psychiatrist Ulf Åsgård, who had a long-established interest in psychological profiling, teamed up with Detective Chief Inspector Jan Olsson, at that time the assistant chief of the forensic division in Stockholm.

Their psychological profile of the Laser Man was the first attempt of its kind in Swedish criminal history. The profile didn't play an important role in the capture of the Laser Man, which was instead the result of skilled and patient police work. But Jan Olsson and Ulf Åsgård's psychological profile was nonetheless seen as a success, because in retrospect it was found to 'correspond by about 75 per cent' with John Ausonius. Analytical police work was the theme tune of the time and profiling was here to stay.

Lennart Häärd, the crime correspondent of *Aftonbladet*, was one of many journalists who visited Säter Hospital in the autumn of 1994.

In the middle of the interview he asked a peculiar question: 'Are you being investigated for a double murder in the Swedish northern mountains?'

He was clearly alluding to the murder of the Stegehuises and Quick kept his answer short: 'No, we haven't spoken about that.'

After the trial for the murder of Charles Zelmanovits there was a great worry that Thomas Quick would stop talking. Birgitta Ståhle emphasised how essential it was that he continued 'his important work' and her instructor Margit Norell wrote letters to Quick, pleading with him: 'Find the strength to go on, Sture!'

The situation was complex.

Quick had confessed to murdering five boys. He had now been found guilty of one murder. Two were statute-barred – those of Thomas Blomgren and Alvar Larsson – and the investigations into the murders of Johan Asplund and Olle Högbom had come to a standstill. So how could he 'go on' with his talking?

Lennart Häärd's question about Appojaure resurfaced now in Quick's mind and on 21 November 1994 he called Seppo Penttinen to tell him about what had come up in the interview.

'I've been thinking about it since then,' said Quick. 'I think it would be good if I were confronted with the facts of that murder.'

Penttinen asked why he thought it would be good.

'Well, because I know I was up there in that region around the time of the murder,' answered Quick.

But then the interview ground to a halt.

'I don't feel like going into it further right now,' he said.

The idea that Quick, the boy murderer, would attack a couple in their thirties went against all serial-killer logic. Nonetheless, the next day Penttinen informed Christer van der Kwast, who, just to be on the safe side, notified the National Criminal Investigation Department. Van der Kwast was told that there was already an investigation under way into the Appojaure murders, and a possible suspect – a fifty-one-year-old male by the name of Johnny Farebrink, a native of Jokkmokk. The individual in question was a drug addict with a violent background who was currently serving a ten-year sentence for murder at Hall, a maximum-security prison. The Criminal Investigation Department had not yet found anything to tie him to the murdered couple and hadn't even had time to question him as yet.

Christer van der Kwast realised that there was a risk of setting up a competing police investigation with a different murder suspect. His thinking on the matter is difficult to understand, but he put forward the bold suggestion that Quick and Farebrink might have murdered the couple together.

A search of the population registry revealed that Johnny was born Johnny Larsson-Auna but nowadays went by the name of Johnny Farebrink. Van der Kwast called Penttinen and told him to ask Thomas Quick if he knew someone called Johnny Larsson-Auna. Or Farebrink.

The following day Seppo Penttinen went to Säter to conduct the first round of questioning about the double murder in Appojaure, in the presence of the lawyer Gunnar Lundgren. Since the successful prosecution in Piteå, Penttinen had been promoted to Detective Inspector, a title that from now on decorated all interrogations and documents where his name appeared, as was required by police procedure. While he was still only a senior police assistant, he and his boss Christer van der Kwast had been less scrupulous in their use of titles – back then Penttinen was usually described as 'chief interrogator'.

'So, Thomas, I want you to get straight to the heart of the matter and not linger too long on the periphery. Start where you feel you have some memories of the actual deed,' he said.

'Hm,' said Quick.

'Can you develop that a bit further?'

The three men sat in silence for a long time in the music room on Ward 36.

'Yeah . . . it was brutal,' said Quick.

Then he ran out of steam and couldn't take the story any further.

'What was the question?' he asked.

'I don't want to influence you,' explained Penttinen, and asked Quick to tell him what first came to mind.

Again there was a long silence.

'Well, the knife is the first thing.'

'What do you remember about it?'

'Its size.'

'OK.'

Quick cleared his throat.

'Try to describe it a bit more.'

They agreed that Quick should try to draw the knife from memory.

The knife in Quick's drawing is large, with a length of about thirty-five centimetres. The blade is slightly curved like a sabre and the top of the blade is shaped so that the tip forms an upward-curving point.

Quick wrote 'cutting edge' on what would normally have been the back of the knife. On the curved side of the blade, the side that would normally have been sharpened, he noted, 'blunt side'.

Seppo Penttinen said that he couldn't understand how a knife could be made in that way. Most likely he realised that no such knife had ever been manufactured, and he suggested that Quick should think about what a standard Mora knife looks like. He made his own drawing of a knife and showed the sharpened side of the blade and the blunt edge of the other side.

But it was no good. Quick stood his ground and said that it was precisely its design that had made his knife different from a Mora knife.

Penttinen carried on questioning the construction of the knife. He asked Quick if he could possibly have made a 'mirror image'.

Eventually Quick agreed that Penttinen could put a question mark beside his note on the drawing about which was the 'blunt side' of the knife.

From a forensic perspective, Penttinen knew perfectly well that the broad-bladed knife that Quick had drawn couldn't by the slightest stretch of the imagination have inflicted the injuries on the murder victims.

'You didn't have any other weapons with you?'

'No.'

'Can you describe a bit how it happened?'

'Well, they were deep stabs. Proper stabs. There was no sort of poking, they were stabs.'

'You're showing that you were stabbing down from above.'

'From above. Hm.'

The interview had been going on for a good while without Penttinen managing to extract any real information about the murder, apart from the unlikely knife.

'What were the conditions in the place you're describing, where you are right now?'

'Lot of mosquitoes.'

'Mosquitoes?'

'A lot.'

Quick said that the camping spot was by a pond in the forest.

'Yes, we both know that it was a tent,' Penttinen filled in.

'Yes.'

'And you've read about that in the newspapers if nothing else.'

'Yes.'

'So where are these people when you're doing this?'

'Well, they're inside the tent. Er . . . apart from, er . . . a part of one of them, er . . . one person's body is outside the tent at first.'

'Completely?'

'No. Yes.'

'You're indicating the upper body.'

'Yes.'

According to Quick, the woman tried to flee from the tent, but he stabbed at her with the knife and forced her back inside.

Thomas Quick made a new sketch, this time of the tent. Shown from the opening, Quick placed the woman on the left and the man on the right.

Quick's description deviated from known facts on every point.

The man had lain on the left, the woman on the right, and the zip of the tent was closed. Janny Stegehuis was still in her sleeping bag and had clearly not ventured outside the tent.

Seppo continued his questioning: 'So how come you ended up there?'

'I was up there and . . . I was up there. And I didn't come by car – that is, to . . . to this . . .'

'Right. So how did you get there?'

'On a bicycle, I did . . .'

'You cycled there?'

'Yes.'

'Were you alone there?'

'Yes.'

Thomas Quick said that he had travelled by train from Falun to Jokkmokk the day before the murder and then cycled eighty kilometres to Appojaure.

'It was a stolen bicycle.'

'OK. What sort of bicycle was it?'

'Er . . . it was a . . . er . . . a . . . it was a three-gear men's bicycle, er . . . which . . . and the two top gears worked on it or it jumped out of gear . . .'

Quick had stolen the bicycle outside the Sami Museum in Jokkmokk. First he went to a food shop, where he bought a fizzy drink, before he set off on the journey to Appojaure. He couldn't come up with any reasons for his cycling off, nor did he have any particular destination in mind.

'Did you have a bag with you?'

'Yeah, I had socks and underpants and that kind of change of clothes . . . I did have that.'

Quick had stopped along the way and slept under the open sky on the road to Appojaure.

'What was the weather like?' wondered Penttinen.

'It was nice weather.'

Later in the questioning they came back to the weather, which was described as fair. It was a troublesome piece of information, as it was well known that there had been light rain in the evening which had then turned into a downpour.

Penttinen knew that the murderer had stolen a bag and a transistor radio from the tent, so he asked, 'Were you in any need of anything from that place, which caused you to remove something from the scene?'

'No.'

'You cast your eyes down when I asked about that,' Penttinen probed, without managing to get Quick to admit that he had stolen something from the tent.

PENTTINEN: If I can return for a while to this . . . to the actual event, I mean, just to touch a little on it . . . er . . . this stabbing you said you did . . .

TQ: Mm.

PENTTINEN: . . . you say you must have stabbed about ten or twelve times. How sure are you about that estimate? Can you . . .

TQ: There were several, er . . . that's sort of what I'm describing . . .

PENTTINEN: Can you give a maximum and a minimum within a wider limit, maybe, so we can rule out this or that number, you see?

TQ: Er . . .

PENTTINEN: [unclear]

TQ: More than ten.

PENTTINEN: Mm.

TQ: Let's put it like that. Not less than ten.

In terms of the number of wounds, Quick is not only vague but also far from correct in his answer. The Stegehuises were murdered with some fifty stab wounds, several of which would have been enough to kill in their own right.

Throughout the interview, Penttinen had been stewing over what Christer van der Kwast had told him to ask Quick. The question came up completely out of the blue after a summary of what Quick had told him in the session.

PENTTINEN: So if I understand you right, you took a train to Jokkmokk. You stole a bicycle and the same day you stole it you cycled up to this area you're talking about . . .

TQ: Mm.

PENTTINEN: Stayed the night at . . . and slept a few hours somewhere.

TQ: Yes, exactly.

PENTTINEN: And then this happens at night.

TQ: Yes.

PENTTINEN: And then after that you leave this place and then you cycle back immediately to Jokkmokk . . .

TQ: Then I carry on back.

PENTTINEN: Down to Falun?

TQ: Yes. It's a long journey.

PENTTINEN: Mm. Do you know a person called Johnny Larsson?

Quick was caught off guard by the question. He realised there must be some circumstance which he was unaware of relating to the Appojaure murder.

'It's not an unfamiliar name,' Quick answered, vaguely.

'It's a double-barrelled name, Johnny Larsson-Auna.'

'Mm.'

'Do you know him?'

'I'm relating to a certain person but I think it could be the wrong person.'

'His name might be Farebrink as well.'

Quick sighed deeply, but however much he pondered on it, he could not discern the role of this Johnny in the story.

Penttinen asked again, 'Do you know who he is?'

'No,' said Quick.

On Saturday, 9 December 1994 Thomas Quick sat at his desk in the evening trying to work out what sort of person Johnny was and what his role had been at Appojaure. Quick often noted down memories or stories which he passed to Birgitta Ståhle and Seppo Penttinen, so that they could be brought up again in the therapy or police interviews. Now he wrote:

> *9/12 1994*
>
> More words.
>
> I was in Norrbotten. A dark man took part in the tent murder, a man from Norrbotten county, 15–20 cm taller than me and with obvious alcohol problems. I was sober, he was drunk. We had met earlier, I can't remember when, where or how.
>
> I felt he was gravely paranoid. He could have been about ten years older than me. Had a bit of a 'worse-for-wear' appearance.
>
> The tent was small, low. If I remember right, there was a smallish car close to the tent – a little Renault or Peugeot – the car was small, anyway. I seem to remember that my companion had some sort of dispute with the Dutchman earlier, as for me I didn't say a word to them.
>
> After the killing was over my companion urged me to drink – but I abstained.

When Quick had gone to bed he turned out the light and fell asleep. But his rest was brief.

'Mikael, Mikael.'

The noise coming from Thomas Quick's room made the care assistant, Mikael, leave his armchair in the day room. Quick was sitting up in bed with a plastic bag over his head. He was hanging by a strap round his neck.

Mikael hurried forward, loosened the strap and ripped off the plastic bag.

Quick slid down and slumped limply on the edge of the bed, running his hands over his aching throat and neck.

'Why, Thomas?' Mikael said. 'Why did you want to kill yourself?'

Mikael tried to make eye contact with Quick, but he got no response. Finally he managed to get his patient to get dressed by proposing a cigarette in the smoking room.

After one and a half cigarettes Quick said in a whisper, 'I'd made my mind up. I was going to try and force material out of myself. Material both for the investigation and for the therapy . . .'

He continued smoking with closed eyes, thinking for a long time before continuing: 'I did it, I managed. But now I've realised that it won't work. I can't do it.'

They had been sitting together in the smoking room for a long time when Mikael went to call Ståhle. Quick spoke to her for an hour. After the telephone call he was able to return to his room, where he was examined by a doctor for possible injuries before going back to bed.

On the following day Quick didn't get out of bed at all, and he was kept under suicide watch.

Mikael made a note in the file:

> This forcing has stirred up material relating to the investigation, which is such hard work for him that he can't quite cope with it. The only way out he saw to avoid the confrontation with these feelings and thoughts was to commit suicide. Right now he is psychotic.

However, the police investigation proceeded as usual and two days later Seppo Penttinen was back for more questioning.

When Seppo Penttinen held the second round of questioning about Appojaure on 12 December, Thomas Quick gave an entirely different account. The long bicycle trip from Jokkmokk to Appojaure had not happened. And now he knew that Johnny Larsson-Auna had taken part in the murder and they had travelled from Jokkmokk to Appojaure in his Volkswagen pickup.

The surprising thing was that Quick, despite the wealth of specific information he was coming up with, was not absolutely sure whether he was actually involved in the murder. Penttinen seemed to share his doubts.

> PENTTINEN: Are you quite sure that you did this?
> TQ: No . . .
> PENTTINEN: What makes you doubt it?
> TQ: (*sighs*) Er . . . what makes me doubt it is . . . is . . . er . . .

partly, er . . . well, the nature of the violence . . . first of all . . .

PENTTINEN: Is there anything else you're thinking about that surprises you at all?

TQ: Yes, that there was a woman involved.

That Thomas Quick had murdered a woman was undoubtedly a deviation from his profile as a murderer of boys. But the fact was there had been a woman inside the tent and, however dubious he was about it, Quick continued describing his memories from Appojaure.

At an early stage of the attack the woman had tried to crawl out of the tent, Quick said. He saw her coming out, her upper body was naked, and he described her long dark hair.

Again Quick's story was about as wrong as it could be. Janny's hair was grey and five centimetres long, she was fully clothed and at no point did she venture outside the tent.

Penttinen asked Quick to make a drawing of the camping place. He put the tent nearest to the lake and the car at the far end. It should have been the other way round.

At the next interview, Thomas Quick, Birgitta Ståhle and Seppo Penttinen were seated, talking and apparently unaware of the fact that they were being recorded and that their words would be transcribed and included in the interrogation report.

'I called you up at that point and said that this wasn't so believable,' Penttinen said to Quick.

In other words, the chief interrogator had phoned the suspect to spill the beans about some of the information being incorrect. According to Sture Bergwall, this sort of informal contact was very common during the investigation, but this was one of the few occasions when I stumbled upon irrefutable evidence of its importance.

I looked for Seppo Penttinen's memo in the investigation notes about the same telephone conversation. According to this, Quick had communicated over the telephone that he had made three erroneous statements during the questioning: that the woman's upper body had been naked, that there were clothes-lines strung up at the scene and that the tent had been yellow. Penttinen wrote that Quick had given this incorrect information on purpose, in the hope that the investigation into Appojaure would be abandoned. The explanation was 'on a psychological level'.

The note gives the impression that Penttinen had passively received the information that Quick offered to him – not that the chief interrogator had called Quick to point out the errors.

In the music room at Säter the interviews continued.

PENTTINEN: This name I gave you about a week ago . . .
TQ: Yeah.
PENTTINEN: Is that the person you're really talking about? Or is it some other person?
TQ: But in that case I want to use the name Johnny, not John.
PENTTINEN: But the surname, is that together with Johnny in that case?
TQ: Yeah, Johnny Larsson.
PENTTINEN: Johnny Larsson-Auna?
TQ: I don't exactly recognise Farebrink.

Unluckily, Seppo Penttinen had asked first about Johnny Larsson-Auna. Johnny Farebrink had had this surname as a child, but he had changed it to Farebrink as early as 1966. Since then he had never used either Larsson or Auna. Not even Detective Inspector Ture Nässén, who had had many run-ins with Johnny ever since the 1960s, recognised the surname Larsson-Auna.

Thomas Quick's doubts about his own involvement did not stop him from flying into a rage when Seppo Penttinen didn't formally place him under suspicion of having murdered the Stegehuises. He called Penttinen on 14 December.

'I deserve more than being questioned "for the sake of information" about these murders! I've told you enough to be considered a suspect for the murders,' he said.

He also declared that he wouldn't take any further part in the investigation, then hung up.

But it wasn't long before he called back to say that he did want to carry on after all. Whether he was jumping on the bandwagon or hopping off, Quick was so tormented by his inner anxiety that it was difficult for him to endure it.

On another occasion during this period, while he was working a night shift, Mikael was sitting in the ward office when he heard a strange sound. At first it was so faint that he wasn't sure if it was just in his mind. He held his breath and tried to sharpen his senses in the silence. Once again he heard a curious, monotonous growling.

It was just after half past twelve when Mikael left the office. At the end of the corridor he could make out a tall figure growling and mumbling as he turned round and staggered towards the office. Quick was out for a night-time prowl again.

'Thomas, what are you doing up in the middle of the night?' said Mikael, without expecting an answer.

Still growling, Quick moved slowly towards him, mumbling, distant and startled at the same time.

Mikael perceived something in the mumbling relating to 'Ellington'. Quick said that he was about to regress and he was afraid that Ellington would show up again.

This Ellington was an elusive phenomenon: sometimes a euphemism for his father, who had hurt him so grievously, sometimes an alien identity who took over Quick's body while he was murdering. It wasn't easy to understand, Mikael thought to himself as he took Quick gently by the arm and led him to the smoking room, where he tried to talk him back down to some sort of reality. When this failed, he fetched a Xanax, which soon calmed Quick down to such an extent that he voluntarily went back to his room.

At about half past two Mikael heard roars of anxiety coming from Quick's room. It was painful to listen to, but according to Quick's express wishes the staff shouldn't come into his room at night when he started screaming.

It wasn't exactly easy to obey this request, as Mikael had a strong sense of compassion for this serial killer who seemed to already be going through all manner of hellish suffering in his earthly existence.

On 19 December Seppo Penttinen went to Säter Hospital for more questioning. This time he got straight to the point.

'So, to begin with, Thomas, I want to ask you if you still stand by your confession to the murders in Appojaure in 1984?'

'Yes,' answered Quick.

The serial killer was back. Order had been restored.

UNIQUE INTERROGATION SITUATION

ONCE THOMAS QUICK decided that he had murdered the Stegehuises with Johnny Farebrink, the investigation gained new momentum.

The very next day Jan Olsson went to Sundsvall to meet with Seppo Penttinen and Christer van der Kwast for a run-through of the case. Penttinen outlined his questioning of Quick to date, omitting some of the stranger aspects of his story.

Up until that point, the Quick investigation team had consisted of Seppo Penttinen and Christer van der Kwast. Now the two investigations into Appojaure were merged into what was dubbed the 'Quick Commission' under the umbrella of the National Criminal Investigation Department.

The head of the investigation, van der Kwast, had virtually unlimited resources in his capacity as the controller of Sweden's first serial-murder case, and Penttinen was appointed to the Criminal Investigation Department as detective superintendent. An action plan was drawn up, and CID Detective Inspectors Jan Karlsson and Stellan Söderman were put in charge of operational matters.

From the Psychological Profiling Group, Detective Chief Inspector Jan Olsson was called in with the psychiatrist Ulf Åsgård to make crime analyses. Olsson also became the forensic expert for the Quick Commission.

Hans Ölvebro was made officer in charge. He was head of the Palme Unit, from which the seasoned investigator Ture Nässén was also summoned. Finally, Detective Inspectors Ann-Helene Gustafsson and Anna Wikström were called in, as was the forensic technician

Lennart Kjellander from the National Police Board Working Group on Forensic Archaeology.

In short, the Quick Commission signed up the most highly qualified crime fighters in the country, who would now roll up their sleeves and get on with the Thomas Quick investigation using every professional and scientific method available to them.

Seppo Penttinen arrived at Säter Hospital at ten in the morning on 17 January 1995. Thomas Quick was waiting in the music room and had already taken so many benzodiazepines that the planned fourth interview on Appojaure hung in the balance.

Penttinen started by trying to establish how Quick and Johnny Farebrink had found their way to the remote picnic spot where the Dutch couple had made their camp.

'It was Johnny who felt slighted by these people,' said Quick.

Farebrink had said that the man had behaved rudely and Quick thought they had insulted him in some way.

Thomas Quick's suggestion that Johnny Farebrink had met the Stegehuises before the murder was problematic. The Dutch couple's journey had been reconstructed in detail, all the way from Holland to Sweden. Their final two days had been mapped out by the police hour by hour.

The Stegehuises drove south on the E45 towards Gällivare shortly after ten o'clock on 12 July. They filled up their car at a Shell petrol station in Skaulo at a quarter to eleven and continued towards Stora Sjöfallets Nationalpark (Great Waterfall National Park).

From Stora Sjöfallet they drove back and made a stop to take photographs forty kilometres west of Appojaure. We know from their travel journal that they put up their tent at half past four in the afternoon.

In other words, Johnny Farebrink's meeting with the Dutch couple couldn't have taken place before they came to Appojaure. For this reason Penttinen steered his questioning away from the subject and asked instead about the knives that had been used in the murder.

Quick maintained that he had used the strange knife with the broad blade which he had sketched in the first interview, while Farebrink's knife had been slightly smaller, with a handle made of reindeer horn.

It was out of the question that the broad blades of these knives could have caused the wounds cut into the victims' bodies. They were made by a knife with a considerably thinner blade, at most twenty millimetres.

A knife exactly like this, the couple's own fillet knife, had been found at the murder scene. In the autopsy report it is stated that this knife could even have caused all of the injuries. For the sake of Quick's credibility, it was now vital to get this knife into his account, and in the continued questioning we see how Penttinen managed this through his unmistakably leading questions.

'Is there a third knife?' he asked.

'I'm feeling that there are three knives involved here, but I'm vague about it.'

'Where would the third knife come from, in that case?'

'Johnny,' answered Quick.

This was an answer Penttinen did not want to hear, so he said,'What did you say?'

'From Johnny in that case,' Quick repeated. 'Or the tent.'

'You seem very disturbed when you say the third knife could have come from the tent,' said Penttinen.

When Quick 'seems disturbed', in the context of the interrogation, it means that he is getting closer to psychologically loaded material – or in other words, the truth, which is often too painful to talk about.

'Well, of course,' Quick answered.

Quick felt so terrible at the thought of the couple's knife that Penttinen had to stop his questioning for rest and medication.

After a break, Quick described how he found the knife inside the tent.

'Why did you need it?' Penttinen wondered. 'You already had a knife each.'

But Quick was no longer with him. He had taken too much medication and wasn't able to keep up.

'You keep trailing off,' said Penttinen.

He wondered if Quick could say where they went after the murders. More uncertainty.

'What complicates it for me is that I seem to remember he gave me a lift to Messaure, or whatever it's called. He dropped me off there.'

That he had been left in the village of Messaure was one more decisive piece of information that Quick had not mentioned earlier. Once the place name had been brought up, he did not have the strength to talk about it any more.

'I can see you've been given medication so you can't go on. Or are you just feeling bad?' asked Penttinen.

'I feel bad,' said Quick. 'There's no problem with the medication . . .'

Questioning was resumed after lunch.

'We were talking about Messaure,' Seppo Penttinen continued. 'How did that enter into the picture?'

'We came to Messaure in the early hours,' said Quick. 'I have a strong memory of taking a railbus from Messaure in the morning.'

Both Quick and Penttinen were unsure whether Messaure was served by a railbus. As usual they had carried on talking about the murder investigation over lunch.

'We were getting on to the fact that you had visited someone there, but it seems difficult for you to talk about it.'

Quick confirmed that this was so.

In the next interview Seppo Penttinen said that he had checked a railway map and confirmed that there was no railbus connection to Messaure. Quick stood his ground.

'He let me off in Messaure and I have a feeling it was from there, later in the morning, that I took a railbus, but here I'm . . .'

'You're unsure,' said Penttinen. 'What about the bicycle alternative, then, you were going to talk about that?'

'I have no memory of cycling from Messaure,' said Quick.

The interviews often seem to take the form of negotiation in this way, where Penttinen and Quick collectively tried to find a solution that was not contradicted by known facts.

On 23 January there was a meeting of the Quick Commission and Stellan Söderman summarised the position: 'As it stands there's a conviction for a murder in Piteå police district dated 1976,' he explained. 'The period of criminal activity is approximately thirty years and the current number of cases is seven. Two are statute-barred, one took place in Norway.'

Next the discussion touched upon the sensitive question of Seppo Penttinen's role in the investigation. There was unanimous agreement at the meeting that it wasn't appropriate for a single interrogator to conduct all the questioning of the suspect. Penttinen explained the 'absolutely extraordinary circumstances' that prevailed during questioning. For the moment, the group agreed to wait before 'briefing' another person into the process.

One week later the Quick Commission had its second meeting at Rikskriminalen (CID) in Stockholm. Jan Olsson, who had made an analysis of the double murder in Appojaure, put forward a proposal to carry out a reconstruction where Quick would demonstrate how the crime had taken place. They would also get Quick and the medical examiner Anders Eriksson together, in order to verify or disprove Quick's information.

A possible reconstruction in Appojaure in the spring was discussed, whereupon Seppo Penttinen again explained to the group 'the unique interrogation situation' that applied to Quick.

'Quick is trying to bring back deeply repressed memories and then reassemble these into a credible sequence of events. According to the therapists this is a part of the work Quick must do in order to go forward.'

He also described the role of the memory expert Sven Åke Christianson in the investigation and explained that Christianson was having regular meetings with Quick. After four years at Säter Hospital Thomas Quick had lost touch with his last few contacts outside the world of forensic psychiatry and the legal system. His contact with people was limited to police interviews and therapy conversations about murder and abuse. He was utterly cut off from the real world.

Sporadic and scanty notes indicate that Quick was feeling increasingly unwell at the beginning of 1995, while at the same time being prescribed more and more benzodiazepines, with worsening side effects as a consequence.

Some examples from the file:

> *26 January 1995*
> Had a panic attack in the smoking room, couldn't get out. Hyperventilated, grew stiff. Breathing into a paper bag. With assistance from staff he made his way back to his room, sat in a wheelchair. Lay down on his bed. Was given Diazepam, 2 suppositories of 10 mg.
>
> *18 February 1995*
> Thomas had a panic attack at 16.00. Sat in the smoking room calling out, 'I can't do it, I can't do it.' Suddenly Thomas charged from his chair and into the stairwell where he threw himself head first into the wall. Thomas tried repeatedly to bang his head against the floor. [. . .]
>
> He was so unsteady on his feet that he couldn't walk, instead he crawled into the smoking room. When he finished smoking he wanted to go back to his room, but he couldn't manage it. He collapsed outside the office door. With another member of staff I fetched the chair from inside the office, I put him in it.
>
> *21 February 1995, Chief Medical Officer Erik Kall*
> The patient has been feeling quite unwell for the last few days. Yesterday he received a letter from the parents of one of the victims who want to know what has happened to their son. The patient has had thoughts about whether it is worth the trouble. But he has decided to continue the process.

Thomas Quick's existence had become a cycle of panic attacks, death wishes, constant medication and conversations about murders and sexual abuse – day in, day out, month after month, year after year.

On 2 March Birgitta Ståhle wrote a summary of the therapy during the period from which the above notes were taken.

> After the trial in Piteå we have continued our work of seeing the earlier contexts and how these have been re-enacted at an adult age. This is taking place in parallel with police interviews. New memories where violence is being directed at adults have started coming up. This information is passed to the police and prosecutor for further development.
>
> Thomas has now been arraigned for the so-called 'tent murder' outside Gällivare in 1984.
>
> His brother Sten-Ove's book on Thomas has caused a strong reaction. At the same time this has made Thomas connect more with memories in which his brother subjected him to extremely violent acts during his childhood.
>
> Thomas made two suicide attempts in the autumn, when intense anxiety awakened a desire to die and avoid the suffering caused by the psychotherapy and police questioning.

Birgitta Ståhle pointed out that as his therapist she remained 'in close cooperation with his ward about his daily psychological status'. Despite Quick's harrowing panic attacks, his longing to die and high intake of medication, Ståhle insisted that the psychotherapeutic process was in a positive phase:

> The images and memory fragments that come up in the therapy are clarifying more and more, and the circumstances around the murders are also becoming clearer. There has been a development towards a deeper ability to make contact both in terms of his own life story and how he has functioned later as an adult. He has also developed contact with difficult feelings such as hatred and fury as well as despair and guilt about what he has subjected other people to. [. . .]

> Through Thomas being open and sharing his extremely difficult situation our communication and the therapy have also been further strengthened.

A few hours after Birgitta Ståhle had written her account of the positive advances in the therapeutic process, a more typical note was added to the file by a nurse:

> Time 19.30: In the evening Thomas had severe panic attacks. He was provided with 2 x 10 mg Diazepam suppositories. Declared that he does not have the strength to live any more. A watch has been put in place.

Late at night on 12 March the telephone rang at the home of Assistant County Police Commissioner Bertil Ståhle. It was immediately clear to him that one of his wife's patients had been given their home telephone number. He called out towards the bedroom:

'There's a crazyman who wants to talk to you. He says his name is Ellington.'

His wife, who had been woken up, reached for the receiver.

'Sture, it's Birgitta,' she said.

A theatrical and mocking laugh was heard.

'This is Ellington and I want to talk to the therapist.'

Birgitta Ståhle recognised the thick voice.

'Sture!'

Afterwards, Birgitta Ståhle summarised the telephone call from memory, inserting her own commentary in square brackets.

'Sture is lying in his bed. He has anxiety. (*Laughs*) They believe in his anxiety and his stories. He's just manipulating.'

'Who are you, then?'

'I'm Ellington and we've met a few times. (*Laughs*)

[Here I get the sense that it's Sten-Ove who's calling, which feels disconcerting. I am used to meeting Sture, but not Sten-Ove. He communicates his contempt for Sture, who is anxious, who is weak. Also contempt for the therapy, the way he calls me 'the therapist'.]

Ellington continued: 'Now I'm going to tell you about the trip to Norway.'

[Now I know that this is Sture in the figure of Ellington. I'm going to listen to what he has to say and try to regain contact with Sture.]

'Me and Patrik. We're travelling towards Oslo. Close, just before . . . (*Starts laughing again*)

'I manipulate and I manage (*triumph in his voice at his power and strength*) to get Patrik to step out of the car. (*Laughs again*) He steps out of the car and he kills the boy. It's he who kills the boy. That was what he wanted! And I'm the one who makes him do it.'

[Here his voice goes into silent crying. I hear Sture say in a whisper, 'Birgitta.' Straight away I know I have to acknowledge Sture, I have to make him clear and strong in comparison to Ellington. Ellington's voice sort of growls in the background but Sture begins to talk to me and I realise that he is back inside himself.]

Margit Norell read Birgitta Ståhle's jottings on the telephone call and was delighted that Ellington had taken shape outside the therapy room. She analysed the significance of this curious incident in the unpublished manuscript on Thomas Quick:

> When Ellington takes form and tries, and fails, to regain power through his disdain for Sture and his weakness, two things occur. Firstly: Sture achieves 'object constancy' for the first time in his life. P and Ellington are the same person. It was highly understandable that Sture wanted to believe that his father needed him, that he meant something to P, and that P was occasionally capable of protecting Sture against the even more dangerous M – after all it was P who pulled Sture out of the hole in the ice. In relation to P there was also, up until the murder of Simon, some sort of predictable framework, as described by Sture himself – from experience Sture came to recognise the sequence of events and could therefore predict when P would ejaculate and the pain would stop and P would become kind again – weeping

a few sentimental tears, patting Sture on the stomach, telling him how much he liked his lad Sture, going into the kitchen and giving Sture lingonberries and milk or something. As a consequence of the murder – as would later be shown – and the cutting up of the foetus Simon, this framework of predictability was broken and Sture experienced the absolutely unbearable terror of P being capable of doing the same thing to him, Sture. Clearly Sture must have seen it like this when M made him directly responsible for the death of the foetus: 'Just see what you have done!' However, what also happens when Ellington takes full form is that his power is broken. He has written down Birgitta's telephone number, Sture's therapist. He calls her and after a few moments of conversation with Ellington, Birgitta establishes contact with Sture and takes his side against Ellington. [. . .] Shortly after, M – Nana – also takes form. This is even more terrifying, as ever since infancy in Sture's experience she has represented anger and, later on, death. The only time when it was not like this seems to have been his gestation in the womb, which was also the only time that Sture was not alone but had a twin.

THE LAST DAM BUILDER

ON 18 MARCH 1995 Thomas Quick was sitting in his room at Säter Hospital when a documentary on the village of Messaure was shown on SVT2.

The place where Thomas Quick had apparently been dropped off after the murder of the Dutch couple is situated some thirty-seven kilometres from Jokkmokk. In 1957 the power company Vattenfall started building a gigantic hydroelectric dam there, on the river known as Stora Luleälv.

The project would keep 1,300 workers in full employment for five years. In the middle of the wilderness a village was built, complete with streets and squares, apartment blocks, shops, a post office, church, school, a community centre, police station, doctor's surgery, café and everything else required by a thriving community. By the early 1960s the village had 3,000 residents.

The power station in Messaure was inaugurated in 1962 with a speech by the prime minister, Tage Erlander. The settlement was later demolished bit by bit and in the end all that remained of the bustling community was the network of roads in the midst of the Lapp/Sami outback.

The TV documentary was about a resident of Messaure, Rune Nilsson, who had worked as a construction foreman until 1971. Once the dam was finished, Vattenfall and Jokkmokk municipality used increasingly strong-arm tactics to get the residents of the village to move away, which most accepted on voluntary terms.

'Vattenfall tried to get me out by hook or crook, but . . . I suppose I'm a bit of a stubborn sort, so I just said "I'm not going anywhere",' Rune Nilsson said.

It turned into a drawn-out battle, with Jokkmokk municipality turning off his water in an attempt to make him move. Ignoring their pleas and threats, he stayed on. After ten years the municipality gave up and let him stay on as Messaure's only inhabitant.

Thomas Quick watched the documentary with amazement and realised what a bad idea the railbus had been. But at least now he knew who Rune Nilsson was and what it looked like where he lived.

This was bad luck for Rune Nilsson, who seemed a peaceful, friendly man.

THE MISSING SIBLINGS

THOMAS QUICK'S SIX siblings had been keeping up with what their crazy brother was saying – with disgust. They were burdened by the Quick story and before long they began to avoid any further information about their serial-killer brother, breaking off all contact with him and staying away from the subject of Sture Bergwall or Thomas Quick altogether. He ceased to exist for them.

Eva, Sture's younger sister, was the one who persevered with him for the longest. When I spoke to Eva, she told me about the nightmarish time they had had after Sture's confession of the murder of Johan Asplund.

'Every time I thought, *Now it can't get any worse* But then it did! It just got worse and worse . . .'

In the end, even Eva realised she had to sever her ties with Sture.

So it was surprising when, early in 1995, Sten-Ove Bergwall emerged as the spokesman for the Bergwall siblings and struck an unforgiving tone towards his brother. In a number of interviews he made a categoric request to the psychiatric care system and the courts: 'Never release Thomas Quick!'

Sten-Ove was ten years older than Sture and had moved away from home when Sture was still a little boy. As adults, the two brothers rekindled their relationship over a shared interest in nature, sighthounds and racing bikes. In June 1982 they took part in 'Den Store Styrkeprøven' (The Great Test of Strength) bicycle race between Trondheim and Oslo, and a few months later they took over a kiosk on Koppartorget (Copper Square) in Hälsinggården,

Falun, a business venture that lasted just short of four years.

Nine years later Sten-Ove regarded his brother as a complete stranger. He wrote the book *Min bror Thomas Quick*, in which he questions who his younger brother really was. He warned of the manipulative Thomas Quick who for all those years managed to hide his evil side from his family. Sten-Ove's conclusion was that his brother had developed a loathsome creature within himself which only his victims had seen.

However, Sten-Ove Bergwall's main reason for publishing the book was to redress the wrongs done to their parents. He maintained that he and his siblings had bright, loving memories of their parental home.

The six children considered it unthinkable that their father could have raped Sture in front of their mother, and absolutely inconceivable that their beloved mother would have tried to drown Sture in a frozen lake.

'I don't doubt that it's true for him,' said Sten-Ove to *Expressen*'s Christian Holmén. 'It's a known fact that people in therapy are encouraged to come up with false memories.'

After the book had been out for a while, Thomas Quick wanted to announce 'certain clarifications' concerning his brother. In a police interview on 10 April 1995 he alleged that Sten-Ove had participated in the murder of Johan Asplund:

> Quick says that, while they were travelling to Sundsvall, Sten-Ove Bergwall was quite aware of the fact that they were looking for a boy who would be their victim. Sten-Ove tried to wind Quick up by saying something to the effect of: 'Show me you have the guts to kill a boy.'
>
> Once they got to the place where they took Johan's life, Sten-Ove behaved in a superior manner and tried to fire Quick up by the things he said, including, 'So kill him then!'

At their second meeting, the Quick Commission had decided to arrange interviews with the people who knew Quick, in order to build up a picture of his credibility. The very highest priority would be given to his siblings, who were to be questioned about their childhood years in the family home. Detectives Jan Olsson and Ture Nässén confirmed to me and Jenny Küttim that the interviews were held in the spring of 1995, in connection with the investigation into the double murder in Appojaure.

The task had been passed to Detective Inspectors Anna Wikström and Ann-Helene Gustafsson, but we did not find a trace of the interviews among the investigation material, not even in the so-called slush. We applied to the district court in Gällivare for copies of the missing documents, but they replied that they didn't have them. We sent a request to the police authority in Sundsvall and received the same answer. Christer van der Kwast passed us over to Seppo Penttinen, who in turn informed us that he did not 'recognise our errand' and so couldn't comment on it and that 'the documentation you are asking for is not found in the material I have at my disposal', both of which were roundabout ways of saying that the interrogation transcripts simply didn't exist.

At the same time Sture Bergwall's siblings informed us individually that they had been questioned by Anna Wikström and Ann-Helene Gustafsson. So what had they said in those interviews?

Ever since the first headlines about Thomas Quick, Örjan Bergwall had been trying to avoid every newspaper article, radio or television report on his brother. But he still knew far more than he would have preferred. The two police officers wanted to know about Örjan's memories of growing up, and he replied that he had recollections of a very secure childhood.

They had moved to Korsnäs, outside Falun, in 1956, just in time for Örjan to start school. The family then consisted of seven children and two adults, who all managed to get along in a ninety-eight-square-metre flat with three rooms and a kitchen. Their father, Ove, worked in a factory making boxes and Thyra, their mother, had found a job as a school caretaker.

Örjan recalled Sture as talented, highly creative and dynamic but with some 'lack of motor skills' in his movements. He was also markedly independent even as a young boy.

Their father was slightly authoritarian, maybe a touch too strict, but also a very friendly person with a good sense of humour. Their mother was a stable and dependable person committed to the well-being of all her children. There were never any long-lasting quarrels in the parental home and Örjan did not recall any real unpleasantness during his childhood. The children never received any corporal punishment at the hands of their parents. Sexual molestation? No, Örjan had never noticed anything like that, and he was utterly dumbfounded at the mere suggestion. There were so many siblings that if anything of that nature had taken place, surely someone would have noticed?

Örjan knew that Sture had committed various crimes. Among other things he had sexually assaulted a young boy at the hospital in Falun and, after that, had been in care at various institutions. In the 1970s, Örjan and his parents had visited Sture at Säter and Sidsjön hospitals. According to Örjan, after that Sture had started improving and he became much more stable in the early 1980s.

By the time of the bank robbery in Grycksbo in 1990, their contact had grown more sporadic. Sture mostly just sent letters about how much he missed his family. The last time Örjan spoke to him was at the beginning of his course of therapy with Kjell Persson. Örjan seemed to recall how, on that occasion, Sture had said that he could see 'a light at the end of the tunnel' and Örjan, interpreting this in a positive sense, told Sture that he hoped he would start finding positive aspects in his life.

Örjan told me that he would never forget the day he swung into a petrol station to refuel his car and saw his brother staring out from the front pages of both the evening newspapers. That was when the nightmare began and it was still looking unlikely to be over in the near future. But he never spoke about this to the two police officers.

Instead he remembered towards the end of the questioning how they brought up a question that ought to have been of great interest to the investigators: Sture's driving skills. Örjan mentioned that Sture got his driving licence very late on, at some point in the late 1980s. Sture had driven with him once as a learner driver, and Örjan's view prior to Sture's test was that he was essentially unable to drive a car.

*

Torvald Bergwall remembered that he met with Detective Inspectors Anna Wikström and Jan Karlsson in the Mikaeli Church in Västerås, where he was the vicar. They explained that the questioning was part of the investigation into the Appojaure murders, while also touching upon the murders of Johan Asplund and Olle Högbom.

Torvald Bergwall also spoke of an untroubled childhood without any memories of sexual molestation or violence. According to him, the version of events circulating in the press was simply untrue. He had always known Sture had mental problems, but their parents hadn't spoken of this openly, because in those times such things were shameful. But they had been very loyal to Sture and never abandoned him. They always took care of him and often visited him at Säter after he was sectioned in the 1970s.

Torvald also remembered Sture's poor coordination while they were growing up – lisping and jumbling his words, which sometimes caused the other children to laugh at him. He mentioned one occasion when the siblings were trying to teach Sture to ride a bicycle but in their eagerness forgot to tell him how to apply the brakes. Sture cycled right into a wall and hurt himself so badly that the children were frightened. This, according to Torvald, was a typical example of their 'inability to grasp his handicap with his motor skills'.

In addition Torvald mentioned that Sture took his driving test very late and had to try several times before he passed. Torvald never saw Sture driving a car before then and had given a great deal of thought to how he had supposedly made his way to all these places where the murders to which he had confessed took place. According to the vicar, it was simply not feasible that Sture had driven himself.

And so it continued: all of Sture Bergwall's siblings confirmed that they had been questioned by the Quick Commission, and all had given a picture of their childhood that departed in every possible way from the stories that had emerged from Quick's therapy at Säter. Some people would say that their unanimous testimony revealed that Thomas Quick had very likely given an untrue description of his childhood and above all had false accused his parents of extremely serious crimes.

So what happened to the transcripts of the interviews with the Bergwall siblings?

They weren't archived at the police authority in Sundsvall, and were clearly kept from the general public, the media, lawyers and law courts that sentenced Thomas Quick.

As far as I can tell they were never evaluated, nor even read except by those who had conducted the interviews, and of course by Seppo Penttinen and Christer van der Kwast.

A MISSING HOUR

ON SUNDAY, 9 JULY 1995 a ten-seater private jet belonging to the dance band the Vikings landed at Gällivare Airport. But instead of Christer Sjögren and his fellow band members, Thomas Quick disembarked with Birgitta Ståhle, four care assistants and a number of police officers.

After staying the night at the psychiatric clinic in Gällivare Hospital, the group set off down the E45, heading south towards Porjus in a Toyota Hiace.

The memory expert Sven Åke Christianson had gained a great deal of influence over the investigation, not least in the methods they used in staging the reconstructions. Quick hadn't wasted any time in getting to grips with these new ideas. For instance, when the minibus was about to turn off towards Appojaure, he insisted that they first had to drive to Porjus and then turn round, as this was the route he had taken with Johnny Farebrink when they drove to the murder scene.

In this way the journey was supposed to correspond with the events of 12 July 1984.

It was 14.15 by the time the white Toyota turned onto Vägen Västerut (the Westerly Road) towards Stora Sjöfallet and Appojaure. Quick's anxiety attacks grew more and more frequent and he claimed that he recognised their whereabouts. They had to stop the minibus so he could get out and throw up.

'It mustn't be true, it can't be true,' he moaned.

The small turn-off to the picnic spot by Appojaure was impossible to miss, as the police had cordoned off the area and posted sentries.

'On arrival, Quick had to take medication, Xanax,' wrote Penttinen in the reconstruction report.

Quick stepped out of the vehicle, wearing a blue baseball cap, a green anorak, black jeans and black trainers. Walking with Seppo Penttinen, he familiarised himself with their surroundings and waited for the forensic technicians to prepare the last few details before the reconstruction could begin.

Every time he'd been asked about it during questioning, Quick had placed the car and the tent incorrectly, while also positioning the man and the woman on the opposite sides to where they had actually been. Yet when they arrived at Appojaure the technicians had arranged everything exactly as it was at the time of the murders.

The police had even specially ordered a tent from the Netherlands and got hold of a green car from the mid-1970s which resembled those belonging to the murder victims.

All this was exactly in line with Sven Åke Christianson's 'cognitive interrogation techniques'. By re-creating the environment in detail, Quick was supposed to gain easier access to his repressed memories. Penttinen started asking the sorts of questions that Christianson had taught him: Do you remember how you were feeling? What can you hear? Can you remember any smells? All this to help Quick bring back memories from the traumatic event.

'If you keep your eyes closed and try to reach back in your thoughts, till you're in 1984,' said Penttinen.

The experienced investigators Ture Nässén and Jan Olsson watched this unfolding spectacle with grim faces. Later, Olsson commented to me: 'It's the suspect who's supposed to place everything as he remembers it. But everything here had been arranged exactly right; the doubles were positioned exactly like the victims. Quick arrived and found his bed already made. It was nothing like how a reconstruction should really be.'

Jan Olsson also found it irritating that Christianson was ordering people around on the crime scene.

'Christianson was pacing about with firm steps and a serious look on his face. He had a lot of influence. "You have to move out of the way so you're out of sight," Christianson told me and other police officers. We were basically pushed away and as a result we couldn't hear much of what Quick and Seppo were saying.'

The figure representing Johnny Farebrink joined Quick. The two murderers, while exchanging whispers, tiptoed up to the little brown tent, each of them holding an implement representing a knife. When Quick reached the tent he made a furious assault on the side of the canvas that was facing the lake. After a few lunges he handed his knife to 'Farebrink', who started stabbing at the tent canvas with two knives at the same time. Quick took his knife back and charged into the opening.

Inside the tent, Hans Ölvebro and Anna Wikström were in position, and she cried out, 'No! No! No!'

As soon as Quick ran into the tent it was chaos. He growled and grunted, now fully regressed and transformed into his murderous Ellington identity. He tossed the tent poles out through the open tent flap. Anna Wikström continued yelling, while Penttinen watched the pandemonium from outside. At that moment Birgitta Ståhle came running with the nurses from Säter, who were ready to intervene.

'Give it up now! Give it up!' shouted Penttinen to Quick.

He seemed to have calmed down somewhat inside the tent, but his guttural, monotonous growling could still be heard as the video camera was switched off. The time shown on the video footage was 16.09.

When the police video of the reconstruction resumed, Thomas Quick seemed much more collected and determined. He and the other figure stole forward towards the tent, while Quick continuously commented on what was happening.

'Here we're sneaking up and checking that it's all quiet. And from this position you go forward and loosen the stays from the middle and back.'

'Johnny Farebrink' loosened the pegs of the outer tent and it folded up. This was an important detail, as a number of slashes from the knife only went through the inner tent and not the outer.

The reconstruction proceeded like a sort of interactive dialogue between Quick and Penttinen, with the chief interrogator providing continuous feedback. He reminded Quick about information he had given in the interviews, clarified and made suggestions of his own.

In all, some thirty bystanders watched Quick convincingly demonstrate how, twelve years earlier, he had murdered two people in cold blood in this deserted place. Six months later, as we know, Gällivare District Court was also convinced when an edited version of the reconstruction was shown in the courtroom. Seppo Penttinen added some voice-over to the video: 'While Quick was immersed in the attack there was a technical fault with the tape recorder. The interruption only lasted for a minute.'

Penttinen's statement about the one-minute interruption was untrue. The camera was restarted at 17.14. What happened in that hour was not recorded on tape, but Jan Olsson remembered.

'Thomas Quick and Seppo Penttinen went off to one side to talk. Then we heard that a decision had been made to prepare the tent again and have another go at the reconstruction.'

According to several of the policemen on the scene, Quick also spoke in the interval to Christianson. Sture Bergwall himself remembered that Penttinen, during their little chat, put his hand on his shoulder and said, 'You do remember telling us that first you loosened the pegs of the outer sheet and folded it up?'

'That little snippet of information meant I could start with that action and take it from there,' said Sture Bergwall.

Jan Olsson described how it went on: 'Thomas Quick seemed very collected, and with imaginary stabbing motions he went through the various sequences exactly according to the analysis we had made.'

But things were going to get considerably worse. Olsson had since been forced to accept that the description he had noted down in his analysis of the sequence of events a year before couldn't actually be correct. The photos he had access to at the beginning showed a bag of rubbish seen inside the tent through a long tear in the canvas. The bag had started tilting and was leaning against the man's sleeping bag. A couple of beer cans seemed to have fallen out of the bag and were lying on the floor. Based on that photo it seemed reasonable that the perpetrator had made his way into the tent through the rip.

However, other photographs had later emerged that were taken by the first police patrol to arrive on the scene. In these, the bulging rubbish bag was still upright and perched on top of it was a beer can. According to Jan Olsson, it was inconceivable that the murderer could have entered the tent through the tear without knocking over that rubbish bag. At least the carefully balanced beer can would have fallen off, he reasoned.

When Jan Olsson saw Quick climbing into the tent through the rip in the canvas and attacking the couple with his knife, he was overwhelmed by the realisation that Quick was replicating the action as described in Olsson's original analysis – not as it must logically have happened. Something was very, very wrong.

Olsson stood at the edge of the trees and watched the reconstruction from a safe distance. He felt extremely uneasy about two important questions that kept coming to mind. Why was Quick acting out a series of events that he in all likelihood had never experienced? And – even more worrying – how had Quick managed to get his hands on the police investigation's own crime analysis?

The probable answers to these questions were appalling.

Jan Olsson controlled his suspicions by telling himself that he didn't know everything about the case. He had not read Quick's interrogation reports and must be unaware of the convincing evidence that already existed.

During the reconstruction Thomas Quick repeated his claim that it was Johnny Farebrink's idea to drive to the picnic spot by Appojaure, where he knew that the Dutch couple were camping. Farebrink wanted to kill them because they had insulted him during an encounter a day or so earlier.

Quick had barely arrived at the picnic spot before he found his own compelling reason for wanting to kill the couple. The day before he had met a German boy on a bicycle, he said, and he believed that the boy was the Dutch couple's son. In his limited English and German, Quick had explained this to the couple, but they had replied saying they didn't have a son.

In Thomas Quick's psychotic mind the couple's denial of their own son was such a betrayal that they deserved to die. Johnny Farebrink had agreed.

'Yeah, see what bloody arseholes they are. Let's sort them out!'

Once Farebrink and Quick had created separate motives, based on their own delusions, for murdering the foreign tourists Quick was left at the picnic spot to keep an eye on the two individuals who had just been given a death sentence, while Johnny drove to Gällivare to borrow a firearm.

By now, Jan Olsson had moved in so close that he could hear what Quick was saying. Olsson took Christer van der Kwast aside and said, 'No one drives off to borrow a shotgun so they can murder two people! Surely you don't believe that?'

Olsson's question was left hanging in the air while Quick continued with his story.

When Farebrink came back to the picnic spot he didn't have a gun. Instead they used three knives to kill the sleeping couple by repeatedly stabbing them. After the murder, Quick and Farebrink went to the 'old man's house' where they had slept the previous night. They made 'the old man' look at the massacred bodies in the tent, to make him understand what could happen to those who did not do what Johnny wanted.

The identity of the old man would not be revealed until the reconnaissance that was scheduled for the following day.

The next morning, Detective Inspector Ture Nässén drove the white Toyota minibus towards Messaure. He had good local knowledge of the area and it bothered him to see Thomas Quick trying to give them directions.

'It was almost embarrassing, it was so clear he didn't have a clue where he was or where he was going,' Nässén told me.

Finally they passed a sign for Messaure. The overgrown roads confirmed the location of the demolished village, but no one in the minibus spoke of what was obvious: the village of Messaure no longer existed.

It was from this place without either houses or people that Thomas Quick claimed he had taken a railbus.

After driving around for a good while, the group finally drew near to the house where Rune Nilsson, the last resident of Messaure, was still living. The minibus stopped and Quick got out, shielding his eyes from the house as if to protect himself from a dreadful sight. With a great deal of drama he dropped to his knees and started weeping in an anxious manner.

When he'd collected himself he said, 'It's nothing personal against you, Seppo.'

'No,' said Penttinen.

'But you, all of you, are killing him!'

Quick cried again with such despair that he started doubling up and groaning.

'It smells musty in there as well.'

'Does it?' said Penttinen.

'And Johnny is really dangerous!'

At the thought of the danger presented by Johnny, Quick started weeping so uncontrollably that he could no longer talk. Finally he managed to speak a few words, while stuttering, '"No!" says the old man. And he . . . says . . . it . . . does not . . . affect . . . him . . . so . . . much.'

A care assistant who was in the minibus suddenly took note of the condition Quick was in and came to his aid with more benzodiazepines. Quick took what was offered.

Birgitta Ståhle also joined the group trying to help Quick through his crisis.

'I can't handle this,' said Quick.

'Is it Johnny who's being wicked to the old man? What's he doing to him that's so wicked?' asked Ståhle.

Quick explained that Johnny Farebrink had threatened the old man with a knife while he stood powerless, unable to help.

'I understand,' said Ståhle. 'You felt paralysed.'

'Promise to be nice to him,' said Quick to Penttinen.

After further discussion outside Rune Nilsson's house, Quick wanted to leave the scene. But when he tried to make his way back to the minibus his legs gave way. He was so drugged that he had to be helped by the nurses, who propped him up and dragged him back.

They got into the minibus and headed back towards Gällivare. This was the conclusion of the trip to Lapland. Ture Nässén left Messaure steeped in gloom.

'That day we were in Messaure I was really ashamed of being a policeman,' he told me, summarising his memories from 11 July 1995.

A month later, at approximately seven in the morning on 17 August, Rune Nilsson was fetched by the police and driven to the station in Jokkmokk to be questioned 'about his activities and observations in the summer of 1984'. When he got there he was fingerprinted and treated as if he were a suspect for the murders in Appojaure.

However, Seppo Penttinen didn't ask anything about Appojaure, Thomas Quick or Johnny Farebrink. Instead, the interrogation focused on the intimate details of Rune Nilsson's life. He was forced to describe his family, his separation from his wife, custody arrangements for their children, his working life, trips abroad, the friends he had, vehicles he had owned, etc. Seppo Penttinen made the following note in his report:

> He was asked whether he is familiar with someone named Larsson in Jokkmokk. Rune responded, 'Not as far as I know.' As a further response to this he said spontaneously, 'You're asking such strange questions.'

Rune Nilsson's comment was absolutely justified. The interrogator's questions were being asked in a manner as if Nilsson were some sort of hardened criminal who had to be outsmarted with devious questions.

Penttinen continued, asking if Nilsson had any poachers among his circle of acquaintances, if he had any connection with the Sami folk high school (where Quick had once been a student), if he knew people who had been in trouble with the police and whether he knew anyone from Mattisudden (Farebrink's place of birth). Nilsson answered patiently but negatively to all the questions.

Penttinen confronted him with eight photographs of various men, one of whom was Farebrink. Nilsson said he did not recognise any of them.

When shown another collection of photographs, Nilsson said that he recognised number seven as 'the person who's had his photo in the papers, the one they call the Säter Man, Thomas Quick'.

Rune Nilsson was not under suspicion for any crime, yet he was interrogated 'for information purposes' for more than four hours.

The following week he was called in for more questioning. 'Today's interview will be about 1984', wrote Penttinen in the interrogation report.

Rune Nilsson told him that when school was finished for the summer, his seventeen-year-old son started working in the turbine hall of the power station in Messaure and lived with him all summer. Nilsson was mostly at home 'waiting with the dinner ready when he came back in the evening'.

Further questioning followed about Nilsson's private life. Earlier he had described how once he tried to distil his own schnapps and almost blew the equipment to smithereens. There was only this one failed attempt, yet he was forced to disclose in detail how he did it, how he pulped the potatoes, what sort of containers he used and so on.

Nilsson was again pressed about what he had done in 1984.

'Look, I don't remember,' he said. 'Nope. And that's all there is to it. I called the boy and asked him if he could remember what he did in '84. Yeah – and he said he was working for Vattenfall. And then we went water-skiing when the work dried up.'

Penttinen explained that Thomas Quick had identified Nilsson from a photograph and even pointed out his property, where he said he had visited.

'Well, that might be so, but I can't recall him ever being there.'

'But can you explain what reason there would have been for him to visit you in 1984?'

'I don't know.'

'It seems pretty unlikely to me that he would just identify you by chance and say that you live in this property in Messaure and then describe certain other things about you that seem to be accurate.'

'Mm. But anyone can describe a house from the outside. And I've been on TV quite a bit and all that.'

Penttinen most likely realised that this wasn't good. He asked, 'On TV and all that?'

What Penttinen didn't know was that at least three TV programmes had been made about Rune Nilsson and that several newspapers had published articles about him as the only inhabitant of Messaure.

'Has there been any filming inside your house?'

'Also that, yeah.'

'And what did they show?'

'They showed the kitchen.'

That was not good either. It was Nilsson's kitchen that Quick had spoken about at such length. Penttinen clutched at the final straw: maybe the films had never actually been broadcast.

'So that's a programme shown on TV? Did they show the kitchen in the programme?'

'Yes.'

In other words, Messaure's last inhabitant was a television celebrity. The value of Quick pointing him out had been rendered null and void in a single stroke. Penttinen evaded the issue – like water running off a duck's back – and continued his questioning as if nothing had happened.

Penttinen explained that in their first interview with Nilsson they had taken his fingerprints because certain things had been stolen from the tent in Appojaure. Had he possibly been given any objects from the Appojaure murders?

'No, I haven't. Absolutely not!'

Nilsson explained that if he had found out anything about the frenzied attack in Appojaure he wouldn't have sat on his hands.

'That person would have been in serious trouble. I'd have contacted the police, of course. People who behave like that shouldn't be allowed to live. They should do what they do in Finland, just gun them down!'

'You think so?'

'Oh yeah! People like that shouldn't be kept alive. It's much too soft here in Sweden, the way we treat them.'

Later, Rune Nilsson's son was visited by the police at his workplace. He was questioned about his father's activities in the summer of 1984. He told them that he'd worked for Vattenfall throughout the summer of 1984 and stayed with his father. He assured them that 'absolutely no strangers came to visit or stay the night'.

The son also told them that the safe in Rune Nilsson's house, which Quick had mentioned, did not and had not ever existed.

Extensive investigation into the Messaure story had clarified that Quick had been wrong about travelling by railbus from the village, that he had somehow been there without realising that the village no longer existed and that he had identified a person who had appeared in a number of reports in the newspapers and on television. Furthermore, a number of specific snippets of information Quick had provided on Rune Nilsson proved to be incorrect.

Nilsson was just a man who loved living a simple life in nature, who lacked any known motivation to protect the frenzied Appojaure killers. So far, he had been treated in the interviews as a liar.

Astonishingly, the police decided to subject him to one more round of questioning, on 1 September 1995, this time in his own home. On this occasion the police found what they considered to be a major breakthrough in the investigation – an old quilt on a chair in the bedroom.

The interrogator confronted Nilsson with the circumstance that made it especially suspicious he should own such a quilt: 'During questioning, Thomas Quick mentioned an old, padded quilt with a checked pattern, possibly blue.'

'But it isn't blue, is it! It's white and blue, you hear! And it isn't checked, it's got a floral pattern.'

'I'm asking you how long you've had that quilt. Can you answer me?'

Nilsson couldn't remember when he bought the quilt. And despite the fact that it was neither blue nor checked, the police confiscated this unique find as evidence of something or other.

Rune Nilsson, meanwhile, had had enough and refused to play any further part in this investigation, which he couldn't understand the point of.

MORE PERSONALITIES

THE PARADOX OF the trip to Appojaure was that Quick's initial, utterly failed reconstruction, the one that played itself out before the video recording was stopped, seemed, in retrospect, to be the triumph of the whole exercise. The sequence where he was transformed into Ellington and threw himself at the tent with a growl, attacking the stand-ins lying there, was shown on television and etched into the collective consciousness of the Swedish public. A cornerstone of the Thomas Quick brand had been established.

On their return to Säter Hospital, Birgitta Ståhle wrote down a few reflections in the file, suggesting that the trip was seen internally as a great success too: confirmation that Quick had made contact with his repressed memories through regression.

> The reconstruction of the first day went very well and Thomas was able to carry out the reconstruction in a very satisfactory way. With an initial regression he came into contact with the event in its entirety and thereby he was able to put out a complete memory sequence. Just like in the therapy, where he regresses in order to establish contact with earlier contexts and emotions, it is also possible to make use of the same process under these circumstances.

One week after the reconstruction in Appojaure a senior physician made a note in the file about Quick's psychological status which went much further than anything we had seen before:

> Clinically speaking the patient has a condition that is comparable to schizophrenia. The patient has a well-functioning superficial layer, he is verbally adept and logical. There are profound fissures in his personality which, on inauspicious occasions, create such disparate reaction patterns that one can could realistically speak of psychosis. One could also speak of MPD [multiple personality disorder].

Multiple personality disorder is a mysterious and much-debated psychiatric condition that was first recognised in the 1500s, when a French nun was possessed by unknown 'personalities'. In 1791 the physician Eberhardt Gmelin published a case study on a twenty-year-old woman from Stuttgart who was capable of suddenly changing identity and turning into an alternate personality who could speak perfect French. When she went back to her original identity she had no memory of what she had done in her guise as 'the Frenchwoman'. In his eighty-seven-page report, Gmelin described how he could make the woman switch between her two personalities with a simple hand gesture.

Up until 1980 there had been 200 known cases of MPD, but with the introduction of a large number of new clinics in the USA for the condition, often attached to larger psychiatric clinics, the number of diagnosed cases increased dramatically – oddly enough. Between 1985 and 1995, 40,000 diagnoses of multiple personality disorder were made, most of which were in North America alone.

This rapid increase has been attributed to high-profile books, films and TV documentaries encouraging and inspiring new cases.

In American literature there are examples of people who have developed more than 1,400 'alternate personalities', each with unique characteristics and names. The various personalities are unaware of the existence or traits of the others.

Specialised forms of therapy that deal with unblocking repressed memories and bringing multiple personalities to light were turned into a highly profitable industry. Unfortunately the golden years were followed by a bad hangover, which started making itself felt in the early 1990s.

In 95 per cent of all cases, clients who developed MPD were 'survivors' of sexual abuse during their childhood. Usually these clients didn't know they had been subjected to such abuse at the outset of therapy, but the therapists helped them recover their repressed memories of the abuse. However, a significant number of patients discovered that the recovered memories were false, and that it was actually the therapists who had made them develop their multiple personalities. A number of therapists were sued in courts of law, accused of inappropriate treatment methods and forced to pay damages amounting to millions of dollars to their clients.

More recently the diagnosis itself has been strongly questioned and many professionals in the field believe that the condition arises due to the influence of the media and irresponsible therapists, combined with medication – especially benzodiazepines. Multiple personality disorder has now been phased out as a diagnosis in itself and instead has been integrated into a broader diagnosis of dissociative identity disorder.

When in 1995 Thomas Quick started switching identity more frequently, it caused a good deal of consternation among the nurses in Ward 36.

One day a nurse found him in the shower with a towel round his head, thrashing his arms about and repeating, 'Nano's coming, Nano's coming.' Two Xanax, two Stesolid suppositories and a few calming words helped him through the crisis. The nurse telephoned Birgitta Ståhle to ask what this 'Nano' was. Ståhle corrected the nurse and explained that *Nana* was the name used for Quick's mother.

'Nana has been present in the therapy for a while and is an even stronger figure than Ellington.'

Quick's new personalities soon become a part of the daily reality of life on the ward. I was able to read in the notes what form they took – for example, during telephone calls using the ward's payphone, which were scrupulously recorded word for word by Ståhle, alongside her own comments.

'Is this the therapist?'

'Yes, it is. Hello, Sture! How are things?'

'This is not Sture. It's Ellington,' grunted Quick, laughing with his hollow Ellington voice.

'Where is Sture?' wondered Ståhle.

'This is Ellington and Sture is in his room. Ha-ha! He's not here. He's a weed who likes to make a victim of himself. Really he'd prefer to go to the music room. Undress himself until he's naked and play the victim. I have something to tell the therapist. Ellington has written a letter.'

'Do you have the letter there that you can read?' Ståhle asked.

Ellington read it out:

> Hello!
>
> Sture is a mythomaniac, a bloody pig.
>
> He doesn't have a chance against me!
>
> Tonight I'll trick him so he hangs himself. Satisfied, oh so satisfied, I'll watch.
>
> I have the truth, Sture doesn't. It was Sture who killed the foetus he calls Simon.
>
> I'll put a stop to his accusations. I don't feel threatened but Sture has lost control and that's because he doesn't listen to me.
>
> I'M STRONG!
>
> He can kill himself, with my help of course, but he doesn't understand that.
>
> I'll play on his so-called anxiety. I need to kill but I can't have that weed at my side.
>
> I wish you a pleasant discovery, hope you enjoy tidying it up.
>
> I don't give a shit if my farewell does not suit your prudish world.
>
> With DEADLY greetings
>
> Ellington
>
> P.S. My regards to his 'excellent' therapist!!!

'Sture . . .'

'I'm Ellington!'

'I want to make contact with Sture.

'Impossible. Only Ellington is here.'

'Can you help me?'

'You mean can I play along in your therapy game? Can I play along in your therapy game?'

Ståhle noted that Ellington suddenly started 'pleading, having earlier had a hard, disdainful tone'.

'You can. But first I want you to open the door of the telephone booth and call the staff over.'

'You mean I should call the people outside? Why?'

'I need to talk to them.'

Ellington opened the door and called out, 'Nurse! Nurse!'

In the file, the staff on duty noted that Thomas had called for them and added, 'The therapist is going to fool you!'

Birgitta Ståhle's written account ends on a very different note:

> Now Ellington's power over Sture has been broken. At first he's quiet and I hear Sture's voice very faintly, then stronger, partly because I am supporting him so he can make contact with reality again. When he leaves the telephone booth he can see the peaceful faces of the dead boys projected against the wall.

The following day Birgitta Ståhle handed Thomas Quick her transcript of Ellington's telephone call. He read what Ellington had got up to in the night. They were both extremely excited about what had happened. Sture told me that he pretended he was unaware of the telephone call, because the alternating identities, at least according to prevailing theories, were not supposed to be aware of one another.

In a note in the file, Birgitta Ståhle explained the underlying mechanisms of Sture's different identities and how they expressed themselves:

> The deep personality rift in his disturbance has emerged in direct form in his therapeutic process. This personality rift can be compared to a multiple personality disorder, because Thomas refers to both figures as having different names and character attributes. Even to an outsider the change is very apparent, because he changes his personality and his voice. Psychologically these divided aspects

> are a way of controlling the serious anxiety he has from his early life. By these inner figures taking form outside himself, it becomes possible in the therapy to see and understand the significance and the context in which Thomas internalises these frightening experiences and how they have been dissociated.
>
> The early traumas in the form of sexual abuse and violence, in addition to the great emotional poverty in which Thomas grew up, have formed his personality and his disturbance. Our work is to join up his life story and confront the early exposure and terror which have been avoided.
>
> Through regression he makes contact with these early experiences and gains an understanding of how these have been responded to and reawakened at an adult age. How as an adult he has handled his early terror by putting other boys in a position of mortal terror and then killing them. Through this, he achieves a temporary decline in his anxiety and a sense of retaining the illusion of life. Through this working process, the picture emerges with more and more clarity, with a gradual move towards a reality that has been averted and contorted.

In the time that followed, the ward staff noted in the file that Quick longed to die, that he cut his throat with a bottle, wept or took medication alternately, stopped eating, 'lives under his blanket', threw himself into walls, tried to cut off his right leg and behaved in generally bizarre ways.

Birgitta Ståhle preferred to refer to it in the file as 'intensive therapeutic work' and continued:

> Clarity and definition about his own life story have resulted in a gradually improved stability and activity – self-development. This takes several different forms. Thomas exists in reality to a greater degree in his therapeutic work and has a deepened connection.

A few days later, Quick's 'self-development' resulted in him completely refusing to eat or drink and being 'in an utter panic about anyone being able to see any part of him'. Whenever he had to venture outside his room in the ward, he covered himself from head to toe and wore a hat pulled down over his face and gloves on his hands.

When I spoke to Sture about this time he remembered above all how obviously pleased his therapist had been when he adopted his alternate personalities. He dug out a newspaper cutting he was given by Birgitta Ståhle to help him understand what he was going through. The article was about multiple personality disorder and, among other things, discussed the case of an American woman, Truddi Chase, who after eight years of therapy had developed ninety-two personalities. There were even examples of the 'alternate identities' within a person's body speaking in foreign languages that the 'host person' had not mastered.

Thomas Quick, who despite several years of therapy had only developed two extra personalities thus far – Ellington and Nana – used the information in his time-honoured fashion. Twelve days after Ståhle had handed him the article, he was able to proudly let her know that a new personality had made itself known to him. His name was 'Cliff' and in the night he had written a letter on his computer – in English! In fact 'Cliff' only spoke English, which was a language that Thomas Quick hadn't mastered. Cliff wrote:

> Hello babyface!
>
> This isn't a dream!
>
> I've looked at you and I find a little crying child – oh I like it!
>
> I'm so glad that you named him Tony . . . *You* can't remember his realname, because you are a tired, uglified fish!
>
> How are you???
>
> I'm fine, because I like the feeling of your deadline!

Birgitta Ståhle was delighted. Now she had even more complexity to pore over, analyse and build new theories around. On a later date she wrote in the manuscript of her book:

> Sture switched personality. He was standing in the corridor of the ward, speaking English and saying that his name was Cliff.

He was in a catatonic state and his face was pale, wax-like. He turned his head away from the staff and said, 'He's afraid [Sture]. Don't look.' Then he asked for Ellington.

After that he said, 'Cliff is strong. He's weak – Sture.' The staff made him take some medicine and he was brought back to reality. Cliff is a shadow of Nana.

AN INCENSED ROAR

A LETTER WITH Norwegian stamps was waiting for Thomas Quick when he came home from the reconstruction in Appojaure. The crime reporter Svein Arne Haavik had written a long series of articles on Quick which had recently been published in Norway's highest-circulation newspaper, *Verdens Gang* (*VG*). Now he was wondering if there might be a possibility of getting an interview as a follow-up.

Quick immediately called Haavik and offered *VG* an interview for a fee of 20,000 Swedish crowns (about £1,800). But first of all he wanted Haavik to send him the material he had published.

VG's article series was no journalistic masterpiece. Yet as we know it was destined to have more impact on the investigation than any other publication.

But the Norwegian adventure was still a way into the future – it was July 1995 and everyone was still fully occupied with the double murder in Appojaure. Quick didn't tell anyone about the articles and stashed them away for a rainy day.

On 1 August 1995 a philatelist was going through an old issue of the Post Office's magazine for stamp collectors, *Nyhets-Posten*, when, in an article on a stamp auction held in Malmö in 1990, he saw a photograph of the audience in which a man with steel-rimmed glasses bore an uncanny resemblance to the serial killer Thomas Quick. Instead of contacting the police – probably because they wouldn't be willing to pay for the tip-off – he called *Expressen*'s news hotline and was put through to the 'Quick expert', Pelle Tagesson.

Tagesson went to visit him in his home and was able to confirm for himself that the man in the photo was indeed Quick.

'Are there any murders that could be connected with the serial killer Thomas Quick's mysterious trip to Skåne?' Tagesson mused. The obvious association was the murder of Helén.

On 20 March 1989 eleven-year-old Helén Nilsson put on her pink jacket and left the dinner table, promising her father she would be home no later than seven. She hurried off to meet her friends Sabina and Linda, who were waiting at the discount store in Hörby town centre.

Six days later Helén's body was found in a plastic sack by a mound of stones in Tollarp, some twenty-five kilometres from her home. The medical examiner concluded that Helén had been held captive by a paedophile who had raped and abused her for several days until she had died.

There were several things that went against any attempt to connect the murder of Helén Nilsson with Quick's presence at the stamp auction. For a start, there was a full year between the two events. But there was an even stronger reason not to publish the story: the bald man in the photo wasn't actually Thomas Quick. The mistake should have been confirmed when Quick was shown the photo, and the whole episode passed over without further embarrassment. But it didn't quite work out that way.

'I was shocked when I saw the photo,' Quick commented to *Expressen*. 'I'd repressed the trip but now I remember it.'

Quick even managed to eliminate the problem of the year between the murder of Helén and the auction in Malmö.

'I went to the auction in Malmö in 1989 and again in 1990,' Quick explained.

The serial killer at Säter assured everyone that he had gone to Skåne to commit another murder, and he did not deny that Helén had been his victim.

Expressen ran the story on two consecutive days. On the first day they ran the headline 'I have murdered in Skåne' and, on the second day, 'The image that shows Quick was in Skåne'. Quick is circled in the photo from the stamp auction and the 'mass murderer's' own comments on it can be read in the article.

One reader almost choked on his coffee when he caught sight of the old photo in the newspaper. He recognised 'Thomas Quick' in the photo and phoned *Kvällsposten*, *Expressen*'s biggest competitor in Skåne.

'I don't think Sven-Olof Karlsson will be very happy about being pointed out as a serial killer in *Expressen*,' he said.

The prediction proved to be absolutely accurate. When the philatelist came back from a business trip to Paris and saw that he had been identified by *Expressen* as a serial killer, he hit the roof. He called *Kvällsposten*.

'This is about as wrong as it gets! It's quite incredible that someone can just sit there and make up a story like this without checking the facts. I'm outraged about being called a murderer like this,' said Karlsson to the reporter at *Kvällsposten*.

He intended to sue *Expressen* for defamation and report Pelle Tagesson to the police, he said.

The erroneous accusations were obviously bad enough, but for the investigators it was even more problematic that Thomas Quick had, once again, lied about making a long-distance trip in order to commit a known murder. He had confirmed *Expressen*'s rather unlikely story even though he must have realised that he was not the person in the photo from the stamp auction.

In the year that followed, Quick continued making remarks that suggested he had a part in Helén Nilsson's death. When the police investigated what Quick had been doing at the time of the murder, it emerged that he had been attending regular therapy sessions with the psychologist Birgitta Rindberg, who had been seeing Sture Bergwall off and on at Säter Hospital throughout the 1970s and 1980s.

Prosecutor Christer van der Kwast despatched Ture Nässén and Ann-Helene Gustafsson to Avesta to interview Birgitta Rindberg. The following is from the interrogation report:

> Birgitta Rindberg was asked if on 21 March 1989 Thomas Quick was at Säter Hospital for a personal visit or if they communicated via telephone. Birgitta Rindberg answered that she believes it was most likely a personal visit. She went on to state that if it had been a telephone consultation she would have made a note to this effect and judging by the notes she made in the file, there was a great likelihood that he was there in person.

With this, Rindberg gave Thomas Quick an alibi for the murder of Helén Nilsson. Ann-Helene Gustafsson wasn't satisfied with asking just this one question, however – she suspected Quick's psychologist might have other valuable information for them. And she certainly did:

> She further described how she saw a programme on Thomas Quick, which was called *The Reporters*. Among other things, Thomas Quick was talking about how he had been subjected to sexual abuse by his father.
>
> Birgitta Rindberg stated that this whole matter of sexual abuse by the father does not concur at all with what emerged during the period when he was her patient. What she recognised from his statements in the TV programme was that he didn't like his father. The memory Birgitta Rindberg retains from their therapeutic conversations was that Quick's father was 'the weak one' and his mother 'dominant' in their family.

Rindberg went on to talk about the time in 1974 when Quick called her to say that he was going to commit suicide. She managed to trace the call and was thereby able to save his life.

In retrospect, considering all that she had read about the murders, she found it odd that he had never lightened the load on his heart by talking to her, particularly when he was calling to say goodbye before his death. She had a clear impression that his suicide attempt was a reaction to the difficulties he had in relating to other people.

> Birgitta Rindberg was then asked how she viewed Thomas Quick as her patient in the mid-1970s and 1989. She said quite

> spontaneously that she never saw him as a murderer. She was never afraid of him, and although there was aggression in him, he never had any violent tendencies towards her. The only violence she encountered was the violence he did against himself. Birgitta Rindberg believes that chief physician Mårten Kalling shared her view on Thomas as a patient.

In the interview, Rindberg said that the Thomas Quick she had witnessed in the media was far more articulate and more of an exhibitionist than he was during the period of his therapy with her. Neither she nor Mårten Kalling believed that Quick was credible as a serial killer.

After returning to Stockholm, Ann-Helene Gustafsson typed up the interview and left it in Chief Inspector Stellan Söderman's room.

Gustafsson told me what happened a few days after that. She heard an incensed roar coming from Stellan Söderman's room and then a voice calling for her. There she found Christer van der Kwast, who had just read the interrogation report and was very upset.

'He gave me a real telling-off, shouting at me that I had exceeded my duties,' she said.

According to van der Kwast, she was only supposed to have asked about Quick's therapy session on 21 March 1989. Nothing else!

'I'm not interested in what some bloody psychologist has to say about Thomas Quick,' he roared.

Ann-Helene Gustafsson was shocked. She had done exactly what she was supposed to do: interview a person and then write down what was said.

'It's never happened to me before or since then. I've never been shouted at because of an interview.'

Christer van der Kwast didn't want to accept the interview in its existing form; instead he demanded a new interrogation report be drawn up that was only about Quick's alibi for the murder of Helén Nilsson.

'I refused to rewrite the interview because it was an official record,' says Gustafsson. 'What he was demanding of me was illegal.'

After discussing the problem of forging source material with her chief, she solved the issue by leaving the report as it was, while also writing a short memo with nothing but the alibi for the murder of Helén.

Only this memo was included in the preliminary investigation file. Van der Kwast's requirement of absolute obedience and loyalty, even at the cost of professionalism, stirs up strong feelings in her to this day.

'We're supposed to be objective and pay attention to whatever speaks in favour of someone or against them. It is not our job to censor interviews!'

CONFRONTATION

MEANWHILE, THE INVESTIGATION into Thomas Quick and Johnny Farebrink was ongoing, although Farebrink had not yet been brought in for questioning. There was no urgency about that, the investigators seemed to feel. Farebrink was safely locked up in the C Wing of Hall Prison. But as usual the Quick investigation was full of leaks and it didn't take long before both Pelle Tagesson and Gubb Jan Stigson were aware of suspicions that Farebrink had been Quick's accomplice in Appojaure.

Johnny Farebrink was one of the most violent criminals in Sweden and had been convicted of serious criminal offences on twenty-four occasions. But the murder in Appojaure was about as far from his usual activities as you could get.

'I'm not the type to murder tourists,' he explained to Tagesson. 'Too many other arseholes need their heads blown off.'

The newspaper speculation was causing serious damage to the investigation, as van der Kwast saw it, and this stirred CID into action. Johnny Farebrink was taken to the CID building on Polhemsgatan in Stockholm, where the first interview was held on 9 May 1995.

Farebrink denied the murders in Appojaure and swore that he had never met Thomas Quick. He also said that he had most likely been locked up at the time. However, it was an indisputable fact that he had been released from Tidaholm Prison two weeks before the murders. Farebrink remembered that his then wife, Ingela, had met him when he was released. They had taken a train down to

Stockholm, where they went directly to Bagarmossen to buy drugs. From the interrogation report:

> When they got to the house, Johnny had the recollection that he and Ingela 'hammered themselves with drugs' and then started 'buzzing' both inside the flat and out on the town. He said that as far as he remembers, there was 'an endless buzz' both at home and out, which is how he put it.

It wasn't much of an alibi. And the ex-wife made things worse by explaining that they went their separate ways after arriving in Stockholm.

Johnny Farebrink had no alibi and was therefore under suspicion for the double murder in Appojaure. Quick pointing him out as an accomplice had put him in a very bad position.

Ingela told me that she was done with Johnny Farebrink when the police contacted her. She had a new life, with a job and house in Norrland. A good life. She was unable to give Johnny an alibi, nor did she particularly want to.

It was only later when the police came and started asking questions about Johnny

The question of Farebrink's sexual orientation made Ingela sense something was amiss. Quick had claimed that he and Farebrink 'had been necking in a sauna'.

'That was when I knew something wasn't right,' says Ingela.

The prosecution of Quick and Farebrink was looming into view when Ingela started ruminating on what had really happened during that mad summer of 1984.

On 30 June 1984 Ingela went to Tidaholm to meet her husband, who was being released from prison that day. After a couple of beers on a park bench, Johnny had asked if he could use a toilet in a branch of Pressbyrån, the newsagents, and as he came out he couldn't help but notice a safe that had been left open. No one was watching! Johnny snatched a couple of bundles of bank notes, some 7,000 or 8,000 Swedish crowns.

After the unexpected cash injection, the couple went to Stockholm, where they purchased a sizeable quantity of amphetamines.

Twelve days later the Dutch couple, the Stegehuises, were murdered in Appojaure. But what was Farebrink doing at that time?

'I don't know how, but suddenly I remembered that I'd had a psychosis in Stockholm,' says Ingela.

Ingela was unsure when exactly it happened, she wasn't even sure it had been in 1984. All she knew was that Farebrink had taken her to the accident and emergency department of Söder Hospital.

Johnny Farebrink would be given a life sentence in prison if he was found guilty of the Appojaure murders and Ingela couldn't keep her thoughts to herself.

She called Ture Nässén at CID and told him about the psychosis which might conceivably give Farebrink an alibi for the murders.

Ingela's medical records were requested from Söder Hospital and all they could do was wait. In the meantime, her memories from July 1984 were becoming more and more clear.

'We'd bought quite a large quantity of amphetamines, bloody good stuff. We left the flat one morning to go and see my friend Eva on Krukmakargatan. At Eva's I started getting really jittery, I got psychotic. In the end Johnny called Jerka. "I can't handle Ingela," he said. Jerka came over – he'd borrowed his mum's car. I put up a fight and all three of them could hardly manage to get me in the car. At the hospital they strapped me down on a bed. I was sure the hospital had been taken over by enemies. Johnny, Jerka and Eva tried to push me down on the bed, and a doctor came with a syringe. I knew it was poison. I looked into Eva's eyes. I could see what she was thinking: "She's going to die!" I fought for my life. Then I got a shot of Haldol and I don't remember anything else. When I woke up the next morning Johnny was standing there. He was wearing my kimono. "Hi, Mum! I've been to Värmland. Where have you been?" Then from his pockets he emptied out loads of amphetamines into two big piles that ended up on the hospital bed. A big pile on either side of me. He turned his pockets inside out and then we left the hospital together. Him in the kimono and me in my bloodstained skirt. The love I felt for Johnny when he stood there in the morning . . . I'll never feel love like that again.'

Just in time for lunch on 26 September 1995, the fax machine at Rikskriminalen spat out Ingela's medical file from the Söder Hospital psychiatric clinic. It confirmed the date and Ingela's account on every point.

Well, I'll be damned, Ture Nässén told me he thought at the time. *Johnny Farebrink has an alibi!*

Farebrink was kept locked up in C Wing at Hall Prison with some of the toughest criminals in the land. When the newspapers started writing about his dealings with Thomas Quick he had asked to be 'boxed up': in other words, placed in an isolation cell. He feared for his life if someone should believe the lunatic from Säter who had pointed him out as his accomplice.

Farebrink was shaken to the core by the realisation that he was seriously at risk of receiving a life sentence for the double murder in Lapland. His voluntary isolation also meant that he was cut off from any information about his unexpected alibi in the form of Ingela's file.

Despite his alibi, Farebrink was driven to Säter Hospital on 12 October for a 'confrontational round of questioning' with Thomas Quick. The video recording shows how he and Thomas Quick were placed directly opposite one another, with lawyers at their sides. Christer van der Kwast, Seppo Penttinen, Anna Wikström and Ture Nässén were also present.

The questioning begins with Penttinen asking Quick if the person sitting opposite him is the one who, in his view, had taken part in the events.

'It's Johnny Larsson, yes,' answered Quick without hesitation.

Again Quick described how he and Farebrink got to know each other in Jokkmokk in the 1970s, naming a number of other people whom they had both known.

Farebrink sat in grim silence during Quick's lengthy story, until he had the opportunity to speak.

'I never met you in Jokkmokk. And I don't know who any of those guys are. But all you have to do is check them out. It's very simple!'

What the police didn't tell him was that they had already interviewed the 'guys'.

All the individuals named by Quick who had supposedly seen him with Farebrink had unequivocally declared that they'd never met Farebrink.

Farebrink turned directly to Thomas Quick.

'You say you've met me,' he said with a barely discernible smile. 'So what sort of car was I driving at that time?'

'I don't know,' said Quick abruptly.

'You must have noticed what sort of car I was driving around in?'

'No,' said Quick, even though in several interviews he had claimed that Johnny Farebrink drove a Volkswagen pickup.

Penttinen changed tack and asked Quick to tell them about his meetings with Farebrink at the folk high school.

'How often did you meet, and was it at the school?'

'It must have been . . . on four or five occasions. We usually met in the evening, then we'd have a couple of beers with GP and J in the school sauna and sit there chatting away,' said Quick.

'So you'd have saunas together?'

'Yes, exactly.'

Farebrink shook his head with an expression that revealed precisely what he thought of Thomas Quick.

'First of all I hate saunas. I wouldn't ever choose to go into a sauna because I can't breathe in there!'

Again Farebrink turned to Quick with a sly smile.

'You say I've been in the sauna with you, drinking beer. Can you remember what tattoo I've got on one of my legs?'

'No,' said Quick.

'Oh really? And what about the tattoo on my back?'

'No, not . . .'

'Once you've seen that tattoo on my thigh, you never forget it.

I promise you! If you were my mate you'd know that tattoo. I can promise you that, you wouldn't have forgotten it.'

Ture Nässén was the only one in the room who knew what Farebrink was talking about. In police circles they used to say of Farebrink, 'Here comes the one who's always armed.' On one of his thighs he has a large tattoo of a revolver.

Quick had no idea what tattoos Farebrink had on his back or his thigh, but he seemed to think about it for a long time after the interview. In one letter to Birgitta Ståhle four months later he wrote that Farebrink had motifs from *The Arabian Nights* on his back. These recovered memories, however, were far from accurate. In actual fact Farebrink's back was covered with an image of an electric chair.

Farebrink kept cool and didn't reveal what his tattoos were during the questioning, well aware that this was one of his few trump cards. Yet Anna Wikström seemed more impressed by what Quick had actually got right about Farebrink.

'He describes your personality, your appearance. He's totally confident when he picks you out. I suppose he must have a really good memory if he's so detailed about it,' said Wikström.

'Absolutely, yeah. I mean, it surprises me. It surprises me that he can just sit there saying stuff like this. That's what I don't get,' Farebrink admitted.

He couldn't come up with any feasible explanation as to why Thomas Quick had involved him, a complete stranger, in the investigation. Farebrink didn't know that Quick had described him as a local tradesman driving round Jokkmokk with tools in the back. And he didn't know that it was Seppo Penttinen who had suggested his name to Quick, not the other way round.

Nor did Anna Wikström present matters in this light during the questioning.

'On 23 November [1994] ten names were verbally put forward, that is ten men's names with both first names and surnames. All of these names had some connection to Norrbotten and on that list was the name of Johnny Larsson.'

Seppo Penttinen and Christer van der Kwast knew as well as

Thomas Quick and Claes Borgström did that this statement was inaccurate. But they all pretended otherwise.

Farebrink was more suspicious than impressed about Quick's knowledge of his name.

'My name wasn't Johnny Larsson then! My name was Johnny Farebrink.'

'But I remember the name Johnny Larsson-Auna. Farebrink I don't recall,' Quick interjected.

That was a mistake. Johnny Farebrink got really fired up this time.

'That name Larsson-Auna, where did you snap that one up?'

'From you, of course.'

'From me? You couldn't have done. My name is Farebrink. And Auna is an old family name my dad used.'

Johnny had never used the Auna family name. Not even his old friends and acquaintances knew it. It only existed in local authority records.

Quick went on to describe a friend who lived in a hut in the forest, where he and Johnny visited.

'I especially remember one time,' said Quick. 'I can't help speculating that this might be a sensitive subject for you . . . We had a sexual encounter, you and me. We masturbated each other in the home of that person.'

'Hey! Can I tell you what I think about fucking pigs like you? Can I tell you?' said Johnny.

'You don't have to,' said Quick.

'Are you suggesting that Johnny's homosexual?' asked van der Kwast.

'No, absolutely not,' answered Quick.

'Christ,' moaned Farebrink.

Anna Wikström turned to Farebrink and suggested that he should respond to what Quick had just said.

'No, I can't respond to stupid things like this. I'm not gonna do it. This is so bloody out there, it's bloody mad.'

Johnny pointed at Quick, eyes narrowing into two slits.

'You better get clear about one thing! To come here and accuse me of being a fag, you know . . .'

'I haven't done that,' said Quick.

'Are you some kind of pathological liar or what? Do you believe what you're saying yourself? Do you?'

Following a break in the proceedings, Quick went on to talk in detail about their meeting in Jokkmokk, the journey to Messaure and the murders in Appojaure. After Quick had given his version of events, Anna Wikström turned to Farebrink.

'To begin with, what do you have to say about running into Thomas Quick in a restaurant across from Konsum?'

'Ah! Bullshit. I was never in Jokkmokk that year.'

'That restaurant opposite Konsum in Jokkmokk, do you know it?' asked Wikström.

'No. I know there's a Konsum supermarket. But there's no restaurant there,' answered Farebrink.

Even the investigators knew that the restaurant mentioned by Quick did not exist, which was a fairly significant fault in Quick's story.

'Are you familiar with the name Rune Nilsson?' Wikström prodded.

'No, absolutely not,' said Farebrink.

'Thomas Quick says that you two were meeting some people you'd seen earlier, who were camping by Appojaure.'

'Which people are you talking about?' asked Farebrink. 'I don't know any bloody Dutch people.'

'The comment Thomas makes here, that you had some idea these people had insulted you, what about that?'

'Ah, he's an idiot, that one! Can't you hear he's crazy? What he's saying is just rubbish. He's a pathological liar!'

At this point Quick told the story of Rune Nilsson in Messaure, whom Farebrink had supposedly threatened with a knife before he'd gone to Appojaure to murder the couple. After the murder, he then fetched Nilsson and showed him the massacred bodies in the tent.

'Johnny was showing him that things don't go well for people who don't treat Johnny well,' explained Quick.

'Who the hell is Rune Nilsson?' asked Farebrink.

'He's a person who lives in Messaure,' answered Christer van der Kwast.

'Have you got hold of him? What's Rune Nilsson saying about all this?'

Everyone on the investigation team knew that Rune Nilsson had denied meeting Quick as adamantly as Farebrink.

'I'm the one asking the questions,' said van der Kwast.

The questioning had been going on for almost three hours and Johnny Farebrink was beginning to understand that the situation was serious. He turned to Thomas Quick.

'You've never met me. How the hell can you get me mixed up in this? And these bloody Dutch people . . . Can you tell me how I'm supposed to know them?'

He turned to van der Kwast and put the question to him.

'When did I meet them?'

'I'm the one who asks the questions!'

Ture Nässén told me he was suffering as he listened to the interview. He knew that van der Kwast was tormenting Johnny Farebrink quite unnecessarily and that the whole spectacle was a forgone conclusion. Once again he was ashamed of being a policeman.

At long last van der Kwast seemed to understand that he'd gone too far and the questioning led on to Farebrink's own version of what had happened in July 1984.

'How was Ingela feeling during this period, the month of July?'

'Ingela was pretty run down when I was released. She'd been taking drugs the whole time while I was locked up. She was in a pretty bad state.'

'How did things work out for her, in general?'

'Well, everything was all fucked up.'

'Nothing in particular happened?'

'No, nothing.'

Christer van der Kwast turned to Anna Wikström. It was time to tell the truth.

'Tell them what we've got,' he said.

While we were looking into the various events here, we came across a file that states Ingela was at Söder Hospital.'

She didn't have to say anything else. Farebrink knew exactly what Wikström was talking about. He had been thinking about it for months, but only now did the whole episode clearly come back to him.

'Yeah, oh yeah!' he said. 'She had the psychosis!'

'Mm.'

'That's good, you know,' he continued. 'I remember that.'

Everyone in the room listened solemnly to Johnny Farebrink's account of Ingela's psychosis. It correlated exactly with Ingela's testimony. He hadn't been able to have any contact with Ingela, so there was no doubt about the truth of the story. Their testimony, combined with the file, meant that Johnny Farebrink had a watertight alibi for the Appojaure murders.

THE 'SHALOM INCIDENT'

IN THE SUMMER of 1995 the *Efterlyst* ('Wanted') series on TV3 aired a lengthy report about the unsolved murder of an Israeli citizen.

Yenon Levi was twenty-four years old when he landed at Arlanda Airport on 3 May 1988 for his dream holiday in Sweden. Just over a month later, on Saturday 11 June, he was found murdered on a forest road in Rörshyttan in the region of Dalarna. The body had been severely battered, with two lethal blows to the skull.

Beside the body lay a 118-centimetre-long wooden stick with its bark cleaned off, which the perpetrator had found on the scene. The stick was flecked with splashes of Yenon Levi's blood and was judged to be the murder weapon. However, the police withheld that detail in the television programme.

The medical examiner could not pinpoint the time of death, but estimated it had been between 8 and 10 June 1988. The last documented trace of Yenon Levi had been at Stockholm Central Station the Sunday before, on 5 June. His movements up until he was found on 11 June remained a mystery, despite the police in Avesta assigning considerable resources to interviewing large numbers of people. The police had no idea when or how he had ended up in the region of Dalarna, where he was finally murdered on the isolated forest road. The murder looked as if it would remain unsolved.

Quick's confession to the murder of Yenon Levi started with cryptic allusions to 'the Shalom incident', two weeks after the report on *Wanted*.

On the evening of 19 August Quick called Seppo Penttinen. He was not feeling well. He described how with the help of an accomplice he had murdered Yenon Levi. They had picked him up in Uppsala and driven towards Garpenberg. There, Quick had held on to Levi while the anonymous helper struck him with 'a heavy object from the boot of the car'. The body had been left at the scene, 'lying on its back more than its side and definitely not on its stomach'.

Later, when Penttinen held the first round of questioning about Yenon Levi, Quick's story had changed on a few vital points. For instance, Quick now stated that he had committed the crime on his own.

> I picked him up in the car in Uppsala . . . offered him a lift. We talked a bit in English, I'm not very good at English. But I told him I'm from Falun, I mentioned the copper mine and said I'd really like to show it to him.

Yenon Levi accepted the offer and travelled to Dalarna with Thomas Quick, where they went to a summer cottage outside Heby. Quick surprised Levi with a punch to the stomach and then he delivered 'the killing blow with a stone to the forehead or the head, maybe two blows'.

After the murder, Quick loaded the dead man onto the back seat of his green Volvo 264 and drove down a forest road, where he dumped the corpse. Levi's luggage – a trunk that resembled a 'sailor's sack' – was left beside the body. Quick remembered that Levi had a watch with a leather strap; he thought of taking it, but in the end he didn't remove anything from the scene.

After two hours, Seppo Penttinen stopped the interview with the intention of coming back to it another day.

'But before you can go on, first we have to analyse what you've told me here,' said Penttinen.

Quick's description of the murder was inconsistent with a number of known facts established by the investigation. Though it did tally very closely with the reconstruction shown on *Wanted*.

STEN-OVE MAKES CONTACT

ON TUESDAY 7 NOVEMBER 1995 the *Expressen* reporter Christian Holmén called Ward 36 at Säter Hospital and asked to speak to Thomas Quick.

'Your brother Sten-Ove has written an open letter to you which is going to be published in *Expressen*. We'd like you to read it before it's published,' said Holmén.

A few moments later Quick picked up Sten-Ove's letter from the fax machine in the reception. He took the letter into his room, closed the door and sat down on his bed to read.

> Open Letter to My Brother Thomas Quick
>
> It has now been a few months since my book *Min bror Thomas Quick* was published [. . .] Since the discussion of what I wrote played out in public I am publishing what you are reading now as an open letter. [. . .]
>
> One of the consequences of the book was that I was reunited with my high school sweetheart and recently we were married. My wife has played a great part in helping me change my view of our kinship.
>
> I put distance between us. I pushed you away as a human being. I even said that your childhood was not my childhood, and that your parents were not my parents.
>
> I do not overlook the things you have done. But deeds do not separate brother from brother. [. . .]

You have yourself in various public forums expressed your consternation over my lack of understanding, my distance, my judgement of you. And you may have your justifications for that. But what I hadn't understood was that having you, 'Thomas Quick', as a brother, meant a lifelong struggle for me.

Now I am able to accept that I am in the middle of this struggle, and that this is about trying to keep you in my heart, trying not to lose faith in our kinship, and not to deny that the same blood flows in our veins.

I stand by your side in the struggle against the evil that exists within you.

I still don't understand the reasons and mechanisms behind your actions when you are transformed into a bloodthirsty monster. [. . .]

But you are my brother, and I love you. [. . .]

Sten-Ove

Sture Bergwall told me that he sat with his brother's letter in his hand, trying to understand what was happening. Was this a trick? Was there some ulterior motive? He read the letter again and was convinced of Sten-Ove's sincerity.

It was as if the letter's conciliatory and loving tone had opened a floodgate; his emotions came pouring out. He was overwhelmed by his longing to see his brother again.

The next day, Quick spoke again with Christian Holmén. They agreed that Sten-Ove would come to Säter a few days later. Quick went into his room and noted in his diary:

Of course I am tense and nervous but I have no doubt that me and Sten-Ove will find a way back to each other. This first meeting will be a little strange, in the sense that there's going to be a journalist there. I imagine S-O will come back later and that we will be able to talk in more depth about all the things that have happened, his situation today and mine.

Quick had neither police interviews nor therapy booked in for the next day. No one at Säter Hospital knew what was in the offing, so the reunion of the two brothers was an untarnished promise that brought much happiness to Quick. In his diary he wrote:

> *9/11 1995*
> Sten-Ove and his open letter have obviously dominated my thoughts. I don't know. My situation has changed since the letter and I am faced with difficult decisions. Tomorrow I am seeing Birgitta again, and maybe it will clarify then.

The morning after, Quick told Birgitta Ståhle about his brother's letter. Her reaction was like an unexpected cold shower for Quick. She was very upset and explained that she had to report what had happened to chief physician Erik Kall.

As soon as Kall found out about Quick's contact with his brother, he told Christer van der Kwast, and it was only a matter of time before Seppo Penttinen and Claes Borgström were informed.

In his diary Thomas Quick wrote:

> Seppo called me up and was really upset. I wasn't prepared for Sten-Ove's visit to cause Kwast and Seppo to get so upset.

But what made a meeting between two brothers so problematic?

Quick had talked about the terrible things that Sten-Ove had subjected him to as a child. He had also pointed him out as an accomplice in the murder of Johan Asplund. His immeasurable enthusiasm at the idea of meeting Sten-Ove was damaging to his credibility, in the opinion of Penttinen, van der Kwast and Ståhle.

Thomas Quick listened to their reasoning, saw the sense in what they were saying, but was not prepared to give in. He wrote in his diary:

> I *want* to see Sten-Ove although I am beginning to see that it might not be appropriate. But I can't and will not say no. Seppo suggested that he could be present, which is out of the question

> for me. The easiest thing would be if Kwast were to arrest me, then I wouldn't have to give this a further thought – I can't say no to Sten-Ove.

When Quick's team realised that the meeting looked as if it would go ahead, there was panic back at camp. 'There's a storm about Sten-Ove's visit,' he wrote in his diary. They all tried their hardest to make him cancel the meeting.

> I don't give a shit about Seppo's talk about credibility in terms of a trial for Johan, the credibility is up to him and Kwast!! For God's sake – does no one understand, deep down, how divided I am about the meeting with Sten-Ove!? I *want* to see him and I can understand it may not be appropriate but my will to do it is much stronger than my intellect.

Sunday was the last chance to stop the meeting, and every bit of firepower was concentrated on Quick to make him back off. If not, Sten-Ove's visit had to be stopped by legal means.

Thomas Quick spent the entire Sunday on the telephone with Ståhle, Penttinen, Kall and Borgström. They were unanimous in their view that Quick should voluntarily cancel his meeting with Sten-Ove.

In the end the matter was settled by Erik Kall, who decided to impose a visitation ban on Sten-Ove Bergwall. Quick accepted the decision. In his diary he noted Penttinen's comment: 'We were lucky to dodge that bullet.'

One might wonder why everyone around Thomas Quick should be so terrified about the meeting of the two brothers. It is a reaction that one associates with very secretive cults.

Sture told me later that he had no doubt about what the consequences would have been if the meeting had taken place.

'If me and Sten-Ove had been allowed to meet and talk, I'm sure the Quick era would have come to an end as early as 1995. There wouldn't have been any more police investigations, because if me and Sten-Ove had been allowed to talk, I couldn't have persisted with my lie. Birgitta Ståhle realised that, maybe even Seppo Penttinen. That's why they were willing to do absolutely anything to stop the meeting.'

In the period that followed, Thomas Quick stopped bothering to get out of bed, answered questions monosyllabically and stopped eating.

THE TRIAL IN GÄLLIVARE DISTRICT COURT

JAN OLSSON AND the medical examiner Anders Eriksson were due to make a joint presentation of the forensic findings that matched Quick's description of the murders in Appojaure.

Olsson told me that he had breakfast with Christer van der Kwast at Hotell Dundret in Gällivare on the day that his and the medical examiner's testimony was being presented. Olsson had appeared in a number of trials as an expert, and in this sense it was just another day at the office. Despite that, and even though their joint presentation was close to airtight and would certainly have a profound effect on the outcome of the case, he felt slightly uneasy about his testimony.

After breakfast, Jan Olsson and van der Kwast walked to the district court together in the Arctic cold. Olsson was consumed by his doubts about the murders in Appojaure and he remembers saying, 'That rubbish bag. The upright bag in the tent. Quick couldn't have gone into the tent and done what he said without overturning it.'

Earlier in the trial Thomas Quick had described making his way into the tent through the rip in the canvas, whereupon the whole tent collapsed.

If Christer van der Kwast thought anything at all about what Jan Olsson was saying, he didn't put it in words. Olsson had studied the photographs from inside the tent with a magnifying glass until he could visualise every detail from memory. It wasn't just the upright rubbish bag that disturbed him. The little schnapps glass was even worse.

Inside the tent on the small area of floor between the two murder victims, where Quick had supposedly positioned himself during the attack, stood a tiny schnapps glass of sherry. The glass had not been knocked over.

'It just couldn't be right,' Jan Olsson told me.

He and van der Kwast, both with similarly grim faces, turned left from Storgatan into Lasarettsgatan. They had reached the district court.

Jan Olsson and Anders Eriksson were well rehearsed for their presentation and, using overhead projectors, they demonstrated both the tears in the canvas and the victims' injuries. The presentation was informative and highly convincing. It seemed clear that over the course of the investigation Thomas Quick had accounted for more or less every wound he had inflicted on the couple with the knife.

Sture Bergwall remembered them in the district court.

'Very strong feelings can come up in a courtroom and that's how it was when Jan Olsson and the medical examiner gave their testimony. It was incredibly significant. That I had described the wounds in Appojaure was almost as important a thing as Therese's bone in Ørje.'

Jan Olsson agreed.

'We did a good job, me and Anders Eriksson.'

He was obviously uneasy about the topic of conversation, although he wasn't avoiding any difficult questions. His own view was that the district court in Gällivare was duped, because so many of the circumstances that strongly refuted Quick's account were never brought up in the courtroom. He was thinking of that schnapps glass; he was thinking about some of the curious events at the reconstruction and the fact that the couple's radio was found in Vittangi. He was also thinking about the rubbish bag, which, he felt, showed that Quick didn't have a clue about the crime and what had actually taken place.

'Afterwards, I thought I should have said all this in the courtroom. But then again – and I guess this is an excuse – I was an expert witness who was supposed to answer questions, not draw my own conclusions. I was expecting questions about it from the defence lawyer. But there was total silence there.'

Jan Olsson knew from experience that the defence lawyer will always attack any point of uncertainty in the technical evidence, so Claes Borgström's passivity came as a surprise to him.

Surely he has to ask about this rubbish bag, I thought. 'It's accounted for in the crime scene report. There has to be a lawyer who questions things – it's a necessity,' he added.

Instead, Olsson and Eriksson received a number of appreciative comments after their joint testimony.

I also read in the trial report that Sven Åke Christianson had been lined up to make a statement on Quick's credibility. Claes Borgström asked him if there was any risk that they were dealing with a false confession. Christianson's answer, by way of a summing-up, was that 'nothing had emerged that might lend support to the notion that this was a false confession by Quick'.

Oddly enough, at this very moment a fax arrived at the district court from a forensic psychiatrist – it was a long and detailed letter warning of the risks of false confessions and false memories. The fax was handed over to the chief judge.

Gubb Jan Stigson, the crime reporter and expert on Quick, referred to the moment in his column in *Dala-Demokraten* the following day:

> There was a bit of a palaver while the judge, prosecutor and defence discussed how to handle the letter. At that point Quick stepped in:
>
> 'I don't even think we should look at that. If some quack from Älmhult sends something here, we obviously have to put it in the bin!'
>
> His request was approved!

Apparently there was an outburst of hilarity in the district court at this elegant solution to the ill-fated letter from a 'quack from Älmhult'. Nils Wiklund, the letter-writer, was in fact a senior lecturer in forensic psychiatry from Stockholm who specialised in witness psychology.

Nils Wiklund still has the letter that the district court chose to consign to the wastepaper basket and showed it to me when I visited him. It concludes with the following lines on the warning signs of false confessions, of which the district court should have been more aware:

> 1. Has the patient for a long period of time not had any memory of events which have 'come back to him' in the therapy process? This increases the risk of false memories.
> 2. Are there tape recordings of the conversations that touch upon the memories? If so, any alleged process of influence can be analysed. If not, the therapist may not realise whether the interaction has called up false memories.
> 3. Are the suspicions backed up in other respects by evidence unrelated to the patient's own account (fingerprints, DNA analysis, technical evidence)?
>
> If only the account itself is considered to give credence to the suspicions, the account should be carefully analysed to see whether it could have been fetched from other sources, such as the mass media.
>
> If there is any risk of memories having been produced in the therapeutic process, the account should be subjected to expert scrutiny by a psychologist with university training in witness psychology. [. . .] If therapy-induced memories are used as a foundation for court judgments without any such analysis, there is a risk of miscarriages of justice.
>
> With kind regards
> Nils Wiklund
> Registered psychologist, senior lecturer in forensic psychiatry, specialist in clinical psychology

Unusually, on the last day of the trial the defendant, Thomas Quick, was given the option to present his own 'plea' – a speech to the courtroom, the audience and the press. He stood up and read from six densely written A4 pages.

'In this court we have experienced and been shown a cruelty which, for most of us, is beyond explanation, a crime with the most horrible ingredients,' Thomas Quick began, with a tremor in his voice, obviously close to tears.

Jan Olsson tells me that he listened with a sense of amazement to Quick's grovelling speech to the gallery.

Quick continued: 'What I have to say should not be seen as a defence of the deeds this lunatic has carried out, nor as some sort of quasi-psychologising reasoning about them, or a tearful attempt to look for my own human worth.'

Quick described how growing up in an emotionally cold family home formed him into a murderer. When he spoke of his constant anxiety and death wish as a child, a number of the younger members of the audience started crying.

Jan Olsson twisted awkwardly in his seat and looked in turn from Quick to the weeping listeners and to the chief judge, Roland Åkne.

'"Why does no one tell him to stop?" I thought. It was so unbearably offensive! It was as if the courtroom had been turned into a place of worship.'

When the emotional speech was over, the district court had to adjourn before defence counsel Borgström could make his closing comments.

Claes Borgström agreed with the prosecutor that Quick's guilt had been overwhelmingly shown in the main proceedings and that the only reasonable punishment would be continued psychiatric care.

The court announced its decision on 25 January 1996. Thomas Quick was found guilty of his second and third murders and sentenced to continued psychiatric care.

Accusations have often been made that Seppo Penttinen and others committed gross perjury in the trials of Thomas Quick. Whatever the truth, this will never be legally proven. In any case, any perjury committed at the court hearing in Gällivare has been statute-barred since January 2006.

However, we can say with confidence that there were many facts surrounding the murders in Appojaure that weren't actually presented to the court, and others that were presented in a confusing way.

The only murder weapon that can with certainty be said to have been used against the Stegehuises was their own fillet knife. Despite fifteen interviews with Thomas Quick amounting to some 713 pages of transcripts, he was never able to describe this knife. This was a palpable weakness in his story, but the district court was never told of it.

The district court was greatly influenced by Seppo Penttinen's testimony that the first time he was questioned, Quick 'was able to sketch out a detailed plan of the camping place'. While this was true, Penttinen failed to mention that Quick had put the car and the tent in completely the wrong positions.

Another significant piece of information, according to the verdict, was the women's bicycle that Quick claimed he had stolen outside the Sami Museum in Jokkmokk. A bicycle like this had been stolen at the time of the murder, as the owner confirmed at the trial. But what Quick originally said during questioning with Seppo Penttinen was that he had stolen a men's bicycle.

Birgitta Ståhle was present at all the murder trials of Thomas Quick. During the proceedings in Gällivare she made extensive notes of what was said, and long excerpts are reproduced in her unpublished book on Thomas Quick. These make it very clear how the court was duped.

> On the second day of court proceedings, statements were made by several parties, including Detective Inspector Seppo Penttinen.
>
> Penttinen has been interviewing Sture since March 1993 and the first interview on the Appojaure murders took place on 23 November 1994.
>
> Penttinen described his experience of the questioning visually. It was as if Sture experienced a lowered French blind, in which some of the flaps have been opened, and he described a story incoherent in terms of time, before a regression took place to another space and time. Sture changed his body language, felt strong anxiety. Penttinen described the course of events, how

> Sture started to have memories of the murders. Sture's way of describing it was similar to previous cases. He described certain fragments of memory but over the course of the interview the sequence of events 'opened up' more and more.
>
> The story wasn't coherent from the beginning. Sture himself explained that because of his feelings of anxiety he had to protect his inner self by making things up that bordered on the truth. Then in the following interview he corrected some details he had given earlier.
>
> Yet Quick's memories are, according to Seppo Penttinen, clear and distinct in terms of the central aspects of an event. Other more peripheral aspects, such as journeys to and from a place, are rather unclear in his narrative.
>
> As for the places where these aforementioned events took place, during questioning Quick provided a detailed sketch of the camping place and the road that leads to it. He further described the type of ground on which the tent stood, the existence of a seating area made of logs as well as the distance between the lake, the tent and the couple's car.

Ståhle's statement clearly shows that her and Margit Norell's theories have been guiding lights for the police investigation: the idea that Thomas Quick makes contact with repressed memories by means of regression. Seppo Penttinen can hardly have been unaware that his testimony under oath had given the court an inaccurate impression of Quick's changing story during the course of the investigation. But we will let Ståhle continue with her account, as Penttinen's deception of the court was about to get even worse.

> During questioning on 23 November and 19 December, Quick mentioned that the tent canvas was cut open and that a long rip was created as well as a smaller rip in the place where he had stabbed at the man.
>
> He also gave a description of the couple and their positions in the tent. Information given was entirely spontaneous. According to Penttinen there was no divergence between what

Quick stated earlier in the investigation and what he has stated here in the main proceedings.

The first interview with Thomas Quick runs to eighty-one pages. Practically all the information Quick gives on this occasion is factually flawed and a number of items are later changed, often more than once, before he reaches his 'final story'. I have italicised all the factual errors from the first interview:

- He steals a *gentlemen's bicycle.*
- Using this, he *cycles* to Appojaure.
- The weather is *fair.*
- He acts on his *own.*
- The picnic spot is situated *between 500 metres and one kilometre* from the main road.
- *In the middle of the open area is a brown four-man tent.*
- The tent is positioned *closest to the lake.*
- A car is parked *next to the forest* facing *away from the lake.*
- *A couple of clothes-lines have been strung up at the scene.*
- Quick kills the couple with *ten to twelve stabs.*
- The murder weapon is a *large hunting knife with a broad blade.*
- *The woman comes out of the tent opening.*
- Her *upper body is naked.*
- She has *long brown hair* and is *about twenty-seven years old.*
- The woman lies on the *right side* inside the tent, the man on the *left.*
- Quick *cuts open one of the long sides of the tent* after the murder.
- He sees that they have their *rucksacks in the tent.*
- The inside of the car *is in disarray.*
- Quick *does not steal anything from the tent* and after the murder *cycles back to Jokkmokk.*
- He does *not* know Johnny Farebrink.
- *He is unsure* if he actually committed the murders.
- *He never spoke to the couple.*

SETBACKS

THE COURT'S VERDICT on the Appojaure murders kicked up a hornets' nest of interest in Quick in Norway, and in the spring of 1996 a number of Norwegian journalists began conferring with the talkative serial killer.

Quick's Norwegian adventure had in fact started in November 1994, when Quick told Penttinen about a murder that had apparently taken place between 1988 and 1990. The victim was a young boy of Slavic appearance with an oversized bicycle. Quick mentioned a place known as Lindesberg and the first name 'Dusjunka'. A month later the boy's name had changed to 'Dusjka' and was being associated with a place called 'Mysa' in Norway.

In December 1994, Penttinen made an enquiry to the Norwegian police about any missing boys who might correspond with the description provided by Quick. The answer, as we already know, was that no one answering to the name of 'Dusjunka' or 'Dusjka' had gone missing, but two African teenage boys had disappeared from a refugee centre in 1989. The journalist Svein Arne Haavik at *Verdens Gang* picked up the story and in July 1995 published further information on the two boys in his series of articles on Thomas Quick – the same articles that tipped off Quick about the disappearance of nine-year-old Therese Johannesen in July 1988.

The Norwegian murder victims – Therese Johannesen and the two African refugees – were added to the police investigation via Quick's 'therapy board', a noticeboard on which symbolic images were pinned up and used in the sessions with Birgitta Ståhle. The board was regularly photographed by Seppo Penttinen, who tried to interpret the more or less codified messages.

By February 1996 the therapy board had been supplemented with a map of Norway and photographs of a blonde nine-year-old girl and two teenage boys of an African appearance. Penttinen understood perfectly well what Quick was trying to say.

After the successful conviction in Gällivare, reconstructions were held in Norway and Sweden so that Thomas Quick could show how the abduction and killing of the two boys had occurred. The Norwegian reconstructions were extensively covered by the media, which did not escape the attention of anyone involved – least of all Quick.

'We bought the newspapers for him, after all. He wanted *Verdens Gang* and *Dagbladet*,' the inspector Ture Nässén told us.

On 23 April 1996, while Quick and his entourage were in Norway, *Dagbladet* ran an article that included photos of the two boys. The investigators were aware of the fact that Quick read the newspapers on a daily basis, but seemed unconcerned about any information he might pick up in this way.

When they stayed the night at Ullevål Hospital in Oslo, one of the nurses gave Quick a baseball cap with ULLEVÅL SYKEHUS printed on it and they established a friendly connection. Quick was careless enough to show the nurse the article in *Dagbladet* where the two boys had been circled in a group photograph. Quick pointed at them and said, 'I recognise those two.' The nurse called the Norwegian police and reported what had happened.

In other words it was a nurse who wasn't even involved in the case, rather than the investigators, who brought the fact that Quick had seen a photograph of the 'Norway boys' to the Norwegian police's attention.

Before they disappeared, both of Quick's alleged victims had had to provide fingerprints in Norway, and while digging for the boys' remains in a place known as Guldsmedshyttan it was decided, just to cover every possibility, to run these fingerprints against the Swedish register. Hits were received for both.

One of the boys had gone to Stockholm, where he had sought political asylum at police headquarters in Kungsholmen. He had been 'dacted', which meant that he had been photographed and had provided fingerprints for electronic dactyloscope scanning and storage. The police were immediately able to call up the name, social security number and registered address of the alleged murder victim, and before long Detective Inspector Ture Nässén was having a chat with him.

'He was a nice chap, living in Fisksätra with his wife and children, but he'd never met Thomas Quick,' Nässén told me.

Quick's second victim had found his way to Ljungby, from where he went on to Canada. Nässén reached him there by telephone, and after that his conclusion about Quick was clear cut: 'The whole thing was just fiction! They said they left Norway because they knew they wouldn't get political asylum there.'

Without describing what they had learned, the police prepared a photo line-up of African boys, in which both of the 'disappeared' boys were included. This was carried out in the police van in Guldsmedshyttan while the forensic technicians were outside the vehicle, digging for the two murder victims who had already been found alive.

Penttinen began by reminding Quick of the number of times he had changed his story.

'If one looks overall at the information you have given in various interviews and the reconstructions we have done, one could end up with a bit of a confused impression.'

After that, Penttinen asked if Quick had seen any photographs of the boys, but he answered very firmly that he had not.

At this point, Christer van der Kwast broke into the interview. This time he put pressure on Quick, but he started cautiously.

'We've had a third-party tip-off from Ullevål Hospital suggesting that you've seen photographs of these boys in the newspaper,' said van der Kwast.

'What newspaper would that have been?' asked Quick, mystified.

Quick wouldn't accept that he had seen a photo, and he wasn't willing to change his story that he had murdered the two boys.

'I'm not quite sure you described what happened to boy number two, the one who was taken from Mysen alive,' van der Kwast probed. 'Where did he die?'

'He died here,' Quick answered without any hesitation.

Quick's message was clear - the boys had been moved from Oslo to Guldsmedshyttan and the police would find the bodies if they just kept digging.

When Quick was shown the photo line-up he carefully scrutinised the faces of the twelve dark-skinned boys.

'There's an immediate recognition of one of the faces,' said Quick, and put his right index finger on photo number five, a youth with a thin face, sad eyes and a half-open mouth.

'And possibly . . .' he said with a certain hesitation, pointing at number ten.

'Five and ten,' Penttinen concluded. 'With number five you said there was an immediate recognition.'

Christer van der Kwast excused himself and said they needed to 'check something', upon which Penttinen turned off the tape recorder and they left the van. Five minutes later they were back again, and it was left to van der Kwast to deliver the crushing blow.

'So I have to tell you something about the person you've just pointed out, number five,' he said in his most authoritative voice.

Quick hummed by way of an answer and realised the news would not be good.

'According to the information I have, this person is still alive,' said van der Kwast. 'This has been possible to confirm using fingerprints.'

Quick had no comment to make on this but he seemed shocked.

Ture Nässén was present throughout the process of the interrogations, the photo line-up and the eventual discovery of Quick's African victims, living in Sweden and Canada respectively.

'There was panic in the ranks! I had to drive Quick back to Säter Hospital. It's a mystery to me that the investigation could go on after the African boys.'

Yet even after this, Christer van der Kwast and Seppo Penttinen kept ignoring the troubling fact that Quick was obtaining his information about murders from newspapers and journalists. But events at Guldsmedshyttan had finally convinced Ture Nässén that Quick was just a big talker.

'The outcome for me was that I resigned from the investigation. I was done with Thomas Quick.'

Alongside the Norwegian investigations, the work on the Yenon Levi murder was still ongoing and it was decided to stage a reconstruction in May 1996.

In the original Levi investigation, extensive forensic work had been done, and this material was carefully examined by Jan Olsson and the forensic technician Östen Eliasson.

Based on this they outlined a likely sequence of events for the murder. However, after their experiences of the reconstructions in Appojaure and the trial in Gällivare, Olsson suspected that Seppo Penttinen was leaking information to Quick. For this reason, he and Eliasson decided not to let Penttinen have access to their findings prior to the reconstruction.

At eleven in the morning on 20 May 1996, Thomas Quick arrived at the alleged crime scene to describe how he had murdered Yenon Levi. The usual entourage – police, nurses from Säter, the therapist, the memory expert, the prosecutor and the forensic technicians – were all assembled.

Thomas Quick, wearing a black baseball cap, blue-and-white bomber jacket, black trousers and trainers, was not in the mood. Before the reconstruction began, he asked to say a few words to everyone. There was no mistaking that he was emotionally fraught.

'To begin with I want to say this to Chief Prosecutor Christer van der Kwast – I am still both upset and frustrated over what happened last Monday. I just don't understand why Christer van der Kwast can't come to me directly and apologise!'

It was only a week since the humiliating fiasco in Guldsmedshyttan. Subsequently Quick had been taken to Stockholm with Birgitta Ståhle for a meeting with van der Kwast. They met late in the evening at the CID offices and van der Kwast took a hard line, demanding tangible evidence and 'mature behaviour' from Quick, who was not used to this kind of treatment. He left the meeting in a fury.

Now there was a golden opportunity to confront van der Kwast before the whole investigation team.

'I don't know if it will make me clam up today. I hope it doesn't. But if it doesn't it's no thanks to Christer van der Kwast. I don't think he's admitted his responsibility in this whole matter. He hasn't found a sense of perspective on himself as a person, and he mixes personal things with his professional role, I feel. I'm really disappointed and I hope Christer van der Kwast has the courage to apologise to me personally.'

Seppo Penttinen ignored the embarrassing prelude and tried to get Quick in a good mood by telling him how they had managed to satisfy all the demands Quick had made prior to the reconstruction. It had not been an easy task to get hold of a Mazda Kombi 929L, an unusual model which Quick had used occasionally in 1988, although it was owned by Patrik Olofsson's mother. Now it stood there, parked.

Also in position was a dummy representing Yenon Levi, and a second person who would be playing the part of Quick's accomplice.

'The basic set-up is that Thomas came into contact with Yenon Levi with an accomplice whom he's named, Patrik Olofsson, and they travelled from Uppsala in this car to the house in Ölsta,' explained Penttinen.

Quick's irritation had passed, and he seemed to be working up an interest in the murder reconstruction.

The reconstruction was intended to start on the road, from which they would drive into the front yard. Everything had to be exactly as it was when they arrived from Uppsala with Yenon Levi.

The accomplice was represented by Anna Wikström, while Seppo Penttinen initially stepped in as Yenon Levi. Later, when Yenon Levi was being beaten to death, Penttinen would be replaced by the dummy.

When Quick, Patrik and Yenon Levi were by the car, Quick said that they had to tear off a shirt sleeve, so that he could bind Penttinen/Levi's hands. It was important to re-create the situation and environment exactly; only then would he remember the events in the right way. All those who were involved knew this very well – it was an integral part of Sven Åke Christianson's well-established interrogation methodology – hence, a shirt sleeve was torn off and handed to Quick.

Admittedly the knot was not very good, but Penttinen sat in the passenger seat with his hands tied while Quick told Anna Wikström to get into the back seat and close the door.

'And from that side you show us you have a knife.'

'OK,' said Wikström/Patrik.

'Can you wind down the window so the camera picks it up better?' said Quick, concerned that the knife threat to Yenon Levi should be clear in the video. 'In the footage while we're moving you should also indicate the knife towards the throat,' he explained to Anna Wikström.

Jan Olsson observed what was taking place and made notes on every stage in the sequence of events.

He was struck by how Quick was behaving like a director in a film production. Sometimes Quick went to one side, lit a cigarette and had a think, then went back to directing his fellow actors in the scene.

It took an incredibly long time to get everything exactly as Quick wanted, but finally a driver who was standing in for Quick, as he was not trusted to take the wheel himself, got into position. The short drive from the road to the house was enacted and filmed with satisfactory results.

During the six rounds of questioning which Quick had been put through about the Levi murder, he had given several different accounts of it and how it took place: with one or two blows of a stone against the skull; by striking a jack against the head, or a crowbar, or a short-handled axe, etc. The place where Yenon Levi was murdered had also varied from one interview to another. Sometimes it took place by the holiday cottage in Ölsta, sometimes in Rörshyttan at the scene where the body was found.

A certain tension was apparent at the reconstruction, as everyone waited to see where Quick would kill Levi this time and with what murder weapon. Jan Olsson was absolutely certain about the place where Levi had been beaten to death and with what murder weapon.

However, he was keeping quiet about this. Quick had to reveal the information himself without any help.

Quick seemed to be struggling with these questions. He told Seppo Penttinen that he wanted 'to feel the jack', while, at the same time, he was trying to build up a sense of himself talking English to Yenon Levi. Despite his poor grasp of English, a certain level of communication was going on.

'I tell him things like "Take it cool", things like that,' he explained.

Seppo Penttinen had fetched the jack so that Quick could try it out, but Quick wasn't happy with what he saw. It was definitely the wrong type of jack, he said, it was supposed to be one of those jacks with 'antennas' on it.

'Does no one here know about jacks?' asked Quick.

'I'm not much good on them,' admitted Penttinen.

A long discussion on jack design broke out between the two men, who both felt they were not particularly well informed on the subject. At long last the reconstruction was resumed.

Quick pulled out his knife substitute and 'cut' Yenon Levi's hands free, and then a rapid and wild chase followed. Levi fled towards the road but was caught by Quick. Levi fell and hurt his shoulder, Quick explained.

His accomplice held on to Levi while Quick gave him 'a couple of nasty blows' and scratched his chest with the tip of his knife.

'And here there's a violent kick to his stomach, and a few more kicks and – the way I'm feeling it – against his side from here. I'd like to have a feel of a stone and the jack,' said Quick, unsure to the last of the murder weapon.

First, Quick wanted to demonstrate how terribly hard he kicked Levi. The dummy lying on the ground weighed about eighty kilos.

Quick summoned all his strength and kicked the dummy as hard as he could. Because of its weight it didn't move an inch; it was like kicking a wall.

'Ouch, ouch, ouch,' Quick moaned, hopping about on one leg, clutching his painful foot.

A number of the onlookers turned away discreetly or suddenly pretended to be interested in other things.

By the time Quick had pulled himself together he had come to a decision about the murder weapon.

'It's a stone. It's a stone,' he said, demonstrating how, using a stone, he struck Levi, who was already unconscious, on the temple.

After this, Quick wanted to take a break and Penttinen took the chance to go over to Jan Olsson.

'How is Thomas doing?'

Olsson muttered something evasive by way of an answer. So far his worst fears had been confirmed, which made him even more concerned that he should not reveal whether Quick's story was consistent with the forensic evidence.

Now Quick had to demonstrate how he and his accomplice had placed Levi's bloody corpse on the back seat, where it was hidden under a blanket.

'What sort of condition did you feel Levi was in?' asked Penttinen.

'Dead,' Quick answered abruptly.

'Did he make any sort of sound or anything?'

'No,' said Quick.

It was the wrong answer, and Penttinen made it clear that he didn't accept this version of Levi being killed here.

'What you've said about him vomiting and coughing up blood, how can you see that?'

Quick had not mentioned this during the reconstruction, but he rapidly fell into line.

'It happened during the car journey.'

The fact that Levi was not dead when he was loaded onto the back seat was greatly significant in terms of the second part of the reconstruction, which would be taking place in the forested area outside Rörshyttan, where Levi's corpse was found.

'So how was his condition then?' asked Penttinen.

'I'll tell you when we get there,' answered Quick cryptically.

Soon a convoy of vehicles was driving along B-road 762 from Rörshyttan towards Ängnäs. A few hundred metres before the end of the road, at a turning area in the middle of the forest, the group stopped. Thomas Quick was now going to demonstrate how he took Yenon Levi's life.

At long last the Mazda estate with Levi in the back seat was parked in the right position and Quick struggled to get the dummy out. With his accomplice he pulled it out by tugging at the blanket on which it was lying. Finally he succeeded.

'So here he's not dead,' said Quick.

In other words, his earlier claim that Levi had already been dead at the holiday cottage in Ölsta no longer applied. Helped by Anna Wikström, Quick got the dummy up on its legs. It was very heavy and after a few seconds Quick simply let it fall, explaining that this was how it had happened. His legs gave way beneath him.

The crowbar was taken from the boot of the car and Quick demonstrated in slow motion how the blow hit the back of Yenon Levi's head.

'I'm sensing that it's a crowbar,' said Quick.

'Are you unsure about that?' asked Seppo.

'I'm unsure about it.'

'What could it be, if it wasn't a crowbar?'

'It could be a spade, but I'm leaning more towards the crowbar.'

Quick sat in the car, which had been moved forward, and tried to 'feel' where he left the body. After a good deal of reasoning, he put the body in the wrong place, facing the wrong way and incorrectly positioned. Quick said that he slid his hand under Levi's jumper and felt the hair on his stomach and chest.

Yenon Levi didn't have any hair whatsoever on his chest, Jan Olsson thought. He made a note in his pad but kept a straight face and didn't show what he was thinking.

The most important find the police had made on the scene in 1988 was a pair of glasses that the murderer had most likely dropped there. Quick hadn't mentioned anything about any glasses. Tests had shown that they didn't belong to Quick and, quite simply, they didn't fit into the story.

Anna Wikström had taken over the role of Yenon Levi and when she was about to lie down, Quick suggested that she should remove her glasses.

The reconstruction continued, but as they were nearing the end, Penttinen asked, 'Did you want to say anything else, Thomas?'

'No.'

'I've been thinking about something you said. Why did you comment on the glasses? You said they were lying here. I mean they are lying there. Did something occur to you and was there something you were thinking about, or anything else?' Penttinen asked.

'Well, they were lying there . . . I don't know why I said it.'

'Are you having difficulties talking about it?'

'No.'

'Was he wearing glasses?'

'No, I don't think so.'

'What made you react to the glasses in particular?'

'I had a feeling when I saw the glasses on him that they were there to one side, but I don't know anything about it,' Quick concluded.

Penttinen's dogged interest in Quick's comment on the glasses worn by the stand-in was not an especially subtle signal. During future questioning Quick would claim that they were bought at a petrol station to disguise Patrik, his sixteen-year-old accomplice.

The spectacles in question had a calibration of +4 dioptres and were therefore intended to correct severe long-sightedness. Why they would have chosen such strong lenses for Patrik when he had perfect vision was never explained. Nor did anyone think to ask. The spectacles were estimated to be about ten years old when they were found, which would have meant that they were purchased when Patrik was six years old. Another peculiarity was the assurance of the sales agent that the model had never been on sale at petrol stations.

As the day drew to a close, Jan Olsson became convinced that the reconstruction they had just carried out would be the end of the entire Quick investigation.

'I was absolutely certain that it had been clarified: Quick had not committed this murder. It was obvious.'

Olsson knew that Quick had pointed out the wrong location for the murder and the wrong murder weapon. Yenon Levi's body had ended up in the wrong place and Quick had also failed to report that the body was searched and the pockets emptied of their contents. The technicians had secured an imprint from one of Yenon Levi's shoes, which not only proved that he was alive but had in fact been fighting so desperately for his life that clumps of grass were torn out of the ground.

All in all, the evidence at the scene suggested that the murder had taken place at the end of a series of events that the murderer would surely be able to describe. Instead, point by point, Quick's story directly contradicted the evidence that had been found. Quick's story was simply untrue, Olsson believed.

When the reconstruction was over, Claes Borgström asked Jan Olsson for a lift to Stockholm.

'I tried to speak to Borgström in the car about the reconstruction and how it showed that Quick had not done it and that none of it had been correct.'

But Borgström answered evasively. Instead he talked about a large sailing yacht he'd just bought. It was a subject he often also discussed with his client, although Quick was uninterested and had no knowledge of sailing and boats.

So what really happened to Yenon Levi?

Two and a half years after the murder, on 10 January 1991, an assistant at the police unit in Borlänge responsible for cases involving foreign nationals made an interesting observation. She believed that a pair of spectacles in a passport photograph were suspiciously similar to the glasses which, as she remembered, had been found by Yenon Levi's body.

The spectacles and the passport photo were sent to the National Laboratory of Forensic Science SKL for analysis. In its statement, SKL wrote that 'there was a high probability' that the spectacles at the murder scene were the same as those in the passport photograph. It was a very firm conclusion, the second strongest indicator on SKL's nine-point scale.

An optical company, Hoya-Optikslip AB, carried out an advanced investigation which showed that the spectacles in the passport photograph had the same strength as those found on the murder scene – in other words, +4.

The passport photograph with the spectacles from the murder scene was of a man we can call Ben Ali, at the time a fifty-year-old of North African origin, who was already in a jail cell in Falun, conveniently enough. He had just been sentenced to a five-year prison term for assault, incitement to grievous bodily harm, criminal threats and theft.

By threats and coercion, Ben Ali had managed to force an acquaintance to slash his girlfriend's face with a knife. The woman's twelve-year-old daughter had witnessed her mother having her face cut to pieces in the brutal attack. The artery on the right side of her throat had been severed and the woman had only just survived. The attacker described how Ben Ali had also asked him to cut out one of the woman's eyes, which he had refused to do.

As a result of the findings at the SKL laboratories, Ben Ali could be connected to the murder scene. Judging by the crimes he had been convicted of, he had shown himself capable of doing violent harm to other people, and even of killing them. Yet it remained to be seen how he might have made contact with Yenon Levi, and perhaps more importantly whether there was a motive.

Among the old investigation material was a tip-off that had been sent to Avesta police barely two weeks after the murder. The anonymous message was carefully handwritten and the short text covered a whole page of A4 paper:

> To the murder investigators
>
> At the Central Station is a group of Arabs with a strong hatred of Jews (they celebrate Hitler).
>
> These Arabs have a connection to Borlänge (among other things a photo company). It would not surprise me if this was a revenge killing, maybe Levy travelled with them from Stockholm.
>
> A far-fetched thought?

A Swedish girlfriend who was questioned described how Ben Ali used to go to the Central Station in Stockholm to look for young Arab men who would work for him. The work consisted of going round knocking on doors in country districts such as Dalarna, the north of Sweden and Norway, selling paintings to the elderly. Often the men worked in pairs, and while one asked to use the telephone or the toilet, the other took the chance to steal valuables from inside.

Many of the young Arabs who had worked for Ben Ali stated during questioning that they had been picked up at the Central Station and promised work, and even Swedish women. Several of the men had lodged with different women in Dalarna.

The investigation confirmed that a large number of young Arab men had worked for Ben Ali between 1986 and 1988. A couple of his female friends claimed during questioning that they had met Yenon Levi in Ben Ali's flat in the summer of 1988.

'I've seen that guy. I remember that nose,' said one of the women when the police showed her a photo of Levi.

According to the woman he had been sitting on the sofa with Ben Ali, watching television.

In early June Ben Ali had been to Stockholm to pick up two young Moroccans, Mohammed and Rashid. As soon as they came to Borlänge they left, and when they came back a few days later, one of them had been wearing a second-hand jacket which he'd not had before. It was red, white and blue and looked exactly like Yenon Levi's missing jacket.

A station inspector at Stockholm Central was the last confirmed witness who saw Yenon Levi alive. He made a statement soon after the murder in 1988: Yenon Levi had been sitting in the waiting area with some Arabic-speaking people. Levi had asked him in English about the train to Mora-Falun.

Another station inspector identified Ben Ali from photographs. He claimed to be '100 per cent certain' that Ben Ali used to come to Stockholm Central, where he sought out other foreigners and pretended to be looking for someone he knew.

Yenon Levi's family came from the Yemen, he had a distinct Arab appearance and spoke Arabic. He could, therefore, easily be mistaken for an Arab, although in actual fact he was an Israeli Jew and had served as a sergeant in the Israeli Army during the war in Lebanon.

Bearing in mind Ben Ali's well-known hatred of Jews, Yenon Levi may have been in danger if it had emerged while they were together that he was really an Israeli Jew.

Ben Ali was arraigned as a suspect in the murder of Yenon Levi but was never formally charged. After he had served his sentence in Sweden he was deported.

In the spring of 1996 the Quick investigation was in its most intensive phase. In addition to questioning, reconstructions and crime scene reconnaissances for the Yenon Levi case and the missing 'Norway boys', Quick was being ferried round Drammen and Ørje Forest as a part of the investigation into the murder of Therese Johannesen. It was during this time that Quick described how he had chopped Therese's body into small pieces and submerged them in a boggy pond in the forest.

On 28 May a huge group assembled at the police station in Ørje: Norwegian National Criminal Police (Kripos), investigators into the Therese case, local police from Ørje, forensic personnel, biologists, a professor of anatomy, dog handlers, cadaver dogs, Norwegian fire fighters, frogmen and members of Norwegian civil defence units. The Swedish investigation was represented by Seppo Penttinen and Anna Wikström, who kept a record of the macabre and costly operation.

On that first day, the pumps were turned on at the edge of Ringentjärnen (Circle Pond). A small army toiled with the various stages of the process. As the water was extracted it passed through a sieve which was carefully monitored, frogmen examined the bottom of the pond, cadaver dogs prowled the area, and the edges of the bog and pond were checked. Wikström noted in her log:

> Shaken glances pass again and again between Seppo and the signatory below the same slightly panicked thought: has he given us correct information?

By the fine-meshed sieve where Therese's body parts were expected to turn up stood Professor Per Holck, the anatomical expert advising the investigation. He had brought the skeleton of a child of Therese's age with him to Ørje in order to show the investigators what they would be looking for.

The work at the pond continued in long shifts, seven days a week, in pouring rain. The absence of any tangible evidence began to worry Wikström and Penttinen early on. In meetings with their Norwegian colleagues they checked their notes from the reconnaissance trips. A sense of doubt was apparent in Wikström's log entries:

> Obviously there are continuous thoughts about TQ's way of expressing himself, his credibility, etc . . . how are we supposed to evaluate this??
>
> Oh . . . if one only had an answer (Saida . . .) [. . .]
>
> Understand that this is difficult to process, I even find it difficult myself to accept that we have to 'stand in line for TQ' but the goal is to give the families an answer. TQ will not be going anywhere anyway.

The agonised notes are interspersed with cheerful descriptions of fun and games between the Norwegian and Swedish colleagues. The log was concluded after eight days, when Wikström and Penttinen temporarily had to return to Sweden for further investigations into the Yenon Levi case.

By this time, Wikström was suffering enormous anxiety about what the consequences would be if no tangible evidence were found after the enormous ordeal of going through the contents of the pond. She quotes a line from Karin Boye, the Swedish poet: 'Yes, there is goal and meaning in our journey – but it's the path that is the labour's worth.'

> The signatory below has to content herself with this, irrespective of the end result.
>
> Seppo and the same signatory have planned the escape route, destination unknown, possibly we will first pass through Säter

[. . .] we find ourselves in a game of 'high stakes', luckily our neighbours do not have a national debt.

This log is hereby concluded on Tuesday, 4 June 1996.

Anna Wikström, Det. Insp.

The work of draining the pond continued from 28 May to 17 July 1996 at a cost of several million crowns, without any evidence being found.

THE QUICK COMMISSION BREAKS DOWN

DESPITE THE DEBACLE of the first reconstruction of the Yenon Levi murder, the investigation kept driving forward and it was with great surprise that Jan Olsson received the news that Quick was participating in a new reconstruction. He tried to explain to me how extraordinary this decision was.

'To repeat a reconstruction is unheard of – you just don't do it. Why would you?'

Ahead of this second reconstruction, Seppo Penttinen had had access to the forensic technicians' crime report for some six months, and this was the period in which he'd been questioning Quick.

Under these circumstances the reconstruction went considerably better for Quick, but his story was still inconsistent on many key points with statements made by the medical examiners and forensic technicians. Christer van der Kwast called a meeting to iron out the problems.

Olsson described it to me: 'It was in the evening at CID and everyone who was involved was there – the medical examiner Anders Eriksson, the investigators from Falun and Stockholm, Christer van der Kwast and me. In that meeting I sensed from the very start that van der Kwast had a different tone.'

Previously Olsson had felt he had the full support of van der Kwast and Penttinen, despite earlier in the investigation having expressed some doubts about Quick's credibility.

'They often said they appreciated my approach, they said it was good that I questioned things. They said I was an asset to the investigation team,' Olsson explained to me.

But he was about to find out that there were limits to van der Kwast's tolerance.

In the meeting at CID, Christer van der Kwast expressed his dissatisfaction with how the medical examiners' report was formulated. Among other things it had been stated quite clearly in writing that most of the explanations given by Thomas Quick during the investigation did not match Yenon Levi's injuries. Nor had Quick provided any credible explanation of a number of the deadly injuries inflicted on Levi. The report was signed by the assistant physician and certified by her chief, Anders Eriksson.

'Christer van der Kwast demanded that Anders Eriksson, who was the chief examiner and a professor at Umeå, should change the report,' Olsson told me.

As head of the department and a professor, Anders Eriksson had the authority to reject the report and write another one, and Jan Olsson was surprised that Eriksson succumbed to van der Kwast's wishes.

Having solved the problem of the medical examiner's report so conveniently, Christer van der Kwast got to grips with the forensic investigation, which in his view fell short in many respects.

'Kwast came at me with a similar attitude. It was almost like a cross-examination in some sort of law court. I realised that he was intending to force this through to prosecution. And then I said to him, "But how are you going to get past the glasses?" And then it all came to an end, and he wouldn't carry on.'

Olsson's apparently innocuous question to van der Kwast was seen as a declaration of war, which would have consequences.

'I've never experienced a prosecutor trying to influence technical experts in that way,' says Olsson.

The suggestion that there was a modified forensic report of Yenon Levi's injuries had circulated in Quick mythology for several years, but despite attempts by journalists and lawyers the original report had never been found either in the preliminary investigation material or at the National Board of Forensic Medicine in Umeå. For this reason I was therefore a little sceptical about Jan Olsson's description of the meeting at CID – that the prosecutor would press the medical examiner to change a scientific report in such a blatant way.

On 23 September 2008 I visited one of the investigators in the Levi case, retired Chief Detective Inspector Lennart Jarlheim, at his home in Avesta. Jarlheim received me on the glass sun porch which he'd built himself. Since retiring from the criminal division of Avesta police, he told me, he'd been busier than ever. He was renovating his children's houses, working in their companies, constantly keeping busy with practical tasks and enjoying life more than ever.

'Oh, so you're interested in Quick,' he said with a wry smile that could have been interpreted in a number of ways. 'You're not the first to come here on that mission,' he added, lighting his freshly prepared pipe and leaning back in his chair.

Jarlheim was the chief investigator at Avesta police when CID came knocking on their door in the autumn of 1995 to let them know that a patient at Säter had confessed to the murder of Levi.

Lennart Jarlheim and his colleague Willy Hammar started a thorough investigation into Thomas Quick's life and social connections at the time of the murder, but it was not long before they discovered that this was an investigation with its own set of rules.

'Usually it's like this: a police district is in charge of its own case and it can request back-up from CID, but in this instance it was the other way round. We had little influence over what should or shouldn't be done.'

Jarlheim and Hammar were extremely surprised when Christer van der Kwast, in his capacity as the head of the investigation, prohibited them from questioning an ex-girlfriend of Quick's alleged accomplice. Lennart Jarlheim also wanted a search warrant for a storage unit in which Quick's belongings were kept, where there might be letters, diaries and other evidence. Van der Kwast put a stop to that, as well as the proposed forensic examination of properties where Quick had previously lived.

Lennart Jarlheim and his colleagues took the view that there were two other likely suspects in the Levi case: 'The Spectacle Man' Ben Ali and a well-known murderer who had been observed in the area at the time of Levi's death. Christer van der Kwast stopped them from investigating these lines of enquiry further.

'The way I saw it was that Christer van der Kwast, Seppo Penttinen and Anna Wikström were completely fixed on Thomas Quick and all they wanted was to bring him to prosecution, even though so very little spoke in favour of Thomas Quick being the guilty party,' said Jarlheim.

He was frustrated about being prevented from conducting as rigorous an investigation as possible. Now he understood the decision of Ture Nässén at CID to resign.

'Me and Willy Hammar also questioned our ongoing participation in the Quick investigation. There was nothing that suggested TQ was guilty of the murder of Levi. Nothing!'

Desplte this, Hammar and Jarlheim stayed on out of loyalty and followed the orders of the head of the investigation, Christer van der Kwast.

The sun was setting on Jarlheim's glass porch and I was just about to take my leave when he got up and disappeared into an adjoining room, returning with a heavy cardboard box.

'You can take this with you. I've been waiting for the right opportunity and I think now is probably the time,' he said, putting down the box on the floor in front of me.

I thanked him, this decent detective inspector, picked up the box and went to my hotel, where I eagerly opened it and looked through its contents.

It was the investigation material from the Yenon Levi case, the African asylum-seeking boys and other relevant matters from the time when Jarlheim was working in the investigation team.

At the top of the pile was the medical examiner's report on Yenon Levi – the one that Olsson had claimed van der Kwast had demanded should be redrafted. It was dated 17 November 1996 and signed by assistant physician Christina Ekström and Professor Anders Eriksson.

On its opening page someone had written in ballpoint pen: 'Working copy. Incorrect according to Kwast, to be revised.'

Another two versions of the statement were in the box, the last copy signed by Anders Eriksson alone.

Now that I had the much sought-after statement in my hand it wasn't difficult finding the passages that prosecutor van der Kwast had perceived as 'incorrect'.

The medical examiner Christina Ekström had checked the forensic findings against information provided by Quick during questioning. By way of a conclusion she wrote, 'In his description of the sequence of events Quick has left many different versions which in many instances are contradictory.'

One troubling circumstance for the investigators was that Yenon Levi had a very special type of injury in the form of a fracture on the right side of his pelvis in the so-called ilium bone. According to this first report, Quick's various explanations could not explain this deadly injury.

Seppo Penttinen had personally gone to see Christina Ekström to try and convince her that Quick was capable of causing the damage to the ilium with a kick or stamping. 'Just think how big Quick's feet are,' Penttinen had said. But Ekström stuck to her conclusion that the injury could only be explained by a fall from a great height, a traffic accident or similar.

I contacted an independent medical examiner who confirmed that the injury to Yenon Levi's ilium bone was unique. It was deadly in its own right and could only have been caused by high-impact violence, most likely through being hit by a car.

Anders Eriksson solved the prosecutor's problem by ignoring about 90 per cent of the information that Christina Ekström had used as the basis for her report. In the final version of the report, attention was given only to what Quick had described in his second reconstruction and the interviews that followed.

The three reports I now had before me suggested very persuasively that Jan Olsson's description of the meeting at CID had been accurate.

*

'But how are you going to get past the glasses?' Jan Olsson had asked Christer van der Kwast.

It was a rhetorical question. There was no way of getting past the glasses.

Despite the fact that Olsson was in charge of forensics in the Levi case, van der Kwast sent Anna Wikström to Avesta to pick up the glasses.

They were handed over to SKL – the state forensic institute – with an enquiry about any possible new methods that might lead to a different conclusion.

However, SKL kept to their earlier assessment that there were 'compelling reasons to suggest that' the spectacles at the murder scene were identical to those worn by Ben Ali in his passport photograph. This was backed up by the investigation carried out by the optical company Hoya-Optikslip AB.

Christer van der Kwast took the decision that he would ignore the detailed investigation conducted by forensic engineers. Instead, he turned to the technical division at Stockholm police, whose conclusions were quite different. In other words, a report from a cooperative policeman, who relied on the expert judgement of an ordinary optician's store on Hantverkargatan in Stockholm (also known for giving discounts to police officers who bought their glasses there), ended up overriding the scientific examination carried out at SKL.

When the Quick Commission was set up at the end of 1995 there was a sincere desire, using scientific methods and the best available investigators, to bring some clarity to the unfathomable Thomas Quick and his murder confessions.

By spring 1997 these ambitious plans had gone awry. A couple of police officers from CID openly said that they did not believe Quick. One person had resigned, experts had been shut out of the investigation and two camps had formed in CID. As the head of investigations, Superintendent Sten Lindström was responsible for personnel and the resource-draining Quick investigation was a significant problem for him.

During the first meeting of the Commission, the matter of Seppo Penttinen's exclusive access to Quick had been brought up. No adjustments had been agreed. On one occasion Lindström had asked whether further thought should be given to the matter.

'No, damn it! No one but Penttinen can interrogate Quick,' van der Kwast had answered.

And so it continued. There had also been suggestions that all interviews with Quick should be analysed. Detective Superintendent Paul Johansson, who was later put in charge of the Psychological Profiling Group and was considered the finest witness testimony analyst in the force, was available to scrutinise all the interviews that had been held in the investigation.

Such far-reaching measures obviously needed to be authorised, which was up to the head of the investigation. Johansson began looking through the interview transcripts, but no authorisation was forthcoming from van der Kwast and eventually the project was abandoned.

However, Paul Johansson did have time to read through the investigation into the Yenon Levi murder. When I got hold of him he was unwilling to make any kind of general statement on the Quick investigation because he hadn't familiarised himself with all the material. But he did have a clear position on the interviews he had read.

'I believe that the investigation shows that Quick had no idea how the murder [of Yenon Levi] happened.'

Johansson was extremely surprised when he read that the court had found Quick guilty as charged.

'Nothing in the verdict matches what Quick was saying in the early stages of the investigation. He changed his story every time. But then once he was given access to the investigation material he was able to talk about it. To me it seems odd that the court should have found him guilty.'

Jan Olsson, who was Paul Johansson's predecessor as the head of the Psychological Profiling Group, wrote a letter to the head of the investigation on 16 February 1997, giving his opinion on the matter.

> To Christer van der Kwast
>
> In my work in the investigation to determine whether Quick murdered Levi, my focus has been to look into this together with colleagues as objectively as possible. [. . .]
>
> Obviously I am aware that the prosecutor makes the final judgement, but I cannot ignore my sense of justice, which has always guided me in my work. For this reason I am deeply shocked to hear that proceedings may be brought against Quick, thus indirectly freeing the person who committed the murder.

The letter continued with a run-through of a number of technical and forensic circumstances that had convinced Olsson that Quick was not guilty of the murder and had no knowledge of it. Olsson did not believe there was anything in Quick's statement to back up the suggestion that he was actually there when Levi was murdered, even though in the investigation he had come close to describing the actual events.

Olsson provided a plausible explanation for this:

> I have taken note of Quick's intense gaze, which is primarily fixed on the interrogation leader, and I am convinced that he has great sensitivity when it comes to interpreting the tone of voice, glances and mood of those around him.

Christer van der Kwast read the letter, filed it and never replied to Jan Olsson.

Despite setbacks which consistently argued against prosecuting Thomas Quick, van der Kwast was determined to bring the investigation to a guilty verdict.

THE LEVI TRIAL

THE TREATMENT REGIME offered to Thomas Quick was the same as always – high levels of benzodiazepine and therapeutic conversations with Birgitta Ståhle three times a week. Quick's patient notes from this period are so alarming that it seems unbelievable that no one should have intervened to help him deal with his terrible dependence on narcotics.

On 19 November 1996 staff found Quick in the music room, where he had tried to hang himself from a belt fixed to a radiator. He was naked and drenched in sweat and switching between different personalities. Next to him, he had left a note: 'I don't want to be Nana because I am Simon.' In the end, care assistants managed to give him more Xanax and Diazepam suppositories.

A week later, Quick woke in the middle of the night with a powerful feeling of anxiety, was 'slipping in and out of different personalities (Ellington among others). Spoke English and all sorts of dialects. After about two hours Thomas came back to reality however, with the help of staff and medication.'

Of this period Birgitta Ståhle wrote:

> Despite this difficult and very heavy existential condition, the psychotherapeutic work is progressing. Hopefully a decision will be made on prosecution concerning Rörshyttan [Levi] before Christmas so that Thomas can enjoy a period of well-earned rest.

But the prosecution was taking its time and Quick's condition deteriorated further after the New Year. Notes in the file constantly speak of severe anxiety, suicidal thoughts and deep lethargy. All afflictions were treated with still more benzodiazepines. One note in the file from 28 January 1997 gives a typical impression of Quick's condition:

> Thomas regressed during the therapy session in the morning with severe anxiety attacks and cramps. Nursing staff had to hold him down and give him two 10 mg Diazepam suppositories. After an hour somewhat better. He was often checked up on. Slept about an hour after lunch. At 14.00 he got up, quickly deteriorated with marked despair and anxiety. Was given Xanax, 1 mg, 2 tablets, a little improvement after about 45 minutes, although exhausted and listless. At about 19.00 Dr Erik Kall prescribed Heminevrin, 300 mg, 3 tablets for the night and supervision as Thomas was having active suicidal thoughts. In the evening he was under the influence of medication but he was capable of controlling himself and listening to music and having normal conversations with the nursing staff. However, at about 18.00 he had another breakdown with heavy weeping and despair. He was given more Xanax, 1 mg, 2 tablets, and with support from the nursing staff he was brought back to his senses. He took 3 capsules of Heminevrin, 300 mg, at 20.50. Slept until 01.00 at night. Woke with a headache. Took 2 paracetamol tablets, supplemented with Voltaren, 50 mg, and 1 Xanax, 1 mg, after about an hour. Goes back to sleep at about 03.00 and woke at 07.00. This morning after therapy he had difficulties walking and moving. His body is not doing what he tells it to do. He was given 2 Xanax, 1 mg. After about an hour he felt better again, he lay on the bed resting. During the doctor's rounds the decision was made to maintain suicide watch until further notice.

At the beginning of April 1997 Christer van der Kwast brought legal proceedings for the murder of Yenon Levi and Quick's condition deteriorated further. The medication was increased even more – he was now being injected with benzodiazepines. On 13 April the chief physician, Jon Gunnlaugsson, ordered an injection of Diazepam, 20 mg, and Quick was 'placed on capsule Heminevrin, 300 mg, 2 x 4, and tablet Rohypnol, 1 mg, 2, for the night'. Despite this heavy medication Quick slept only an hour and a half that night. A care assistant wrote in the file: 'Now in the morning he is more or less catatonic. He trembles, sweats and has difficulties talking.'

At 08.45 a doctor came to give Quick an injection of Diazepam, 20 mg, 'which had no marked effect'. At 10.30 he came back to administer another injection. 'After about half an hour the enormous tension was released.' The doctor prescribed an increase in Quick's intake of the very strong drug Heminevrin to 3 x 4 capsules, as well as another injection at night.

Just before the trial Thomas Quick received a number of death threats. Hedemora District Court therefore decided that the main proceedings would take place in the police station in Falun.

On the first day, 5 May 1997, several family members of Quick's victims were among the spectators in the courtroom. Johan Asplund's parents doubted Quick and wanted to see for themselves how his trials were conducted. Olle Högbom's father, Ruben, was there for the same reason.

'He says that he is driven to confess out of a sense of moral obligation to the families. If that's the case he should tell us where Johan is, give us some evidence. Instead he just plants new seeds of doubt,' Björn Asplund commented to *Expressen* the following day.

Also in attendance was Detective Inspector Lennart Jarlheim, helping van der Kwast keep order among all the maps, the photographs, the murder weapon and other evidence. Jarlheim had put together the preliminary investigation report himself and knew it inside out. Jarlheim was surprised that a prosecution had been brought at all. In his opinion there was not enough evidence to establish guilt.

Because of a lack of technical evidence to connect Quick to the crime, the evidence comprised statements he had made during the investigation, as well as his confession. Quick's different identities also played a part in the trial. When questioned about his ability to communicate with Yenon Levi in his poor English, Quick came up with an unexpected answer: 'I turned into Cliff and he speaks excellent English.'

In his testimony, Seppo Penttinen described how the investigation had been run: 'Thomas Quick changed his story as the investigation proceeded. These changes have come about without any coercion. In other words Thomas Quick cannot have become aware of "errors" by investigators persistently repeating the same question or asking whether he was really sure about his version of events.' The district court placed great emphasis on Penttinen's positive evaluation of the quality of his own interviews.

But when I actually read the interviews, an entirely different picture emerged.

In their first interview sessions, Quick had claimed that he met Yenon Levi in Uppsala and that Levi wanted to accompany him to Falun. However, Penttinen knew that Levi had gone missing in Stockholm. How Quick's erroneous statement was corrected is a blatant example of how Penttinen was constantly interpreting and commenting upon Quick's psychological signals. This psychological reasoning could not hide the fact that in reality Penttinen was telling Quick that his answers were wrong.

PENTTINEN: Are you 100 per cent certain that you met Yenon Levi in Uppsala?

TQ: Yes.

PENTTINEN: No doubt at all?

TQ: No.

PENTTINEN: Well, I have to read your reaction here again. When I asked you in that way you reacted in a manner that I interpret as a sort of doubt in your method of expressing yourself, your facial expression gives me that impression.

TQ: Hmm.

PENTTINEN: This is a very important question if you've been telling me for a long time now that the meeting took place in Uppsala and then somehow you signal that there could be some doubt about it.

A few pages later in the interview Quick changed his mind and said that he had met Levi in Stockholm. In this laborious way the investigation was dragged forward, one detail after another modified so that Quick's story didn't depart too much from known facts.

Christer van der Kwast also couldn't resist giving Quick a helping hand. In the first two interviews Quick had stated that Levi's bag was left on the scene. Yet in the third interview Quick was again asked what had happened to the bag. He answered that it had been left by the body. This answer was not accepted and van der Kwast came back to the question a little later:

KWAST: Again, what happened to those things?
TQ: They're by the body.

Next, Quick explained where the body had been left, and wrongly stated that it could not be seen from the road. Van der Kwast took this opportunity to ask again about the bag:

KWAST: And the bag, then? That large bag?
TQ: Yes.
KWAST: Where was that?
QUICK: It was behind him.

Despite Quick's clear statement, van der Kwast didn't give up. The question was too important and therefore he asked it a fourth time:

KWAST: What about when you leave the scene? What happens to the bag?
TQ: It's left there.
KWAST: Well, right there, you see, we have a problem. In fact this bag has never been found.

In the next interview Quick described how the bag was removed from the scene. The district court was unaware and remained unaware of these circumstances. Lennart Jarlheim places much of the responsibility for this on Quick's defence lawyer.

'The trial was an absolute farce! Claes Borgström didn't ask a single critical question in the whole trial. It was so clear that all they wanted was to make sure TQ was found guilty,' he said.

Nor did the proceedings in the district court convince Johan Asplund's parents. Quite the opposite: they added further fuel to the fire.

'The entire trial was a piece of theatre directed by Quick,' Björn Asplund commented in *Expressen* on 8 May.

The chief judge and jurors in Hedemora District Court didn't share the Asplunds' opinion. Thomas Quick was unanimously found guilty of the murder of Yenon Levi. In its verdict, the district court wrote that it had been 'established by the testimony of Seppo Penttinen that the questioning has been conducted in an exemplary way without any leading questions or insistent repetitions'.

Claes Borgström commented on the Asplunds' dubious reaction in the same *Expressen* article, in which he admitted that their feelings about Thomas Quick's credibility were understandable.

'But the crucial question is: Where has he got the information from, how does he know all these details?' said Borgström.

The reporter Pelle Tagesson let a few well-chosen quotes from Christer van der Kwast's closing argument round off the debate: 'He leaves us with a concrete and accurate picture, far removed from any guesswork [. . .] What more could one ask for? This must be viewed as probable beyond any reasonable doubt.'

TO ØRJE FOREST!

A FEW WEEKS LATER, a fax came through to Ward 36 at Säter Hospital from the Department of Psychology at Stockholm University addressed for the attention of Thomas Quick. The front sheet, with a personal message from the sender to the recipient, was slowly fed out. A seven-page document followed, under the heading 'Guidelines for the reconnaissance of the crime scene by Thomas Quick in Norway on 11 June in connection with the disappearance of Therese Johannesen in 1988'.

A year had gone by since the Norwegian fiasco with the fruitless inspections and the equally fruitless draining of the lake, and now eyebrows were being raised here and there over the fact that Quick was once again being driven to Ørje Forest to lead them to the location of Therese's body.

The renewed hopes of the investigators were based on the fact that Christer van der Kwast had paid for the services of a private dog handler and cadaver dog which had been taken to Ørje Forest to search a large wooded area at the end of May 1997. The result was staggering.

Earlier the police had concentrated on the immediate surroundings of the small lake known as Ringen, but the search had now been expanded to cover several square kilometres and divided into areas designated as 'Skumpen' (the Bump), 'Torget' (the Square) and 'Kal Sten' (Bare Rock). The dog had reacted to the presence of human remains in all three places. After this breakthrough all they had to do was loosen Quick's psychological barriers so that he could lead them to where he had hidden Therese's body. Sven Åke Christianson had been given carte blanche to create the optimum conditions for Quick to remember and find the 'courage' to make it all the way to Therese's grave.

The pages juddering out of the fax machine now were the results of Christianson's intellectual labour. That I was able to see them at all was the result of an improbable discovery.

Sture Bergwall is like a squirrel and over the years he has gathered an impressive number of documents which are kept in storage in the basement at Säter Hospital. Every time he visited his storage space he brought up astonishing material that provided new insights into the investigations. One day he told me in an excited voice that he had found this fax.

The document is too long to be reproduced here in its entirety, but it's also too unbelievable to be summarised in a credible way. Instead, what follows are some excerpts from Christianson's guiding principles, which were very broad in scope. First there were some instructions that some might have interpreted as an insult to the investigators:

> In order for the reconnaissance and identification of the place/places where Therese lies buried to take place in an optimal [way] two basic conditions must be observed:
>
> 1) Thomas Quick's (TQ) approach: 'I can do this, I might not be able to do this, we'll see.' [. . .]
>
> 2) We should endeavour to make the inspection as simple as possible. We should leave Säter Hospital and go to the hiding place in Norway. TQ should lead us there and we should in principle only function as a support to him (perhaps just make him feel less lonely in the process).

The small details are also of great importance in creating optimal conditions:

> Carefully prepare clothes, provisions and other equipment. To bring on the journey: coffee, water/drinks, sandwiches, chocolate biscuits (sweets) and cigarettes.

To help the investigators understand better, Christianson wrote a 'feasible sequence of events on the day of TQ's reconnaissance':

> Departure from Säter Hospital by car as early as possible in the morning. Ask TQ to step inside the car. 'We're leaving now.' TQ's attitude: Let this happen now, and he goes and sits in the car and we depart without any decisions being taken or talk of what lies ahead. [. . .]
>
> A Walkman can be brought as a means of relaxation.
>
> Once we have passed the Norwegian border we should start activating TQ. 'We're passing the Norwegian border. Hello! Wake up!' Ask TQ to remove his Walkman.

On the way to the 'hiding place' Christianson was in favour of Quick choosing the route himself, without any leading questions. If he directed them to the right when Seppo Penttinen knew it should be left, he should not be corrected.

> When TQ says: 'Stop the car, we're getting out', it is important to do so, and to respect that it is TQ who is in charge of the car stopping or reversing.

Christianson imagined that Quick, once they started moving forward on foot, might 'break into a sweat, feel anxious or slow his steps'.

> In the event of this some mild coercion may be needed. A physical push of a gentle kind. This is the decisive stage of making one's body cross the threshold of anxiety. Seppo or Anna could give him a little shove.

Christianson recommended that Quick should have unlimited access to narcotics-strength medications, and he reminded the investigators not to forget the very strongest of these:

> Medicines Xanol (?) in doses decided by TQ. Also a medical readiness if TQ finds he is capable of showing us the hiding place, for instance Heminivrin (?) if his reaction is too strong.

Professor Christianson's recommendations about 'Xanol' and 'Heminivrin' do not seem to be based on any pharmacological knowledge (both Xanax and Heminevrin are misspelt) but rather seem to be Quick's own preferences.

'I'd probably told him they weren't to fuss about the Xanax. I wanted to have as much as I wanted,' said Sture. 'I mean, Heminevrin is a very strong drug that has a very rapid effect. It's pretty much like knocking back a quarter-bottle of schnapps. A nurse here at Säter told me recently that I used to sing to her when she gave me Heminevrin. It's exactly like being drunk.'

Christianson added that all conditions that could disturb TQ's concentration and focus on the place where Therese lay buried must be eliminated. Police questions about the event or sequence of events at the time of the murder were to be saved for a later date. On the day of the reconnaissance, on 11 June, the only priority was to find where the corpse had been hidden.

One of the disruptive elements Christianson worried about most was the intrusion of journalists and he advocated extreme measures to keep them at bay:

> Evade media monitoring. Close off the whole area, including aerial surveillance. Any awareness of the presence of the media will adversely affect concentration.

Unlike other reconstructions with Quick, this inspection in Ørje Forest was not recorded on video, which was in accordance with Sven Åke Christianson's guidelines.

'If possible we shouldn't film TQ as he makes his way to his hiding place,' the professor wrote. 'It will disturb his focus on Therese.'

In Christianson's imagined sequence of events, Quick was now approaching his hiding place:

> If TQ comes this far, he should be able to say, 'Now I open this grave' or 'Can you open it . . . Pick that up, give me a moment to feel.'

Christianson realised that it would be annoying not to be able to open the grave once they had reached it. Therefore he suggested the following:

> Certain tools may be required if the ground has hardened, for instance something to turn the ground, a metal spit, a smaller spade or similar.
>
> [. . .]
>
> If TQ actually goes all the way to a hiding place (grave) he should be given the opportunity to take a short moment in private. Allow TQ the chance to open the hiding place himself or assign this to someone else (if he wants this) and then TQ should have the chance to physically touch a piece of bone, for instance a rib bone. It is important that we respect this desire and he should not be made to feel any shame about it.
>
> Nor should we ask him why.

In his book *I huvudet på en seriemördare* ('In the Mind of a Serial Killer'), Christianson suggested that retained body parts help the serial killer 'relive the aspect of lust in the attack' and 'create intimacy and give sexual excitation'.

According to Christianson, body parts might be 'used as stimulants for masturbation or Satanic symbols'.

In view of these possible scenarios, the suggestion that Ørje Forest should be sealed off, including aerial surveillance, seemed like reasonable measures.

But the reconstruction didn't play itself out as Christianson had imagined.

*

On the morning of 11 June the expedition set off for Norway. Quick was travelling in a minibus with his nurses and Birgitta Ståhle, so that he wouldn't feel any pressure from the investigators. Anna Wikström, Sven Åke Christianson and Seppo Penttinen were in a car behind them. At first, Christianson's guidelines were followed scrupulously. The medicines had been brought, as had coffee, sandwiches and sweets. Wikström kept continuous notes on what was happening.

> A short pause was made halfway there, when all partook of coffee and sandwiches. By 12.00 we were approaching Örje Forest and the vehicles entered the so-called 'Ringen area'.

The reconstruction began at 13.20 and various passengers switched places in the vehicles. Travelling in the CID minibus were Quick, Borgström, Ståhle, Penttinen, Christianson, Wikström, a sound technician and driver called Håkon Grøttland from Drammen police.

Progress was slow, with a stop by the pond that had been drained the preceding summer. The convoy moved on and passed another bog on the left-hand side. 'Thomas Quick shied away abruptly from this by looking to the right,' noted Wikström.

The police minibus drove along the narrow lanes of this vast forest and Quick reacted with anxiety at the sight of a ridge. After various manoeuvres they stopped and Quick uttered the words, 'Yes, we're here now.'

> At 14.00 we had a coffee break in the so-called 'Skumpen'. At this point Thomas Quick wandered about 50 metres away from the car towards the rock formation and was given his coffee while sitting in the road. Thomas Quick cried desperately in his loneliness and maintained a dialogue with himself. Exactly what Thomas was saying wasn't clear to the undersigned but my sense of it was that he was speculating in the sense that he has arrived at the place and it may possibly be 'the time'.

Quick wandered around in deep anxiety. He appealed for help from the therapist.

> In connection with this, Thomas Quick clearly cried out his anxiety, 'Nomis, come and help me!' Thomas Quick's calls echoed loudly across the landscape. Nomis is the name Simon backwards. The name Simon is a frequently recurring theme in Thomas Quick's therapy world.

'At 14.25 we left this place of anxiety,' noted Wikström, and the journey continued a kilometre or so to a rock formation which Quick wanted to climb. There he started 'an anxiety game' which seemed to be about exchanging a few words with his alleged accomplice, Patrik. He carried on into the forest, where he smelt and tasted the bark of a tree, then lay down in a foetal position. 'Powerful anxiety came to the fore in Thomas Quick and care assistants intervened,' according to the report.

Afterwards Quick revealed that he had been between only twenty and twenty-five metres from a hiding place.

The police minibus drove on to 'Torget', a place Quick claimed he recognised very well. He told Penttinen about 'some of the cutting activities'. Repeatedly he called out the words 'five intestines'. The significance of this was left to the interpretation of the spectators. Suddenly Quick rushed up a slope towards a drop, then he fell at the steepest part and smacked his cheek and nose against a boulder.

> Thomas Quick remained lying down in a powerful fit of anxiety and told us during this anxiety attack after he had calmed himself down somewhat about what he has hidden in the different places. At 16.30 he said, when he woke from his fall and the shock of it, 'Now I'm close.' Then he spoke in an anxious voice about place one, i.e. the first place we went in the reconstruction, where one can find the torso and ribs. In place number two, i.e. at the edge of the rock with a gravel and sand pit, the head of Therese can be found. Further in place three, where we are now, Therese's thigh bones, feet and arms should be found. He mentioned: 'I have cut off her feet.'

Quick was informed that Norwegian police had found a tree 'with markings carved on the trunk'. This was destined to be one of the stronger items of evidence weighing in against Quick. However, he went on to say that he was 'slightly unsure where the tree is'.

He was also informed that a cadaver dog had reacted to the area and was asked to make a last attempt to approach one of his hiding places. 'Thomas Quick took note of this, a clear reaction was seen, but he didn't have much strength left,' wrote Wikström.

Quick told them that Therese's hand should be 'nearby' and made an unsuccessful attempt to go to the place. 'He fell into deep anxiety and cried uncontrollably some 10–15 metres from the team.'

After five and a half hours in Ørje Forest, the group begin their retreat for Säter, without having had occasion to use either the metal spit or the spade.

After the second reconstruction in Ørje Forest, an extensive search of the terrain was carried out. In the places where Quick had stated that Therese's head, torso, ribs, arms and hands were hidden, nothing at all was found.

When this was reported to him, Quick changed his story again. He said that he had returned to the area the following year and removed Therese's remains from the scene. Quick was told that a cadaver dog had reacted to the area. Quick said that perhaps some smaller pieces of the body had been left behind.

Professor Per Holck, who had been the investigation's anatomical expert during the process of draining the pond, returned to work in Ørje Forest with renewed energy. In October and November 1997 he collected a very large number of samples from the areas pointed out by Quick or picked out by the cadaver dog.

The samples consisted primarily of charred wood, but among the hundreds of pieces Per Holck believed a few that had been found in old fire sites in 'Torget' were very likely burnt pieces of bone. His judgement was that they were fragments of tubular bone with a hard surface and an inner porous material, scientifically known as *spongiosa*. According to Professor Holck, the transition between the inner porous material and the hard surface of the bone was indicative of human bone. On one of the bone fragments there was a 'growth ridge' that suggested it belonged to a human being aged between five and fifteen.

The alleged bone pieces were sent to one of Holck's colleagues in Germany, Professor Richard Helmer, who confirmed that in all probability these came from a child.

The bone fragment with the growth ridge was so badly charred that no DNA could be extracted from it; nor could it be established in any other way that it came from Therese. Despite this, the discovery of the bone was felt to be the greatest triumph of the Quick investigation.

As soon as the news reached Gubb Jan Stigson's ears, on 14 November, it was served up on the front page of *Dala-Demokraten*:

> QUICK VICTIM FOUND
>
> The investigation has made a breakthrough
>
> This discovery means that the investigators, for the first time in the five-year history of the Quick investigation, have been able to follow Quick's fragmentary confession right through to the actual remains of his victim.
>
> In other words, this is the breakthrough the investigators, Quick and perhaps most importantly the doubters have needed for so long.

It is easy to understand the triumph of the investigators and 'Quick believers' at the discovery of the bone. Equally it was a setback for the doubters. The bone fragment seemed, in retrospect, one of the greatest mysteries of the Quick investigation.

It also became a very real problem for me. Everything in the investigation consistently showed that Quick lacked any knowledge of Therese and the location of her body. So how could one explain the discovery of the burnt bone fragments in a place where Quick claimed he had incinerated Therese?

If it really was a human bone at all.

A TIGHT-KNIT TEAM

FOR TWO DAYS the chief judges of Hedemora District Court, Lennart Furufors and Mats Friberg, had listened to the testimonies of Therese's mother, Inger-Lise Johannesen, members of the Norwegian police and Thomas Quick. It had emerged that Quick had taken sixteen-year-old Patrik Olofsson with him to Norway, and that he had participated in the abduction and murder of Therese. According to Quick, Patrik had raped Therese at a viewpoint on the way to Ørje Forest.

After hearing this, the judges called Christer van der Kwast and Claes Borgström to ask why Patrik had not been summoned. Van der Kwast and Borgström firmly dismissed any such possibility, and Lennart Furufors seemed willing to leave it at that.

Notably, neither van der Kwast nor Borgström had ever been interested in questioning any of Quick's alleged witnesses or accomplices in a court of law.

Johnny Farebrink, who according to Quick had been his driver and accomplice in the murder in Appojaure, was not prosecuted or allowed to testify – even though he wanted to appear, not least because he was mentioned in the crime description and therefore wanted the chance to clear his name. Not even Rune Nilsson in Messaure, who had allegedly been taken to the murder scene and shown the murdered couple, was called as a witness.

Patrik was also named as an accomplice in the murder of Yenon

Levi, and the district court had expressed a desire to question him. The same thing happened on that occasion – the prosecutor and defence agreed there was no need for it and the matter was dropped.

The individual named by Quick as a witness who was present during the murder of Charles Zelmanovits was, conveniently enough, dead by the time of the trial. But Quick had also pointed out other accomplices in murders for which prosecution had never been brought.

All these people who had supposedly participated in or had knowledge of Quick's murders give rise to an interesting question: how common is it for serial killers to work with an accomplice?

The psychiatric expert of the Pscyhological Profiling Group, Ulf Åsgård, was assigned by CID to investigate the feasibility of Quick's alleged accomplices.

'In order to be able to tackle this I have to know exactly how many accomplices we are talking about,' Åsgård said to Jan Olsson. 'I also have to know exactly what relationship the accomplices had to Quick. And most importantly I have to read the interrogation reports.'

Olsson passed on Åsgård's requirements to van der Kwast and Penttinen, but after conferring with them he had to put the brakes on Åsgård.

'They say it's impossible,' said Olsson.

After collecting available data on collaborations between serial killers from all over the world, Åsgård was nonetheless able to answer the question of how common the occurrence is, generally speaking. He summed up the report he had handed in to the Quick Commission to me like this: 'Quick had five different accomplices and that's a world record, without a doubt. The conclusion to be drawn from this is that it wasn't true, simple as that.'

The damning report was received without comment. No one from the investigation contacted Åsgård.

'In this investigation freethinkers weren't tolerated,' he said. 'Anyone who indulged in that sort of thing was thrown out.'

Ulf Åsgård wasn't given anything else to do by the Quick investigation and he described a strange, icy silence after 'I'd sworn in church', as he put it.

'I'm not suggesting this was a cult, but they had certain cult-like mechanisms; there was no openness to discussion and certain people's authority was raised to a level above what they actually had.'

After Ulf Åsgård had completed this single task, only to find that he was never again contacted by the Quick investigators, he continued examining the verdicts and investigations. He soon became convinced that Quick couldn't possibly be the serial killer he claimed to be.

'Nothing fits with our police experience of perpetrators. The physical evidence is non-existent and our collective understanding of serial killers speaks strongly against Thomas Quick being one himself.'

Sven Åke Christianson's exact role in the Thomas Quick investigation continued to be unclear, but he did have an assignment as a consultant working for the prosecutor. In the Therese trial he had made a statement on Quick's memory functions, which he found to be normal.

There were two aspects to Quick's story that seemed inconsistent: in the initial interviews, his descriptions of Therese and the area of Fjell where she lived were incorrect in every respect. Yet he was still able to recall details about the victim, the environment and the crime which, to a layman, might seem unlikely so many years later.

Christianson solved the problem by explaining to Hedemora District Court that 'traumatic events are well preserved in the memory, but there can be protective mechanisms that subconsciously repress any memories of them', which was a scientific explanation for why Quick sometimes remembered things surprisingly inaccurately and sometimes suspiciously well.

Between his assignments for the Quick investigation, Sven Åke Christianson busied himself giving lectures on his patient, conversation partner and research subject. After his testimony under oath at the Therese trial – but before the trial had come to an end – he lectured to a packed auditorium in Gothenburg on the subject 'How to Understand a Serial Killer'.

The audience was faced with a projected image on a large white screen of Thomas Quick and his twin sister. It is summertime in the photo and the roses in the flower beds by their grandparents' cottage are in full bloom. The twins, wearing their Sunday best – shorts and skirt – are holding hands and smiling at the camera.

'Can we see which of these two children is going to become a serial killer?' Christianson asked rhetorically. 'My view is that a person develops into a serial killer, they aren't born to it. What Quick did to Therese Johannesen is incomprehensible. But we can understand how it came to that. This is the logic of the perpetrator. Crimes are often about acting out thoughts, feelings and memories that cannot be dealt with.'

No one seemed to react to the fact that Christianson was exposing his patient publicly in this way, or that he was showing a photograph of the twin sister, who at this point in time was doing everything she could to keep from being associated with her brother.

The audience was spellbound by Christianson's explanations for all this evil, explanations that closely echoed the object relations theory which was being practised at Säter Hospital.

'Hence we see that the murders are the serial killer's story about his own traumatic experience,' Christianson asserted, using a turn of phrase that could just as well have been spoken by his supervisor, Margit Norell.

The team around Thomas Quick were tightly forged together; everyone shared the same vision of Quick and his guilt and there was a sense of absolute rigidity about their position. In his book *Avancerad förhörs- och intervjumetodik* ('Advanced Interrogation and Interview Methodology') Sven Åke Christianson offers his 'very special thanks' to Margit Norell and Birgitta Ståhle for 'the comprehensive expertise you have contributed'.

There was only one way forward – more investigations and more guilty verdicts.

Quick was found guilty of the murder of Therese. The verdict was thorough and seemed well substantiated. The odd thing about the case was that there were very strong indications that Quick had constructed his story using information obtained from Norwegian newspapers. In addition, the whole story was absurd. He had given incorrect statements on pretty much everything. One mistake after another had been corrected during endless questioning with Penttinen in a process that had been going on for three and a half years.

So how could the verdict seem so well substantiated?

Again I went through the 'evidence' and was able to confirm to myself that most of it was utterly worthless.

The investigators claimed that Quick had carved a symbol into a tree, which was later found as described in Ørje Forest. What Quick had actually said was that there was a tree about as thick as a man's thigh at the pond known as Ringen. He had carved a symbol of a square into this tree. Within this square there was a 'Y' which had been carved on its side. The investigators searched repeatedly for this tree without finding it. At long last a birch tree with some form of damage or marking on it was found, but in an entirely different place in the forest. The mark on the tree bore no resemblance to what Quick had described. Considering the number of years that had passed since Therese's disappearance, the birch must have been extremely spindly in 1988, possibly no more than a few centimetres in diameter, which would seem an odd choice for someone who wanted to carve a symbol into a tree for posterity.

Another piece of evidence was Quick's description of a pile of wooden planks in Fjell, some of which had been scattered by children. In fact the planks turned out to have been delivered in the days after Therese's disappearance.

Quick had described Fjell as a small rural village consisting of single-family homes. He had also said there was a bank or shop there.

In his usual way, Seppo Penttinen had attached importance only to the bank, and he made a great deal of the fact that Quick knew the bank had closed down.

Things continued in this vein until the introduction of what the district court viewed as the most significant piece of evidence in the whole case. From the verdict of the district court:

> However, an absolutely unique circumstance is his statement on Therese's eczema in the crooks of her arms. This had not been known even by the police, and Therese's mother had not mentioned it until she was asked by the police after Thomas Quick had referenced it.

So what was revealed in the investigation material about this matter, which certainly did seem highly important?

At a reconstruction in Fjell on 25 April 1996 Quick had said that he had 'a memory of Therese having scar tissue on the arm and he pointed, when he said this, at his right arm'. He couldn't say anything more about it.

When she disappeared, her mother had detailed all of Therese's physical characteristics on a form. In the box for 'scars and other defining marks' she noted a birth mark on her cheek but nothing about any scars in the crooks of her arms. The Norwegian investigators immediately contacted Therese's mother, who told them that her daughter had atopic dermatitis on the inside of her arms. The condition bothered her less during the summer and she couldn't say whether Therese had had eczema at the time of her disappearance, or scars in the crooks of her arms.

By the next interview, on 9 September 1996, the Norwegians had passed on the information to Seppo Penttinen that Therese had eczema on the insides of her arms, and he brought up the matter with Quick.

> PENTTINEN: In connection with that inspection we did, you offered some information on Therese's appearance. You mentioned among other things that she supposedly had some sort of scars on her arm or arms, I can't quite remember, but anyway in that region of the body.
>
> TQ: Yes.
>
> PENTTINEN: What's your memory of that today?
>
> TQ: Oh, I don't know.
>
> PENTTINEN: Do you remember mentioning it?
>
> TQ: No, I don't.

In other words, Penttinen mentions 'arms' in his question, while Quick had only spoken of a scar on her right arm. He also gives Quick a hint that something to do with Therese's arms could be important.

During questioning on 14 October Penttinen returned again to the matter.

PENTTINEN: I've asked you this before, you mentioned something during this inspection, that you had a memory concerning her arms, some sort of skin condition or similar?

TQ: I never said that . . . a bit inflamed . . .

PENTTINEN: Yes, but you have not described it, like, you haven't said in a concrete way what you mean, you've said you have a memory about this.

TQ: Yes.

PENTTINEN: If you can develop it a bit that would be good.

TQ: It's a, a flare-up. I'm hoping we mean the same thing by flare-up.

PENTTINEN: Is it something that passes or is it something lasting, something that she, is it an illness or some kind of natural flare-up just for the moment or . . .

TQ: I don't know, I don't know. It could be she had just flared up for the moment. It could also be something she has, because it's a clear, a clear flare-up.

PENTTINEN: You're indicating the upper side of your arm now?

TQ: Yes.

PENTTINEN: Is that where you see it or is it over the whole arm or is it both arms?

TQ: It's on both arms, yeah.

PENTTINEN: It's on both arms?

TQ: Yes.

PENTTINEN: Is it round the whole arm or is it, is it something that's patchy or . . .

TQ: It's a patchy mark. A patchy redness, I mean.

Even though Quick was given the information about 'arms' and 'skin condition' he couldn't come up with the right answer. But his answer was 'right enough' for the investigators, in their testimonies in the courtroom, to be able to turn Quick's extremely vague but increasingly correct description of eczema into the notion that he had described how Therese had scars from eczema on the inside of her arms at the very beginning of the investigation. Whether she actually had them at the time of her disappearance was something that even her own mother was unsure about. Nonetheless it was regarded as compelling evidence.

Among all of Quick's information which was interpreted by the district court as evidence for his murder of Therese, I found only one detail that wasn't incorrect or sourced from a newspaper or transmitted via Seppo Penttinen: during the reconstruction in Fjell, Quick had said that the balconies of the apartment block used to be a different colour.

> TQ: Mm, mm, I don't remember exactly if the houses had the colour they have, have now . . . uh . . .
>
> PENTTINEN: What colour would you suggest then, if there was a change?
>
> TQ: I'd like to say the edges of the balconies were white . . . then you have to remember as well that the trees here . . . and everything was . . . another colour, it was green, wasn't it . . . uh . . . it throws me off to some extent . . . also the memory . . . uh . . . if I think of the houses further off over there . . . uh . . . there isn't a . . . [inaudible] like this . . . high-rise.

Quick's description of the repainted balconies is correct. It seems notable in itself that Quick would be able to remember their colour eight years later after a few moments spent in a residential area, especially as they weren't especially eye-catching but neutrally white.

Today, Quick can't even remember that he was taken on an inspection to Fjell – which is easily understood when one considers the heavy doses of medication he was on – and he can't think of an explanation as to why he was right about the balconies.

'If I've come up with a hundred descriptions then maybe ninety-eight are wrong and two right,' he tells me. 'I've given them such an incredible amount of information that of course I have to get it right sometimes.'

That's as far as I got – Quick was right about the balconies. Hardly evidence compelling enough to find a man guilty of murder.

And then there was that little piece of bone . . .

ARCHAEOLOGICAL EXCAVATIONS

THE EVIDENTIAL VALUE of the bone fragments was toned down in the verdict of Hedemora District Court on 2 June 1998, on the basis of technical legal considerations. Quick had said that he wouldn't exclude the possibility of 'other body parts than those from Therese' being found in the places he had pointed out in Ørje Forest. In other words, the court wanted to insure itself against the possibility of the bone at some point in the future being identified as that of another child who was also disposed of by Quick in the same place. The verdict mentions the boy 'Dusjka', whom Quick claimed he had abducted, murdered and cut up in Norway.

But the value of the bone as evidence was not questioned.

'It was obviously a very important element that they found the remains of a child who'd been incinerated in Ørje Forest, in precisely the place indicated by Quick,' said the chief judge, Lennart Furufors.

The verdict declared: 'Even if the remains of organic material found in the abovementioned forest cannot tie Thomas Quick to Therese, they nonetheless suggest that his story is true.'

'Clearly it made a big impression on us that burnt human remains had been found in the forest. It was important evidence,' Furufors confirmed to me.

In the heated debate that flared up in 1998 over the Quick investigation, the bone found in Ørje Forest was effectively used as a bat against anyone who questioned the role of the prosecution – such as the attacks from the witness psychologist Astrid Holgersson, who was critical in general of the handling of the Quick investigation, and from

Nils Wiklund, the senior lecturer in forensic psychiatry, who questioned the role of Claes Borgström as a lawyer and the subsequent lack of an adversarial process. Borgström responded as follows, in a polemical piece in *DN Debatt* on 6 June of the same year:

> In Örje Forest, south-east of Oslo, someone has buried organic material in a variety of places. In one place burnt pieces of bone have been found. Professors Per Holck from Norway and Richard Helmer from Germany have independently confirmed that the pieces of bone are of human origin, most likely a younger person.
>
> It is Thomas Quick who told us where in that huge forest we should dig to find the remains of a human being, the Norwegian girl Therese Johannesen.
>
> The psychologist Nils Wiklund is concerned (*DN Debatt* 8/5) that Quick's confessions are false and produced partly in conversation therapy and partly through leading questions asked by police. I hope that Wiklund will now rest easier.
>
> Surely not even he could believe that someone has revealed to Quick where he should stick his finger in the ground and say, 'Dig!'

Equally, for Seppo Penttinen writing in the *Nordisk kriminalkrönika* ('Nordic Crime Chronicle') and Gubb Jan Stigson – in article after article – the bone fragments were the primary line of defence against the doubters.

While doing research before the broadcasting of my documentary, Jenny Küttim was tipped off by SVT veteran Tom Alandh, who suggested that she should dig out the TV series *Tidningsliv* ('Newspaper Life'). The twelve-part documentary series, shown on SVT1 at the end of 2003, was a portrait of the newspaper *Dala-Demokraten*, Gubb Jan Stigson's employer. In the penultimate episode Christer van der Kwast gives a talk at the Crime Journalists' Club (KJK) in Stockholm. The driving force behind the evening had been Gubb Jan Stigson, who had invited the prosecutor so that he could talk about the Thomas Quick investigations.

In a long introduction, van der Kwast condemned the journalists who had taken a critical stance to the investigation, but he also mentioned the great problem over the years: that the prosecutions had been based on circumstantial evidence.

The documentary film-maker Tom Alandh was not a member of the Crime Journalists' Club, but he was in attendance and he was the only one who reacted to what had just been said: 'So is that really the case, there's no technical evidence at all for any of the eight murders he's been convicted of? Is that right?'

The question caused van der Kwast to lose his footing slightly, despite this being a relatively well-known fact.

'Well, what is technical evidence? I mean . . . One has to . . . I say . . . it's a bit sloppy, so to speak, if one says, "There is no technical evidence." Normally by technical evidence one means things like DNA matching between the victim and perpetrator. This type of thing we do not have. But on the other hand, there are other things, so to speak, of a technical nature, such as, for instance, burnt human remains which have been cut into as he described.'

Again, the fragments of bone. But not only that. Van der Kwast described the finds in Ørje Forest as if there were no room for doubt. He assumed that the information was correct.

The forensic investigation report shows that van der Kwast's 'human remains' consist of small burnt fragments of a total weight of less than half a gram. The largest piece, 'cut into as he described', weighs 0.36 grams.

Was it really possible to determine from such a small burnt particle that it was human bone? And that it came from a child aged between five and fifteen?

The discovery of the burnt fragments of bone in Ørje Forest gave the investigators new hope of also finding body parts in Sweden, and they especially pinned their hopes on finding Johan Asplund's remains. Thomas Quick had announced that he was going into phase two of the investigation, in which he would be able to give information so that body parts could be found.

While the debate on Quick was raging in the press, the main

character in the drama was being ferried around Sweden for various inspections. He pinpointed hiding places outside Sundsvall, but also in the vicinity of Korsnäs, Grycksbo and other places in Dalarna where he had lived in the 1980s. In the end, the list comprised some twenty-four locations.

The next stage was to let Zampo, the cadaver dog, examine the places specified by Quick with his owner and handler John Sjöberg. To everyone's great joy, Zampo signalled the presence of corpses almost everywhere he was taken. In all, he reacted positively in some forty-five different places.

To assure himself of the dog's ability, Professor Per Holck dug six pits in Ørje Forest and filled five of them with different materials: three were filled with organic material from humans, one with burnt animal bone and one with charcoal, while in the sixth pit there was nothing at all. Zampo reacted to human remains in all of the pits except the one containing burnt animal bone. This high incidence of error should have given cause for concern, but the dog's owner explained that most likely the spade had contaminated the pits with olfactory molecules. The test results were dismissed and no other test of Zampo's reliability was ever carried out.

After the test, the policeman Håkon Grøttland wrote an appreciative letter to the dog handler: 'You should know that we would never have solved this [the Therese murder] without you and Zampo.'

Wherever in Sweden Zampo had reacted, suspicious material was removed and the location was excavated by an archaeological unit.

In view of the fact that Quick claimed to have cut up a number of bodies in small pieces and spread them around, large quantities of soil were handed in for analysis at the Naturhistoriska Riksmuseet (Natural History Museum) in Stockholm, where Rita Larje, the CID's osteologist at the Working Group on Forensic Archaeology, studied the finds with a magnifying lens and microscope.

She said to me, 'I received lots of bags and was told that there were supposedly human remains in there, because a so-called cadaver dog had reacted to it. Osteologists just scrape through whatever they're given. If it's soil it's sieved and then we look for organic elements. And in this case I was supposed to be looking for bones.'

Rita Larje did not find any pieces of bone, so she went back to scrutinising the material through a microscope, as there might have been traces of organic material which had been burned – flesh then forms small, porous balls. But she found none of these either.

With Rita Larje's help I went through the reports of her soil analyses on behalf of the Quick investigation – in all, some twenty of them. In one place bones had been found that were visible to the naked eye.

'In this case we found they were rib bones from a cow, with signs of gnawing by rodents. And then we found teeth from cattle.'

One might think that the investigators would have drawn the logical conclusion, when the massive effort delivered so little: Quick was lying and Zampo reacted a little too readily. But the investigations kept rolling on.

Rita Larje and I reached the last report, which was from Sågmyra, where Sture Bergwall had lived the last time he was a free man. When hiding place after hiding place had proved entirely devoid of human remains, Quick implied that he had taken his trophies with him as he moved to different homes. Hopes were therefore high that 'Quick's mausoleum' would be found in Sågmyra, with pieces of many of his victims.

Larje looked over her report from 1998: 'Apparently there were 39 units, 39 bags of soil to go through. And most of the contents were wood, charcoal, resinous bark and pebbles – all naturally occurring in a wooded area.'

Rita Larje wrote a report to the effect that there were no bone fragments or anything else of interest. At this point Seppo Penttinen must apparently have snapped. He would not accept the negative result of the last excavations; instead he despatched all the material to Oslo, to Per Holck, who had found Therese's bone fragments in Ørje Forest. Penttinen wanted a 'second opinion'. After a few weeks, Holck's answer came back: 'No bone remains have been found in the material.'

It was the first time Rita Larje had seen all the documentation together: location searches, excavations, thousands of tests for phosphate levels in the soil in the hunt for body parts, and her own investigations.

She shook her head and said, 'It leaves you speechless when you see how much work has been put into this. Nothing is ever found and still they go on believing it will be found in the next place right until the very end. And still they find nothing!'

To my great joy, Larje was willing to discuss the Norwegian bone finds with me. I shared all of my material with her and she examined the documentation and the statements made by the professors.

Having read everything, Larje wasn't willing to make a statement on what the burnt pieces might consist of, but she was highly critical of the opinions expressed by professors Holck and Helmer. She believed they had reached conclusions which the material didn't support. According to Larje, Holck and Helmer hadn't identified the bone pieces. In their statements they didn't specify from what bone or from what part of a bone the largest fragment came.

'If you can't say where in the skeleton a piece of bone is from, then you can't determine what kind of bone it is either.'

Rita Larje asserted that the professors' statements included a number of conclusions that were not supported by scientific literature and were in part based on absolutely incorrect reasoning.

'The conclusion that this bone came from a young person was based on very shaky foundations,' said Larje.

She wouldn't go any further than this without having access to the bone fragments. However, she was willing to go to Drammen with another osteologist to analyse the fragments.

I contacted Christer van der Kwast, who, according to the Norwegians, had to give his permission for such an examination. He was not wholly dismissive, so I contacted Therese Johannesen's mother, who also supported a second analysis of the bone fragments.

But no further word was heard and we started running out of time.

After a good deal of chasing, van der Kwast's answer came back: no independent osteologists were permitted to look at the bones.

THE CRACKED CODE

THE TWO VERDICTS that remained for me to scrutinise were the most unlikely of all.

When it came to both the disappearance of both Johan Asplund and the murders of Trine Jensen and Gry Storvik, the legal cases presupposed that Thomas Quick had driven very long distances on his own before he was even capable of driving a vehicle. The courts confirmed that there was no technical evidence and that the final verdicts for both were therefore entirely based on Quick's own accounts. In these cases previous murder convictions were given as one reason among very few others to regard Quick as the perpetrator, an argument that was curious even if you ignored the fact that the earlier court cases were hogwash: according to Swedish law, every alleged crime must be judged without reference to any other criminal activity.

So how could the court arrive at a judgment based only on Quick's own story?

The trial for Thomas Quick's sixth and seventh murders opened in Falu District Court on 18 May 2000 but for security reasons was transferred to the high-security courtroom of Stockholm District Court. Wearing a light grey summer blazer, Quick was brought into the courtroom from a side entrance and took his seat next to Claes Borgström and Birgitta Ståhle. Everything followed the usual routine. The players of the drama were so confident in their roles that on this occasion they seem to have lowered their guard somewhat and taken slightly bigger risks than before.

Prosecutor van der Kwast stated his case and read out the first point of the prosecution.

'On 21 August 1981 in an area by Svartskog [Black Forest], in the municipality of Oppegård in Norway, Thomas Quick took Trine Jensen's life by subjecting her to blows to the head and strangulation.'

After declaring his guilt, Quick was supposed to describe the events, but he was interrupted by van der Kwast, who first wanted to play a video recording from the reconstruction, as well as describe what Quick had stated during questioning. Only after Quick had listened to Kwast's repetition of the whole story was he allowed to give his own account.

Quick had driven to Oslo to find a boy, but instead it was seventeen-year-old Trine who crossed his path. He asked her to show him the way to the Royal Castle.

'And unfortunately the girl got into the car,' said Quick in a cracked voice.

He snivelled and had to take long pauses while he described his 'grotesque and bizarre behaviour', which in this case consisted of assaulting, undressing and then strangling Trine with the strap of her handbag.

By this time it was widely known that the investigators' big problem with Quick's murder confessions was how to connect him to the crimes.

'Our checking of his story has been rigorous,' said van der Kwast, and his assertion was backed up by Claes Borgström.

'When he was taken for a tour of the area he was able to point out within a thirty-metre margin of error where the body had been left. This was in a big forest in Norway, eighteen years after the event,' explained Claes Borgström to the journalists covering the trial.

Birgitta Ståhle was there to explain to the court the underlying mechanisms of Quick's development into the serial killer he was.

'In his formative years and up to the age of thirteen, Thomas Quick's father abused him sexually. His father's ruthlessness and cruelty were frightening and horrendous. Yet his fear of his mother is far stronger.'

Next she described how at the age of four Quick witnessed the birth of his younger brother Simon, who was then killed by his parents. Afterwards he went with his father into the forest to bury the remains.

'When Thomas Quick was about four years and ten months old, his mother tried to drown him in a hole in the ice,' Birgitta said, continuing the apparently endless depiction of misery from Quick's childhood.

The chief judge of the court, Hans Sjöquist, listened with growing astonishment to the testimony and when it was over he asked, 'Has it been possible to verify this information?'

'No. But if something is incorrect it usually emerges in the therapy sooner or later,' answered Ståhle.

It was undoubtedly difficult to understand why a homosexual paedophile and serial killer had driven twice from Falun to Oslo in order to commit sexually motivated murders of women. The therapist was also able to answer this, in the form of a motive for the murders.

'Murdering women and girls is a form of revenge, a hatred directed at women who become a representation of the mother. His twin sister has also been mentioned and the aggression in regard to her is based on jealousy,' explained Ståhle, before going on to conclude her testimony with the following words: 'It requires moral sense to speak of the ultimate immorality which these murders represent.'

Bengt Eklund – the ward head from Säter Hospital – was also in attendance so that he could assure the court (as described in the reports) that 'Thomas Quick had very limited access to Norwegian newspapers and could not have got hold of more than the odd newspaper without my knowledge.'

To lend further support to Quick's credibility, Sven Åke Christianson made a statement on an experiment he had conducted with ten volunteers in the Department of Psychology at Stockholm University. First they were instructed to read a number of Norwegian newspaper articles on both murders. Afterwards they were asked to describe the main details of the crimes from memory. This was compared with both the facts known to the police and those contained in the newspaper articles. Unsurprisingly, the volunteers' descriptions contained more or less the same number of correct details, irrespective of what sorts of comparisons were made. However, when Thomas Quick's statements were subjected to the same test, a clear difference was evident: his story contained more information known to the police than could have been obtained from media sources.

The court was greatly impressed by Christianson's ingenuity and included a lengthy description of the test in its verdict. The paragraph concluded with the following: 'The result supports the assertion that Thomas Quick has had access to considerably more factual information than has been published in the newspapers.'

So that the court would not be misled into drawing one of two possible conclusions from this summary – namely that Quick had acquired the information elsewhere, most likely from the investigators and his own therapist – both Seppo Penttinen and Birgitta Ståhle testified that they had not conveyed factual information to him in any way whatsoever.

All in all, the court was left with an impression that was very far from the truth.

On one of my trips to Norway I met with Kåre Hunstad, the crime reporter who had been the first to supply Thomas Quick with information about Trine Jensen, thereby connecting her murder with the Quick investigation.

We met in a hotel bar in Drammen. Hunstad had written more articles on Thomas Quick than any other Norwegian journalist during the golden 'Quick era' between 1996 and 2000. At the time he had closely monitored developments. But his interest in the Swedish serial killer went further back than that.

'It was in the early 90s and I was the crime correspondent at *Dagbladet.* I used to read *Aftonbladet* and *Expressen* every day.'

During the trial relating to the Appojaure murders, Hunstad had been in attendance in Gällivare, not to report on it but as a spectator.

'Because I wanted to try and understand Quick,' he explained.

'For a hungry reporter it was natural to hope that Thomas Quick had also been in Norway, and maybe one could connect him to unsolved murders there too.'

The hungry reporter's dream came true soon after he'd returned from Gällivare, when Quick unexpectedly – thanks to the information he had obtained from Hunstad's Norwegian colleague Svein Arne Haavik – confessed to the murder of Therese Johannesen. It was a significant development.

Hunstad tried to make me understand how enormous the Therese case had been in Norway, and he told me about the unfolding story on which he and his colleagues had reported over the years.

'Then Quick comes along and confesses to the murder! I already knew a lot about the Swedish cases. The whole story was a proper farce, lacking in evidence and with weak sequences of events stitched together. It didn't seem credible. It was like a big travelling circus.'

Hunstad had written countless conventional articles simply reporting the latest news on the serial killer Quick, so his sceptical stance surprised me. He was Norway's foremost reporter on the subject; he was often the one to break new stories on the investigations.

Hunstad wrote about Quick's inspection of the refugee centre in Norway, from where he claimed to have abducted the two boys. The day after this article, on 24 April 1996, Thomas Quick was able to read for himself in *Dagbladet* about other Norwegian murders that might be attributed to him.

Bearing in mind Quick's earlier focus on young boys, Hunstad wrote that investigations should be resumed into thirteen-year-old Frode Fahle Ljøen, who had disappeared in July 1974. A police source also stated that the murder of seventeen-year-old Trine Jensen in Oslo in 1981 and the disappearance of seven-year-old Marianne Rugaas Knutsen from Risør that same year would be looked into as soon as possible.

After his return to Säter Hospital, during severe convulsions in a therapy session, Thomas Quick regained the first memory fragments of his alleged murders of Trine, Marianne and Frode – all of which he had read about in *Dagbladet*.

However, Quick was having problems articulating the name of Frode and for the time being he referred to him as 'Björn'.

The author of the useful article gained the privilege of becoming Thomas Quick's very good friend – a friendship that would prove mutually beneficial.

'I had his telephone number and could call whenever I liked. I built up a good relationship with him. We had a great deal of contact and . . . he was a dealer. Every time we met he wanted to get something out of it,' said Kåre Hunstad.

On one occasion Quick wanted a high-end new computer as payment for an interview. In a fax retained from 20 May 1996, Hunstad wrote that *Dagbladet* had turned down his demand but the radio station P4 was willing to provide it instead. In a letter Quick wrote later on he said, 'You can have a good interview with me before then, but my conditions are a bit tough. I'll meet you on the condition that I get 20,000 crowns [about £2,000]. Claes [Borgström] knows about this so you don't have to run it past him.'

According to Hunstad, it was rarely a case of more than a few thousand crowns, but even so the newspaper found it problematic.

'I still have a letter he wrote that says if he's paid he'll confess to new crimes. That was the payback. He could be like that.'

During one of his visits to Säter, Kåre Hunstad had brought along a video camera so he could film the interview. Quick understood that the most interesting thing for a Norwegian audience was his Norwegian murders. The interview began with Quick describing how he had driven to Norway in 1987 and had caught sight of a boy of about thirteen.

'I stopped the car and he stopped cycling. It was early autumn, August or September, about seven in the evening. The boy understood there was something strange going on. He tried to dodge me and run away. He was wearing a thin jacket which I grabbed. And then I hit him across the jaw and he fell to the ground and I smashed his head against the asphalt until he passed out or died. Then I took the body and put it alongside the car and arranged the bicycle in a special way. There were apartment blocks around, a crossroads. Then I went back to the car and ran the bicycle over. The car was not noticeably damaged, but the bicycle was really badly damaged.'

The murder had supposedly taken place in Lillestrøm, just north of Oslo, and had been seen as a traffic accident, Quick went on. Kåre Hunstad realised that what he had here on video was a confession to a previously unknown murder. *It's a scoop*, he thought to himself.

Quick carried on talking about another Norwegian murder, of a prostitute in Oslo. Already one such person featured in the investigation – Gry Storvik – but this was someone else.

'Have you told the police about it?' asked Kåre Hunstad.

'I think I'll talk about it in the autumn. Then I'll tell them about the prostitute,' said Quick, and took a slurp of his coffee. 'I can say this much: as far as I could tell she was a narcotics . . . user. A junkie.'

'Can you describe her?'

'About twenty-five years old. Quite down at heel, dark, and she was murdered with three stabs of a knife. I met her in Oslo. I can't quite say where.'

'You're sure she was a drug user? Did you pick her up like any other customer?'

'Yes, yes. We went a short distance in the car to a place in Oslo I don't really know so well. A place with some vacant flats. That's where she was killed.'

'So you attacked her? Was she raped?'

'No.'

Quick couldn't remember the exact year but he thought it was probably 1987.

After this they spoke about the murder of Marianne Rugaas Knutsen. Quick had already confessed and was under investigation for this murder, but there were others.

Quick described how he had driven to Bergen in the 1970s, where he met a boy of about sixteen or seventeen.

'One of your first victims in Norway?'

'Yes, my first victim with a deadly outcome,' Quick confirmed in a matter-of-fact way. 'He got into the car voluntarily and we drove just outside Bergen. I stopped the car in the forest and raped and strangled him. I drove back to Bergen and left him at the port. In a different place to where I'd picked him up.'

'So you had the body inside the car?'

'Yes, I had the body inside the car. And I left the body fully clothed.'

'Which means you put the clothes back on the body.'

When Kåre Hunstad left Säter Hospital he wondered whether he had a scoop or had just revealed a pathological liar.

Hunstad approached his contacts in the police force and made some enquiries of his own based on the information Quick had given him. He was soon able to confirm that there had not been any deaths, disappearances or murders in Norway that fitted with the three murders Quick had described on camera. It was highly likely that Quick had just made it all up.

I was struck by the fact that Quick had once again been caught out confessing to murders that had never taken place. But why hadn't Hunstad taken a more critical stance to Quick's confessions?

'I never believed Quick,' said Hunstad. 'I tried to understand serial killers and learned that they kill specific kinds of people. But here we're talking about boys and girls, young and old. To this you have to add that there are never any witnesses, no technical evidence and everything is a goddamn mysterious circus.'

Hunstad said that as a journalist he was trying to 'crack the code', which didn't make a great deal of sense to me. 'The more people who dig around in the Quick case the better,' said Hunstad, wishing me the very best of luck before we parted.

When it comes to the verdicts for the murders of Trine Jensen and Gry Storvik from 22 June 2000, there is not much of a code to crack. A close reading of the investigation shows how the stories, as usual, are modified as they emerge in a close interchange between Thomas Quick and his circle. In the numerous interviews, Quick variously attacks his Norwegian female victims with a knife, a piece of firewood, an axe or a metal dildo, or – when his imagination is found lacking – head butts or elbows or slams them against some part of the car. Crucial information that proves to be erroneous is followed up and corrected, though it is often still not quite right and so is repeatedly followed up in subsequent interviews.

Despite this, Quick's assertions even in the very latest statements were so difficult to match with the forensic conclusions that Christer van der Kwast made do with presenting a report in which medical examiners Anders Eriksson and Kari Ormstad only listed factors that more or less acceptably matched the story to the facts. The autopsy report was never cited, nor the DNA analysis of the sperm found inside Gry Storvik, who had been raped. This detail was dealt with by Quick claiming in the courtroom that his 'clear memory' of the event was that he 'had not ejaculated' during the rape – despite having said precisely the opposite during questioning.

The prosecutor, defence counsel, doctors, therapists and members of the court were satisfied to leave it at that.

One supporting factor for Quick's story that was particularly emphasised in the verdict was the fabric handbag strap tied into a strangling knot which had been found next to Trine Jensen's decomposed body and was very likely the murder weapon. It came from her handbag and this had not been conveyed to the mass media, which was why the court placed such importance on Quick's disclosure of this specific detail.

The first time Quick mentioned Trine Jensen's name to the investigators was on 4 October 1996. That was the day the entire Quick entourage was conducting the second reconstruction of the murder of Yenon Levi.

Quick surprised them by requesting a special interview. He had some information to impart to them and it couldn't wait.

Seppo Penttinen, Claes Borgström and Thomas Quick were sitting in a makeshift interview room at Säter when Penttinen turned on the tape recorder at 10.15.

'Go ahead, Thomas,' he said.

'I just wanted to give you some information. Very briefly. I'm not going to answer any questions about what I'm telling you, but I do want to leave this with you before we start on the Rörshyttan story, so I don't have to carry this inside me like a burden. I want to mention that two seasons after Johan's death, in other words in the summer of 1981, I was in Oslo, where I abducted a woman who, I think, was in her late teens. Her name was Trine Jensen.

I took her away and murdered her. And that's all for today.'

Penttinen called a close to the audience. The time was 10.17. It had lasted two minutes.

The 'interview' where Quick confessed to the murder of Trine Jensen is remarkable in several respects. Obviously first and foremost because it is so brief and the suspect would not accept any questions. Even more irregular is that at a first interview Quick was able to offer such concrete information about a murder: that the victim's name was Trine Jensen, that she was in her late teens and disappeared from central Oslo in the summer of 1981. All of these details were correct, and they were all available to read in a number of newspaper articles.

In February 1997, on his own initiative, Thomas Quick brought up the question of Trine Jensen's disappearance, but the investigators let it lie, presumably because they were too busy with other things. In March 1998 it was time again – in an interview with Kåre Hunstad, Quick said that he would 'soon be talking about the murder of Trine'.

On 27 January 1999 the name came up during questioning, when Quick was being interviewed about a large number of alleged murder victims. He provided another few details, such as the fact that he had left Trine's body by a forest road near a shed.

Seppo Penttinen tried to press him for more: 'You say you violated her, what do you mean by that?'

'I violated her body in different ways.'

'In different ways, you say?'

'Mm.'

'You're talking in quite a low voice here so I'll clarify it. Can you describe any of the ways that . . .'

'No.'

It was like talking to a brick wall, but when Quick was pressed he handed over another few snippets of information, for example that Trine was left completely naked in the forest, probably north of Oslo – 'Well, you know me and my sense of direction, it's hopeless' – before he put an end to further questions with the words 'Well, well, that's all, we'll leave it at that.'

During questioning two weeks later he asserted that he killed Trine with a blow to the back of her head, but not much more. On 17 May it was time for another interview.

> PENTTINEN: What about her age and appearance?
>
> TQ: No, I can't cope with that now.
>
> PENTTINEN: What's stopping you from describing her? Appearance, fair or dark, tall or short, fat or thin?
>
> TQ: Fairer than dark, taller than short, chubbier than slim.

Thomas Quick drew a map of the area which was completely wrong unless, as certain interpreters have suggested, it was an example of Quick's 'right–left problem'. If inverted it wasn't so bad.

Penttinen asked what parts of the body had been subjected to violence.

'Around the stomach,' said Quick.

'Do you remember if you've said anything else in earlier questioning?' asked Penttinen.

'No,' said Quick.

Penttinen wondered if he could possibly be remembering any other woman than Trine.

'Doubtful,' answered Quick.

'So I'm notifying you now that you're under suspicion for the murder of Trine Jensen,' said Penttinen.

On 28 May 1999, six days before a planned interview with Thomas Quick regarding the murder of Trine Jensen, Seppo Penttinen telephoned Quick so that he could 'pass on information about clothes and any items that he connects with the victim'. The most important 'item' of the case was obviously the strap from Trine's handbag, which had most likely been used to strangle her.

The telephone call was not recorded, so we do not know what exact words were spoken, but the fact is that in this exchange Seppo

Penttinen also chose to discuss the most crucial matter of all – without the tape recorder being switched on. Quick told him, according to Penttinen's note, that Trine Jensen had a 'handbag with straps that were longer than just a handle'. If one knows that a handbag has long carrying straps, which are considered significant in some way, it does not seem excessively difficult to work out what the straps might have been used for.

When, on 3 June 1999, Thomas Quick was questioned about the murder, he once again drew a map which, with some goodwill, could be correct – provided one reversed it. Quick described how Trine had got out of the car and was moving on her own when he attacked her with a knife and stabbed her several times. He claimed that there would have been a trail of blood some thirty metres long.

Finally Trine collapsed and Quick could see that she was dying. At this point he started attacking her again. She died while lying on the ground. He stabbed the front of her body.

'I'd locate it in the chest or possibly the stomach,' he said.

Despite being aware of the long carrying straps of the bag, Quick gave an entirely inaccurate account of how Trine had been killed. Instead of just asking him to continue with his story, Seppo Penttinen steered the conversation on to items she had brought with her.

Quick mentioned that he remembered 'the handbag with . . . er . . . that strap'. Penttinen immediately took the bait.

'What's this handbag strap you're talking about?'

Quick wasn't able to answer; he sat there in silence, sighing.

Seppo Penttinen reacted with the same signal that he always used when Quick was on the right track.

'Do you have some memory associated with that strap? I can see by your face that this is difficult for you to talk about.'

'Yes, it's difficult,' answered Quick.

'What do you associate with that handbag and the strap?'

'Well, I take the strap and I use it, I was going to say . . . uh . . .'

'You were going to say you used it? In what way did you use it? Can you explain that to me?' asked Penttinen. 'If that's right . . .' he added, just to be safe.

Quick sighed and said that he couldn't remember. But by now Penttinen was in full swing and he wasn't about to let this one go.

'Do you remember if something happened with it?'

'Well, I remember holding the strap . . . er . . .'

Quick indicated that the strap was a few centimetres wide. This did not tally very well with Trine's bag, but Penttinen egged him on.

'What was it made of? Do you have some sort of sense memory of the whole thing?' he asked.

'Yeah, I have a sense memory and . . . uh . . .'

'If you're thinking of the texture,' Penttinen prodded.

'Well, it's some sort of leather or skin, or whatever it's called,' Quick attempted.

This was completely wrong. Penttinen knew it was a fabric strap. Quickly he changed the subject.

'What happened with this strap you keep bringing up?'

'I could say that I bound her feet with it, but that would be the wrong information.'

Penttinen's questions were endless and Quick offered the alternative that Trine found it distressing when he was holding the strap. In the end Penttinen went in hard to get Quick's statement into order.

'If you just try to speak in plain language, Thomas! There's something you're avoiding. You want to get it out, but I can see that it's very hard for you.'

'Yeah, it's very hard,' Quick confirmed.

'You don't bind her legs, but it comes into use in some other way if I'm understanding you right.'

Again Thomas Quick tried to explain how frightened Trine was of the strap and then he went back to the knife. But Penttinen didn't want to hear this.

'If I interpret you now with your body language and so on, I'd say something happens with that handbag strap. At what stage is it useful to you? Where were you at this point? If you can try to develop that.'

The question was no longer *if* the strap was of use, but *where* and *how*.

By the time the next interview came around, on 1 September 1999, Quick had been mulling it over for two months. He'd also been able to fish for information and snap up various tips from the Swedish and Norwegian police who took part in the August reconnaissance to the places where Trine Jensen and Gry Storvik were found.

And sure enough, in a therapy session with Birgitta Ståhle, Quick revealed that important memories had been reawakened.

In the interview, Thomas Quick, Seppo Penttinen and Christer van der Kwast managed through their collective efforts to reach the conclusion that the strap had been used as a strangling knot.

At long last – two years and eleven months after Thomas Quick had first admitted to the murder of Trine Jensen – they had finally obtained a piece of evidence that would hold up in court.

And the inspection video? This notorious film that had such an effect on the conviction shows Thomas Quick, on 16 August 1999, leading a number of Swedish and Norwegian police and other individuals to almost the exact spot where Trine Jensen's body was found. On the way the car also passed close to the car park where Gry Storvik was found. Quick reacted strongly, with a severe anxiety attack. The others in the car later claimed they were not aware at this time of the other murder – as stated in court, only at this stage did suspicions arise that Quick had also murdered Gry Storvik.

Remarkably enough, my Norwegian colleagues told me that Oslo police had connected the two sexually motivated murders at an early stage and suspected that Trine and Gry had fallen prey to the same assailant. I also discovered that Gry had already featured in newspaper coverage of the Quick investigation just as much as Trine Jensen.

Bearing in mind the leaks and Quick's generous allowance of full clearance, what was the value of leading the police to two crime scenes that were fifteen and almost twenty years old, and not in any way secret or unknown?

DA CAPO

AT SÄTER HOSPITAL Christmas and New Year were not usually a big deal, and exceptions weren't made for the eve of the new millennium. Around the time of the New Year Thomas Quick was 'tense and shaky', according to his file. His carers reported 'weeping and despair'. Quick was unable to sleep because of his 'high-level anxiety'.

In March a meeting was held to discuss Quick's treatment regime, but he was too ill to attend. The chief physician Erik Kall was optimistic as always, noting in the file that there had been 'positive developments in the patient. He has progressed in his psychotherapeutic process and become more integrated as a person'.

Birgitta Ståhle went even further when she wrote in the file of the beneficial effects of the long-term therapeutic treatment. As usual she began her entry by describing the recent advances in the therapy, then moved on to developments in murders currently being investigated and how these related to Quick's traumatic childhood experiences.

> Our continued therapeutic work has implied a broadened and deepened seeing and understanding of both the significance of the various murders and also how the earlier experiences are narrated/expressed in the murders.
>
> In the later part of the autumn there was a clear integration which means that the contexts, both earlier and later, are connected in a clearer way. The differentiation between the various murders has been one of the things of importance to work on.

> This has become very clear in the meaning and significance of the murders of boys and those of women.

Chief physician Erik Kall and Birgitta Ståhle's enthusiastic judgements are in heart-rending contrast to the notes made by the ward staff at this time:

> Thomas is having a particularly difficult period at the moment with a lot of existential brooding. On 6/4 he was told that he would be formally arraigned for prosecution within two weeks, which led to additional pressure and increasing anxiety as a consequence. Has taken extra amounts of benzodiazepine to reduce his anxiety and to be able to sleep. On the night of 8/4 he slept only two hours. Much despair with crying and screaming in the night despite extra on-demand medications.

In the weeks that followed there were dreadful scenes of sleepless 'scream-nights', anxiety and a parade of Thomas Quick's multiple personalities, who took turns making appearances on the ward – with high dosages of medication as a result.

On 30 June Birgitta Ståhle made another triumphant note in the file, this time on the subject of how the previous week Thomas Quick had managed to get himself convicted of the murders of Gry Storvik and Trine Jensen.

> Continued therapy 3 times a week. Ongoing constructive development of the psychotherapeutic process. Trial in Stockholm 18–30 May.
>
> The trial was regarding prosecution for the murder of two girls, committed in 1981 and 1985. During the trial this positive development takes the form of Thomas managing to conduct himself throughout the trial in a much more collected way than before.

Birgitta Ståhle observed that Thomas Quick needed 'a relatively short time to recuperate himself after the trial' and that the therapy 'has taken a huge step forward'.

Even before the verdict had been given, Seppo Penttinen and Christer van der Kwast were back at Säter for the next murder investigation.

Eight years after Thomas Quick had assumed responsibility for the murder of Johan Asplund it was finally time to bring the whole thing across the finishing line.

Quick's repeated failure to show where he had hidden Johan's body had led to van der Kwast being forced, after every fresh attempt, to admit that the foundations were not yet in place to bring the Johan murder inquiry before a court. Now the investigation was going to be brought to a close, so that Quick could be put on trial.

On 26 November 2000 Birgitta Ståhle described what happened to Quick during the reconstructions and the mechanisms of a serial killer.

> These tours have resulted in a strong, active and very constructive inner therapeutic process. The earlier defensive structures have been exposed and it is possible to both see and understand in a more complete sense.

She continued:

> A prerequisite for this inner work is a deepened connection with reality, both his own early vulnerability and the vulnerability of the victims.

That Thomas Quick, despite this 'deepened connection with reality', was in free fall in a personal sense can hardly be doubted. On 12 December 2000 a psychiatric nurse wrote in the file:

> Thomas came out of his room at about 02.30 crying inconsolably and in despair. He stayed in the day room until about 04.00 with staff. Thomas paced back and forth and was at times very torn up and in despair. He held his head and said repeatedly that he 'can't take the pressure'.

The staff resolved the crisis with the help of Xanax and Panocod, but a few hours later the situation was just as bad again.

> In the morning, Thomas felt a bottomless despair. He cried uncontrollably. Sat with the staff. Calming conversation and medication as needed. Conversations with Birgitta Ståhle on the telephone. 'The bottomless despair runs parallel to the severe anxiety.'

A little later in the day, Thomas Quick was paralysed by cramps in the doorway of the smoking room and was quite unable to move. The hospital staff solved the problem with even more Xanax and Panocod. 'Part of it is that on Thursday, 14 December that is, a documentary on the so-called "Johan case" will be on TV. It's obviously going to be difficult for Thomas,' a nurse noted.

During rounds, Dr Kall was informed that Quick hadn't slept in three nights. He suggested a mammoth additional dose of tranquillisers, 50 mg of Diazepam. It worked and Quick managed to sleep for between four and five hours and declared himself satisfied with the effect of the Diazepam, which was still working when he woke up, as he 'managed to get out of bed despite crippling despair'.

During the period that followed he grew worse and worse and was constantly speaking of suicide.

The hospital staff frequently wrote in the file about his 'significant anxiety which he tries to control by taking additional on-demand medication'. Many times the maximum intake was exceeded. According to the nursing staff, police questioning in the run-up to the trial for the murder of Johan Asplund was 'tougher than expected' and Thomas Quick was once again mentioning suicide. In the following days it was noted in the file that he felt 'especially bad' with 'a great deal of anxiety' and was 'trembling, pale, slurring his words'.

A few days later, on 16 February, it was once again time for Birgitta Ståhle to sum up the situation:

> A psychotherapeutic 'wheel spin' after the Christmas break has brought a further emotional deepening and connection as well

> as the ability to see and embrace both his earlier activities and how these earlier activities have been acted out in his adult life and have taken form, among other things, in the murdering of boys.

While plans were being hatched for three new prosecutions for the murders of Johan Asplund, Olle Högbom and Marianne Rugaas Knutsen, a man in another wing of the hospital sat down to scrutinise Thomas Quick's files and medication logs. This was the previous chief physician Göran Källberg, who after a few years in other professional fields had now taken up his former position as head of the clinic. Realising that Quick's consumption of narcotics-strength medications was exceeding recommended doses by a significant amount, he was seriously alarmed. In his view, what he was seeing here was a consumption of pharmaceutical drugs for the sake of 'kicks'. And it had been going on for a terribly long time. Ultimately, it was Källberg who was responsible for this clear case of negligent care.

In a conversation with Göran Källberg on 25 April 2001, Thomas Quick denied that this was a case of outright drug abuse and grew very worried when Källberg communicated his decision: benzodiazepine medication would be gradually reduced and then phased out completely. Quick told me that at this time he had been dreading the approaching trial for the murder of Johan, which was due to start a few weeks later.

Göran Källberg's decision had immediate consequences for the murder investigations. There is an interesting note from a nurse from 5 May which gives an insight into Quick's withdrawal problems. The note also reveals that he was sitting with the investigation notes, as if studying them in order to be able to give a coherent story in the forthcoming district court proceedings.

> [Thomas Quick] did not sleep last night. Sat trying to 'work' in preparation for the coming trial. Has investigation notes he needs to read. Because of feeling unwell, due to withdrawals and anxiety, he can't do this. Asked me to contact Dr Kall or another

> doctor on duty to get a one-off prescription of a Xanax tablet and two soluble Panocod tablets.

But Göran Källberg's decision was strictly adhered to and Quick was not given any extra dosage of the medication, neither on this occasion nor on the following day. However, chief physician Erik Kall realised that his patient would not be able to manage the trial unless he was given temporary reprieve from the planned cutback. He wrote:

> For the duration of the trial it is necessary to impose a temporary needs-based medication regime, as follows:
>
> At times of high anxiety affecting the patient to the extent of endangering his ability to complete the trial, a Xanax tablet, 1 mg, can be given when required.
>
> At times of such serious tense headache that the completion of the trial hangs in the balance, a Treo comp tablet can be given, or two if required.
>
> If the patient's general condition is affected in such a way that oral medication cannot be administered, Diazepam Prefill 5 mg/ml 2 ml can be given when required.

The trial for the murder of Johan Asplund started in Stockholm on 14 May 2001. Because Claes Borgström had taken up the position as Sweden's new Ombudsman for Equality, Thomas Quick was being defended by a new lawyer, Sten-Åke Larsson from Växjö. Aside from this change, he was flanked by the usual group: Seppo Penttinen, Christer van der Kwast, Sven Åke Christianson and Birgitta Ståhle.

On the first day Quick recounted his extremely detailed memories of the abduction of Johan some twenty years earlier: how he had tricked Johan into getting into his car by telling him he had run over a cat, how he rendered him unconscious by slamming his head against the dashboard, how he drove him up to Norra Stadsberget and how there he assaulted him sexually.

After this, how he drove Johan to a place in the area of Åvike, where he strangled him, undressed him and then cut up the body using a saw and a knife. And lastly how he scattered the different body parts in various places around central Sweden.

Again, Sven Åke Christianson was brought in to talk about his invention – the memory test which, it was believed, demonstrated that Quick hadn't simply acquired his facts from the newspapers. As usual, Birgitta Ståhle testified about Thomas Quick's horrendous formative years and how the reawakened memories of them were capable of explaining his transformation into a serial killer. Once again she made a statement under oath that as a general rule she is not present during police questioning and also that the police were not party to what was mentioned in the therapy sessions. Seppo Penttinen also testified about the 'airtight seals' between the therapists and the investigators and claimed that Quick, despite having changed his mind on some of the points over the course of the eight-year investigation, had retained 'clearly defined memories' on the crucial aspects and 'stayed true to the central parts of his information'.

John Sjöberg told the court about his splendid cadaver dog Zampo and how the dog had reacted to a number of the places where Quick claimed to have scattered Johan's body parts. And in case the court wondered why none of these body parts had been found, the geologist Kjell Persson made a statement on his measurements of levels of phosphates in the ground, which indicated that 'some form of organic material' was decomposing in the spot pointed out as the murder scene in the Åvike area.

Furthermore, Christianson put forward a psychological explanation for the same puzzle: that serial killers have a need to both talk about their actions and preserve the body parts. These dual needs lead to conflicting emotions.

In its verdict on 21 June 2001, Sundsvall District Court made a slightly hesitant start: 'Quick has confessed to the deed which is the subject of prosecution. For a confession to form a basis for a guilty verdict, however, there must be additional support from the other parts of the investigation.'

By way of an opening statement the court acknowledged that

there was no technical evidence to connect Quick to Sundsvall at the time of the murder, nor was there anything to establish what had happened to Johan Asplund.

After this, it was stated that more than twenty years had passed and that this was problematic in itself. Furthermore, the district court declared that Quick's claims of having borrowed a car from his homosexual acquaintance Tord Ljungström were not adequately supported by the prosecution. Having got all this out of the way, the guns started blazing: 'Nevertheless the district court believes that in view of what has been established in earlier verdicts regarding Quick's long-distance travel by car, the question is not of significant importance.'

The document goes on to note how closely Thomas Quick's observations from Bosvedjan match the established facts of that particular morning and accepts Christianson, Ståhle and Persson's explanations as to the missing body parts as well as Quick's unpredictable but at times razor-sharp power of recall.

After this came the court's one and only substantial argument, namely that Quick had been able to describe two physical characteristics on Johan Asplund's body which were not previously known even to the investigators, and that this seemed to indicate that his story was true: a small birthmark on his back and a hernia in his testicle.

Checking through hundreds of pages of interrogation transcripts on the Johan Asplund case, I was soon struck by a strong sense of déjà vu.

The first time Quick mentioned anything about any of Johan Asplund's physical characteristics was during the Zelmanovits reconstruction on 21 August 1994, when he said that Johan had a scar. Penttinen picked up the thread in questioning nine days later, when Quick clarified that it was a surgical scar on the stomach, 'maybe five centimetres long'.

Seppo Penttinen asked if there were any other 'factors' about the body.

Quick answered negatively twice, but when Penttinen would not let it go, he said, 'Er . . . the testicles.'

'What about them . . . is there something special about them?'

'Well, like this, I have a sense that they're very shrivelled . . . uh . . .'

'Is it the testicles that have shrivelled, or what?'

'Yes, exactly.'

Seppo wouldn't drop the subject, and in the end asked 'if there was a difference between the testicles'.

'Yes, there could be, but then I'm a bit . . . uh . . . more uncertain . . . uh . . . it's like . . . well, as if one, at least one of the testicles is . . . is pulled up . . .'

Seppo wondered if it might be the case that the scrotum held only one testicle, and Quick said that this was possible.

'Was one more prominent than the other?' Penttinen clarified.

'Yes, exactly,' said Quick.

One month later Penttinen returned to the subject.

This time, Quick found it 'difficult to describe in detail what the exact situation was with the testicle', but that there was something about the testicles that made him think that Johan's body was 'asymmetrical'. Quick also drew a sketch of the scar on the front of Johan's body, which was placed in the region of his groin and described as red and inflamed.

Two days later the chief interrogator was at the home of Anna-Clara Asplund, asking whether there were any unreported peculiarities about Johan's body. Anna-Clara produced a sketch showing a birthmark which was like a faint shadow at the base of the back.

On 14 October Penttinen held his next interview with Quick. The interrogator was now speaking of a 'skin condition', not a scar, and explained that he wanted to discuss its position. Quick wasn't quite keeping up with all this and pointed out that he had already given 'quite a close description'.

Penttinen grew impatient after a few questions and then blurted it right out: 'Is there any possibility that it could be on the other side of the body? You've said that it's on one particular side of a central line of the body.'

'Mm,' answered Quick.

'Is there any possibility that it's on the other side of the body?'

'I think one should always factor in that it could be like a mirror, a sort of reverse perspective,' said Quick.

'What makes you say that?' wondered Penttinen.

'Because I'm identifying myself with the victim as well and I am the victim and I also see the victim from the victim's point of view, so to speak.'

Quick and Penttinen ruminated a little on this interesting psychological mechanism, before Penttinen came back to the skin condition that had now been placed on the appropriate side of the body.

'So try that description again, if you close your eyes and think back on how you saw that skin condition.'

But Quick didn't get any further. Not that time.

When the investigators checked Johan Asplund's medical records they discovered that he had been troubled by a testicular hernia. His mother assured them that it was completely healed and not at all visible at the time of Johan's disappearance, but this didn't make any difference.

In an interview on 3 June 1998 the news had somehow got through to Thomas Quick. After a long description of how he had abducted Johan and cut him into small pieces, Penttinen steered the questioning on to his 'physical characteristics'.

'The way I'm feeling it today, he had some sort of testicular hernia,' answered Quick pretty much instantaneously.

A little later Penttinen reminded Quick about the skin condition and Quick pointed at his back.

'You're pointing at yourself as you're sitting there, you're pointing at the right-hand side of your back just above your buttocks,' said Penttinen helpfully.

And with this, it was done and dusted – just like with the strap that was used to strangle the victim outside Oslo. The chief interrogator, thanks to an impressive amount of work on this case for almost four years, had reached a point where indisputable evidence could be presented to the court.

That Quick's initial descriptions of these 'physical characteristics' were fundamentally different obviously wasn't a matter that was brought before the court.

Sture Bergwall had an alibi on the day of Johan's disappearance. His mother came home from hospital on 7 November 1980, which was confirmed by both his diary from that time and the hospital's own records. Secondly, on that same day he picked up a month's supply of Oxazepam on prescription.

So how did he get hold of information about the crime which was, after all, correct?

Sture told me that he remembered at a very early stage seeing an episode of *Efterlyst* ('Missing') on Johan Asplund. He borrowed an annual from 1980 that contained quite a lot of detail. To help him find his way around Sundsvall, he tore the map out of a telephone book in a phone box when he was on leave in Stockholm. Then, after he started confessing in 1993, he read all the newspaper articles about the case. Closer to the trial he was given access to the investigation material.

At some point in 2000 he was also allowed to borrow a book, Göran Elwin's *Fallet Johan* ('The Case of Johan'), published in 1986. It helped him fine-tune the last details. Sture found his study notes for me. Among other things he had copied the book's descriptions of the clothes Johan Asplund had been wearing at the time of his disappearance – information he had been lacking earlier that he could now slot into his story ahead of the trial.

And who lent him the book?

Gubb Jan Stigson.

INTERVIEW WITH THE PROSECUTOR

THE GUILTY VERDICTS against Thomas Quick acted as a springboard for the career of Christer van der Kwast, who was promoted to chief prosecutor and head of the Anti-Corruption Unit when it was set up in 2005. Since then, he hasn't been interested in talking about Thomas Quick. 'I've parted ways from that inquiry', is how he has put it.

He was willing to make an exception for me – very likely Gubb Jan Stigson's recommendations had played a part in this.

Right until the very last minute I was worried that the interview I had scheduled with Christer van der Kwast on 13 November 2008 would be cancelled, and my fears were only assuaged once I was inside the modern premises of the Office of the Prosecutor-General by the Kungsbron (King's Bridge) in Stockholm and was shown into van der Kwast's office.

In the interest of brevity we had agreed to limit the interview to three of the cases: those of Therese Johannesen, Yenon Levi and the Stegehuises.

Lars Granstrand, the cameraman, rigged up the lights and camera, while I sat with Christer van der Kwast and engaged in small talk. He found it curious that I should be interested in such an old story as the Quick case.

'I wonder if you'll get any viewers for a subject like that. The case is so old now anyway, there's no way of assessing it.'

I answered that there might be one or two interested viewers, but above all I was the one who found the case interesting. Soon I felt

Lars giving my shoulder a poke, which meant that the camera was running.

'How convinced are you that Thomas Quick is guilty of the eight murders you had him convicted of?' I asked.

'I am convinced that the evidence I presented in the law court was enough for a guilty verdict to be reached.'

'Clearly,' I said, 'but that's not an answer to my question.'

Thus the interview began and thus it continued. I felt that he was taking cover behind legal formalities, or, when did this not work, rejecting the relevance of my claims and questions.

Van der Kwast described how the investigation began with the case of Johan Asplund and then moved on to the murder of Thomas Blomgren in Växjö.

'In the Blomgren case you have said that Quick is connected to the crime.'

'Yes, that's how I remember it, that was my judgement – that if it had not been ruled out by the statute of limitation I would have been in a position to put it before a court of law.'

'What made you so convinced of that?'

'Really the same main ingredients as in all the Quick investigations. He gradually provided information in a number of ways, information that connected him to the victim, knowledge of the victim, so that we could rule out any other possibility than his having been there and in contact with the victim.'

Van der Kwast continued: 'There was clearly a connection between him and the place, above all the place where the body was found. According to the medical examiner, everything was explained and nothing was left unexplained. His description of the wounds was very compelling. He could place Blomgren, the victim, very precisely in a shed of some sort. I'm trying to describe this so you can understand how we worked.'

I listened and nodded to indicate that I knew how they worked. At the same time I had to bite my tongue to stop myself blurting out that Quick had an alibi for the murder. Not yet. As soon as I said this, there would be a serious risk of the interview being called to a halt.

Instead we started quarrelling about the double murder in Appojaure. I asked how he felt about Quick's first statement, in which he claimed to have cycled from Jokkmokk to Appojaure and back again, only to say in the next interview that he had come by car with Johnny Farebrink, who had been his accomplice in the murder.

'This has been a recurring problem, that the events are wholly or partially fuzzy,' said van der Kwast.

'Surely it's not so fuzzy,' I ventured.

'In the sense that his story emerges exactly as you're describing now.'

'Is it really possible to talk of a story "emerging" if the original story is completely replaced by a different one?'

'Well, it can be described any way one likes,' said van der Kwast.

The interview had been in progress for over an hour when I asked van der Kwast why at the time of the investigation he had allowed Quick leave and full clearance despite the fact that he was under investigation for the murder of several young boys.

'Of course one could say it's not understandable. But the basic question is if it was proper. Are there other aspects to the question? You see, the thing is there are other aspects,' he answered cryptically.

'Yes, you wanted Quick to tell you as much as possible,' I tried.

'Of course. It was my job to get him to talk.'

'Do you have any memory of being at all interested in what Thomas Quick got up to during his trips to Stockholm while he was on leave?'

'I don't remember that. We tried to keep tabs on him as much as possible.'

'Did you ever ask him?'

'How could I know that, eight years later?'

'What if I told you he went to the library in Stockholm? To the press archive?'

'I don't know what he did – is that what he did?'

'He did.'

'You know a lot, don't you?'

'Yes, I do know a lot.'

For the first time in the interview, Christer van der Kwast was visibly flustered and I felt uncomfortable when I looked at his troubled expression. His eyes were watering and he rubbed his hands together nervously, while saying with supposed indifference, 'And so, what did he read?'

'About Thomas Blomgren, among other things.'

'Still, the crucial evidence was not that sort of material. That's the whole point.'

We both knew that it was precisely the 'whole point' – that Quick had repeated what he had read in the newspapers from 1964. Van der Kwast realised this and changed tack in the middle of his answer.

'If it can be shown that we were wrong the whole situation will have to be reviewed.'

'He travelled down to Stockholm with the express purpose of doing research on Thomas Blomgren,' I clarified.

'I have a kind of recollection I've heard this story before. But no more than that,' said van der Kwast.

It was an extraordinary comment. As if it were just a minor detail that a serial confessor was researching the murders he was being interviewed about. I made no further comment on it. Instead I pulled out a photograph of Sture Bergwall and his twin sister posing in folk costume in front of Stora Kopparberg Church in Falun and gave it to van der Kwast.

'This photograph was taken on the same day that Thomas Blomgren was murdered,' I said.

Christer van der Kwast gave the photo a cursory glance.

'And?'

'Thomas Quick and his twin sister were confirmed on that day. You actually interviewed the sister about this, so I'm wondering where that information is. Where is the interrogation report?'

'I'll have to ask Seppo about that. I can't remember. I'd be extremely surprised if such a simple fact had been overlooked. I'm not going to sit here and defend this, but I won't accept anything until I have it in black and white right under my nose.'

Christer van der Kwast knew he couldn't pass any of the blame on to Seppo Penttinen or anyone else. As the head of the investigation he had approved the interviews that were held and bore ultimate responsibility for the impartiality of the inquiry. Material that weighed in against his prosecution could absolutely not be withheld. For this reason he assured me that he had conducted the investigation to the very best of his abilities.

'I'm quite open – if something comes up that's wrong – then I'll say, "This is wrong, we've taken a wrong turn there, this is all over the place, we've had the wool pulled over our eyes." But before anyone can say that something is fundamentally wrong it really has to hold water. In all these years I've never met anyone who's come up with something convincing. Not for any of the cases.'

It was now time for me to reveal the secret I had been incubating for more than two months.

'You see, the thing is, Sture Bergwall has taken back his confessions,' I said as calmly as I could.

'Well, he can do that if he wants to,' said van der Kwast with a shrug of the shoulder. 'I worked on the premise that even if he did this, the court judgments would still hold firm.'

He thought about it.

'So that is the opening of your programme? On film, is it?'

'Yes. Everyone will have the opportunity to say their own piece,' was all I could think of saying in my dazed condition.

'Ha, ha, ha! Well, that's certainly interesting news for me. He retracted his confessions, did he? To you? Just like that?'

'Yes.'

'So he never did anything?'

'No.'

'The thing is, there's no guarantee that what he's saying now is true and what he said before was false. In that case he has to explain how it was possible. I'd be surprised if he claimed he'd been fed the information which led to his convictions.'

'One thing we know for certain is that he's been fed with medications,' I said.

'Yes, absolutely . . . I'm not disputing that he was given medications of various kinds, but I'm not in a position to know their effects.'

'Some doctors have said that this goes far beyond drug abuse. I mean, you can even hear in your reconstructions the way he says, "I have to have more Xanax. I don't care if I overdose."'

'I'm sure he did. He was in such bad shape that he had to seek help. That's how it was perceived, rightly or wrongly . . .'

While we were on the subject of hospital care and medications, I asked van der Kwast what he thought of the fact that Quick had not had any memories of his childhood or the murders – that all the memories had been repressed and then reawakened. And what was his opinion of object relations theory and Birgitta Ståhle's therapy?

'I'm extremely sceptical of all that! I've not bought into those models, I've only acted on hard facts. Those were just working methods to get the job done. Using various techniques like cognitive interviewing was worth a try.'

'You're familiar with the Simon illusion?'

'Yes, and the whole dilemma. I mean, some people are Freudians and they're engaged in all sorts of ideas. I'd say it's more up to her to answer professionally for her approach. It never had the slightest importance for me in my role as prosecutor.'

'But it had importance in terms of Quick talking about what happened.'

'Yes, it made it possible to . . . I don't know how the people on the therapy side have worked together. I couldn't have insight into that.'

'But you did have insight!'

'Yes, I understood more or less. But I maintain that it did not have any significance. What was important was what came out of it.'

Prosecutor Christer van der Kwast had taken memories extracted in therapy and used them as a foundation for murder prosecutions, yet now he claimed to be 'extremely sceptical' about the notion of repressed memories reawakened in therapy. Clearly, he was anxious to disassociate himself from anything that might be interpreted as psychological hocus-pocus.

'I maintain that the courts made their decisions based on hard facts. And I reject the idea – and also feel it is disrespectful to come here and claim that we were so bewildered that we believed Quick's stories based on some general psychological theories. Or that we would have intentionally manipulated situations so we could get evidence. I mean, that's rubbish!'

The interview continued, swinging between discussions of details and out-and-out rows about interpretations and assessments. In retrospect, Christer van der Kwast describes the experience as being 'interrogated for four hours'. It is true that the interview went on for that length of time. At the end, we were both tired and crestfallen. Christer van der Kwast repeated that there was no longer a need for him to take a stand on the case. But he raised his finger in a warning gesture, as if to point out the risks I was facing.

'Just jumping on the bandwagon of one story or another that he chooses to tell for mysterious reasons, I would be very careful about that!'

'Thanks for the advice,' I said politely.

'I mean, he's an extraordinarily manipulative person,' explained van der Kwast.

Lars Granstrand packed up the lights, tripods and leads. After he had gone I stayed for another hour and carried on discussing the subject with van der Kwast. I realised that we were both facing a significant risk. By this stage I was absolutely sure that Sture Bergwall was innocent of the eight murders for which he had been found guilty. I felt quite confident about the material I would present on television. Nonetheless it was hard to question six unanimous courts of law, the Office of the Attorney General and the chief prosecutor of the Anti-Corruption Unit. In the end, I would damage either van der Kwast or myself; it wasn't possible that both of us could emerge with our honour intact.

Christer van der Kwast seemed immersed in a similar train of thought.

'So what's the end result of all this, then? Will he be there on camera saying he's innocent and he just made it all up as he went along?'

I confirmed that this was what Sture Bergwall could be expected to say in the documentaries.

After that, we established that there wasn't much we agreed on, and on that note said our farewells.

INTERVIEW WITH THE LAWYER

QUICK WAS FOUND guilty of six murders while being defended by Claes Borgström. Many critics argued that Borgström had not defended Quick, that in fact he had failed in his duty to scrutinise Christer van der Kwast's evidence.

That Borgström had also sent out invoices to the tune of several million Swedish crowns just to have his client found guilty had also created some bad blood. Maybe this was the reason why Borgström had so feverishly defended the verdicts against Quick and, with more aggression than anyone else, had attacked whoever dared question the investigation.

Just after lunch on Friday, 14 November 2008 I installed myself in a dingy café not far from the Swedish Trade Union Confederation (LO) building on Norra Bantorget in Stockholm. I was waiting for the hour to strike two, which was the time we had agreed for my long-standing appointment with Claes Borgström.

I didn't know if Christer van der Kwast had had time to let Borgström into the secret that Sture Bergwall had retracted all of his murder confessions. To avoid being caught up in small talk with Borgström – and risk giving away the news before the interview – I killed time in the café while Lars Granstrand rigged up the camera and lights. When I came to the office we were supposed to be ready to start on the dot of two.

For months I had studied Claes Borgström's participation in almost all of the interrogation sessions and reconnaissances in the Quick investigations. In the video recordings I had watched Thomas

Quick being led around in forests, so drugged that he could barely talk or walk without being propped up by his therapist and interrogator. Claes Borgström walked beside them, but he never brought up the fact that his client was high as a kite. On a number of occasions Borgström had also seen Quick confess to murders that had obviously never happened. He had heard facts being distorted or concealed in the courts without intervening. Why?

After all, the lawyer Claes Borgström had always taken a stand against repression, he spoke up for human rights and was a committed type with left-leaning sympathies at heart who had always protected the weaker members of society. The picture of him did not add up. Who was he?

When the Social Democratic government of 2000 offered Borgström the job as Sweden's first male Equality Ombudsman he resigned as Quick's defence lawyer just before the trial for the murder of Johan Asplund. After seven years as Equality Ombudsman, Borgström joined forces with Thomas Bodström (the former Minister for Justice) and set up the law firm Borgström & Bodström, with offices at Västmannagatan 4. Borgström's new venture – with the previous Minister for Justice as his partner, in an imposing building with an upmarket address, with LO's Stockholm District and Unga Örnar (Young Eagles) as neighbours – could certainly be interpreted as a means to an end.

At a quarter to two, as I was standing up to leave, my mobile rang.

'Claes Borgström called! He hasn't spoken to Kwast and he doesn't know anything,' said an unusually excited Sture Bergwall.

Borgström had told him that he was about to be interviewed by SVT and that he was nervous about the interview.

'But then he looked at his invoices for three of the cases and it calmed him down. He invoiced for a thousand hours' work for those three cases you'll be talking about.'

With a thousand invoiced working hours, Borgström felt safe in the conviction that he had an unbeatable advantage in terms of knowledge of those cases.

'He was guessing that you had probably put in forty hours of preparation,' said Sture with a laugh.

I thought to myself that if I had been sending out invoices as a lawyer for my hours I'd be financially independent by this stage.

'You know what else he told me? He's become a party member and he's aiming for a ministerial post after the election. Imagine him telling me something like that! Isn't it strange?'

'Really strange,' I replied, but my thoughts were elsewhere.

I found myself standing at the front entrance of Västmannagatan 4. We finished our call and I walked up the palatial staircase and rang the doorbell of Borgström & Bodström.

Everything had been rigged up and prepared, so when Claes Borgström appeared a few minutes later we got on with it right away. He asked me what my points of reference were for the interview. What was my angle?

I told him quite truthfully that I had not held any firm opinions on the matter at the beginning, but that as time passed I had grown increasingly sceptical about the investigation. He looked at me searchingly with his sharp blue-grey eyes.

'How much time have you put into this?' he asked.

'About seven months,' I said, and thought of Sture's telephone call.

'Seven months? Full-time?'

Borgström gave me a dubious glance while I explained that I worked longer hours than a standard working week.

'I looked at three of the trials I took part in, Therese, Appojaure and Levi,' said Borgström. 'When I checked my remuneration I had a thousand hours logged for all three.'

'So you're well prepared,' I said encouragingly.

'Yes, it means I have a certain amount of insight.'

I started carefully and asked Borgström to describe how he came to be Quick's lawyer.

'He called me during the ongoing investigation into the so-called Appojaure murders and asked if I wanted to represent him. Obviously I agreed that I would. And then I ended up representing him in four trials over a period of several years.'

Borgström talked without needing to be prompted, and before long he brought up the subject of the unique situation of defending a serial killer who was voluntarily talking about his own crimes.

'As a defence lawyer it isn't unprecedented. I have defended other people who have confessed to murders.'

'Even when they weren't under suspicion?'

'No, in general there has been suspicion and then a confession has come,' Borgström admitted.

Claes Borgström particularly emphasised that a confession on its own wasn't enough; it had to be backed up by other evidence. In Thomas Quick's case the supporting evidence was that time and time again he had described things that only the perpetrator could have known. Borgström cited the murder of Therese Johannesen as an example.

I answered by showing Borgström a photograph of the concrete suburb of Fjell, which Quick had described as a country hamlet with low-rise family homes. Then I showed him the photograph of Therese, black-haired and with an olive complexion, described by Quick as a blonde girl, and after that a reconstruction of Therese's clothes at the time of her disappearance.

'Why was Quick so wrong when he tried to talk about his murders?' I asked.

'If you go through the investigation material you'll find a lot more inaccuracies. Those are just a couple,' said Borgström.

Quick also said that Therese wore pink velour trousers, patent-leather shoes and had large front teeth. Borgström looked at my photos of Therese from the relevant time: a denim skirt, mocassins and a wide gap where those big front teeth were supposed to be.

'But he changed his mind, I seem to remember. He said she had dark hair. And he talked about buckles on her sandals. He was convicted on the basis of providing information that when checked proved to be accurate and impossible to explain in any other way than that he was there at the time of the crime being committed.'

Claes Borgström was a man of striking intelligence and I wanted to believe that he was also intellectually honest. In my eagerness to make him understand, I tried to explain how Quick had been provided with information. I told him about the series of articles from the Norwegian newspaper *VG*, where evidently Quick obtained the information he needed to make his first confession.

'Not all the information,' protested Borgström.

'Yes,' I said.

'Not the atopic eczema on her arms,' Borgström objected.

'No, but that came much later!'

'But you were saying that he got all the information!'

'I said he got all the information he needed to confess to the murder,' I said with a certain measure of despair. 'He said that she was blonde! And he said that she was wearing entirely different clothes from the ones she was actually wearing. Everything was wrong!'

'Not everything,' protested Borgström. 'The hairclips were not wrong, nor the buckles on her shoes.'

In actual fact, when she disappeared, Therese's hair had been put up with a blue hairgrip and a rubber band. After eight months of police questioning, Quick, on 14 October 1996, said that Therese had a hairband – in other words, neither a hairgrip nor a rubber band – which may possibly have been orange. After another year of questioning, on 30 October 1997 he still maintained that she had worn a hairband.

I realised that my strategy of outlining a set of circumstances and letting the interview subjects explain their view of it was not working.

How could Claes Borgström, after invoicing for a thousand hours of work, have been so ill-informed? Was it really possible that he had failed to see that Quick had provided so much incorrect information that even chance might have resulted in a story that was, at the very least, no further from the truth?

I had turned into one of those litigious freaks that fussed about details no one outside our little circle understood or had any interest in. And it made for really, really bad television.

'The devil is in the details,' I muttered quietly to myself, and persisted in my idiotic attempt to explain how the media had supplied Quick with information. Borgström wasn't interested. As far as he was concerned, the case was in the past and Quick had been found guilty of eight murders. He was clearly even regretting his decision to take part in this televised interview.

I handed over the letter written by Thomas Quick to the Norwegian journalist Kåre Hunstad. Borgström read:

> I'll meet you on the condition that I get 20,000 (my speakers have broken and I need new ones) and that when you come you bring a receipt showing that the money has been deposited in my account. Claes knows about this so there's no need to run it past him. If you agree to these terms I promise you a good interview – I get paid for my efforts and in return you get a good story.

After reading the letter, which showed that Borgström had also been aware of the commercial aspects of Quick's confessions, he looked at me and said with forced indifference, 'How sick are you if you do something like that? "Give me twenty thousand and I'll confess to a murder I never committed." And get locked up for the rest of your life. People who think he's innocent are describing a human being virtually as sick as someone who could commit these murders.'

The lawyer seemed to feel that it didn't make a great deal of difference whether his client was guilty or not – clearly he was just as crazy in either case. Borgström's argument led us seamlessly on to the next subject.

'Were you aware that Quick was abusing benzodiazepines during the entire investigation?'

'I wouldn't put it like that,' answered Borgström truculently. 'But I knew he had a drug problem, yes. Though not while he was at Säter,' he added.

'Yes, he did.'

'Drug abuse?'

'Yes. At Säter Hospital it was referred to as needs-based medication. He was able to graze freely on various kinds of benzodiazepines,' I said.

'I don't accept that statement!'

'It's the view of the chief physician at the time, it's not my own,' I explained.

'I don't accept that statement,' repeated Borgström, and thereby put a stop to any further questioning on medication.

*

I changed tack, turning to the investigation into the Yenon Levi murder and Christer van der Kwast's actions regarding the spectacles found on the scene. Why had he ignored the findings of SKL (the Swedish National Laboratory of Forensic Science) and procured an opinion elsewhere, so that Quick could be presented as the assailant?

'I'm not here to defend the prosecutor, but I can't help noticing an insinuation that the prosecutor wasn't satisfied until he had an outcome that moved things in that general direction,' said Borgström.

'It surprises me that you didn't use the SKL findings in the courtroom.'

'Yes, I hear that it surprises you,' answered Borgström sarcastically. 'No comment!'

I pulled out the next document, a list of eighteen circumstances which, according to the forensic technicians, directly contradicted Quick's Levi story. This was all hard evidence, such as confirmed tyre marks on the scene that did not correspond with the tyres of the car Quick claimed to have been using; Quick said that he had rolled up Levi's body in a dog blanket, but no dog hairs or fibres from the blanket were found on Levi's body; the bloodstains on Levi's shoes did not conform with Quick's version of events; the soil on Levi's clothes came from the place where the body was found, not the place referred to by Quick.

The forensic technician Östen Eliasson had summed up the forensic evidence as follows: 'Nothing concrete in the forensic investigation backs up Quick's story.'

'There are eighteen forensic conclusions that go against your client's story,' I said to Borgström.

'Really? Maybe there are even more,' answered Borgström.

'Was this list something you made use of?'

'How would I use it?'

'I can think of a number of ways, but as a lawyer you know better than me.'

'Well, as you can't seem to tell me how I should have used the list, I won't answer your question.'

Borgström simply rejected the relevance of whatever I asked him.

As he saw it, the investigation material was so complicated that it could be used to back up any hypothesis at all. It made no difference if I found ninety circumstances that were wrong and ten that were right.

'Just one correct detail could be enough,' said Borgström.

I wondered if I had really understood him correctly, so asked, 'Ninety-nine that are wrong and one that's correct?'

'Yes, if that one circumstance is strong enough to connect a person to a crime. Ultimately it is up to the court to make that judgement.'

'Can you suggest one such circumstance?'

'I'm not going to do that, no, but of course there are many. You'll just have to read the verdicts. That's all there is to it.'

Claes Borgström could confidently fall back on the six unanimous court verdicts that had firmly established Sture Bergwall's guilt in the murder of eight people. Whether Quick had been wrong in ninety-eight or ninety-nine instances out of a hundred, it didn't change the fact that a Swedish court judgment was immovable.

'JK says that the verdicts are very well formulated. They show the underlying arguments of the verdicts, by what route they arrived at the conclusion that guilt had been established beyond any reasonable doubt. My views have no importance in the matter. It's the view of the court that counts,' said Borgström modestly.

'In certain respects the reasoning of the court doesn't reflect the actual reality,' I pointed out. 'The verdicts don't give a very fair picture of the evidence.'

'Maybe you have made poor judgements yourself, just as you deem others have done,' Borgström objected.

'They're based on easily checked facts,' I said.

'No,' Borgström protested. 'They are *difficult* to check. You're talking about such extensive material that it's easy to pull out bits that fit with any given hypothesis.'

The interview had been going on for over an hour and we were not getting anywhere. Borgström seemed to feel that I was way off target, although he did admit that I had done my homework.

I saved my most dramatic information until the moment when the interview was almost over. I tried to control my voice and facial expression as I said, 'Your former client Thomas Quick has retracted all of his confessions and says he's innocent.'

'Well . . . yes, he may have done,' said Borgström, confused.

He tried to grasp the meaning of this unexpected turn, rapidly running through the likely consequences for him and devising a strategy for the rest of the interview. Having spoken to Sture Bergwall just a few minutes before the interview, it must have been difficult for him to process the information.

Borgström stared at me and asked, 'So that's his view today? That he's been wrongly convicted?'

I confirmed that this was indeed the case. Borgström gave the matter some serious thought. A little smile hovered somewhere on his face. I could see his usual combative self re-emerging.

'You shouldn't be so sure that this is his *current* position.'

'I am sure of it,' I said.

An anxious look crossed Borgström's face.

'Have you spoken to him today?' he asked nervously.

'Yes, I have.'

'At what time?'

Now you're really clutching at straws, I thought, before replying, 'I'm not going into that. It's not important. I know this is Sture's current position.'

'Typical,' said Borgström, looking quite downcast. 'You have no obligation of confidentiality, have you?'

The interview was turning into a conversation, probably because neither of us had the energy for much else. I told him about Quick's medication and the actual reasons for his 'time out' some seven years earlier.

Just as Christer van der Kwast had behaved the day before, Borgström now swung between great humility at the idea that Quick might have been wrongly convicted and an insistent defence of the legal process in which he had played a decisive part.

'Whatever position Thomas Quick takes in future, neither you nor I nor anyone else will be able to know for certain what has happened here. For the time being it's the court rulings that matter.'

Admittedly he was right about this.

'Are you confident about your performance in the Thomas Quick case?' I asked.

'I have not collaborated in putting an innocent person behind bars,' Borgström answered.

'That's quite a bold statement,' I said.

'OK. I'll add one word: I have not *consciously* collaborated in putting an innocent person behind bars.'

Borgström felt I should spend some time reflecting on Quick's reasons for doing what he had done. I replied that I had put months of work into trying to understand precisely this.

Borgström had his doubts about that, but he wanted to finish things off by giving me something to think about.

'Quick came to Säter Hospital after being found guilty of aggravated robbery. It is now 2008 and he'll *never* be released, even if he pushes for a review.'

'Isn't that a little outside your field of expertise?'

'Yes, but I'm entitled to my opinion.'

'When did you last see Sture?'

'A long time ago.'

And yet you are quite happy to condemn your former client to a life sentence, I thought, keeping silent.

The atmosphere in Borgström & Bodström's law firm was more than a little frosty when I took my leave.

SYSTEMIC FAULTS

CLAES BORGSTRÖM SEEMED to me the greatest mystery in the case of Thomas Quick. He was much too intelligent not to have seen the fraud in what had been going on for all these years, and at the same time too honest to have consciously taken part in a miscarriage of justice such as this one.

Who was he? And what was really going on behind those eyes?

After the interviews with Christer van der Kwast and Claes Borgström, we had only another four weeks before broadcast. It was now a question of putting the last pieces into place. I made a final attempt to have the bone fragments released for independent examination and Jenny Küttim hunted for the missing interrogation reports.

Sture's twin sister, Gun, found a note in a diary where she had written down the time, date and name of the interviewer who had come to see her. On the morning of Friday, 19 May 1995 she had been questioned by Anna Wikström and a local policeman. We had already tried several times to get our hands on this interview – like all the other transcripts of the interviews with Sture's siblings. Finally, validated by Gun's specific information, Jenny called Seppo Penttinen to inform him that it was an offence not to hand over official documents of this kind.

Late that same evening the interview transcript came juddering out of the fax machine at SVT and we were able to confirm that it pertained to the investigation into the Appojaure murders.

The next day I immersed myself in it.

Gun began by describing the members of the family and where they had lived. She said that their 'school years and time with the family were positive on the whole'.

> Gun mentioned that she has always viewed Sture as very gifted and knowledgeable. Among other things she mentioned that Sture always kept up with the news and newspapers, which has given him a very good general knowledge. She also says that he was politically interested from an early age.
>
> Further, Sture wasn't very interested in sport, which meant that he didn't socialise very much with the other boys in his class.
>
> As a result Sture was often outside the circle of his classmates and most of his social interaction was with Gun.
>
> Gun sometimes felt that Sture was maybe bullied a little by his classmates and she had a recollection of some of the boys locking Sture into an outhouse in a barn.
>
> Gun can't remember if Sture suffered as a result of this bullying.
>
> The socialising in the family was also frequent and Gun mentioned that she mainly spent time with the boys in the family.
>
> Gun says that during high school Sture spent a lot of his time on the school newspaper.
>
> Concerning her family Gun sees her childhood as very positive. She mentioned that her father was very hot-tempered and has memories of him at various times throwing saucepans on the floor. She can't remember what the arguments were about, but she said that they resolved themselves in due course.
>
> Sture has mentioned in therapy that he had been subjected to sexual molestation by his parents and Gun's comment on this is that 'it's shocking'. She says that it is inexplicable that something like this has happened. When she looks back and really analyses her childhood she can't imagine that anything like this could have happened.

Gun also gave a positive view of the time they spent in Jokkmokk, where she and Sture attended the folk high school. On one occasion she noticed that Sture had gone outside the student hall of residence and was standing there screaming. She took care of him but never found out what had happened. By this time she had already begun to suspect he was under the influence of drugs. Also Sture's periods within various institutions were, as she saw it, largely caused by Sture's drug problems.

> In terms of the confessions made by Sture during the investigation Gun is dubious about the information she has got partly from the investigating team and also in the mass media. She says there is a question mark hanging over the whole thing for the siblings, as far as Sture's behaviour is concerned during these years. Their reason for this is that they never really noticed anything worthy of comment about Sture, apart from his drug abuse, which they all confirm he has struggled with.
>
> Earlier in the interview we touched upon the claim of sexual molestation made by Sture against his parents. Gun feels that this statement seems overblown and that there must be other reasons for Sture behaving as he has done. She also mentions that she has given thought to various occasions in the past when Sture fell and hurt himself and was even rendered unconscious.
>
> Finally Gun was asked to describe her family very briefly.
>
> Mother, Thyra: Very caring about her family. Cheerful, always willing to help.
>
> Father, Ove: Silent and brooding, but always fair.
>
> Oldest sister, Runa: Happy, nice person.
>
> Sten-Ove: Complicated, difficult to understand, analytical and hot-tempered but a nice person.
>
> Torvald: Lovely person getting on with his life.
>
> Örjan: A person who never grows up but wants the best for everyone.
>
> Sture: Pleasant, an extrovert and a smart person.
>
> Eva: Always chatting, happy and extroverted.

As far as Jenny and I were concerned, the document was an encouraging sign that the missing interviews from the investigation had in fact been kept, and were most likely in the possession of Seppo Penttinen. However, he had sent only one of the two interviews with Gun Bergwall we had asked for – the one which we had been able to specify by date and time.

And we hadn't seen any sign of the interview where she had spoken of their confirmation, which would verify Sture's alibi for the murder of Thomas Blomgren.

Travelling up to Stockholm on the train one morning in November 2008, an idea suddenly occurred to me to call the Chancellor of Justice, Göran Lambertz, and ask if he might have time for a cup of coffee that same morning. He replied that I was welcome to come up to his office.

It was a beautiful winter's day when I walked from the Central Station across the bridge to Riddarholmen and the elegant palace of the Office of the Chancellor of Justice. Lambertz received me in his impressive room on the first floor.

The duties of the Chancellor of Justice are highly diverse and often contradictory in their scope.

The chancellor is the government's highest-ranking ombudsman and effectively functions as the lawyer of the state. As such, he or she acts as the legal adviser and representative of the government and state. If, for instance, the state has in some way infringed upon the rights of a citizen who is now demanding compensation, the chancellor will defend the state against that citizen. At the same time the chancellor is supposed to keep an eye on the workings of public authorities and law courts on behalf of the government, while also playing the part of ultimate guarantor in protecting the rights of the citizens against abuses of power. If the state has done something wrong – such as sending an innocent person to prison – the Chancellor of Justice determines the level of financial compensation that should be paid out.

In short, the Office of the Chancellor of Justice is a very odd concept – a manifestation of the decent state: the chancellor is the incorruptible Swedish public servant who represents benign authority and the best interests of the citizens, while being elevated above the most impossible conflicts of interest.

Faced with Chancellor of Justice Hans Regner's plans to step down from the job in 2001, the Justice Minister Laila Freivalds had wanted to see a list of possible applicants for the vacant position. This preparatory task was given to Göran Lambertz, head of the legal secretariat at the Foreign Office, who commented some time after, 'I presented a number of names to Laila Freivalds and outlined the various abilities of each candidate. Then as the presentation came to a close I added, "I'd rather just have the job myself."'

This was precisely how it turned out. Göran Lambertz had shown himself to be a champion of the legal rights of the individual. He publicly commented on the fact that many innocent people were incarcerated, that the police sometimes lied to protect their colleagues and that judges were occasionally lazy. To everyone's surprise, Lambertz got involved in specific case reviews and even drafted a petition calling for the review of a murder conviction that he considered wrong. It seemed that Sweden had got itself a fearless Chancellor of Justice, one who often appeared in the media and was prepared to challenge powerful interests. It is probably fair to say that he won the love of the people.

In May 2004 Göran Lambertz started the 'Chancellor of Justice Legal Rights Project' and two years later his department published a report entitled 'Wrongly Convicted'. The report was based on all retrials since 1990 where the prison term had exceeded three years and the convicted person had subsequently been cleared of all charges.

The report stated that up until the 1990s retrials of this kind had been extremely rare. Three of the convictions that had been overturned had been very much in the news. The remaining cases in the report made it pure dynamite: eight of the eleven wrongful convictions were for sexual crimes, mostly sexual abuse of children and teenagers. In most of the cases, teenage girls had made accusations against their fathers and stepfathers while seeing psychologists and therapists.

A number of prominent jurists – including Madeleine Leijonhufvud and Christian Diesen – with a long-established commitment to fighting the sexual exploitation of minors, attacked the report fiercely and demanded Göran Lambertz's resignation.

I should probably add at this stage that I can't be considered as unbiased on the subject, given that two of the retrials in the chancellor's report were the direct result of a case I had investigated and made the subject of a television documentary. 'The Case of Ulf' told the story of a young girl who, in therapy, had described being subjected to extremely disturbing assaults with aspects of Satanic practices and even ritual murder. A large amount of evidence that showed the girl wasn't telling the truth had been withheld by the police, prosecutor and Prosecutor-General.

The battle lines in the debate on the chancellor's report were well defined. What sort of testimony should be seen as reliable? What was the proper role of therapists and prosecutors in the legal system? The debate was highly relevant to the legal process in the case of Thomas Quick. Most of the critics who had defended Lambertz in this debate on rule of law were also sceptical about Quick's convictions.

For this reason it wasn't surprising that in the early days of his term of office, Göran Lambertz had expressed strong doubts about Thomas Quick's convictions. Johan Asplund's parents met Göran Lambertz and for the first time felt that a public official understood them and was taking them seriously.

'He encouraged us to bring him a statement so that he could make enquiries into all eight of Thomas Quick's convictions,' Anna-Clara Asplund told me.

The lawyer Pelle Svensson – the Asplunds' representative in 1984, when they brought civil proceedings against Anna-Clara's ex-partner – was assigned to draft the petition.

On 20 November 2006 Svensson handed in a 'legal inquiry' of sixty-three pages to the Chancellor of Justice, with supporting material in cardboard boxes containing all of the court verdicts, investigation material, video tapes and so on.

Pelle Svensson's report was supported by Anna-Clara and Björn Asplund, as well as by Charles Zelmanovits's brother Frederick, who had never believed in Quick's guilt.

When the Chancellor of Justice announced his decision on Thomas Quick a week later, it came as a surprise to everyone. Had he really been able to review all the material and draft a decision on it in just a week? His decision was as follows:

> The Chancellor of Justice will not start an investigation nor in other respects implement any further measures in this matter.

The Chancellor's decision ran to eight pages and concluded with the following claim:

> The verdicts imposed on TQ are in all essential respects very well written and solid. They contain among other things extensive descriptions of the assessment of evidence by the courts.

Even Christer van der Kwast and Seppo Penttinen earned praise from Lambertz:

> In terms of the serious allegations directed at the prosecutor and head of the preliminary enquiries, I particularly want to emphasise that the investigation gives no cause for any other conclusion than that these persons have conducted themselves with skill under difficult circumstances.

Göran Lambertz's decision gave rise to speculation about the real motives behind him dropping the whole matter of Thomas Quick so quickly and readily. Especially surprising were Lambertz's laudatory comments on the excellent work of the police, prosecutor and courts.

At the time, Göran Lambertz was under fierce attack and had made enemies among the police, the Office of Prosecutions and the country's judiciary. To this one could also add certain groups of journalists in the wake of his prosecution of the publisher of *Expressen* in a press freedom case. His enemies also included various groups who were campaigning against sexual crime in general. In other words, his future as the Chancellor of Justice could not be taken for granted.

Göran Lambertz categorically denied that he was ever influenced by such considerations. At the time I had been one of the people who were unsure of his motives. Now I had the opportunity to ask him whether he had really been able to properly review the details before his hasty decision.

'I only had time to read the verdicts,' he admitted. 'I read them twice and the second time I had a red marker pen in my hand.'

He had also relied on assistants who read the supporting material, or at least parts of it. While I was there I met one of the underlings whose services Lambertz had relied on – an apparently newly hatched lawyer who, it seemed, had found Pelle Svensson's 'legal inquiry' far from impressive.

When we bumped into him at the coffee machine, Göran Lambertz called out cheerfully, 'You two have an interest in common!'

As we shook hands the young lawyer said, with a certain chill in his voice, 'Yes, but we don't agree about anything.'

'Really,' I said. 'Come back in a year or so and then we'll see.'

I almost felt sorry for him. At most he had been given five days to form an opinion on a massive and complex body of material. His significantly more experienced legal colleague Thomas Olsson had put in months of work just to review one of the murder cases. Yet it was this rosy-cheeked lawyer who had provided the grounds which, without a doubt, formed the basis of Lambertz's most catastrophic decision as Chancellor of Justice.

Lambertz's verdict was the final nail in the coffin, extinguishing any lingering hope of Pelle Svensson, the Asplunds and many others who had believed that Lambertz would be the one to finally correct this miscarriage of justice. In the meantime, Lambertz's approval was used by the prosecution as a trump card in the debate: the legal process had been reviewed and praised at the very highest level. I had already seen the argument deployed by Gubb Jan Stigson when we met in Falun right at the beginning of my research, and most recently it had also been repeated by Claes Borgström in his office.

I was astonished by Göran Lambertz's thoughtless approach to the whole matter. After outlining my findings, I began by talking about the first verdict and how I had come to the conclusion that there was actually no proper evidence at all. There were overwhelming indications that Quick had nothing at all to do with Charles Zelmanovits's disappearance, yet the prosecutor had avoided the entire problem.

Lambertz listened with interest. The meeting was amicable in tone. I told him about Sture withdrawing his confessions and then summarised one investigation after another. Finally, just before lunch when I had to leave, Lambertz explained that everything I had said was interesting but did not really make very much difference. Because the biggest mystery remained. How could Quick have talked about Trine and Gry? How could he have led the police to where the bodies were found?

I had to admit that those were the cases on which I had done the least research and that I didn't have the answers at my fingertips.

I left the meeting with a deep sense of disappointment. Personally, I have always liked Göran Lambertz and regarded him as a man of honour. What I had told him should have resulted in some kind of remorse, but I couldn't see the slightest trace of that.

As I walked away from the Office of the Chancellor of Justice, I understood two things. First, the forces defending the infallibility of the legal system were much more entrenched than I had realised. Second, the Quick story would keep rumbling along until the very last question mark had been straightened out. This meant that, at least as far as I was concerned, the job was far from done.

THE SVT DOCUMENTARIES

MY FIRST TWO documentaries on Thomas Quick were aired on SVT's *Dokument inifrån* ('Inside Document') on 14 and 21 December 2008.

So what was the story I was telling?

More or less this: a psychiatric hospital had drugged a sectioned patient, effectively turning him into a drug addict. He had then been subjected to intensive therapy. With the help of a good deal of cajoling and free access to narcotics, he had confessed to about thirty murders.

Despite the patient constantly being caught out lying, the prosecutor, investigators, therapists and all manner of specialists managed to bring eight confessed murders to prosecution. Six courts had unanimously found the patient guilty in each case.

In my documentary the patient took back all of his confessions and declared that he had never murdered anyone.

The first two documentaries told in some detail the oddities of the investigations into the murders of Therese Johannesen, the Stegehuises in Appojaure and Yenon Levi in Rörshyttan. But the most important new information was obviously that Sture Bergwall, the serial confessor, was now claiming that he was innocent.

PART III

'The criticism is pure nonsense. I see nothing wrong in what I have done, just because the arguments are made very loudly.'

Chief Prosecutor Christer van der Kwast to TT, 20 April 2009

THE WIND CHANGES

THE FINDINGS IN my documentaries meant that the Thomas Quick case was once again dominating the national media. By the Sunday evening on 14 December 2008, just after Sture Bergwall had retracted his confessions at the end of the first documentary, the lawyer Thomas Olsson made a statement to TT (Tidningarnas Telegrambyrå), Sweden's leading news service, that Sture Bergwall was intending to apply for a judicial review of all the murders for which he had been convicted. The first petition for a new trial regarding the murder of Yenon Levi would be sent to Svea High Court in the New Year.

Christer van der Kwast counterattacked the following day on a national radio programme known as *Studio Ett*.

'These are unfounded claims,' he said, responding to the suggestion that he and Seppo Penttinen had misled the courts. 'Everything has been openly accounted for in the investigations. It is not true that we have fed Quick with information.'

He also insisted that he was still absolutely convinced of Quick's guilt.

'What weighs in most heavily is that in every case he has been able to give us information that could only have been known to the perpetrator. This has been cross-checked with forensic evidence and certification from medical examiners among other things. There has been supporting evidence for every one of his confessions.'

Seppo Penttinen chose not to comment on the matter. 'There's a petition for a judicial review under way and I don't want to make any comment before that process has come to a close,' he told TT.

The same strategy was chosen by Birgitta Ståhle, Sven Åke Christianson and Claes Borgström.

Legal experts such as the lawyer Per E. Samuelsson and the General Secretary of Advokatsamfundet (the Bar Association) Anne Ramberg made a statement on Sture Bergwall's prospects of being cleared, which, in their view, were not favourable because withdrawal of the confessions did not constitute enough of a reason in itself. 'In order to be cleared, there must be some sort of new information which the court can take a position on,' Anne Ramberg commented to TT.

A few days later van der Kwast popped up again in a rare interview in *Svenska Dagbladet*. He referred to my documentaries as a 'low point' of investigative journalism and dismissed various reporters who had wanted to interview him, suggesting that they 'didn't have a clue' what it was all about. In his view, nothing new of any substance had turned up, apart from the fact that Sture Bergwall had retracted his confessions.

Van der Kwast embarked on a series of arguments that seemed a little strange, at least to anyone who was informed on the subject. He said it was nonsense that the case of the refugee boys demonstrated how Quick was making up murders after being fed with information from the media.

'In actual fact he started talking about one of the boys on 16 November 1994, before anything had even turned up in the media,' he told the newspaper.

I was having a hard time believing what I was reading. On 16 November 1994 Seppo Penttinen visited Säter Hospital to hear what in his own notes he described as 'association material' which 'very likely bears a relation to reality'.

On this occasion Thomas Quick mentioned the murder of a 'younger boy' at some time around '1988–1990'.

From Penttinen's notes: 'In this context the place name of Lindesberg is hovering in his mind. The boy couldn't speak Swedish. Quick mentioned some Slavic-sounding name like "Dusjunka". The boy was wearing a denim jacket, a moss-green jumper and oversized jeans with turned-up trouser legs. He had black hair and a southern appearance.'

How could Christer van der Kwast seriously suggest that this bore any relation to the story of the African refugee boys in Norway?

Kwast continued listing the 'unique details' Quick had provided during the investigation, which proved his guilt: Johan Asplund's testicular hernia and unusual birthmark, Therese Johannesen's atopic eczema and that Quick had been able to describe 'the wounds of the Appojaure murder victims, which were not known outside the circle of investigators'. And then came the trump card: that in the Therese case, Thomas Quick had been able to lead police to a place in the forest where he had cut up and burnt bodies, a place where a cadaver dog reacted to the presence of human remains – and when they dug, they uncovered fragments of burnt bone.

Van der Kwast also found it difficult to believe that any of the cases would be overturned.

'What's happening now is a soap opera spectacle. I am counting on the courts keeping a cool head. There will not be any retrials,' he said.

In the tidal wave of news, feature articles and editorials that followed, one of Sture Bergwall's real victims came forward: the man whom he came close to murdering in 1974 in a student residence in Uppsala. In a piece on *Newsmill* the man described the traumatic event and went on to express his disappointment in me:

> When I saw the programme on Thomas Quick on SVT yesterday I felt it was very biased – it gave the impression that he was innocent of the murders he'd been convicted of. I was a hair's breadth away from being murdered by Quick, or Sture Bergwall as he was called in those days, and it's difficult for me to believe that he's just a pathetic "petty criminal" as he's been described by Jan Guillou and other writers in the evening newspapers. [. . .] For the sake of my family I've not said very much about what happened to me almost 35 years ago. I've paid a price for my silence. When I now see the skewed image of Quick that is being presented I feel I have a responsibility to tell my story. Hannes Råstam's programme and the writers in the evening press make me feel sick.

The man, who was also interviewed in *Dagens Nyheter*, wrote, 'In fact I called Hannes Råstam when I heard about his documentary project. I wanted to tell him that I still had the police report from the attempted murder of me and that Råstam was welcome to read it. But Råstam wasn't interested in meeting me – he only wanted to know if Quick had been under the influence of drugs at the time.'

A few days later, on 17 December, *Expressen* published an interview with the stepfather of the nine-year-old whom Sture Bergwall had sexually molested at the age of nineteen while working as a nursing assistant in 1969. 'He is capable of murdering any number of people,' said the stepfather, who was coming forward because, in his view, 'it is important to highlight that Thomas Quick has been found guilty of violent acts before'.

As well as describing the assault at the hospital, the quotation was once again given from the psychiatric examination of 1970, stating that Quick suffered from a 'high-grade sexual perversion of the type known as *paedophilia cum sadismus*' and, under certain circumstances, would be 'extremely dangerous to the safety, well-being and lives of others'.

Even some of my colleagues felt that I had painted the picture of Sture Bergwall in a somewhat rosy light by not delving deeper into his earlier wrongdoings in the documentaries, where they were only briefly alluded to. The criticism was not unexpected and yet it was palpable. At the same time, it couldn't have been done in any other way: the aim of my investigation was to uncover whether Sture Bergwall had committed the eight murders he had been convicted of, not to go deeper into crimes we already knew he had committed. As it was, it had been almost impossible to compress the enormously complex story into two hours of television.

Soon the situation was very much like the Quick feud raging at its worst about ten years before, with the difference that the doubters, who earlier had been in a noisy minority, now made up the majority. Those who still believed that Quick was guilty as charged were a rapidly shrinking group.

On 17 December *Dagens Nyheter* ran the following editorial:

That Thomas Quick has been convicted of eight murders and accepted the blame for many more may well be one of our country's greatest miscarriages of justice. But it could also be a case of a guilty murderer. Whatever the crime status of Thomas Quick, one thing can be said unequivocally: in the Quick case, the Swedish legal system has shown some worrying weaknesses, weaknesses that remind one of the legal rot of the 1950s. A legal review should now take place in accordance with legal practice and common sense. Such investigations should have as their purpose to clarify what has happened, what the role of the alleged guilty party has been and, above all – they must be unprejudiced.

The case of Thomas Quick shows many departures from accepted procedure. Attention is also being directed at the prosecutor, interrogator, defence counsel, law courts, and the whole line-up around the murderer Thomas Quick. This attention is hardly flattering.

It is quite clear that Thomas Quick has been 'helped to remember', that therapeutic treatment has been combined with a police investigation, and that any circumstances that might put a 'dent' in his guilt have been removed from sight. Arguably, it is problematic for the legal system as a whole that this can happen. Now there must be an investigation into how a number of people in positions of responsibility have conducted themselves in the case of Quick. His lawyer's awaited petition for a new trial will hopefully be granted. Any faults and/or omissions can thereby be exposed and blame apportioned.

The broader question is whether the treatment of Thomas Quick says something about our legal system in general. The role of the theory of repressed memories is striking. This theory has been discredited to some extent in recent years, but for a few years it was accepted in Swedish law courts and a number of people were found guilty and sentenced to long prison terms on the basis of allegations apparently based on memories. The fact that many years had passed and that there were no witnesses or other evidence to back up these memories seemed to have no

> importance. Even more troubling is that legal authorities whose task it is to watch over order in the legal system have also been pulled along and lost their sense of critical awareness.
>
> The Chancellor of Justice allowed himself to be convinced by the sheer number of convictions against Thomas Quick and dismissed the objections by declaring that they touched upon circumstances that by and large had little significance. So what happened to that elegant phrase 'beyond all reasonable doubt'?

In addition to the heated state of public opinion and the fact that Sture Bergwall intended to petition for a retrial, there was another awkward issue for those who had worked to convict Thomas Quick or insisted on emphasising his guilt: now even the Prosecutor-General, Anders Perklev, was looking at the case, after two civilians in Sundsvall had reported Seppo Penttinen and Christer van der Kwast for gross professional misconduct.

Clearly even the Chancellor of Justice, Göran Lambertz, was increasingly aware of the ground moving beneath his feet. On Monday, 22 December, the morning after the second documentary had been aired, he appeared on TV4's *Nyhetsmorgon* ('News Morning').

'I don't know if he was guilty but I'm quite sure that he's guilty of at least some of these murders. There is absolutely overwhelming evidence for a few of the sentences,' he said in his appearance.

'So you're certain that he's guilty?' the presenter asked.

'Yes, for a couple of the murders I am certain,' said Lambertz. 'And one also has to bear in mind that it has been established beyond all doubt that he has the capacity to do this. He has been judged by many psychiatrists to be a highly dangerous person with a sadistic and paedophilic nature and he has evidently committed a couple of extremely serious violent crimes, which he's already been convicted of.'

This was undoubtedly quite a significant step away from the opinion he presented in his decision of 2006. In a debate article in *Aftonbladet* on 6 January 2009 he went one step further. After outlining the factors that spoke in favour of Quick's guilt, he wrote:

> 1. It is absolutely possible that he decided to 'become a mass murderer', memorised as much as possible from the media and managed to portray himself as guilty by continually modifying his story and behaviour to what was required so that he would be believed. The influence of drugs and psychotherapy may have played a role. His current story may be the correct one.
>
> 2. For at least a few of the eight murders there are other persons under strong suspicion.
>
> 3. Certain highly significant parts of Quick's stories seem to have been absolutely incorrect. These errors are difficult to explain in any other way than that he made them up.

Lambertz went on to write that there was not 'a vestige of evidence' to suggest that the investigators 'had tried to mislead the courts and the general public into believing that Thomas Quick was guilty of crimes that they did not themselves believe he had committed'. However: 'The police and prosecution may have proceeded a little hastily at times, possibly not taking enough account of the circumstances that argued against Quick's implication in the crimes. This would not be a good thing, but it could be seen as a human error given the investigation process in which they found themselves.'

The Chancellor of Justice simply had no idea any more on which foot he should stand.

> It is easy to come to the conclusion that everything is black or white. That either the psychotherapist Birgitta Ståhle, the policeman Seppo Penttinen, the prosecutor Christer van der Kwast, the lawyer Claes Borgström or a couple of journalists, such as for instance *Dala-Demokraten*'s Gubb Jan Stigson, are utterly mistaken and may even have conspired in certain ways. Or that those who are totally misguided include Leif G.W. Persson, Jan Guillou, the psychiatrist Ulf Åsgård, the lawyer Pelle Svensson, the policeman Jan Olsson and the journalist Hannes Råstam. In fact it need not be one or the other. All these people could have done a good job and drawn fairly reasonable, though quite different, conclusions.

Göran Lambertz's conclusion was symptomatic: 'If Thomas Quick has been wrongly convicted, then surely it is a huge miscarriage of justice? Yes, all commentators seem to be agreed about that. But obviously the conviction could also be correct, and we'll have to wait for the answer that may eventually emerge. But one has to emphasise that in principle it is less serious if the legal system convicts an innocent person who has confessed and wishes to be convicted, than if it convicts an innocent person who maintains his innocence.'

This was undoubtedly an interesting thought from the country's highest-ranking lawyer.

Anne Ramberg of Advokatsamfundet was every bit as wavering in her arguments when she tried to present her position in *Advokaten* magazine's first editorial of 2009, where she suggested that Thomas Quick could very well 'be correctly sentenced even if innocent'.

On 16 February 2009 the Prosecutor-General announced that he did not intend to press for any investigation into the conduct of responsible parties behind the Thomas Quick convictions.

His reason for this was that most of the alleged instances of professional misconduct had taken place more than ten years earlier and therefore fell outside the statute of limitation. Even misconduct at a later stage, which could therefore be relevant to an investigation of this kind, would have been made before the Chancellor's assessment of 2006. And: 'The Chancellor of Justice found after a thorough review that a preliminary investigation should not be initiated' as there had not been any 'significant failings from the prosecutor's side, or that of the police'.

Because the Chancellor of Justice was the country's highest-ranking lawyer, the Prosecutor-General noted that he didn't have the authority to question his decision. And with this, the matter had run its course.

The two individuals who had pressed charges against the police also wanted the Office of Prosecution to take a position on whether it would be justified in initiating its own court process to re-examine the Quick judgments. On this point Perklev conceded that they had good reason to do so and the matter was handed over to the

National Authority for Police Court Cases in Malmö, where the Chief Prosecutor Björn Ericson put together a group consisting of himself, three other prosecutors and a fact-finder to scrutinise the entire Quick investigation.

THIRTEEN BINDERS

ON 20 APRIL 2009 Thomas Olsson and his colleague Martin Cullberg handed in Sture Bergwall's petition for a retrial of the Yenon Levi murder. The document, seventy-three pages long and consisting of 274 bullet points, listed all the peculiarities over the course of the investigation: the bypassing of SKL's findings and everything else that strongly spoke in favour of an alternative perpetrator, 'Ben Ali', the first unsuccessful reconstruction, the obvious lie about his accomplice – Patrik – and how Quick had changed pretty much every statement he had made in a meandering journey spanning fourteen long interviews to the courtroom where his final story was presented.

Because Björn Ericson's group had already been charged with examining the Quick investigation, they were asked to take a position on Sture Bergwall's first petition for a new hearing.

In principle it is impossible to overturn verdicts once they have been adjudicated. This principle is one of the cornerstones of the Swedish legal system and also goes by another name, *orubblighetsprincipen* – the principle of immovability.

During the entire twentieth century there had only been four retrials of murder convictions – one in every twenty-five years. In the 2000s there hadn't as yet been a single retrial. Now Sture Bergwall was hoping to have *eight* murder convictions overturned. The odds were worse than lousy, but I never doubted that this was what eventually would happen. The more I dug around in the case, the more indications I had of Sture Bergwall's innocence.

What was clear, however, was that the process would take time.

Sweden doesn't have a separate institution for retrials, so prosecutors looking at petitions must do so when they have a spare moment from their usual tasks.

In a legal system where trials are postponed for months and years because of staff shortages, it goes without saying that a petition for a retrial of a case more than ten years old will not be given very high priority.

In addition, as there is no legal aid for the plaintiff in such an application, this means that the lawyer who takes on the case will be doing so on a *pro bono* basis – and thus, like the prosecutor reviewing the case, will have to squeeze it in whenever possible.

In the spring of 2009 Johan Brånstad, the editor of *Dokument inifrån* and I decided to go ahead with a third documentary on Thomas Quick to tell the full story of the cases there had not been time to deal with in the first two films. The intention was also to take some of the focus away from Sture Bergwall and to point the spotlight more on the circle that facilitated the miscarriages of justice.

At the same time I kept searching for the missing interviews.

Gun Bergwall remembered a few more things about the interview in which she gave her brother an alibi for the murder of Thomas Blomgren. She couldn't be precise about the date, only that it took place in the early 1990s, and that the police officer came from Luleå and recorded it on tape. His name was Barsk, she remembered, and there was also another person present.

'He asked a lot about the Whitsun weekend in 1964. I wondered why, what had happened that weekend, but they didn't want to tell me. They wanted to look at photos as well,' said Gun Bergwall.

She had shown them one in which Sture could be seen in his confirmation clothes at the same time as he was supposedly murdering a child in Växjö. When Gun found out that Sture had confessed to the murder of Thomas Blomgren that weekend she firmly stated that Sture had not left Falun. Not that weekend and not at any other time during this period. Sture was always at home.

To have person after person telling me how they had given the police information that firmly spoke against the possibility of Quick being the murderer was one thing – certainly it was enough in its own right to show on television. But to have the thing confirmed in writing in an archived and withheld interrogation report would obviously put everything in a different light.

I sent letter after letter to the police authority in Sundsvall, but either they didn't answer at all or issued denials via Seppo Penttinen.

At the same time the Chief Prosecutor Björn Ericson's group entrusted with the inquiry began to slowly close in. Soon Ericson was demanding to have all investigation materials held by the police in Sundsvall sent to him.

In mid-October 2009 out of the blue I received a fairly grovelling letter from Seppo Penttinen, with copies of the two interrogation reports I had been searching for. Penttinen explained that these two interviews with Örjan Bergwall hadn't been included in the investigation files because they had been judged to be a part of the so-called 'slush'.

In response to my repeated question about the contents of this slush and where it was kept, he wrote, 'The undersigned is aware of the existence of a small number of interviews which, like Örjan Bergwall's interview, have been judged to be a part of the "slush". These interviews have no particular connection to any specific matter. They are interviews of persons in Sture Bergwall's circle of acquaintances and were part of the process of researching his general background. [. . .] We are now informing you that all the investigation materials in the concluded proceedings have been sent to the National Authority for Police Court Cases in Malmö.'

I wasn't all that convinced that Seppo Penttinen would actually send all the materials to Björn Ericson, so I sent Ericson a list of eight interviews which I knew existed and had requested from the police in Sundsvall. Had they succeeded where I had failed, had they been given these interviews?

When it turned out that Penttinen had not sent them, the internal investigators contacted him and politely asked him if there was a possibility that he had some additional material in his study – oddly enough, this was where all the Quick material was stored.

My third documentary on Thomas Quick was aired on 8 November 2009.

After that, no further programmes had been planned, but I couldn't let go of the question of the missing interviews. It had become a personal matter for me.

After a number of nudges the internal investigators seemed to have received all of the material. In total, there were thirteen binders, which for many years had been kept out of sight of the courts, the public and journalists. Because the documents were not registered they had been impossible to track through police authority filing.

On 16 December I went to Malmö to look through the thirteen files. Their contents decisively changed the overall picture of the investigation. Here were the interviews that showed that the man who had supposedly driven the young Sture to Växjö couldn't possibly have done so, along with other similarly impossible accomplices and helpers. In a file marked 'Other Interviews' I found, among other things, fourteen interviews with all of Thomas Quick's siblings, who unanimously gave a picture that completely contradicted the terrifying childhood memories elicited in the climate of Säter's drug-induced object relations therapy. The interviews also ruled out the possibility that Sture Bergwall could have driven a car before 1987.

What defined all these interviews – which were regarded by Seppo Penttinen as irrelevant – was quite simply that they showed the extent to which Quick was making it all up.

The most interesting thing in the files was an interrogation of Thomas Quick on 27 January 1999, showing that Quick was systematically making up murders and that the investigators were aware of it. Two weeks earlier, in conversation with Detective Inspector Anna Wikström and Birgitta Ståhle, Thomas Quick had spoken about a 'breakthrough in the therapy'. For the first time, Quick had drawn up a list of all his murders in chronological order.

From the verdict on the Trine and Gry proceedings I knew that on the second day of the main hearing in Falu District Court Christer van der Kwast had handed in a similar list containing some twenty-nine people.

When Thomas Quick came to the interview on 27 January he had this list in his back pocket. It is worth pointing out that Quick's lawyer, Claes Borgström, and Jan Karlsson from the CID were present during the entire interview.

After a long opening exchange with Penttinen, Quick began his story:

> TQ: This is a chronological list starting in 1964: Thomas Blomgren.
>
> PENTTINEN: Mm. So the first name is Thomas, then you've listed Lars, Alvar, the Hospital boy, Björn, 'Michael', 'Per', Björn – Norway, Reine, Martin, Charles, Benny, Johan, the Värmland boy, the car boy, Olle, the Stegehuises, Magnus, the West Coast, Levi, Marianne – Norway, the woman by the road, Therese – Norway, Trine – Norway, the woman in the car park – Norway [. . .] And then up on the right M–Z. Duska – Norway, J. Tony – Finland.

Penttinen carried on reading Quick's note: 'I have a sacred place between Sågmyra and Grycksbo. I have a place of massacre by and around Främby Point. I have a small but very valuable hiding place in Ölsta.'

The first name on the list after Thomas Blomgren was 'Lars', who had supposedly been murdered by Quick in 'central Sweden' in 1965. The truth, however, is that 'Lars' was feeding ducks with a friend on the ice when the ice broke and the boy drowned. There were witnesses to the accident and the family is absolutely certain that it was nothing but pure misfortune. I knew this because Jenny Küttim and I had already looked through all the confessions Quick had made over the years – not just the ones that led to proceedings in law courts. Therefore I knew that this confession was regarded as so unbelievable by the Quick investigators, they didn't even bother to contact the family of 'Lars'.

A 'named youth', according to the list, had been abducted in 1985 in Norrland, from where, according to Thomas Quick, he was brought to Falun and his body placed in one of Quick's 'hides'.

'We know who he is,' Christer van der Kwast said mysteriously in an interview with TT in the spring of 2000.

In one of the withheld interviews it emerged that this was about a fifteen-year-old boy, Magnus Jonsson, who had disappeared in Örnsköldsvik early in 1985. However, the truth was that the police had found Magnus's lone footprints on the ice leading to open water, where he had obviously fallen in and drowned. A few years later Magnus Jonsson's remains were found and identified with the help of DNA analysis.

The list of Quick's victims also included a number of confessed murders that, according to local police authorities, lacked all foundation in reality – there were no disappearances that matched the given times and places.

When van der Kwast handed in the list to the district court in May 2000 he commented to TT, 'We have gone through all the murders, accidents and disappearances that could be possible Quick cases. We have a lot of material that is difficult to check. The clearest ones are these given in the list, that is, where he himself has provided us with the information.'

For members of the district court the list must have suggested that they were dealing with a criminal who was absolutely unique and that the current case was just one in a line that could be expected to grow longer and longer.

The question is, how would the district court have judged the murders of Trine Jensen and Gry Storvik if they had been informed that a large number of the murders on the list were evidently figments of Quick's imagination?

THE CRIME JOURNALIST

BJÖRN ERICSON'S CHIEF prosecutor's group didn't get very far in terms of their own decision on a retrial for Sture Bergwall, but on 17 December 2009 they finished their review of the petition for a new trial in the Yenon Levi case. Björn Ericson announced that it had been accepted.

Meanwhile, Ericson kept requesting materials on each case and had now reached the famous bone fragments from the Therese Johannesen inquiry. The Norwegians handed them over and before long they had been sent to SKL for analysis.

One of the osteologists who studied the bone pieces was Ylva Svenfelt, an independent research scientist and a specialist in burnt bones from the Iron Age. She was very surprised when she saw the bone fragments, which were allegedly from a human child.

On Thursday, 18 March 2010 a number of media sources revealed that the bones had only been subjected to a visual inspection ahead of the first trial: in other words, professors Per Holck and Richard Helmer had only looked at them before announcing their expert, scientific findings. This time, however, they were examined at molecular and biological levels. They proved not to be bones at all, but were actually wood with an added component of glue – most likely fibreboard.

'Anyone who has worked with burnt bone fragments can see straight away that this is not bone. I can't interpret it in any other way than scientific fraud,' Ylva Svenfelt commented to *Aftonbladet*.

Thomas Olsson made a statement to *Expressen*: 'It's so incredible, even we couldn't have anticipated this. But it's symptomatic of the Quick case, where people of academic repute have offered their services to the whole circus.'

Two days after this news, which perhaps more than any other had added a sheen of ridicule to the whole investigation, I received the Guldspaden Prize (the Golden Spade) from Föreningen Grävande Journalisters (the Association of Investigative Journalists) for my Quick documentaries.

Their annual three-day conference was held that year at Radiohuset (SVT's main building) in Stockholm, and on the Sunday the whole event was rounded off with a debate between me and Gubb Jan Stigson on the role of the media in the Quick scandal. Among the audience in the auditorium of the Radio Symphony Hall were about a hundred colleagues, including Jenny Küttim, Johan Brånstad and Thomas Olsson.

It was with mixed feelings that I waited for the debate to begin on the podium.

I owed Gubb Jan a great debt of thanks. Not only had he in some sense persuaded me to take on the case, but he had also helped me to get hold of significant amounts of material and opened many doors with his recommendations.

He was now the only one who still adhered to the view that Quick was guilty, but he was still willing to defend that view in an open forum. He had therefore become something of a spokesman for van der Kwast and Penttinen, as well as Ståhle, Christianson and Borgström. He received no other reward for this than the increasing mirth of his peers.

And to a very large extent this was my fault.

At the same time his obstinate refusal to accept proven facts was beginning to come across as quite extraordinary. Strangely enough, he was also blind to the role he had played in the story. During my research for the third documentary I continued to delve into material, including the preliminary investigation notes on Trine and Gry, in an attempt to find out who exactly, other than Kåre Hunstad, had provided Quick with the original tip-off for the murder.

In a document from 26 January 2000 I found an inventory, the result of a Sisyphean task completed by a poor policeman by the name of Jan Karlsson, who had trawled through every Swedish newspaper that might have mentioned Gry Storvik's name after she was found murdered on 25 June 1985. After fruitlessly scanning every edition of *Aftonbladet*, *Dagens Nyheter* and *Expressen* he came to *Dala-Demokraten*.

And there – on 2 October 1998, ten months before the famed visit to the crime scene – was an article on the subject written by none other than Gubb Jan Stigson.

Dala-Demokraten was one of the newspapers which Ward 36 at Säter Hospital subscribed to, and in interrogations relating to other cases it had emerged that Quick read it daily. I sought out the article in question at the Kurs- och tidskriftsbiblioteket (Academic and Newspaper Library) in Gothenburg. Under the headline 'Thomas Quick Now Being Linked to Sex Murders in Norway', Stigson went on to write, 'Currently interest is being focused primarily on two murders of women and one disappearance, all three of them Norwegian crime classics.'

After a short outline of the Trine Jensen and Marianne Rugaas Knutsen cases came the crucial information:

> The third case concerns 23-year-old Gry Storvik, who went missing in central Oslo and was found murdered in a car park in Myrvoll on 25 June 1985. The discovery was not far from the place where Trine's body was found. The cases have several similarities. The victim's bodies bear signs of violence with many similarities. And furthermore, both girls disappeared within a radius of just a few hundred metres.

The information on the murder of Gry which Quick was able to read in *Dala-Demokraten* was undoubtedly quite a good start, given how the questioning was carried out and how Quick's stories were usually 'developed' over the course of an investigation.

For some unknown reason, when during my initial research Gubb Jan Stigson was kind enough to photocopy around three hundred of his articles on Quick, he chose not to include this one in the collection.

The fact that the article was entered into the CID investigation report didn't prevent the district court from being kept in the dark about its existence.

The podium debate began with the moderator, Monica Saarinen, also the presenter of *Studio Ett*, pointing out the irony of Gubb Jan Stigson having received the Grand Prize of Publicistklubben (the Publicists' Club) in 1995 for his journalism on Quick – the very same subject as mine.

After some small talk about how we had first come into contact with one another, and clarifying that we had taken radically opposed positions on the question of Quick's guilt, Stigson explained: 'You get to a point where you can't get any further, you just have to accept that he's guilty. I'd like to say that I've maintained a critical outlook all along. And then all this happens, all this nonsense. This suggestion that he was just a clown. There's been complete silence about his background, which is unique in Swedish criminal history.'

'Hannes, how can you be so sure he's innocent?' Saarinen asked.

'I've read all the material,' I explained. 'Above all I've lined up everything that spoke in favour of his guilt. And there's nothing left. There's not a shred of evidence. These judgments only rest on Quick's testimony, and once you read his stories and realise how they've emerged, you see how in the beginning he knew absolutely nothing about these murders. He's wrong about practically everything.'

At this point Stigson started shaking his head and I felt a stab of irritation.

'You're shaking your head and you're doing it even though you know better. The audience hasn't read these interrogation reports, but you have. So what circumstances is he aware of, then, in the early interviews, for even one of his murders?'

'The point is . . . in every case he says something early on that sort of makes it worth carrying on with it, and then he complicates it and in the end you uncover astonishing information. How did he end up in Ørje Forest?'

'He read about it in *Verdens Gang*.'

'About Ørje Forest? No one knew anything about Ørje Forest before he . . .'

'Ørje Forest is mentioned in *Verdens Gang*. As is all the information he gives about the Therese murder.'

'No, no . . .'

'Perhaps you don't know any better, but you are mistaken.'

Gubb Jan Stigson changed the subject and asked why I seemed unconcerned about Sture Bergwall's previous criminal record. I answered that I was looking into how the Swedish legal system and the Swedish system of psychiatric care were capable of dealing with a mentally ill person, who was also drugged, who confessed to murders – not what his prior criminal record had been.

This didn't prevent Stigson from going on. Instead he launched into a description of 'ten to twelve sexual attacks of varying degrees of severity' which Sture Bergwall had apparently begun committing at the age of fifteen, followed by the stabbing in 1974. Monica Saarinen interjected that Stigson, ahead of the debate, had sent her eighty articles which she had read, and that he mentioned these earlier crimes in an estimated 80 to 90 per cent of them.

'I mean they are the prerequisite for what comes after,' Stigson claimed.

'How do you mean?' asked Saarinen.

'Yeah, but I mean . . . he has suffered with this . . . these are perversions that are virtually incurable.'

'How do you know that?' asked Saarinen.

'Well . . . I mean . . . that's what the statistics say.'

Stigson alluded to two other cases and the doctors he had spoken to.

'You mean that because he did this he could very well be guilty?' asked Saarinen.

'No, but because he's got this thing it's worth investigating to see if he's guilty. But it says . . . Fransson checks his background and comes to the conclusion that . . .'

At this stage I could no longer hold my silence, and I interrupted him.

'What Gubb Jan is talking about is a mix of hearsay, uninvestigated incidents, alleged incidents and so on. There are two prosecutions where he confessed and he was found guilty. That is correct. And

I've mentioned that he has been found guilty of two extremely serious violent crimes. I don't think there's much point going over events that go back decades. What's incredible is that he has been found guilty of eight murders which I and many others are saying he never committed. If we could just leave the 1960s behind and make our way into modern times it would be a huge relief. To keep stirring and stirring and stirring the pot as Gubb Jan Stigson has been doing now for twenty years about these various statements made by doctors, about events that happened when he was only nineteen, these so-called . . .'

'Fourteen.'

'What?'

'Don't the oldest go back to when he's fourteen? About fourteen. That's what he says, anyway.'

'Oh, I see, you're going even further back now. Soon you'll be back in the 1950s. I think it's shameful, actually. Gubb Jan Stigson's journalism is a character assassination of a psychiatric patient.'

'Character assassination? But this is . . . this is . . .'

'Gubb Jan Stigson has copied three hundred of his articles for me and there's this constant dwelling on this . . .'

I was forced to turn towards him, rather than the audience.

'I really don't understand what you are doing, because it doesn't have a bloody thing to do with the actual verdicts.'

'Oh, it absolutely does!'

'The question of his guilt in these murders?'

'No, no, it's not as simple as that!'

'The question of guilt in murders? That is what we're supposed to be discussing here. A person who's been wrongly convicted of murder.'

'Oh, but it's so easy to wriggle out of this one. It's almost fraudulent not to include his background . . .'

Monica Saarinen tried to break the poisonous atmosphere by changing the subject, but Stigson and I quickly launched into a new argument. He insisted that Quick was also guilty of the murder of Thomas Blomgren and I tried in vain to convince him that it was absolutely impossible, while at the same time informing the audience of Quick's visits to the Kungliga biblioteket (the Royal National Library) in Stockholm to revise his facts.

'Hannes, are you saying that Gubb Jan also helped Thomas Quick acquire information so he could keep confessing?'

'Gubb Jan has published articles where he's named victims, detailed where the victims disappeared, described the sort of violence the victim was subjected to, where the victim was found and so on, before Thomas Quick had even mentioned anything about it, and . . .'

'What case are you talking about?' Gubb Jan cut in.

'Gry Storvik, for example.'

'Yes . . . but . . . surely . . .'

'Surprisingly enough, that's one of the articles you chose not to copy for me. I found it in a newspaper archive. On 2 October 1998 you published an article that described everything Thomas Quick needed to know to make a confession. Before this point he had never even mentioned the name Gry Storvik.'

'I knew nothing about Gry Storvik until I heard that he'd named her!' Stigson hissed.

'So it must be a forgery that's found its way into the archived microfilm, then?' Stigson slumped a little over the lectern where we were standing.

'I have it on my computer. I'll show it to you immediately afterwards,' I said.

'Have you yourself given any thought to the possibility that Thomas Quick could have got information from your articles?' asked Saarinen.

'There is nothing in my articles that has any bearing on these cases,' Stigson insisted. 'He says I gave him this book . . . Göran Elwin's book on the Johan case. Nothing in that book has any bearing on the court verdict!'

'Well, it contains descriptions of all his clothes and his red rucksack,' I said. 'These are the types of things I know for a fact that Thomas Quick carefully made a note of so that he could talk about it. So of course you've given him information.'

'Yeah, but . . .'

'And you gave him that book.'

'But if he could go to the library anyway, why would he come to me for a book?'

Stigson changed tack again with a long description of his contact with Quick and how he had frequently had telephone contact with him because he felt 'sorry for him'.

I tried to hit the rewind button: 'It's important to grasp that these murder investigations, the entire Thomas Quick story, is driven by the media, the police and his therapy in a strange process of collusion. In which the media is used by the police in order to . . .'

'Bloody hell . . .' Stigson shook his head.

'What are you trying to say?' I asked.

'Well, bloody hell! You think I've been colluding with the police?'

'Every time Thomas Quick starts talking or suggesting anything it's immediately leaked to you or other journalists who start publishing photos of the victims, of . . .'

'Who's leaking?'

'Well, clearly someone on the inside of the police investigation. Sometimes van der Kwast, sometimes Seppo Penttinen. Why would anyone do that during an ongoing police investigation?'

'That's rubbish. I've never had anything like that . . .'

'Look me in the eye! Is this really just rubbish?'

'Yes, that I . . . yes, yes! That on a regular basis they were supplying me with something so he'd be able to . . . yes, it's rubbish. Not in any way!'

'But you've had information from day one!' I protested.

Stigson started talking about an interview he did with Lars-Inge Svartenbrandt, and all the positive things he had said about repressed memories and therapy.

'You've totally lost touch with reality,' I said.

But Stigson just carried on talking about Svartenbrandt. Monica Saarinen wanted us to start rounding things off, and I asked what – if anything – might make Gubb Jan Stigson change his mind about the case of Thomas Quick. He said that he hadn't seen 'anything that explains anything away'.

'Nothing?' I wondered.

'Nothing.'

'But what could make you . . .'

'In the end you reach an end point. I've reached that point as far as these cases go.'

I was starting to feel faint. So it really was that simple: it was about faith.

Having it or not having it.

The discussion was thrown open to the audience and the first question was familiar: could Swedish courts of law really be so lax that they imposed sentences without any technical evidence?

Stigson put his foot down: 'Not technical evidence in the sense of fingerprints and DNA. But there's other technical evidence. Like marks cut into birch trees and things like that. Phosphate mapping. Sniffer dogs.'

'Yeah, that dog is pretty interesting,' I said. 'A privately owned cadaver dog that reacts to human remains in an incredibly large number of places. Archaeological excavations have been carried out in over twenty locations, earth has been put through a sieve, a lake has been emptied, but nothing has been found except for this tiny little fragment weighing half a gram which, it's now been revealed, is not even bone. Don't you draw any conclusions from that?'

'Well, you know . . .'

'Gubb Jan Stigson, you're the only one who still believes this.'

'Yes, I seem to be.'

After the debate had ended I stayed on with a few colleagues up by the stage.

At the same time, Gubb Jan Stigson packed up his things and quickly walked away through the audience.

Before I'd had time to react, he'd left the auditorium. He clearly wasn't interested in the article I had offered to show him on my computer.

THE LAST PIECE OF THE PUZZLE

ON 20 APRIL 2010 Thomas Olsson and Martin Cullberg handed in Sture Bergwall's second petition for a new trial, this time regarding the Therese Johannesen case. About a month later, on 27 May, Chief Prosecutor Eva Finné announced her decision in the Yenon Levi case. Although the retrial was accepted, no trial was scheduled. The evidence was so paltry that there was simply no point in holding new proceedings, as would normally happen.

'After reviewing the case I have come to the conclusion that the evidence does not hold any possibility of corroborating a crime,' she wrote. 'Bergwall denies the crime. Certainly over the course of the investigation he has offered some information that tallies with some of the evidence, but his statement is characterised by contradictions and changes to such an extent that a conviction cannot be considered as likely. For these reasons I am dropping all charges against Sture Bergwall.'

Christer van der Kwast was furious.

'I think it's rubbish not to seize the opportunity of a full examination out in the open where Quick can explain his earlier confessions. It's an easy way out of a substantial and difficult new legal process. Quick was convicted on proper grounds and the petition for a retrial has been improperly approved. I believe that media pressure has played a role in this capitulation,' he commented to TT.

After the summer Björn Ericson announced his decision regarding the Therese retrial. He did not oppose a review.

It was only a matter of time before Sture Bergwall would be freed of all eight murder convictions. He would go down in history – though in an entirely different way to how Birgitta Ståhle, Sven Åke Christianson, Christer van der Kwast, Seppo Penttinen and other participants in the Quick scandal could possibly have imagined.

On 2 September 2010 Chief Prosecutor Bo Lindgren, appointed by Björn Ericson to review the Trine and Gry verdicts, received the original raw footage behind the edited version of the reconnaissance that had been shown to the Falu District Court at the trial in Stockholm.

They were delivered in two boxes. There were thirteen VHS tapes and eight mini-cassettes, in total some thirty-nine hours of recorded video. The technical division transferred the films to DVDs and, before long, copies were delivered to Thomas Olsson at the Leif Silbersky law firm in Stockholm. There, Jenny Küttim burned her own copies, which she transferred to a server in order for me to download them and burn my own copies right away.

There was something almost ceremonial about the way I fed that first film into my laptop. For me, I felt like I had reached the end of my investigation. I had checked all the information I could check, straightened out all the other question marks – the inspection film from the trial for the murders of Trine Jensen and Gry Storvik was all that remained.

The films had been shot using two cameras. One showed the road in front of the car in which, among others, Thomas Quick, Seppo Penttinen, Christer van der Kwast and Sven Åke Christianson were travelling. Another filmed Quick's face during the journey, with Penttinen clearly visible in the seat in front.

I quickly realised that this was the footage that was most interesting.

The films were desperately dull for the most part. They showed the trip from Säter to Oslo, then around and around Oslo and then out of the city again. A few of the films showed the reconstructions at the murder scenes, where Thomas Quick tried to demonstrate how he had murdered the women. Basically he didn't do anything at all right, and sure enough none of these scenes were included in the edited version shown to the district court.

But the most interesting thing was of course to be able at last to see whether Quick, at the inspection in August 1999, eighteen years after the murder of Trine Jensen, was really able to 'direct the car without any significant difficulty to within a few yards of the place where she was found', as well as the famous sequence where he spontaneously reacted with powerful anxiety as the convoy of vehicles passed the car park where Gry Storvik's corpse had been left. In the films shown to the district court there was no doubt about either of these supposed facts.

In the unedited film the cars drove around Oslo for an absolute eternity. Sture sat in the back, high as a kite and with staring eyes. He held up his index finger and slowly wagged it back and forth. Seppo Penttinen was in front, stony-faced.

At long last the police grew tired of driving around aimlessly and decided to go to Kolbotn, which is closer to where the bodies were found. Even here Quick wasn't able to find his way. Once it was clear that he didn't have a clue where they were supposed to go, Penttinen took charge.

'So the suggestion now is that we turn round and go back to the last junction, where we waited for a long time while you were deciding, and then we take the alternative road to the left, because you were looking quite steadily in that direction, and then we've covered that possibility as well.'

After this, they turned on to the road leading to the crime scene, but Quick led them the wrong direction.

'There's an exit here now onto the E18 again, Thomas,' Penttinen finally pointed out.

After this, he announced, 'Christer has an idea that you should stay here, in this area, if you could turn off a bit . . . Yes, stop. I think we should take a short break, if you don't mind? OK, turn off the sound.'

When sound and image were turned back on the car was travelling along the same road, but heading in the right direction this time. Thomas Quick moved his finger hither and thither. Then suddenly Seppo Penttinen said that he had pointed to the right and the car turned off at the correct junction. Was he pointing to the right? Maybe. Certainly he was also pointing to the left. And straight ahead. But only when they were at the correct turn-off did Penttinen react and explain where Quick was really pointing. Soon the procedure was repeated, but in the opposite direction, because Quick had once again missed a junction and the vehicle had to turn round – after the interrogator had discreetly asked if it might not be better to turn back.

As they were passing the actual place where Gry's body had been found, Penttinen said, 'Should we stop?'

But Thomas Quick didn't pick up on this; he wanted to carry on.

Before long Penttinen said, 'What do you say, do you want to turn round?'

Finally Quick realised what was going on. He agreed that they should turn round. Soon he asked them to stop in more or less the place where Penttinen had just suggested it might be good to stop for a while.

To say that Thomas Quick was able to lead the investigators to the scene is to really conjure things out of thin air. It was quite the opposite; they were the ones who led him to the scene, through their hints and helpful interpretations as well as clear instructions and manoeuvres.

Sture Bergwall said to me, 'There was always information to pick up on. I was reading not just Seppo but also the other police in the minibus, and the driver. If Seppo got a bit strained I knew we were heading in the wrong direction. And if the driver applied the brakes I knew we had to turn off very soon, and then I had time to say so. The whole time I had these small, small signs. With little details they let me know where we were going. But it sounded as if I was telling them.'

And what about that spontaneous reaction to the spot where Gry Storvik had been found?

First of all, Thomas Quick was aware of the basic facts, already given away by Gubb Jan Stigson in *Dala-Demokraten*. Furthermore his fellow travellers – contrary to what they later claimed in the district court – were long since aware of the similarities between the two cases and how close together the two crime scenes were.

Stigson wrote as follows, 'The third case concerns 23-year-old Gry Storvik, who disappeared in central Oslo and was found murdered in a small car park in Myrvoll on 25 June 1985. The spot was not far from the place where Trine's body was found.'

The following exchange from the reconnaissance took place when the vehicle passed a sign for 'Myrvoll':

> PENTTINEN: You're thinking about something, Thomas. Tell me. How do you feel?
> TQ: Yeah, I'm OK.
> PENTTINEN: Really?
> TQ: Mm. Yes, there's the name of a town that I don't connect to the place where I saw the name.
> PENTTINEN: Was it just now?
> TQ: Yes.
> PENTTINEN: What town was it, then?
> TQ: I can't remember.
> PENTTINEN: Was it in connection with the crossroads we passed?
> TQ: Mm.

And sure enough, soon they passed the car park in question in Myrvoll, where for some unknown reason the car stopped and remained stationary at a junction. Quick was encouraged to keep showing them the way, but he chose the wrong direction and soon they turned round and went back, this time stopping at the other end of the car park. In the district court film, the video recording was cut there and a voice-over announced, 'This view of the car park is what Thomas Quick focused our attention on. It's where Gry Storvik was found.'

Yet the film I was now watching continued with Penttinen sitting there talking to Quick in the car park where they had brought him.

'There's something here,' said Quick.

'Is there something here?' said Penttinen.

'Yes.'

'Where? You're indicating the whole area?'

'No, not the whole area.'

'So, what then?'

'That shed . . .'

Thomas Quick pointed to the right from the direction they were facing, while the car park was the other way.

'What?' said Seppo Penttinen, sounding quite surprised.

'. . . behind here, there and here . . .'

Quick didn't point out the car park with a single word or gesture. On the contrary, he seemed to want to focus the investigators' attention on a place on the other side of the road.

As for Thomas Quick's anxious reaction, which the investigators seemed to feel was so enormously significant, it actually occurred on a nearby roundabout as they once again passed a road sign for 'Myrvoll'. On the film, one can hear Quick explaining that they were 'close to the Trine place'.

He didn't mention Gry Storvik at all. Only Seppo brought her up, in a voice-over recording in the edited version of the film.

MEETING WITH THE JOURNALIST

STURE BERGWALL WOKE at 05.29, one minute before his alarm clock went off. A report on *Ekot* was talking about a member of parliament, Fredrick Federley, whose salad bar had gone bankrupt, and how suppliers and tax payers were affected, which didn't interest Sture very much.

After washing and getting dressed, he went to the canteen to pick up coffee and buttermilk, which he took in his room. Ten minutes later, at exactly five past six, he rang the bell to be let outside.

It was a nice day. The fresh morning air brought with it a scent of bird cherry as he emerged into the exercise yard. Sture took a deep breath, closed his eyes and held his breath.

At twenty-five to eight he was back in his room, where he showered and then drank the second cup of coffee of the day in the company of *Dagens Nyheter*.

He noted in his calendar that he had completed his two thousand, three hundred and fifty-sixth day in a row. It was the only entry he made that day, despite having agreed to meet another human being for the first time in seven years.

After this he immersed himself for a few hours in 'Crossword Fun' in the magazine *Bra Korsord* ('Good Crosswords') until he ground to a halt on a difficult clue. He had a few letters pinned down and was unsure about the rest until he finally gave up.

It was a strange coincidence that he had seen the journalist's SVT documentary on the Falun pyromaniac: nine children and young people who had confessed to starting several fires even though they were innocent. There was something in the tone of it that had appealed to him. The subject of the reportage, false confessions, had also given him a vague sense of hope. But no more than that. He wasn't particularly thinking about it.

On Ward 36, the care assistants knew that Sture was having a visitor in the afternoon. They had spoken among themselves and agreed that it had to mean Sture had made a decision and that something had changed. Why else would he break his silence now?

As Sture came out to fetch his lunch, one of the old-timer nurses from Ward 36 came up to him, took him gently by the arm and said to him in a confiding voice, almost whispering, 'Sture, you're having a visitor today?'

'Yes,' confirmed Sture.

'Are you going on with the criminal investigations?' said the nurse optimistically.

Sture hummed by way of an answer, a vaguely communicative hum that could mean almost anything. *So that's what they think. That's what the staff are saying*, he thought.

He would go to his meeting without expectation or anxiety. *Maybe some sort of possibility would appear*, he thought, but he pushed this away as soon as it occurred to him.

Ten minutes before the appointment, two care assistants came to Sture's room and said it was time to go.

CHRONOLOGY OF STURE BERGWALL/ THOMAS QUICK

1969 Sture molests four young boys
1970 Sentenced to closed psychiatric care, admitted to Sidsjön Hospital
1971 Studies for a year at Jokkmokk Folk High School
1972 Back to Sidsjön Hospital
1973 Moves to Säter
Trial release
1974 Stabs a man in Uppsala, back to Säter
1976 Charles Zelmanovits disappears in Piteå
1977 Discharged from Säter
Death of father
1980 Johan Asplund disappears
1981 Trine Jensen murdered
1982 Opens a tobacconist's with his brother Sten-Ove
1983 Death of mother
Begins contact with Patrik Olofsson
1984 Murders in Appojaure
1985 Gry Storvik murdered
1986 Closure of tobacconist's kiosk
Opens a new kiosk with Patrik Olofsson's mother
1987 Obtains driving licence
Moves to Falun, then to Grycksbo
1988 Yenon Levi murdered
Therese Johannesen disappears
1989 Two Somali boys go missing from refugee centre in Oslo

1990 Moves to Falun
Robs a bank
1991 Convicted of aggravated robbery and theft
Admitted to Säter
Starts therapy with Kjell Persson
1992 Plans move into own flat
Change of name to Thomas Quick
Goes with Kjell Persson to Bosvedjan
1993 First meeting with Birgitta Ståhle
Confesses to murder of Johan Asplund
Reconnaissance of the crime scene
Remains of Charles Zelmanovits found
Kjell Persson requests leave of absence
Göran Fransson hands in his notice
1994 Confesses to murder of Charles Zelmanovits
Admitted to forensic psychiatric clinic in Växjö for a few weeks
Birgitta Ståhle takes over the therapy at Säter
First meeting with Sven Åke Christianson
Reconnaissance in Piteå
Convicted of the murder of Charles Zelmanovits
Confesses to murders in Appojaure
Establishment of the Quick Commission
1995 Reconnaisance in Appojaure
Reconnaissance in Messaure
Changes lawyer to Claes Borgström
Confesses to murder of Levi
1996 Convicted of murders in Appojaure
Confesses to murder of Therese Johannesen
Reconnaissances in Drammen, Ørje Forest and Lindesberg
Confesses to murder of Trine Jensen
1997 Convicted of the murder of Yenon Levi
Reconnaissance in Ørje Forest to point out burial sites
1998 Quick feud begins
Convicted of the murder of Therese Johannesen
1999 Reconnaisance for Trine Jensen murder
2000 Convicted of the murders of Trine Jensen and Gry Storvik

2001 Convicted of the murder of Johan Asplund
Thomas Quick takes time out
2002 Takes back the name of Sture Bergwall
Ends his therapy with Birgitta Ståhle
2008 Meets Hannes Råstam for the first time
Thomas Olsson accepts the case
2009 Retrial approved for the murder of Yenon Levi
2010 Charges dropped for the murder of Yenon Levi
Retrial approved for the murder of Therese Johannesen
2011 Charges dropped for the murder of Therese Johannesen
2012 Retrial approved for the murder of Johan Asplund
Charges dropped for the murder of Johan Asplund
Retrial approved for the murders of Trine Jensen and Gry Storvik
Charges dropped for the murders of Trine Jensen and Gry Storvik
2013 Retrial approved for the murder of Charles Zelmanovits
Retrial approved for the murders in Appojaure
Charges dropped for the murders in Appojaure